ABLAZE

Ten Years That Shook the World

Peter Rowe

Library of Congress Cataloguing in Publication Data

ISBN 978-1-09839-802-6
eBook ISBN 978-1-09839-803-3

Rowe, Peter 1947 –

Ablaze – Ten Years That Shook The World / Peter Rowe

www.peterrowe.tv

Cover image – Patricia Hearst, by Peter Rowe

Pinewood Press

TABLE OF CONTENTS

INTRODUCTION

The years 1965 to 1975 bracketed a wild and tumultuous period. It was a decade of revolution and experimentation, one that worshiped change and loved the new. There were battles—between young and old, swingers and squares, black and white, gay and straight, Green Beret and Viet Cong. There were conflagrations, coups, skirmishes, movements, wars, and revolutions. There was chaos and disruption almost everywhere.

There is a chapter for each year of the decade. The book focuses on political and military activity, but it also chronicles the new ideas that had such a profound impact—in music, journalism, art, aviation, drugs, education, and architecture. Famous revolutionaries of the period like Mao Zedong and Che Guevara get top billing, but also featured are Jane Fonda, Timothy Leary, Warren Beatty, Abbie Hoffman, Oliver Stone, Patricia Hearst, Bernadette Devlin, Carlos the Jackal, Steve Jobs, and Joan Baez. There are political leaders like Lyndon Johnson, Richard Nixon, Harold Wilson, Ian Smith, Pierre Trudeau, and there are eccentric dictators like Idi Amin Dada, Haile Selassie and 'Papa Doc' Duvalier. There are also the soldiers, terrorists, bomb-disposal experts, spies, draft-evaders, informers, hostages, and heroes whose names are not well known, but who dramatically and often secretly participated in the struggles of the era.

Ireland, Uruguay, Greece, Canada, France, and China get plenty of attention but as usual, the U.S. gets more. It should be no surprise as the movements of this era—Black Power, Gay Liberation, the students' movement, the women's movement, the counterculture—all, at least arguably, began in the United States.

America sees herself as a country born in revolution. In truth, the American Revolution of 1765 – 1783 was not really a revolution but rather an insurrection. The rebels did not have goals and aspirations to change society; they simply objected to the taxes that England tried to impose on the colonies to pay for the costs of defending them during the French and Indian Wars. The popular conception that American revolutionaries were an egalitarian bunch fighting a mad King George III to create a democratic country is simply not true. George III was not mad *during* the war. He only began to suffer from porphyria five years after it ended. In any case, he was not the sole ruler of England, which was run by a parliament and a Prime Minister. In the rebellious American colonies, the lives of the people without any power or freedom before the Revolution—women, African Americans, Indigenous, recent immigrants, the poor—remained totally unchanged by it.

In many ways the years 1965 – 75 were more revolutionary in America than the years 1765 – 1783. They were certainly violent. In a single eighteen-month period between 1971 and 1972 for instance, there were over 2,500 bombings in the U.S. More importantly, there were changes to many aspects of life and to many different parts of society—changes that influenced, and were influenced by, many other parts of the globe. People in this era, in America and around the world, were truly revolutionary in spirit, and thought they could, and would, change the world. In some ways, they did. In other ways they were hopelessly naïve, sometimes idiotically foolish. They did make big changes, some of which were permanent, some not. Much of the heady radicalism of the period ended by the mid 1970s, and the world politically shifted dramatically in the '80s. Other conflicts and struggles of the 1965 – 1975 decade are still being fought today.

Ablaze – Ten Years That Shook The World approaches the story chronologically. It begins on January 1, 1965 and ends on December 31, 1975. It dances from Athens to Oakland, from Montréal to Montevideo, and deals with the changes and events in the order they happened. It was a druggy era. The mélange may at times feel like a psychedelic kaleidoscope. Just like a daily newspaper, every story is not necessarily related (except by date) to the one beside it.

The years 1965 – 75 created a crazy steaming jambalaya of action and change.

Dig in…and dig it.

1965

China Goes to Africa, Dylan Goes Electric, Flaming Dart,
Malcolm X Killed, Che Goes to the Congo, McLuhan, LSD-25,
FLQ, Fanny Hill Goes On Trial, Dominican Republic Invaded,
Cosmo Re-imagined, Color TV Broadcast, Baby Boomers,
Kilgallen Dies, Rhodesia Rebels, Burn Baby Burn.

As the second half of the memorable decade of the 1960s dawned, American movie star Warren Beatty started reading the new book he had just been given during the holiday season. The incendiary tract was American communist writer John Reed's account of the 1917 Russian Revolution, *Ten Days That Shook The World*. Reed was a journalist for the socialist magazine *The Masses,* and one of very few outsiders who had witnessed the monumental revolution. On his return to the U.S., Department of Justice officials interrogated him for hours and confiscated all his notes and research materials from Russia. It was only when the notes were returned that he could write the book, which he did in a crazed coffee-fueled day-and-night marathon. The response to the book was positive from both left and right. Historian George Kennan said it had "blazing honesty." Vladimir Lenin himself wrote a glowing foreword to the Russian edition. New York University placed it at number six on their list of the "Top 100 Works of Journalism." of the 20th Century.

In 1965 Warren Beatty was a well-known actor with films like *Splendor in the Grass* and *Mickey One* under his belt, but he was not, by any means, the biggest male movie star in the world, a title that would arguably be his within just a few years. He began thinking that Reed's memoir might make a great movie, one with a great starring role for him. It seemed, however, an impossible task. It would surely be most unlikely that capitalist Hollywood would finance a movie glorifying not just the Russian Revolution but American communists who had actively been a part of it. Somehow, in the new revolutionary period beginning in 1965, he pulled it off. It took a while, but he eventually managed to get $32 million from Gulf + Western's Paramount Pictures and made his epic film, *Reds*. It was a remarkable thing to accomplish, and it spoke volumes about this new, intoxicating, revolutionary era of the 1960s and '70s.

Before he could persuade Hollywood to bankroll *Reds*, though, Beatty had to demonstrate that he was a bankable moneymaking hyphenate—a Star, Director, Writer, and Producer. He did that with *Bonnie and Clyde*, the film he would release in 1967. It was a film that was loathed by the studios and by the elderly film critics of the era, but it would make millions, win Oscars, and have a wildly disruptive influence on the youthful revolutionary zeitgeist of the times.

• • •

Another film was playing in January of 1965 that, while little remembered today, was possibly seen by more people than all the Warren Beatty films ever made. The film, *Collective Enemy of the World's People* was widely distributed to the Chinese population, which was then half what it is today, but still a substantial 725 million. The plot swiveled from Asia to the Middle East to Africa to Latin America to the White House, with the narrator furiously telling the viewers that "from the Indochina Peninsula to the Congolese jungle, from the Caribbean Sea to Cyprus, from Japan in the Pacific Ocean to Zanzibar at the edge of the Indian Ocean, the anti-American struggle of all the world's people is right now rolling like a furious billow rushing towards imperialism causing it to sink down lower and lower until it is surrounded on all sides."

In the same first month of the year, Zhou Enlai, the Premier of the People's Republic of China, was touring Africa, announcing that "it is in an exceedingly favorable situation for revolution…a mighty torrent pounding with great momentum the foundations of the rule of imperialism, colonialism and neo-colonialism."

Meanwhile, the Voice of America and Radio Free Europe were pumping out American anti-communist propaganda. Both the Chinese and American efforts worked. In this volatile ten-year period of 1965 – 75, there were revolutionary wars, movements, coups, or attempted overthrows often inspired by or supported by the U.S., China, or the Soviet Union erupting in Greece, Guatemala, Chile, Uganda, Dominican Republic, Ireland, Québec, England, France, Angola, Czechoslovakia, Algeria, Togo, Mali, Congo, Germany, Libya, Rhodesia (today Zimbabwe), and of course Vietnam, Laos, and Cambodia.

China began pouring vast amounts of aid into Africa. One of their favorite recipients was Tanzania, a country created following the Zanzibar Revolution that had overthrown the old Arab rulers of the island. But Tanzania, with its socialist revolutionary president, was only the most visible prize-winner in Africa. Almost every African nation that wanted help from China got it, much to the dismay and anger of the United States. This largesse would continue, even during the unbelievably disruptive years of the upcoming Cultural Revolution—an extraordinary phenomenon that would begin in 1966 and then continue right through these 'ten years that shook the world.' It was one of the strangest and most extreme of the many revolutions of this period, with the different sides taking turns wielding strength; primary school students and peasants elevated to extraordinary positions of power, civic leaders being defiled and imprisoned; communist officials purging and being purged.

• • •

Revolutionary activity was also very much in the air in the world's most powerful nation. On January 3rd, after weeks of sit-ins, protests, and arrests regarding the Free Speech Movement led by Mario Savio, the new acting chancellor of the University of California at Berkeley, Martin Meyerson designated the Sproul Hall steps as an open discussion area. Political activity, including canvassing for the Civil Rights Movement, which until then had been forbidden, was now permitted. It began a period of intense student activism that would be opposed by forces led by the future Governor Ronald Reagan. The fight between an aging right-wing B-Movie star and the young students typified most of the battles of the period. Not all, but many, were battles of young versus old. The young certainly had numbers on their side. At the dawn of 1965, because of the post-war baby boom, half the population of the world was younger than 25. Unlike previous generations, who had come of age more-or-less as clones of their parents, the Baby Boomers had their own heroes, their own attitudes, their own lingo, and their own music. One of their biggest icons was Bob Dylan.

• • •

From the perspective of the late 70s, Bob Dylan observed that "I guess the '50s ended in about '65." It was an accurate observation. 'The Sixties' in the way we usually think about them, really started with the rev-olutionary year of 1965. It was certainly true that Bob Dylan went through some shockingly radical changes himself in '65, starting with his album *Bringing It All Back Home*, recorded in January. For starters, his producer Tom Wilson, a black man (unusual for the time) assembled a group of electric rock and jazz musicians to play with Dylan. One of them, bassist

William Lee, was the father of filmmaker Spike Lee. This was a complete change from all his earlier recordings, which were just Dylan, his raspy voice, and his guitar and harmonica. The studio musicians were new to him, and certainly new to Dylan's giant base of folk fans. They didn't rehearse the songs, but just played, with what guitarist Bruce Langhorne called "telepathic chemistry." Wilson had been saying for two years that if they matched Dylan with a band, they "might have a white Ray Charles with a message." They certainly had something.

The album crackles with enigmatic originality—a bit too much originality for many listeners at the time, though almost all would eventually come under its radical sway. It included two unquestionable classics: *Mr. Tambourine Man* and *It's All Over Now, Baby Blue*. Musicologist Andrew Grant Jackson, in his *1965: The Most Revolutionary Year in Music*, describes it as "the first rock album that sucked the art of poetry into its bloodstream, the moment when LPs became not just collections of pop songs but works to stand alongside masterpieces of any form, from Picasso's *Guernica* to James Joyce's *Ulysses*. But unlike those works, Dylan's songs would soon be heard by youth across the planet, listening, as Ginsberg put it, 'to the crack of doom on the hydrogen jukebox.'"

• • •

Black Americans in the south had won the right to vote following the Civil War, but largely lost these rights after the southern states in the early 20th Century created a series of laws to prevent blacks from registering to vote. On January 15th, Martin Luther King travelled to Washington to inform President Johnson of his plans for action to try to restore voting rights for black Americans. Johnson, who was preoccupied with *Operation Flaming Dart*, his new bombing initiative against North Vietnam, wasn't totally focused on King's plans but he was not unsympathetic. He had already told his Attorney General to draft, "the goddamndest, toughest voting rights act that you can." He was warned by advisors that such a move would lose the Democrats votes from white Southerners, but he also knew that African Americans were getting impatient with the lack of real change in their lives and might become militant if nothing happened.

Some blacks were already searching for revolutionary answers. Robert Collier, along with a small group of others travelled to Cuba in violation of the State Department ban. On their return, they started the Black Liberation Front. Through their fledgling radical group, they met two very disparate people who would bring an end to the BLF before it really got a chance to get going. Raymond Wood was a black undercover cop for the NYPD who was assigned the task of infiltrating the organization. Michelle Duclos was a 26-year-old television personality for Montréal's CFTM-TV, and a member of the radical Québec separatist group the *Rassemblement pour l'Indépendance Nationale*. It is remarkable how many women were central to revolutionary movements throughout the 1965 – 75 period—Michelle Duclos was the first, but by no means the last. She began a love affair with Wood, and then conspired with Collier to help him with his first big mission. He planned to blow up the Statue of Liberty. [1]

On January 29 Wood and Collier drove to Montréal to hang out with Duclos, and then on February 15th she drove her 1961 Nash Rambler to New York City carrying in it 30 sticks of dynamite and three blasting caps. She was not aware that she was now under the surveillance of the RCMP, the FBI, and the NYPD, and that she was being tailed by her lover, Raymond Wood. Once in New York, Duclos delivered the bomb-making materials to Collier, and the next day both of them and two others were arrested in Manhattan. The conspirators all received the maximum sentences—ten years for the three men, five for Duclos. One might ask why her sentence was half the length of theirs since she was the central figure in the conspiracy, but there is an obvious answer—they were black men, she was a white woman. In any case all their terms were eventually reduced. After spending only three months in prison Duclos was simply deported back to Canada. The men were given probation after serving between 18 months and three years. And the Statue of Liberty is still standing.

• • •

On February 18th, two days after the arrests in New York, while on a peaceful march from the Zion United Methodist Church to the city jailhouse in Marion, Alabama, the deacon of the church, Jimmie Lee Jackson was fatally shot by an Alabama State Trooper named James Fowler. The night rally had turned into a melee after police shot out the streetlights and then attacked not only the marchers but also journalists, including an NBC correspondent who was hospitalized. Jackson had been trying to protect his mother, who was beaten by other police as she ran from the rally. They were both trapped in a café by troopers and Jackson was shot at point blank range. The officer was investigated but not indicted. In 2010, though, he was finally charged and found guilty of manslaughter. The incident triggered the attempted march in Alabama from Selma to Montgomery on March 7th that became known as "Bloody Sunday."

• • •

Another killing would have equal effect on race relations in the United States. Malcolm X was born in 1925, the son of Earl and Louise Little. Both were leaders in the Universal Negro Improvement Association. White men killed four of Earl's brothers, and then an offshoot of the Klan called the Black Legion (similar to today's Proud Boys) burned down the Little's home. When Malcolm was six, his father was killed in Lansing, Michigan in what was described as a streetcar accident but was widely believed to be a murder by the Black Legion. The family was broken up and Malcolm and his siblings were sent to separate foster homes. After being told by a teacher that his goal of becoming a lawyer was "no realistic goal for a nigger," he dropped out of school. By the 1940s he was a pimp, drug dealer, thief, and sometime male hustler. In 1946 he was sentenced to ten years for burglary. In prison, he became a member of the Nation of Islam, turned his life around, changed his name, and on release became one of the leaders of the movement. The FBI, suspecting him of being a communist, began surveillance of him in 1953.

On February 21, Malcolm X was assassinated by three Black Muslims at a Harlem rally. The rift between Malcolm and Elijah Muhammad, the leader of the Nation of Islam was accepted as the cause for the murder, but like all the assassinations of the sixties there was widespread feeling that a larger conspiracy was involved, especially when it was revealed that John Ali, the National Secretary for the Nation, was an undercover agent for the FBI's secret Cointelpro Program.

• • •

The most dedicated revolutionary of the period, Che Guevara, had a hard time settling into civilian life following the heady days of the 1959 Cuban Revolution. He was Fidel Castro's first lieutenant, and actually led his team of guerrillas into Havana before Castro. He was a great revolutionary fighter but was not really suited to the more sedentary task of running the country. Divvying up tasks among his comrades following his defeat of Batista, Castro asked, "Who here is an economist?" Guevara's arm shot up, so Castro appointed him Minister of Industry and Head of the National Bank. Years later Guevara, who had a degree in medicine, but no training whatsoever in economics, confessed that he thought Castro had asked, "Who here is a communist?"

Although highly intellectual, Guevara was just about the least likely person on earth to be a banker. His idea of running the Industry Department was to get out with the workers in the hot sun, strip off his shirt and help them lay walls of concrete blocks. It was vastly more genuine than Donald Trump hurling paper towels at Puerto Rican hurricane victims, but perhaps not much more useful. It probably did more for Che's image than it did for the overall state of Cuban industry. As head of the national bank, Guevara was required to sign his name to the banknotes.

He simply signed them *Che*, which horrified the traditional banking community. As Argentinian Ricardo Rojo wrote in his tribute *My Friend Che*, "the day he signed *Che* on the bills, he literally knocked the props from the widespread belief that money was sacred." [2] Che went further. He believed that all money, interest, mercantile relationships, and the market economy should be destroyed.

On February 24th, Che spoke at a conference on Afro-Asian revolutionary solidarity in Algiers, denouncing imperialism by both the U.S. and the U.S.S.R. It was the last public speech he ever gave. After returning to Cuba he was given a long dressing-down by Castro. With the U.S. blockading all trade with the relatively small country, Cuba could hardly afford to be tweaking the nose of its patrons in Moscow. Castro stripped Che of his titles in the government and sent his friend to do what he did best—be a revolutionary guerrilla fighter. Che and a group of his old comrades left for the Congo to attempt to export the Cuban Revolution to Africa. Che's efforts in Africa were not immediately successful, but they did lay the groundwork for the huge push that Cuba made ten years later to involve itself in the Angolan Civil War, a Cold War proxy conflict between the U.S. and South Africa, and the U.S.S.R. and Cuba.

It isn't a surprise that the ultra-charismatic Che became a hero to the young in the 60s even though he was nearly 40 years old. It appeared that the generation who had been commanded to "never trust anyone over 30," had made an enthusiastic exception for Che. It is, though, somewhat surprising that a German philosopher, born way back in 1898, became the hero of the young. Sixty-seven-year-old Herbert Marcuse was a Marxist but a fierce critic of the Soviet brand of Marxism. He had worked for the Office of Strategic Services (the predecessor of the CIA) through the 40s, and by the 60s he was a professor at the University of California San Diego. California Governor Ronald Reagan tried to get him fired but the 'Father of the New Left', as he was called remained until 1970. He was a frequent and lionized key speaker at student, free speech, and anti-war rallies through the period.

• • •

Meanwhile radical Canadian philosopher (and University of Toronto professor) Marshall McLuhan became an even more popular intellectual darling of the era. His *Understanding Media* became the most influential book of the year and of the upcoming period. His dense academic prose, full of startling and sometimes confusing aphorisms was not always understood but was widely appreciated for its enthusiasm for the new, and for change. McLuhan coined the phrases 'The Medium is the Message' and the 'Global Village' and he accurately predicted the Internet, 30 years before it appeared on the world stage.

Unknown to McLuhan at the time, or indeed to almost anyone, was a technological breakthrough that would ultimately prove to be more transformative and revolutionary to the world than any of the political developments of the period. Welsh computer scientist Donald Davies began work on the concept of 'packet switching', the central concept that allowed the construction of what would allow the linking of computers. Four years later, this very humble and experimental beginning led to what would eventually become the Internet. By 1966 Davis had also developed the concept of computer 'protocols' and what he called the 'Interface computer', later termed the 'router'.

• • •

On March 2nd, the United States began *Operation Rolling Thunder*, the massive bombing of North Vietnam. Curtis LeMay, the Chief of Staff of the United States Air Force described what he thought the U.S. should do to the tiny country, saying "we are going to bomb them back to the Stone Age." The bombastic Lemay was happy that Kennedy was gone, and that Johnson was now his boss. While no politicians would ever be as ready to push the nuclear button as Lemay himself (he was the model for the insane "General Jack D. Ripper" in the hit film, *Dr. Strangelove or: How I Learned to Stop Worrying and Love the Bomb*), at least he knew that Johnson wasn't likely to pull back from a war in Southeast Asia as Kennedy had planned. Johnson based his policy on what the Germans call *realpolitik*. "There are three billion people in the world," he once told his military advisors, "and we have only two hundred million of them. We are outnumbered fifteen to one. If might did make right, they would sweep over the United States and take what we have. We have what they want." [3]

• • •

Back in Selma, in response to the death of Jimmie Lee Jackson, civil rights activists planned a march to the state capitol in the style of Mahatma Gandhi. Governor George Wallace forbade the event, but 525 protestors led by John Lewis began the march regardless. They were almost immediately stopped by 200 state troopers, many on horseback at the Edmund Pettus Bridge. The bridge, tellingly, was named after a Confederate General and Grand Dragon of the Alabama Ku Klux Klan. When the protestors attempted to cross, they were attacked by the troopers who were armed with bull whips, clubs, tear gas and rubber tubes wrapped in barb wire. White crowds cheered on the police. Over 50 marchers were seriously injured in the melee which was filmed by television news cameras. That evening, ABC interrupted the Sunday Night Movie, ironically *Judgement in Nuremberg*, to broadcast the disturbing images of the demonstrators being beaten by the Alabama state troopers. The next day, March 8th, the iconic picture of demonstrator Amelia Boynton lying unconscious and bleeding on the bridge was on the front page of newspapers around the world.

• • •

Also, that day, Vietnam saw the first deployment of U.S. ground troops when 3,500 Marines landed at Da Nang. President Johnson assured

America that American troops would be in Vietnam for only six months. The number would grow to 210,000 by December and 485,000 by 1967. America would be embroiled in Vietnam for the next ten years.

• • •

On March 11th, three clergymen who were in Selma to support the civil rights marchers were attacked and beaten by a group of white men. One of them, James Reeb, an activist Unitarian minister from Philadelphia, was seriously wounded and required hospitalization, but the Selma hospital refused to admit him. By the time he got to a hospital in Birmingham he was in a coma, and two days later he died of his injuries. The men charged with the attack were, naturally, acquitted by an all-white Alabama jury.

Four days after the attack, President Johnson addressed the nation on TV, telling the country, "At times, history and fate meet at a single time in a single place to shape a turning point in man's unending search for freedom. So it was at Lexington and Concord. So it was a century ago at Appomattox. So it was last week in Selma, Alabama." He announced that he would be sending Congress a new voting rights bill, and then said, "Their cause must be our cause too. Because it is not just Negroes, but it's all of us who must overcome the crippling legacy of bigotry and injustice. And *we shall overcome.*"

On March 21st, the attempted march to Montgomery was repeated, this time with 3,200 activists, 3,000 National Guardsmen protecting them, and Dr. Martin Luther King leading the protest. With the protection of the Guardsmen, this march successfully made it to Montgomery. Governor Wallace would not accept their petition, but eventually a secretary took it, and Dr. King gave his famous "How long? Not long." speech. The very night of his speech, though, some Ku Klux Klansmen saw a white female activist, Viola Liuzzo, a housewife from Michigan, driving black marchers back to Selma. They chased her down and shot her. One of the Klansmen was revealed to be an FBI informant who did nothing to stop the murder. FBI Director J. Edgar Hoover through his COINTELPRO unit spread the rumor that Liuzzo was a communist who had left her kids to have sex with black men.

President Johnson presented the Voting Rights Act to Congress as a result of the actions in Alabama, and liberal whites and moderate blacks were pleased that King's non-violent tactics seemed to have worked. Young black activists were not at all so convinced that these moderate moves would bring any real change. On March 23rd, Stokely Carmichael formed the Lowndes County Freedom Organization, which in turn inspired Huey Newton and Bobby Seale to form the Black Panther Party for Self Defense.

• • •

On March 27th, Curtis Mayfield and the Impressions' *People Get Ready*, the very prescient song about the coming struggles of the next few years, peaked at number three on the Billboard R&B chart. Martin Luther King named the song "the unofficial anthem of the civil rights movement," and *Rolling Stone* Magazine named it the 24th greatest song of all time. The same day, *Bringing it All Back Home* was released. Also that day, in England, John and Cynthia Lennon and George Harrison and wife Patty Boyd were secretly dosed with LSD-25 by Harrison's dentist, John Riley. Though they responded badly to this first, unexpected trip, they soon became acolytes, with Lennon claiming that he took "over a thousand" acid trips over the next few years, and that it was the inspiration for much of his music.

• • •

Dr. Albert Hofmann, a chemist in the Sandoz drug company in Switzerland first made Lysergic Acid Diethylamide (LSD) in 1938 from the ergot fungus that grows on rye bread. It remained virtually unknown to the public until the mid-60s but was of great interest to the American spy agency, the Office for Strategic Services during World War II and then to the CIA through the '50s and early '60s. Wild Bill Donovan of the OSS, and later Richard Helms, head of the "Dirty Tricks Department" of the

CIA, were fascinated by the drug's potential for mind control and as a potential truth serum. In the mid-50s the CIA purchased from Sandoz ten *kilograms* of the drug, virtually the entire world's supply, for a quarter of a million dollars. It was enough for a staggering 100 million doses. Albert Hofmann's friend Walter Vogt, a Swiss poet and physician, called LSD, "the only joyous invention of the 20th century," but much of its history in this period was anything but joyous.

The CIA experimented with the drug in a variety of ways, most of them illegal. One major program used San Francisco prostitutes to administer the drug unknowingly to their johns so that CIA agents could observe the results in a program called *Operation Midnight Climax*. To run it they hired an old-school DEA agent named Colonel George White, who infamously had once killed a (likely innocent) suspect with his bare hands and had been the man who orchestrated the death of jazz singer Billie Holiday. White used equally brutal methods to investigate LSD. They explored the possibility that acid could be used to create programmed assassins, à la *The Manchurian Candidate*.

The agency also investigated the idea of secretly feeding foreign leaders LSD so that they would babble incoherently while trying to make important speeches and thus lose the respect of their followers. Colonel White was involved in attempts to unwittingly dose both Egyptian President Gamal Abdel Nasser and Cuban Premier Fidel Castro. The LSD program was wildly controversial even within the CIA, and in 1966 the agency parted ways with loose cannon Colonel White. He had no regrets. He reflected on his service to one of the senior doctors attached to the agency, saying, "I was a very minor missionary, actually a heretic, but I toiled wholeheartedly in the vineyards because it was fun, fun, fun. Where else could a red-blooded American boy lie, kill, cheat, rape, and pillage with the sanction and blessing of the All-Highest?"

The CIA's LSD testing attracted a very eclectic collection of people, such as Captain Albert Hubbard, another graduate of the OSS school of wild covert operations. During the early years of World War II,

Kentucky-born Hubbard secretly transported ships and planes from the U.S. to Vancouver, where they were chopped up, militarized, and shipped across Canada or through Panama to be used by the Canadian and British forces to fight the Germans. Since America was at the time neutral, it was all highly illegal. Hubbard was given cover by secret agencies in the U.S. and mock Canadian citizenship by Canada. He got turned on to hallucinogenic drugs through his covert missions during the war and in the 1950s he became known as the 'Johnny Appleseed of LSD.' He was still involved with American secret agencies, though he claimed the CIA "lied so much, cheated so much, I don't like 'em—they're lousy deceivers, sons of the devils themselves." Nonetheless, he connected the agency with Dr. Humphrey Osmond, who was doing extensive testing of LSD at the Weyburn Hospital in Weyburn, Saskatchewan. Osmond is the person who created the word "psychedelic" to describe these revolutionary new drugs. He also first turned on the British writer Aldous Huxley to mescaline and LSD. Huxley wrote the famous essay *The Doors of Perception* about the psychedelic experience. The book had a huge impact on the growing counterculture of the 1960s, not least on Jim Morrison and John Densmore, who were inspired by it to name their rock group The Doors. Hubbard, always the keen champion of LSD even tried in the '60s to turn his pal J. Edgar Hoover on to the drug, but the FBI chief stubbornly declined. "That old bugger was tough, really tough," lamented Hubbard.

Probably the most important testing of the drug was done when the CIA got involved with Dr. Ewen Cameron, a respected psychiatrist who was president of the American, Canadian, and World Psychiatric organizations. The Agency provided Cameron with both LSD and extensive financing to try it out on his patients in the Allan Memorial Institute in Montréal. The doctor knocked out patients for months at a time, giving them repeated doses of LSD-25 to explore whether he and his staff could permanently modify their behavior.

Nine of Cameron's patients later sued the CIA, the Allan Institute, and the Canadian government for a million dollars each, claiming they never agreed to act as guinea pigs for the drug and were still suffering from its effects. Ironically, the CIA had violated the Nuremberg Code for medical ethics by sponsoring experiments on unwitting subjects in the Montréal hospital, even though Dr. Cameron himself had been a member of the Nuremberg tribunal that had heard the case against Nazi war criminals who committed atrocities during the Second World War.

The CIA eventually began to lose faith in the drug as an interrogation tool, finding its effects on people paradoxically both too benign and too unpredictable. Some of the braver operatives, though, began to experiment with LSD themselves and to hypothesize about the possibility of using it not on individual subjects, but rather on wide swaths of the population, perhaps either foreign or domestic adversaries. The U.S. Army became particularly intrigued by the possibility of dispersing acid as a gas (they called it 'madness gas') or dumping it into drinking reservoirs. The spooks and soldiers also began to spill the beans about the amazing trippiness of the drug, the hallucinations and the mind-expanding experience when taken in comfortable situations (i.e. willingly, and not in psychiatric wards). As Hubbard would say to people, "If you don't think it's amazing, all I've got to say is go ahead and try it." The word got out to the academic community, most famously to two Harvard researchers, Dr. Richard Alpert and Dr. Timothy Leary, who began to take a very different interest in the drug. Leary's famous acid mantra (which he actually attributed to Marshall McLuhan) was "Turn on, Tune in, Drop out". In early 1965 relatively few people had even heard of LSD-25. By the end of 1967, largely due to his proselytizing, virtually everyone knew about it, and many had taken a trip themselves with the powerful mind-bending psychedelic.

LSD seems to have caused trouble wherever it went. Leary and Alpert got into a giant wrangle with the Harvard Administration who demanded that they stop their experimentation and turn over their psychedelics. "These drugs apparently cause panic and temporary insanity in many officials who have not taken them," quipped Leary. Eventually the two professors were fired. With their teaching gigs gone, they connected with Billy Hitchcock, a rich heir to the Mellon Foundation, who gave them a mansion called the Millbrook Estate in Dutchess County, New York. They planned to use it to set up a "church" to explore the mind-blowing new drugs like LSD, mescaline and psilocybin, along with other passions of the era like group therapy, yoga and meditation. They first called the church the Original Kleptonian Neo-American Church and later changed the name to the League for Spiritual Discovery. LSD, still at that point legal, was considered a 'sacrament' of the church. They began to attract artists who attempted to both re-create and enhance the psychedelic experience with swirling artwork and audio-visual light shows.

The Army and CIA had no use for this sort of thing. By now, they had moved on from LSD to testing a much more powerful super hallucinogen called BZ – Quinuclidinyl Benzilate. Some believe it was the drug CIA operatives in Russia used to incapacitate singer Paul Robeson. The army scientists were also somewhat amazed to learn that grunts in Vietnam were stealing LSD from military stores and dropping acid for fun before going out on jungle missions. Reports from Southeast Asia were that most American infantry soldiers were stoned most of the time either on acid or on highly potent Thai marijuana during battles with the Viet Cong and the NVLA. They got pumped for combat by listening to their favorite rock groups—The Stones, and later The Doors.

Eighty per cent of American servicemen smoked grass. Military police didn't even try to crack down. Some moved on to Southeast Asian heroin and 15% came back from Vietnam addicted. The favorite crazy thing to do before going into battle was to drop acid. "*Apocalypse Now*— that's how it really was," said one past member of the supersecret Army Security Agency. "After a while, Vietnam was an acid trip. Vietnam was psychedelic, even when you weren't tripping." [4]

• • •

The *Front de Liberation de Québec* (the FLQ) had first appeared a few years earlier but became increasingly visible in 1965. Its bombing campaign continued until 1970, when it escalated to kidnapping and murder and threw Canada into the biggest internal crisis the country had ever seen. On April 15th, *La Cognée*, the sect's newsletter, showed its true colors by providing detailed instructions on how to create bombs using dynamite, a detonator, an alarm clock, and a battery. The instructions were not only used by young Québeçois terrorists but later by their American and European counterparts, once they had been translated into English and re-printed in a manual called *The Anarchist Cookbook*.

The FLQ members had grown up in the years of *La Grande Noirceur* (the Great Darkness). At the time, a thuggish reactionary politician named Maurice Duplessis was Premier, society was largely ruled by the highly repressive Roman Catholic Church, most of the bosses were English speaking, and French workers were looked down upon and very poorly paid. When French-speaking Québecers spoke their own language, they were often told to "Speak white." Both Duplessis and the Catholic priests demanded giant families so kids were frequently brought up in intense poverty. Jean Chrétien, just for instance, who in 1965 was Parliamentary Secretary to the Prime Minister and would go on to eventually become Prime Minister himself, was the 18th of 19 children—not atypical in that era. Québec saw extreme change in the 60s. Within one generation, it went from being the most religious society in the world with the largest families, to the least religious with the smallest families.

The FLQ represented the most radical fringe of Québec society, which by 1965 was a stew of anti-Anglo nationalism, separatism, and a Marxist or at least Social-Democratic demand for a change in the economy of the province. When their April newsletter printed the bomb-building directions, it suggested they were veering into very dangerous waters.

• • •

1965 saw some of the opening salvos of the battle over censorship, erotica, and pornography that would continue through the next ten years. *Fanny Hill – Memoirs of a Woman of Pleasure* was originally written by

John Cleland in 1748 and became one of the most prosecuted and banned books in history. In the early 60s it was re-published by Mayflower Books in England and Putnam in the U.S. and was seized by police in both jurisdictions. Boston, a city famous for its puritanical law enforcement, was especially zealous in going after the book. (Boston had once banned the US $5 bill, because a new version of it included images of half-clad Roman sculptures and its draconian laws once forbade the exchange of Christmas presents). The Boston trial of *Fanny Hill* was seen as an important milestone in the rapidly changing mores of the times. However, even though almost unanimous testimony was given on behalf of the novel's literary worth, the judge ruled the book obscene, and the Massachusetts Judicial Court agreed with him. Putnam appealed to the US Supreme Court, and even though Chief Justice Earl Warren resisted taking the case, saying he didn't want the court "to have to read all the prurient material in the country to determine if it has social value," the court did eventually take it on. In a landmark decision the court ruled in the spring of 1966 that *Fanny Hill* was not obscene. The floodgates were open, and attitudes towards sexual material very rapidly changed. In less than a year, books, magazines, and movies far more risqué than *Fanny Hill* were available across America and around the world.

• • •

On April 24th, rebel members of the Dominican Republic military, in tandem with the Dominican Revolutionary Party, seized the Radio Santo Domingo building, thus beginning the Dominican Civil War. The next day the rebels stormed the presidential palace and began bombing it with four P-51 Mustangs, and from a military vessel, the *Mella*, in the Ozama River. On April 26th, rebel leader José Rafael Molina Ureña was declared provisional president.

The following day the US began airlifting American civilians out of the country, and U.S. President Johnson unleashed the rhetoric that his administration saw this as a second version of the Cuban Revolution.

He had already made it clear that he had abandoned Kennedy's goal of reform and protection of human rights in Latin America. His new "Mann Doctrine" demanded that Latin American countries be judged by how well they protected American financial interests, not by how well they protected the rights of their own people. It was evident the U.S. would no longer discriminate against military dictatorships, and instead would support many over the upcoming years. In the Dominican Republic, Johnson crushed a popular uprising intended to restore constitutional order and return to power the democratically elected President Juan Bosch. Johnson described his reasoning as simply being "There ain't no doubt about this being Castro now," and claimed that "It may be part of a whole communistic pattern tied in with Vietnam." [5]

On April 30th, the 3rd Brigade of the 82nd Airborne Division of the U.S. Army landed at San Isidro Air Base in the Dominican Republic. The U.S. government was widely damned both internally and around the world for its invasion of the Dominican Republic. The leader of the invasion, Vice Admiral John S. McCain Jr. (father of the future Senator and Presidential aspirant of the same name), defended the country's actions, saying, "Some people condemned this as an 'unwarranted intervention', but the communists were set to move in and take over. People may not love you for being strong when you have to be, but they respect you for it and learn to behave themselves when you are." [6]

•   •   •

On May 21st, the last day of the first major trials of members of the *Front de Liberation de Québec* (the FLQ), Justice André Sabourin of the Court of Queen's Bench sentenced Edmond Guénette and François Schirm to be "hanged by the neck till death ensues." The pair had been leaders of an attempted robbery of a Montréal gun store that ended up with the death of the vice-president of the company. Schirm, even though he was a Hungarian (and ex-member of the French Foreign Legion), not a Québecer, announced that "As a revolutionary, I was prepared to sacrifice my life and am still prepared to do so for the liberation of the people of Québec."

• • •

While planning a major conference of revolutionary third world leaders, Algerian President Ahmed Ben Bella, who had led the Algerian Revolution of 1954, was overthrown by his defense minister Houari Boumédiène, and jailed for the next 14 years. The organization of the planned revolutionary conference was taken over by exiled Moroccan opposition leader Mehdi Ben Barka until his capture and (presumed) assassination, at which point leadership was taken over by Fidel Castro. The conference was held in Havana in 1966. The killing of Ben Barka, who was known as the "travelling salesman of the revolution" became a national scandal in France when *L'Express* magazine revealed details of his abduction and death. Two French police officers went to jail for their role in his kidnapping, and the Prefect of Police, Maurice Papon, (later convicted of crimes against humanity for his role in the Nazi-collaborating Vichy regime of World War II) was forced to resign. It went much further than that. Also implicated were the Israeli secret security agency Mossad, a major French crime figure named Georges Figon, former Moroccan Interior Minister Colonel Mohamed Oufkir, the CIA, and even King Hassan of Morocco, and President Charles de Gaulle of France. It is alleged that Colonel Oufkir tortured Ben Barka to death and that a CIA operative code-named "Colonel Martin" dissolved his body in a vat of acid.

• • •

International travel was becoming increasingly difficult in this Cold War period. In 1963 the U.S. made it illegal for American citizens to travel to Cuba. It became the longest trade and travel embargo in the history of the world. When black civil rights activist Robert F. Williams wanted to visit Cuba, he had to go via Canada and Mexico. Once he had travelled, as he did in 1965 to North Vietnam and China, there was little chance he could ever go back to the U.S. without getting arrested.

In Berlin it was much worse. The wall separating the city into two halves had been built by the East Germans to prevent their people from leaving. It had started in 1961 as a wire barrier. In 1965 the East Germans began building a much more robust concrete wall. Over 5,000 people attempted to escape the country by climbing over, digging under, or breaking through the wall. More than 200 died, shot by guards as they attempted to get to the West. The official instructions given to the soldiers was, "Do not hesitate to use your firearm, not even when the border is breached by the company of women and children, which is a tactic the traitors have often used."

• • •

There was some good news when one restriction was not allowed. On June 7th, the U.S. Supreme Court ruled in *Griswold vs Connecticut* that states could not outlaw the birth control pill (aka The Pill) because the Constitution guarantees "marital privacy." It was an important ruling that affected the Sexual Revolution of the mid '60s and the Women's Liberation movement of the late '60s and early '70s. Women's ability to control their reproductive life played a great role in defining their role in society. Of course, then, as now, the religious right opposed this freedom.

• • •

Two weeks later, a battle between the U.S. Army, the Brazilian Army, and the Dominican Republic rebels resulted in the death of more than 75 soldiers. The foreign troops remained on the island for the next year, until on July 1, 1966, Reformist Party candidate Joaquin Balaguer was elected as President. Radical folksinger Phil Ochs penned and recorded a song about the American incursion into the Dominican Republic titled *Cops of the World* that sarcastically portrayed the U.S. as a global bully.

• • •

Musicians were constantly getting into trouble with The Man in these years. In one of the goofier contretemps, country star Johnny Cash managed to light three mountains ablaze while on a camping trip with his nephew. Cash claimed that the fire, that destroyed over 500 acres in the Los Padres National Forest in California was caused by sparks from a defective exhaust system on his camper. His nephew later stated that it started from a fire Cash had lit to keep warm and, in his drugged-out state, failed to notice was burning out of control. Cash was charged. When the judge asked him why he did it, the unrepentant singer replied, "I didn't do it, my truck did, and it's dead, so you can't question it." [7] When the prosecutor also noted that the fire had driven off 49 of the refuge's 53 endangered California Condors, Cash replied, "I don't care about your damned yellow buzzards." He was found guilty and paid a fine of $82,001. The incident would contribute to his outlaw image, though in fact his brushes with the law were relatively minor. Earlier in the year he had been arrested for trespassing on a private lawn to pick flowers, an incident he would turn into a song, *Starkville City Jail,* that he would sing before an audience of hardcore inmates incarcerated for far more serious crimes in California's San Quentin Prison.

• • •

In June, a little-known agency called the U.S. Public Safety Program began secretly funding forces in Guatemala to fight against urban guerrillas. They started a program that would last for years with the ultimate elimination by murder or 'disappearance' of over 42,000 Guatemalan citizens between 1965 and 1973. [8]

• • •

In Canada, the FLQ bombing campaign escalated through June. Following an intense day of seven bomb attacks and false alarms on the national holiday of Queen Victoria's birthday (May 24), separatist bombers in early June derailed two CN trains and attacked a third with Molotov cocktails.

• • •

The July issue of *Cosmopolitan* Magazine proved to be another bombshell landing with a bang on the fast-disappearing traditions of old-style North American culture. The magazine had been around since 1886 and was promoted as a 'First Class Family Magazine.' By the early 60s, it had become, like so much else from the past, bland and boring. The owners took the radical step of hiring Helen Gurley Brown, an outspoken, liberated feminist with a recent best-selling book, *Sex and the Single Girl*, as the new editor of the magazine. Brown made it very clear from her first July issue that this was a whole new *Cosmo*—one that aggressively promoted the point of view that women, whether married or not, could engage in and enjoy sex without guilt. The lead story was all about The Pill, the highly contentious contraceptive drug that was still being described as an "evil" product by the Roman Catholic Church. *Cosmo* wrote about sex in a bold manner that might have made the male readers of *Playboy* blush. Brown's liberal views on women's rights, and issues like rape, one-night stands, and the right to abortion unquestionably changed the mores of the times.

• • •

Also in July, Jane Fonda returned to America from France with her boyfriend, director Roger Vadim. She too became a potent symbol of the sexual revolution especially when, above Times Square, the Walter Reade Theater chain erected a giant 80-foot poster of her lying naked to promote her movie *Circle of Love*. After returning to California, she began to change, as she began to learn for the first time about politics and

America's increasing involvement in Vietnam. Her Malibu beach home became a hub for a new group of actors, filmmakers, and musicians who were creating the revolutionary "New Hollywood"—people like Warren Beatty, Francis Coppola, her brother Peter Fonda, kingpin young producer Bert Schneider and visitors from the East Coast like Andy Warhol and his underground star Viva. The crowd saw themselves as central to wiping away elements of the 'old' America with its repression and Puritanism and replacing it with a new subculture based on peace, free love, rebellion, ecstasy, psychedelic drugs, and a commitment to social change, civil rights, and resistance to the Vietnam War.

In 1965 drugs like marijuana and hashish were still in the purview of only a very limited number of people. That would completely change within these 'ten years that shook the world' so that by 1975 they had completely permeated society—or at very least the society of the young. The fact that these drugs were fun *and* illegal, and that there was a whole communal and necessarily secretive ritual that developed around their use, combined to create much of the revolutionary ethos of the era.

"When a young person took his first puff of psychoactive smoke," said Berkeley Free Speech Movement veteran Michael Rossman, "he also drew in the psychoactive culture as a whole, the entire matrix of law and association surrounding the drug, its induction and transaction. One inhaled a certain way of dressing, talking, acting—a certain attitude. One became a youth criminal against the State."

• • •

In Africa, the word 'revolution' did not mean young vs old, or stoned vs straight. It meant trying to find a way to pull the people of the huge continent out of hunger, poverty, and a colonial past. Zambia had been known as Northern Rhodesia until only six months earlier when it became its own nation, independent of Great Britain. It was rich in resources, particularly copper, but as a landlocked country it was unable to export them without shipping them through the antagonistic whites-only regimes of Rhodesia and South Africa. Since the beginning of the year, it had been exploring a way of building a railroad to carry goods instead through sympathetic socialist Tanzania to the port of Dar es Salaam. An expert engineer, John Leslie Charles, builder of much of the Canadian National Railway, studied the route and in July declared it to be "feasible and economic", and estimated the cost to be 353 million U.S. dollars.

The two African countries needed financial assistance to build the giant project, though, and were turned down by Britain, Japan, the United States, the World Bank, West Germany, and the United Nations. Even the Soviet Union, usually keen to export its revolution around the world, declined to get involved. Tanzanian President Julius Nyerere visited China to discuss relations, but he was hesitant to bring up the railway, knowing that China was itself such a poor country. To his surprise, Mao told him, "You have difficulties as we do, but our difficulties are different. To help you build the railway, we are willing to forsake building railways for ourselves."

Within a year, Nyerere had a commitment from China for a 400-million-dollar loan for the building of the railway. The U.S. was not only contemptuous of the railway, claiming that it would be built of bamboo, but also angry that the African countries accepted the huge loan from China. Said Nyerere, "All the money in the world is either Red or Blue. I do not have my own Green money, so where am I going to get some from? I am not taking a cold war position. All I want is money to build it."

The railway was only one of dozens of projects begun in the 1960s to export the Chinese revolution and to attempt to fight colonialism in Africa. Teams of Chinese doctors travelled deep into the continent to treat fevers, malaria, and rheumatism. Chinese engineers built roads, bridges, and buildings. Chinese sent out radio broadcasts in dozens of African languages. In Mali, an estimated four million copies of Mao's Little Red Book were distributed—one for every inhabitant. More contentiously, China also provided military training and equipment to freedom fighters-—revolutionary guerrillas pledging to liberate their countries from the vestiges of colonialism and imperialism.

• • •

On July 1ˢᵗ, Canada's Dominion Day, a dynamite bomb was exploded outside the city hall of Westmount, blowing out the windows of nearby homes in this Anglo enclave of Montréal. On the same day, a separatist march of several thousand opposing the national holiday led by ex-boxer Reggie Chartrand and his group the *Chevaliers de l'Indépendence* ended with over a hundred arrests, and the transmission tower of English-language radio station CKTS in Shawinigan, Québec destroyed by a bomb. Shortly thereafter, seven heavily armed FLQ militants headed for the Canadian Air Force station at La Macasa, 110 kilometers north of Montréal in the Laurentian Mountains. The station was the Cold War site of 28 Bomarc missiles in underground silos, designed to be equipped with either nuclear or conventional warheads as a part of NORAD's anti-Soviet defense system. The separatists, all in their early 20s, thought they could get international attention for their movement if they could take out the missiles. On July 16ᵗʰ, before they could take on the daunting task of taking on the missile site, the rifle-toting militants were spotted by a local cottager, who alerted police. The subsequent investigation by two *Sûreté du Québec* policemen ended with the gunmen shooting one officer, taking the other hostage, and accidently shooting one of their own gang. A massive manhunt ended with the eventual capture of the group, who were eventually found guilty of various crimes and received sentences of from six months to four years.

• • •

On July 20ᵗʰ, *Like a Rolling Stone* was released, a violent, angry, vitriolic song by Bob Dylan. Considered revolutionary at the time for both its six-minute length, its nasty rock and roll beat, and its subject matter, it became an anthem for radicals and the song of the summer of '65. To this day, it remains Dylan's biggest hit. Five days later, Dylan was almost booed off the stage at the Newport Folk Festival. Backed by an electric rock band, his appearance was considered sacrilege by his followers, yet another shock in the ever-changing 1960s. Many of those who booed him in Newport would soon be buying his next radical, visionary masterpiece, released in late August – *Highway 61 Revisited*. British musicologist Michael Gray makes the audacious claim that the '60s only started with the release of *Highway 61*.

If even young music-lovers sometimes had trouble keeping up with all the changes in the world in 1965, the older generations were often completely lost. Singer/Songwriter Arlo Guthrie describes how he remembers it: "The corporations, the businessmen and women who were controlling the entertainment business, did not understand the lyrics of the songs that they were selling. The guys on the radio didn't get it. The guys that owned the radio had no connection with the music, in terms of understanding it. For the first time, there was an explosion of all different kinds of music being played. And the lyrics were unintelligible. Not just the lyrics—the philosophy, the heart of it, was unreadable, unknowable, to the people who controlled the industry. All of a sudden, all around the world, for a very short time, imagine a world where everybody's got a radio, and all of a sudden everybody's saying what they really think, in words you could understand, but your parents couldn't. A floodgate had opened, because we were using a language that couldn't be understood over the system we were using to communicate it. And it was so wonderful. People were walking down the street plain laughing, just having a great time, because all of a sudden, it was free." [9]

• • •

Television lagged far behind other media as a force for social progress, but two technological advances were about to change that. In 1965, television was still almost entirely seen in black and white. Color TV technology did exist (unbelievably, inventors had been experimenting with it as early as 1880) but there was the chicken-or-egg issue. TV set manufacturers wouldn't make color TV sets because broadcasters weren't broadcasting in color, and TV networks wouldn't broadcast in color because no-one owned color sets to receive it. In 1964, only 3.1 % of television households in America had a color set. Finally, in the summer of 1965 NBC broke the log jam by announcing they would be photographing and broadcasting their 1965/66 season in color. The two other American networks soon followed suit, as did other countries. The CBC in Canada went color in 1966, BBC-2 in England in 1967. Color sets were expensive—the equivalent of about $12,000 in today's money—but people wanted them and started to buy them.

Color television had an unexpected and profound effect on the ever-contentious issue of race. The simple truth is that black faces do not photograph well in black and white without extra care and artificial lighting. Especially in the outdoor settings of protest marches, African Americans appeared on the television screens prior to 1965 as being dark, underexposed, difficult to see and thus scary figures. Once television news began broadcasting in color, with its far more nuanced range of contrast and tone, it was remarkable how the new medium presented black faces in a much more complimentary manner, and how this contributed to the changing attitudes of whites towards people of color.

The second technological change that had an effect on society had to do with the way that television news was recorded. Prior to 1965 news was captured with giant, heavy tripod-mounted Mitchell cameras with fixed focal length lenses, and huge thousand-foot magazines sitting on top. The cameras were virtually impossible to handhold, and did not record sound, so they had to be cabled to equally large 16mm sound recording units. The cumbersome set-ups were okay for getting out the official word of the establishment authorities, in staged government press conferences. They were almost useless for capturing the feelings of the rest of society. It is true that the German company Arriflex made relatively small cameras that could be handheld, but these had the contradicting features of both being noisy and silent – 'MOS', in the parlance of the day – *Mit Out Sound*. Pretty useless for news or television documentaries, since they could not record voices.

That changed in the 60s, with three new inventions. British-born American filmmaker Richard Leacock came up with a way of installing a quartz crystal in a handheld blimped camera so that the cameraman no longer had to be linked to the sound recordist by cable. Meanwhile, Polish inventor Stefan Kudelski created the Nagra tape recorder, a unit so lightweight, portable, and rugged that it could easily be carried over the shoulder. Finally, the Éclair company of France began building the shoulder-mounted NPR (Noiseless Portable Reflex) camera. The world of television news and documentary features was transformed. Instead of just recording the sanitized reports of what had happened from police, military, or civic officials, cameramen were out on the streets, fields, or jungles documenting it. News coverage of Little Rock and Selma, *cinema-verité* films like *The Mills of the Gods* (about Vietnam), *Primary* (about American politics), *Don't Look Back* (about Bob Dylan) and *Warrendale* (about disturbed, institutionalized kids) changed the way people saw the world. They also transformed what was going on in the world. Civil rights activists knew it was the television coverage that made their sit-ins and demonstrations meaningful, so they began to feel their possible bloodshed might be worthwhile. Vietnam was called 'the first television war', and it was these new lightweight cameras and tape recorders that brought the war into viewers' living rooms. Protestors at the 1968 Chicago Convention, knowing they were being filmed, chanted, "The whole world's watching! The whole world's watching!" Norman Mailer, in his Pulitzer Prize-winning book about his participation in the October 1967 anti-Vietnam Washington demonstration, *The Armies of the Night*, described how meaningful and important it was to him that when he broke through the lines of the National Guard to walk towards the Pentagon, the Canadian *cinema verité* cameraman Richard

Leiterman slipped through with him and then walked (backwards) filming the writer until Mailer was finally arrested.

• • •

The world's oldest political alliance, between the U.S. and the U.K., began to fray in this period. J. Edgar Hoover at the FBI had never liked the British, and though the CIA was filled with East Coast Anglophiles, the many shocking failures of British Intelligence—Kim Philby, George Blake, Donald Maclean, Guy Burgess—meant that even the CIA was losing faith in Great Britain. Suspicious of the newly elected socialist Labour government, President Johnson encouraged the President's Foreign Intelligence Advisory Board to snoop on British Intelligence systems. James Angleton, the cadaverous and feared head of Counter-Intelligence at the CIA, modified CAZAB, also known as the "Five Eyes"—a super-secret counter-intelligence organization of the secret agencies of Canada, America, New Zealand, Australia, and Great Britain so that Harold Wilson's British government was kept out of the loop of its intelligence-sharing. [10]

• • •

During the summer, Chairman Mao went into a long retreat away from Beijing to plan his anarchic attack on his own Communist Party. His plan was based on his readings about the descriptions in classical Chinese literature of a character that has been called, "one of the most memorable reprobates of world literature", the rebellious, irreverent, kung fu-practicing 'Monkey King'. Within a year, Mao's millions of young followers would be quoting his words: "Revolutionaries are like the Monkey King: their golden staff is powerful, their supernatural powers are sweeping…we use our sorcery to turn the old world on its head, crush it to pieces, turn it into dust, create chaos and great disorder, the bigger the better!" From his self-imposed retreat Mao came up with his idea of *jixu geming*—continuous revolution—ceaseless, violent shake-up of the political establishment.

It was an idea that would shake up the lives of millions of his country-men, and of people around the world. "Bombard the headquarters," he proclaimed. "Don't be afraid of making trouble. The bigger the trouble we make, the better…There is great chaos under heaven; the situation is excellent."

• • •

In America there was also someone who believed in making trouble—"Good trouble", as he called it. John Lewis and the Student Nonviolent Coordinating Committee (SNCC) Freedom Riders cooked up what Lewis called their "Good trouble" throughout the American south in the summer of 1965. Their activism ultimately led President Johnson to sign the Voting Rights Act on August 6th. Within a year Black voter registration dramatically increased from less than a third to more than a half. The act also had the effect of turning southern whites away from the Democratic Party and into Republicans and revolutionizing and polariz-ing American politics along black/white and liberal/conservative divides.

The battle over race in America erupted into one of the most explosive battles ever on August 11th with what Blacks called the Watts Rebellion and whites called the Watts Riots. Even though far away from the volatile, deep south, Southern California had since the 1940s profound racial issues, mostly regarding real estate. Ninety-five per cent of Southern Californian housing was off-limits to Black and Asian citizens. A referen-dum called Proposition 14 sponsored by the real estate industry and sup-ported by most white Californians effectively ended efforts by the Federal government to stop housing restrictions in California.

On top of that, the Los Angeles Police Department was widely accused of police brutality and of actively recruiting from the deep south to get a paramilitary police force that was filled with officers who held strong racist, anti-black and anti-Latino sentiments. On the evening of August 11, a dispute over a traffic violation grew into a combat between blacks and the LAPD, with 14,000 National Guard eventually joining in. The fight stretched across a massive 46-square-mile zone of South-Central Los Angeles. Sergeant Ben Dunn later described it as resembling "an all-out war zone in some far-out country. It bore no resemblance to the United States of America."[11] The insurrection even popularized a new catch-phrase, first attributed to KGFJ disc jockey Nataniel "Magnificent" Montague, which went on to become the rallying cry of this entire 1965 – 1975 era: "Burn, baby, burn!" The phrase even became part of the software code that took Apollo 11 to the moon in 1969—"Burn, baby, burn – Master Ignition On."

The four days of unrest resulted in over 1000 injuries, $40 million dollars damage to burnt-out buildings, 3,400 arrests, and 23 people shot dead by LAPD officers or National Guardsmen. Two LAPD officers were accidentally killed by gunfire from other officers.

President Johnson decried the riots. Also, a few days later on August 31st, the President decreed that the burning of draft cards was now a crime punishable by a five-year prison term and a one thousand dollar fine. Singer Glen Campbell, who just had a hit with Buffy Ste. Marie's powerful anti-war song *Universal Soldier*, went one further, declaring that draft card burners should be hanged.

• • •

In September, Cesar Chavez, with a large group of mainly Mexican American farmworkers linked forces with Filipino grape pickers to begin the Delano Grape Strike. Chavez consolidated his position as a powerful labor leader and became the face of labor activism for the next ten years. He enlisted the support of the Student Free Speech protest movement in Berkeley, California, then met and got advice on boycotts from SNNC, the Student Nonviolent Coordinating Committee, and received support from Walter Reuther's enormous and powerful United Automobile Workers union. For his efforts, the FBI labeled him a communist and began active surveillance of him and his farm-workers union.

• • •

Things were still pretty square in 1965, nowhere more so that in the field of education. Most teachers, administrators and school boards were doing things the way they had been done for the past 75 years, and most jurisdictions had no interest in changing. The government of Ontario, though, felt the winds of change blowing and so set up a commission to review education and propose new ideas. The commission stated, "Today, on every side, there is heard a growing demand for a fresh look at education. The committee was told of inflexible programs, outdated curricula, unrealistic regulations, regimented organization, and mistaken aims of education. We heard from alienated students, frustrated teachers, irate parents, and concerned educators. Many public organizations and private individuals have told us of their growing discontent and lack of confidence in a school system which, in their opinion, has become outmoded and is failing those it exists to serve." The commission eventually produced *The Hall-Dennis Report*, a study that would lead to big changes in public education.

In the U.S., Paul Goodman published an incendiary book about young people and education called *Growing Up Absurd*. The best-seller told young people they were completely right to feel disaffected about growing up in a square society without meaningful community, spirit, sexual freedom, work, or, certainly, education. Juvenile delinquency was constantly under the microscope in this period. Unlike the conventional establishment thinking that blamed the phenomenon on comic books or rock and roll or simply on the kids themselves, sociologist Goodman argued that delinquency was a totally understandable valid response to what he saw as the vapid, conformist unfulfilling nature of American society.

• • •

Much of the violent, rebellious sometimes criminal activity of the 1965 – 75 period can perhaps be attributed to the baby boom. There were a huge number of babies born between 1945 and 1950. By no means were all of them wanted. Just consider the number of pregnancies in Germany due to rape by Russian soldiers – which historians place as high as two million.[12] The number of rapes by American soldiers of German (and French) women was much less, but it was not insignificant. The U.S. Army had a policy of non-fraternization with the enemy, but American soldiers joked that "copulation without conversation is not fraternization." The German army set up brothels in all the countries they conquered and occupied. The local women forced to work in them serviced up to 32 men a day and were only released if they became visibly pregnant and were thus no longer suitable. During the "Rape of Nanking", tens of thousands of Chinese girls and women were raped by Japanese soldiers, which doubtless again led to many thousands of unwanted pregnancies. In part to reduce further atrocities, the Japanese Army created what were known as 'comfort stations' for their troops. Huge numbers of Korean, Chinese, and Filipina women were forced into servicing the Japanese soldiers with again the result of many thousands of unwanted pregnancies. Beyond these instances of forced sex, there was lots of consensual sex during World War II, much of it followed by soldiers heading off to battle leaving behind unwed mothers or pregnant widows.

There was no birth control pill in the 1940s and abortion was illegal almost everywhere. Large numbers of unwanted boys were being brought up in the '50s by single mothers, or in orphanages, or foster homes. It is little wonder that from 1965, when these boys were between 15 and 20 years old, and 1975, when they were between 25 and 30, there was a huge issue of angry rebellion and delinquency. The crime rate was enormous in this period, and only began to decline in the mid 80s, exactly 15 to 20 years after the introduction of The Pill and of *Roe vs Wade* and similar laws around the world permitting abortion.

• • •

Schools in 1965 were perceived by some as being little more than jails for young people. Corporal punishment was still widely exercised. Students were totally under the control of teachers and administration. The most authoritarian of teachers would be promoted to the role of vice-principal, and these men had total dictatorial control of student (and teacher) conduct. Students who were thought to be troublemakers, or dumb, or outsiders, or simply were not liked, could be punished in various ways. They were strapped, received detentions, were failed, were held back so they were in classes with kids younger (and usually shorter) than them, or were expelled. Schools were judged by their overall performance of their students in standardized tests, so principals would often kick out the ones with the lowest marks, or strongly encourage them to leave on their own. Teenage pregnancy was certainly a reason for girls to be kicked out of school.

The most outrageous and evil educational institutions, the Residential Indian Schools run by the Canadian government and by the Catholic and Anglican churches, were still very much alive in this period. Large numbers of Native children were forcibly taken from their parents and enrolled in schools hundreds of miles away, with the goal of "taking the Indian out of the child." The kids were not allowed to speak their own language, and suffered a massive amount of corporal punishment, starvation, physical, emotional, and sexual abuse, and even death at the hands of the teachers, priests and nuns who ran the schools.

In the U.S., boys who were in school were protected from the draft, but as soon as they were expelled and were no longer in an educational institution, they were most definitely subject to it, and would likely soon be on their way to Vietnam. Of course, long hair was not allowed, and there was a strict dress code not just for students but for teachers. For instance, it was absolutely forbidden for female teachers to wear pants.

Within the next ten years much of this changed. Even in 1965, there were progressive movements working to liberalize education. Most notably, in England, A.S. Neil had started the Summerhill School, a progressive institution that would have a big effect helping create the 'free schools' that would proliferate in this period. Neil's 1960 book, *Summerhill* became the bible for this new movement. "The function of the child is to live his own life," said Neil. "not the life that anxious parents think he should live, not a life according to the purpose of an educator who thinks he knows best."

The central idea of Summerhill was that students participated in the governing of the schools. All decisions were made by the entire community, with students, teachers, and administrators all getting an equal vote. Students, of course, were always in the majority. Classes were not compulsory at Summerhill; students were free to study whatever subject matter they chose. Naturally there was pushback from traditionalists, especially when it was learned that older students at the school engaged in mock weddings, and then slept with each other, and when older students and younger teachers had open relationships.

Free schools began to open in 1965 in North America, modelled on the British Summerhill school. In October, 'Free Universities' began opening across the US, offering courses in Marx, Lenin and Revolution. Even the most traditional schools began to change. Yale University, after much handwringing from conservatives, dropped its strict dress code in October.

In 1968, the largest, most radical and most controversial experiment in education anywhere opened, Toronto's Rochdale College. By 1972, there were around 600 'open' or 'free' schools across the U.S., but they soon began to die away due to the Nixon Administration's education policies and the conservative backlash of the late '70s.

• • •

On October 1st, in an attempted coup, members of the Indonesian National Armed Forces assassinated six Indonesian Army generals. It was a highly complicated affair, involving President Sukarno, who even though he had been President since 1945, now declared himself, in the spirit of the mid-Sixties, to be "infatuated by the rhythm of revolution." Also very involved were the Indonesian communist party, China, Mao, and the CIA. Earlier in the year Sukarno had pulled out of the United Nations and told Lyndon Johnson to "go to hell with your aid." Major-General Suharto managed to manipulate the coup, depose Sukarno, and appoint himself the new President of Indonesia. Within a year more than half a million people were killed by the Army and paramilitary groups in giant orgies of violence. Thousands of homes of suspected communists were burned. In Bali, 6,000 people were killed in three days. The violent bloodletting was cheered by the American government and media, who saw the events as a Cold War victory. In Washington, the coup was hailed as the CIA's greatest operation in its history, although by 1968 they did admit it was also one of the worst mass murders of the 20th century. The violence, opined the *New York Times*, was simply due to "a strange Malay streak, that inner frenzied blood-lust which has given to other languages one of their few Malay words: *amok*."

• • •

On October 16th, the Hells Angels ran amok at a major antiwar protest in Oakland, attacking the protestors who were trying to block troop trains carrying draftees destined for Vietnam (and this despite Allen Ginsberg's peaceful chanting of *Hare Krishna*). The violent motorcycle gang had an ambivalent attitude towards the youth movement. Sometimes the neo-Fascist gang thought hippies and war protestors were un-American. Other times, especially when LSD got involved, the unpredictable motorcycle gang championed the long-haired student rebels. The weekend protest had been a confusing event, with Bob Dylan, who had been invited to lead the demonstration, puckishly refusing to participate unless the protest signs were images of lemons or watermelons or words like 'orange' or 'automobile.' Famed counterculture novelist Ken Kesey further complicated the proceedings when instead of giving the expected rabble-rousing speech against the war he shouted at the huge audience, "Do you want to know how to stop the war? Just turn your backs on it. Fuck it!" and then stalked off the stage.

Radical activist Jerry Rubin was jailed for his political shenanigans in California, then was subpoenaed by the House Un-American Activities Committee (HUAC). Instead of pleading the Fifth Amendment as most did when forced to testify to HUAC, Rubin entered the hearing room dressed in an American Revolutionary War uniform. "I wear this uniform," he announced, "to symbolize the fact that America was born in revolution, but today America does violence to her own past by denying the right of others to revolution." As the stern Congressmen grilled him about his activities, Rubin, in his Paul Revere getup, lightheartedly blew soap bubbles at them. He showed up to later appearances dressed first as a bare-chested guerrilla in Viet Cong pajamas and carrying a toy M-16 rifle, then as Santa Claus. He made the newspapers every day, to the chagrin of the maddened politicians.

• • •

In October, Charles Gagnon, a former lecturer in politics and economics at the Université de Montréal, and Pierre Vallières, an ex-reporter at *La Presse*, now lead writer for the FLQ newsletter *La Cognée*, organized a totally new central committee for the semi-moribund FLQ and began recruiting young members willing to participate in violence "to lay the foundations of a revolutionary movement that would exclusively serve the exploited of Quebec." The FLQ told Quebec students that "it is time to melt your pens and turn them into plastic bombs."

The Canadian government, perceiving that separatism was becoming a serious threat to the country, and believing that France was supporting the movement, authorized the RCMP to spy on the Gaullist government, which they elevated to the rank of an 'enemy power.' The federal government did *not* want the RCMP spying on Canadian university students, and forbade the Mounties from doing this, but just as in the U.S., the police force began using spies and informers on campuses, and violently broke up anti-war protests by Canadian students.

• • •

On November 8th, a woman called "the most powerful female voice in America," was found dead in her New York apartment, apparently from a fatal combination of alcohol and barbiturates. Dorothy Kilgallen was a widely read reporter and columnist, syndicated to more than 140 newspapers, and longtime panelist on the television game show, *What's My Line?* Kilgallen had been investigating new theories about the assassination of John F. Kennedy. She had developed a close relationship with Jack Ruby, the killer of Lee Harvey Oswald, and was about to conduct another interview with him in his Dallas jail cell in which he promised to "tell all." She was also writing a major story about New Orleans mafia don Carlos Marcello's purported role in the assassination. Two weeks before her death she told her lawyer, "I'm going to break the real story and have the scoop of the century," and she confided in her hairdresser Charles Simpson, "If the wrong people knew what I know about the JFK assassination, it could cost me my life."[13] Questions about Kilgallen's death became yet another mystery being investigated by the growing number of people questioning the official version of what happened in Dallas in 1963.

• • •

The day after Kilgallen's death, November 9th, was the date of the so-called "Great Black-Out of 1965". The tripping of a mis-programmed safety relay at the Sir Adam Beck Hydroelectric Power Station at Queenston, Ontario, just north of Niagara Falls led to a cascading series of events in the North American power grid that resulted in a total loss of power for 30 million people and a 13-hour blackout across Ontario, New York, New Jersey, and most of New England. It proved to be a mostly benign event. There was a widespread urban legend that there was a mini-baby-boom nine months later, but the veracity of this has never been confirmed. What the black-out did indicate, though, was how close the world was to unintentional nuclear Armageddon. Major cities like New York and Boston were equipped with nuclear bomb detectors, and the power outage set these off, putting the Command Center of the Office of Emergency Planning on full alert and triggering to NORAD the illusion of a Soviet nuclear attack, which they were frightened by, but fortunately, ultimately did not respond to.

• • •

The so-called "culture wars" started to heat up in 1965, particularly in terms of the new permissiveness seen in literature, art galleries, the stage, and even television. Various Mrs. Grundy's, either government-appointed or self-appointed, set themselves up to fight this change. In England, a woman named Mary Whitehouse made a name for herself by leading the charge against what she called, "the propaganda of disbelief, doubt and dirt…promiscuity, infidelity and drinking." In November, the prominent and flamboyant critic Kenneth Tynan, during a live debate on BBC about sexual explicitness on stage, said he doubted if many theatregoers would be shocked by the word 'fuck'. Maybe not, but television viewers were. It is thought to be the first time the word was ever heard on British television, and it caused a giant uproar. Mary Whitehouse wrote to the Queen about the scandalous event, suggesting to Her Majesty that Tynan should have "his bottom spanked" over it, presumably unaware that S&M flagellation was one of Tynan's favorite vices.

• • •

On November 11th, the 'white settlers' of Rhodesia, led by Ian Smith, unilaterally declared independence from Great Britain and became a rogue nation because of its refusal to allow majority rule. Smith's government introduced a State of Emergency, banned both the black political parties—ZANU, the Zimbabwe African National Union, and ZAPU, the Zimbabwe African People's Union—and jailed all black nationalist leaders. Unlike most of the many other African countries that had gained independence fairly peacefully in the previous ten years, it was clear a majority-ruled Rhodesia would only happen through armed struggle. In the buildup to the 'Bush Wars' of Southern Africa that would become after Vietnam the most violent battles of the next ten years, a loose federation of revolutionary groups began to coalesce in Southern Africa—ZAPU in Rhodesia, *uMkhonto we Sizwe (Spear of the Nation)*, the military arm of the African National Congress in South Africa, SWAPO (the South West Africa People's Organization) in South West Africa (now Namibia), FRELIMO (the *Frente de Libertação de Moçambique)* in Mozambique and the MPLA (the *Movimento Popular de Libertação de Angola)* in Angola.

Immediately upon the declaration of independence, the new white-only Rhodesia was condemned by Great Britain and sanctioned by the United Nations. These measures, though, were slow to happen and weakly implemented. Harold Wilson's British government was accused of "throwing the book at Rhodesia, one page at a time." Rhodesia was shunned by every country in the world, except for South Africa, and the countries of black Africa were united in their resolve to crush Ian Smith's rebellion. Ian Smith was viewed as an outlaw on the world stage, especially after he bluntly, publicly, stated his position in a radio broadcast, proclaiming, "Let me say it again. I don't believe in black majority rule ever in Rhodesia, not now, not in a thousand years."

Rhodesia was the most contentious departure but by no means the only British colony to gain its independence from England in the period. In 1965, Gambia also became independent. In 1966, Botswana, Lesotho, Barbados, and Guyana. In 1967, Aden and South Yemen. In '68, Mauritius and Swaziland. In '71, Fiji, Tonga, Bahrain, Qatar, and the United Arab Emirates. In 1973, The Bahamas; and in 1974, Grenada. Former U.S. Secretary of State Dean Acheson described the new state of affairs: "Great Britain has lost an empire and not yet found a role for itself."

• • •

Che Guevara's African adventure had proven to be nowhere near as successful as he had hoped. After seven months in the Congo, he had been unable to plant the seeds of revolution in the country. Egypt's President Nassar had warned him he would simply become a 'Tarzan' figure in central Africa, doomed to failure, and the warning turned out to be true. Guevara found that the local Simba rebels, who he tried to assist, were wracked with tribal rivalries, and had, he eventually found, "no will to fight…we cannot liberate, all by ourselves, a country that does not want to fight." He also found he had three formidable enemies. The United States National Security Agency had a spy ship cruising the Indian Ocean listening to all his radio transmissions. The Congolese government hired British/South African mercenary Mad Mike Hoare to fight against him. And thirdly, tropical diseases like malaria and dysentery decimated his troops. Hoare claimed to be the first man to have defeated Che Guevara. He was also once quoted saying, "killing communists is like killing vermin, killing African nationalists is as if one is killing an animal. My men and I have killed between five and ten thousand Congo rebels in the twenty months that I have spent in the Congo. But that's not enough. There are 20 million Congolese you know, and I assume that about half of them at one time or another were rebels whilst I was down here." [14]

Che was prepared to die in the Congo, but he was eventually convinced to abandon the lost cause. He left on November 20th and hid out in the Cuban embassy in Dar es Salaam for six months While there, he wrote three books, and then went to the famous spa in Karlovy Vary,

Czechoslovakia to try and shake the tropical diseases that he had contracted in Africa.

• • •

On November 27th, four new groups, the Women Strike for Peace, the Students for a Democratic Society, the Committee for Sane Nuclear Policy, and the National Coordinating Committee to End the War in Vietnam, led 250,000 people demonstrating in Washington against the Vietnam War. It was the first of many giant protests against the war. The fall of 1965 also saw the first of many "Teach-Ins" in which students would take over their campuses to discuss, learn about, and protest the war.

Young people were also involved in battles over the length of hair and over attempts to liberalize archaic laws. On December 7th, the Massachusetts Supreme Court upheld high school officials' right to suspend students with long hair.

The next day, two new acts came into force in Great Britain. The Race Relations Act made it illegal to discriminate on the basis of race, color, or national origin in public places. It was derided by critics as being a bit toothless, as it did not cover housing, employment, or stores, but amendments to cover these were added three years later. The same day, another act abolishing the death penalty for murder was also adopted. They were the first of a number of new liberal laws enacted in Britain in the period. In 1967 a new law legalized abortion, and another decriminalized homosexual acts. In 1968 the Theatres Act ended the censorship by the Lord Chamberlain's office that had existed in England since 1737, and in 1969 the Divorce Reform Act ended equally archaic rules about divorce. In England, if not in Massachusetts, the times, they were a changin'.

• • •

On December 23rd, Timothy Leary was busted crossing from Nuevo Laredo, Mexico into Texas. His girlfriend, Rosemary Woodruff, had a small bag of marijuana which U.S. Customs found hidden in her panties, and for which Leary took the rap. The charges for this tiny amount of weed, combined with a subsequent California arrest for possession of two roaches would ultimately lead to the equivalent of a life sentence, as well as a break-out from prison, a re-capture, and then more charges against the Harvard professor.

•　•　•

What would 1966 bring? The answer, my friend was blowing in the wind.

1966

Carlos the Jackal, Tunnel Warfare, Is God Dead?
Papa Doc Rules, Rastafarians Smoke, London Swings,
Idi Amin Dada, The Cultural Revolution, South Africa,
Women's Liberation, Merry Pranksters, Red Guards,
The Battle of Algiers Excites, Andy Warhol Shocks,
Eldridge Cleaver Frightens, Madame Mao Bites.

The new year began with the grand Tricontinental Conference, where 500 delegates from 82 countries met in Havana from January 3-16 to discuss anti-colonial and anti-imperialist revolutionary strategies. Many prominent revolutionaries attended, but none of the three men who had originally planned the event. Algerian revolutionary President Ahmed Ben Bella was deposed in a coup and jailed. Exiled Moroccan opposition leader Mehdi Ben Barka was arrested, imprisoned, and is presumed to have been killed. Che Guevara (though his image was waving everywhere on banners across Havana) was still in a medical spa in Czechoslovakia, recovering from the tropical diseases he had contracted on his recent revolutionary adventure in the Congo.

Instead, Fidel Castro, Chile's Salvador Allende, and representatives from the Viet Cong were the revolutionary stars of the conference. The

CIA secretly monitored the event, and widely reported to sympathetic news media a speech by the chief of the Soviet delegation, S.P. Rashidov, in which he announced that the U.S.S.R. was backing liberation movements in Puerto Rico, Peru, Guatemala, the Dominican Republic, Venezuela, and Guyana.

One of the youngest and least noticed delegates was a 17-year-old Venezuelan named Ilich Ramirez Sánchez. The teenager, named "Ilich" after Vladimir Ilich Lenin, had been taken to the conference by his father. Within four years he would be known as Carlos the Jackal, arguably the most infamous political terrorist in the world. He continued his revolutionary training in the summer of 1966 at the Camp Matanzas, a guerrilla warfare school run by the Cuban Intelligence Agency.

• • •

If left-wing revolutionary groups weren't trying to take over countries in the 1960s, then right-wing Army Colonels were. On January 3rd, in Ouagadougou, Upper Volta (now Burkina Faso) army officers forced President Maurice Yaméogo to resign, threw him in jail, and took over the government. His son unsuccessfully tried to break Yaméogo out of prison, and for his efforts received a seven-year sentence in the same institution.

• • •

In nearby Nigeria, a group of Army officers murdered the Prime Minister and took control of the oil-rich West African nation. Their coup ended democracy in Nigeria and led to the Biafran War, a deadly conflict that resulted in some 100,000 military casualties and as many as two million deaths from starvation.

• • •

No other military forces could throw their weight around like the United States. On January 7th, the U.S. Air Force used dozens of B-52 bombers to drop 30-ton loads of bombs on the Cū Chi region of Vietnam. They turned the lush jungle into a pockmarked moonscape. Their goal was to destroy the vast system of tunnels that the Viet Cong had built in the area to move soldiers and supplies closer to Saigon. Following the bombing campaign, American and Australian 'tunnel rats' entered the tiny tunnels that were filled with booby traps and poisonous cobras to attempt to find and kill Viet Cong soldiers.

At about the same time the First Cavalry Airmobile unit began an experimental action called *Operation White Wing*. Against a Viet Cong battalion, they deployed grenades containing BZ, an extremely powerful hallucinogen and poison developed as an alternative to LSD-25. Less than a hundred of the VC were believed to have escaped alive. According to Dutch author Will Vervey, the super hallucinogen chemical was used on at least five other occasions by the U.S. in Vietnam. Despite the fact that Defense Department officials admitted that the unstable drugs "have dosage ranges into lethality. They can clobber people," the army stockpiled as much as fifty tons of BZ, or enough to turn every single person in the world into a crazed maniac.

While the army scientists were experimenting with hallucinogens as weapons, infantry soldiers were playing with them just to get through the war. "I was stoned every day of my life in Vietnam," one GI acid-head confessed, "stoned to the gourd. It was the only way to deal with all the horror and the insanity, and that's what everyone did. Everyone was stoned on something." [15]

• • •

People were definitely also stoned at the three-day Trips Festival staged by Ken Kesey and his Merry Pranksters in San Francisco on January 21, 22 and 23. The festival was the event that made the city the acknowledged center of the psychedelic revolution. It was a wide-open LSD-laced party, the likes of which the world had never seen. There were thousands in attendance, day-glo bodies bouncing on trampolines, mime exhibitions, rock and roll, a "Congress of Wonders", live mikes, sound equipment and closed-circuit television cameras littered around for anyone to play with. At one point M.C. Kesey requested, "If anybody knows he is God, please come up on stage."

The Grateful Dead leader Jerry Garcia called it, "something like organized chaos...everybody was high and flashing and going through insane changes during which everything would be *demolished*, man, and spilled and broken and affected...and after that, another thing would happen, maybe smoothing out the chaos, then another...thousands of people, man, all hopelessly stoned, all finding themselves in a room of thousands of people, none of whom any of them were afraid of. It was magic— far-out beautiful magic."

• • •

Some of the Trips Festival celebrants were no doubt dancing the 'Watusi', a popular dance in the dance-crazy 60s. Meanwhile, the real Watusis (today called the Tutsis) were massing on the Burundi border preparing to attack Rwanda, overthrow the government, and establish a base for revolutionary activity within central Africa. The guerrillas had been trained by the Chinese for the revolutionary action.

• • •

In March, Cesar Chavez led a group of about 50 striking grape-pickers from Delano, California, to the state capital of Sacramento 300 miles away. They marched behind a banner of the Virgin of Guadaloupe, carried crucifixes, and used the slogan, *Peregrinaçion, Penitencia, Revolucón (Pilgrimage, Penitence, Revolution)*. By the time they got to Sacramento, their pilgrimage had swollen to 8,000. At each stop they proclaimed a *Plan de Delano* written for the event by Latino playwright/screenwriter Luis Valdez and modeled of the *Plan de Ayala* of Mexican revolutionary Emiliano Zapata.

"We Shall Overcome! Across the San Joaquin Valley, across

California, across the entire Southwest of the United States,
Wherever there are Mexican people, wherever there are farm
workers, our movement is spreading like flames across a
dry plain. Our Pilgrimage is the match that will light our
cause for all farm workers to see what is happening here,
so that they may do as we have done.
The time has come for the liberation of the poor farm worker.
History is on our side.
MAY THE STRUGGLE GO ON! VIVA LA CAUSA!

• • •

On March 4th, John Lennon was quoted in the London *Evening Standard* saying that the Beatles were now more popular than Jesus. The comment set off a wave of protests including the crushing and burning of Beatles records across the U.S. Bible Belt.

• • •

A week later, on March 11th, Timothy Leary was convicted of possession for the Laredo, Texas bust (for less than an ounce of grass) under the Marihuana Tax Act of 1937. He was sentenced to 30 years in prison, fined $30,000, and ordered to undergo psychiatric treatment. He appealed the decision on the basis that the Marihuana Tax Act was unconstitutional, as it required self-incrimination in blatant violation of the Fifth Amendment. It was obvious that the establishment's beef with Leary was not possession of grass, but rather his revolutionary provocative proselytizing about LSD and the hopelessness of Western society. "You have to go out of your mind to use your head," he declaimed. "I would say that at present our society is so insane that even if the risks were 50-50 that if you took LSD you would be permanently insane, I still think the risk is worth taking, as long as the person knows that that's the risk."

The battles over LSD continued in the U.S. Government. Led by Robert Kennedy, the Senate opened an inquiry into the controversial drug. Kennedy's wife Ethel had recently undergone LSD therapy in Vancouver. The Senator from New York fiercely cross-examined officials of the FDA and the National Institute of Mental Health, who were suddenly back-pedaling, arguing for new restrictions, and demanding that research projects on the drug be shut down. "Why, if they were worthwhile six months ago, why aren't they worthwhile now?" asked Kennedy. "Why didn't you just let them continue? We keep going around and around…if I could get a flat answer about that, I would be happy. Is there a misunderstanding about my question?" He continued by arguing, "I think we have given too much emphasis and so much attention to the fact it can be dangerous and that it can hurt an individual who uses it…that perhaps to some extent we have lost sight of the fact that it can be very, very helpful in our society if used properly."

Kennedy's pleas fell on deaf ears. Within two years the U.S. had made possession of acid a misdemeanor and the sale a felony. Most of the rest of the world followed suit. The new 1960s version of Prohibition put people in jail but did not substantially slow down the widespread use of the hallucinogen. Even NASA joined in, reportedly giving LSD to astronauts as a way of preparing them for the weightlessness of outer space. After all, the most common description used for the effect of the drug was "Spacey!"

LSD was also popular amongst the engineers of Silicon Valley. Al Hubbard had an amazingly eclectic group of associates and acolytes. Richard Nixon called him a friend. George H.W. Bush, the future CIA Director and President, communicated with him. Hubbard, always playing his role as the Johnny Appleseed of Acid, also turned on many of the straightest and most brilliant of American engineers to the drug. Peter Schwartz, a senior engineer at Ampex and later a leading futurist, says that "problem solving in engineering always involves irreducible complexity. You're always balancing complex variables you can never get perfect, so you're desperately searching to find patterns. LSD shows you patterns. I have no doubt that all that Hubbard LSD all of us had taken had a big effect on the birth of Silicon Valley." LSD had a profound effect on many California engineers like Schwartz and was instrumental in changing the computer from a top-down tool of the military-industrial complex to a tool of personal liberation (with a countercultural vibe) and then helped drive the new concepts of cybernetics and virtual reality.

· · ·

All that was rapidly coming but was still in the future. In the very real, violent present of the '60s, the revolutions continued. On April 1, a group of ZANU fighters crossed the Zambezi River with the goal of sabotaging the Feruka oil refinery and pipeline. It wasn't an April Fool's joke, but it played like one. Within mere hours of their arrival, the Rhodesian authorities had captured them and beaten the plans out of them. The Rhodesians, realizing this was just the beginning of the movement, rolled out a security operation codenamed *Pagoda*, effectively marking the beginning of a shooting war in the country.

· · ·

There was talk of radical political change and separation all over the world. Frequently, the only difference of opinion was whether the change would be made violently or democratically. In Québec, future Premier René Lévesque promoted separatism at the 1966 convention of the province's Liberal Party. When the party rejected it, he walked out of the convention and soon thereafter founded the *Mouvement Souveraineté-Association*, an important organization that later morphed into the *Parti Québecois*, a powerful non-violent separatist party that came close (twice) to taking Québec out of Canada.

· · ·

TIME Magazine's April 8th cover was the first ever without a photo or illustration but instead the question IS GOD DEAD? in stark red text against a black background. Both the cover and the article created a firestorm. The *Los Angeles Times* later listed the issue as among the "Twelve Magazine Covers That Shook the World." *TIME* received 3,500 letters about the story—the largest it has ever received in response to a story in the entire history of the magazine. The story presented some bitter truths that many found difficult to accept—science and secularism in the 1960s were making people, even priests and theologians, question the existence of God. Church-going and traditional piety were in steep decline and were being replaced by the new passions of this revolutionary age.

• • •

God may have been dead, but Mao was not. Chinese publishers began selling "Quotations from the Works of Mao Tse-tung", familiarly known as the "Little Red Book". It is now considered the second best-selling book in the history of the world. There were at least one billion copies sold or given away. Some estimates put the number at over six billion, which would put it in the Number One spot, ahead of the Bible. Lin Biao, the Chinese Minister of Defense, called the book "a spiritual atom bomb of infinite power," and proclaimed "Mao Zedong's thought is a common asset to the revolutionary people of the whole world. This is the great international significance of the thought of Mao Zedong…Hold aloft the just banner of people's war…Victory will certainly go to the people of the world!"

• • •

The mid-60s were a period of censorship and turmoil in television. In England, a faux documentary about nuclear war titled *The War Game* had been pulled by the BBC from its planned 1965 telecast, either because the broadcaster was too squeamish to allow it to be shown, or because it was deemed to be not in tune with the government's foreign policy, or both. In April it was shown at the National Film Theatre in London. It went on to win the Best Documentary Academy Award and was described by Roger Ebert as "one of the most skillful documentaries ever made" with a portrayal of bombing that is "certainly the most horrifying ever put on film although, to be sure, greater suffering has taken place in real life, and is taking place today."

There was even more controversy at the Canadian public broadcaster. In April, the brass of the CBC fired the two hosts of the newsmagazine show *This Hour Has Seven Days*, which led to weeks of protest and acrimony in the Canadian press and parliament. *Seven Days* had gone on the air in October 1964 and many of its stories had been controversial. In one, they created a bear-pit confrontation between a leader of the Ku Klux Klan and a Black Power activist. In another, they uncovered an East German prostitute named Gerda Munsinger believed to be a spy ('the Cold War Mata Hari') who had conducted affairs with two members of the Federal Cabinet. The show was totally cancelled in the summer by conservative elements in the CBC executive offices, but it inspired a similar show, *W5* on CTV (the rival, private network) which in turn became the model for *60 Minutes*, that began on CBS in 1968.

South Africa totally banned television, to prevent the transmission of seditious ideas about freedom and equality. Albert Hertzog, the government minister responsible for communications announced that television would be allowed in the country "over [his] dead body." Only after an outcry from the white population that they were unable to watch the moon landings, and the removal of Hertzog from office, was television finally introduced in 1976.

● ● ●

China, which also did not yet have television, was instead starting to be bombarded with posters of Mao leading an adoring crowd of multiracial followers and words like, "The socialist system will eventually replace the capitalist system; this is an objective law independent of man's will. However much the reactionaries try to hold back the wheel of history, eventually revolution will inevitably triumph." Other posters quoted his poems, which he had been writing since the 1920s. For example, *The four seas are rising, clouds and waters raging / The five continents are rocking, wind and thunder roaring / Away with all pests / Our force is irresistible.*

• • •

There was no shortage of weird charismatic political leaders in this 1965 – 1975 period. Two of the most colorful met on April 20th. François "Papa Doc" Duvalier had been dictator of Haiti since 1957. He attained power, and hung on to it, by portraying himself as a voodoo spirit. He modelled himself on Baron Samedi, the most powerful and evil of voodoo gods, the spirit of the dead and the leader of the zombies. Duvalier dressed like Samedi, wearing a black tailcoat and top hat, and thick, dark spectacles. He created his own Praetorian Guard, known as the Tontons Macoute. The Tontons were a violent paramilitary force named after another voodoo bogeyman whose specialty was carrying unruly children off in a *macoute* (gunny sack) and eating them for breakfast. They were led by a man named Luckner Cambronne, nicknamed "the Vampire of the Caribbean". Luckner and his Macoutes protected Duvalier and murdered between 30 and 60 thousand Haitians, often selling their plasma to American clinics or their cadavers to American medical schools.

Duvalier had a number of titles, including *The Greatest Patriot of All Time, The Emancipator of the Masses, The Renovator of the Haitian Nation, The Champion of National Dignity,* and *Chief of the Revolution and President for Life of Haiti.* On April 20th he greeted Haile Selassie at the newly renamed Aéroport François Duvalier and accompanied him along newly named Avenue Haile Selassie to his palace in Port-au-Prince. Selassie was equally grandly titled. He was not merely Emperor and Regent Plenipotentiary of Ethiopia, but also *King of Kings, Lord of Lords, Elect of God,* and *Conquering Lion of the Tribe of Judah.* His regalia was also considerably grander than

Duvalier's—his chest was completely covered with medals and gold braid, and he was also literally believed by many people to be the Son of God, descended from Jesus Christ. Selassie had ruled Ethiopia since 1916 and acted in a manner to put Roman emperors to shame. He once travelled to Europe and presented both the President of France and King of England with presents—lions from his personal pride.

Following his meeting with the creepy and frightening Haitian dictator, Emperor Selassie flew to Jamaica, where he was greeted by over 100,000 ganja-smoking Rastaferians. In an era that was full of examples of the cult of personality, this was surely one of the strangest. The Rastaferi took their name from Selassie's, as before he was all those other titles listed above, he was simply Ras (meaning "Duke") Selassie. In 1966 there were about 600,000 in the quasi-religious group, who believed Selassie was the Second Coming of Jesus and Jah incarnate; that Africa was Zion, the Promised Land; and that Western society was oppressive and evil—'Babylon'. Most especially, they believed that marijuana was a sacrament and should be smoked on a virtually non-stop basis.

When Selassie's plane landed in Jamaica, it was rushed by such a huge crowd of ganja-smoking, dreadlock-crowned Rastaferians that their hero refused to leave the safety of the cabin. After leaders cleared the crowd, Selassie finally had the nerve to descend from the plane, and he eventually met with many of them. Rita Marley, the wife of reggae star Bob Marley, was convinced she saw stigmata on Selassie's hand as he waved to the crowd. The markings, that looked like the scars on Jesus' hands after the crucifixion, were enough to convince her that he really was the Messiah. Soon after, she converted Bob Marley to the cult and he became not just its best-known member, but the conduit through which the world learned about this groovy new sect.

• • •

Jamaica would soon acquire a certain cachet from the ganja-fueled reggae of Marley, Jimmy Cliff, and others, but for now London was ordained as the swinging center of all things hip. A *TIME* magazine cover article proclaimed that there had been a "bloodless revolution" in Britain that had created "a kind of classlessness and a verve which has not been seen before." But for all the hoopla about how "Eng-a-land swings like a pendulum do", about the Beatles and Carnaby Street, Mini-Coopers and miniskirts, many aspects of British life remained unchanged. One of the most popular TV shows of the day, believe it or not, was the *Black and White Minstrel Show*, in which white singers and dancers blackened their faces to perform over-the-top caricatures of black performers. BBC provided the only radio to the country, and it too seemed stuck in the 1940s. In reaction, hip entrepreneurs set up what became known as pirate radio stations on ships moored just outside British territorial waters. The best known were Radio Caroline, moored off the Suffolk coast, and Radio Atlanta, off Essex. These stations, playing the kind of rock and roll that young people wanted to hear, became wildly popular. The Postmaster General introduced a bill to Parliament outlawing the pirate stations, and the Marine Offences Act became law in August of 1967.

The Beatles, freed from the intense five-year grind of touring, performing, and making records and films, took the opportunity to go into swinging London's EMI Abbey Road Studios for a luxurious 70 days to create what many believe was their masterpiece. According to musicologist Russell Reising, "*Revolver* has assumed the status of cultural icon, approaching in its many avatars, its impact, and its endurance the status of some of the definitive works of Anglo-American culture such as Herman Melville's *Moby Dick* and James Joyce's *Ulysses.*" Many "All-Time Best" lists in magazines from *Entertainment Weekly* to the official newspaper of the Holy See, *L'Observatore Romano,* call it the greatest album of all time. The word "revolutionary" was frequently used to describe the Beatles' new offering. In the *Village Voice,* one of America's preeminent rock critics, Richard Goldstein, described *Revolver* as "revolutionary". Tony Hall in the *Record Mirror* called the songs on the record "the most revolutionary ever made by a pop group." The music, as indeed indicated by the title of the album *was* revolutionary, partially due to the mind-altering LSD-25 that the band was now ingesting in quantity, partially simply due to the incredible originality and talent of the band's three song writers. The Beatles certainly had a revolutionary effect on millions of young people in the Western world, but perhaps their greatest influence was not in England, Europe, or the Americas, but in Russia.

The Beatles' records were banned in the Soviet Union. It was forbidden to bring a Beatles record into the country, and if anyone tried, customs officials were equipped with special scratching devices to deface the discs so they wouldn't play. President Nikita Khrushchev declared the electric guitar "the enemy of the Soviet people," and the group was derided in the Soviet press as "the Bugs". However, Soviet youth fought back. The rare Beatles albums that made it into the country, usually smuggled by sailors into ports like Leningrad (now St. Petersburg), were secretly copied onto discarded medical X-Ray acetates, and sold on the black market as 'flexis.' It was a dangerous business—some sellers of Beatles flexis were sent off to the Siberian gulag for seven-year prison terms. It was illegal to listen to the Beatles, but one way or another, hundreds of thousands did. It was strictly запрещено (forbidden) to even jokingly mention the similarity between the names Vladimir Lenin and John Lennon, but the braver of young people liked to tweak the authorities by doing exactly that. Hundreds created homemade guitars and stripped propaganda poles of their speakers to build amplifiers so that they could create underground tribute rock bands.

Russian historians are convinced that the effects of the Beatles on Russian society were profound and eventually contributed to the end of the Soviet Union, "Beatlemania washed away the foundations of Soviet society," said the august Institute of Russian History. "They helped a generation of free people grow up in the Soviet Union."

"Russia was held together by fear and belief," says Russian TV journalist Vladimir Pozner, "and the Beatles played a role in overcoming the fear and in showing that the belief was actually stupid."

Artemy Troitsky, the Russian rock historian, adds, "In the big bad west they had massive institutions that spent tens of millions of dollars to undermine the Soviet system, and I'm sure that the impact of all those dumb cold war institutions had a much smaller effect than the impact of the Beatles, who turned millions of young people to another religion. And by the end of the '80s, the whole of Soviet ideology and Soviet power disappeared like fog in the morning."

• • •

On April 28th, as the Beatles were recording *Revolver* in London and the Russians were trying their hardest to prevent other Russians from listening to Beatles music, seven members of the Zimbabwean African National Liberation Army surreptitiously crossed from training camps in Zambia deep into what was then Ian Smith's Southern Rhodesia searching for transmission towers to bomb. They were spotted by Rhodesian helicopters and shot to death before they did much damage. They were soon mythologized as martyrs in the cause of the Chimurenga (Revolutionary) War of Liberation against Smith's white Rhodesian government. The guerrilla leader who had sent the group in, Joseph Khumalo, defended his action by quoting Mao: "Where there is war, there is sacrifice…Fight, Fail, Fight, Fail. Until you succeed." The African would-be freedom fighters, though, realized they needed much more training if they were to try to take on the might of the Rhodesian security forces. They began to be schooled by the Chinese at the Nanjing Military College in China, and at revolutionary training camps in Zambia. At first, remembers John Mawema, who would later become head of security for ZANU, the training was "a sort of an adventure. What we saw in the films. People shooting at each other. You know, wanting to become cowboys of some sort. But as you go for training you are given the political line of the party, the ideology, and the objectives of the armed struggle. Then you realized that all you were thinking was wrong…the party was more concerned with political education than military training. The Chinese believed you have got to be mature politically in your head before you go and shoot…You know the Chinese are very particular about such behavior."

In contrast, the Rhodesian army was staunchly non-political and non-philosophical. Paul Moorcroft, a journalist who reported on the war, wrote that the Rhodesian's "vague conservatism and hole-in-the-corner racism" could not compete with ZANU's sense of mission and commitment to the cause of Maoist revolution. The freedom fighters needed every ounce of discipline, as the Rhodesians used all manner of brutal warfare against them. In the war zone, they left caches of cigarette boxes soaked in poison, containers of corned beef and jam injected with thallium, and clothes soaked with parathion, an extremely powerful toxin created by the Nazis and known in Germany as *Schwiegermuttergift* (mother-in-law present). It was not only the guerrilla fighters but also curious civilians and children who consumed the poisons and ended up dying gruesome deaths in the bush.

• • •

In Québec, the FLQ bombing campaign moved from attacks on symbols of federalism and Anglo domination to assaults on local companies engaged in labor disputes. The unfortunately named H. B. Lagrenade Shoe Company was a family-owned business that had been embroiled in a labor dispute for over a year, claiming it could not increase wages paid to their workers ($1.05 an hour for men, 90 cents for women) and still be able to compete with low-cost foreign shoemakers. Eventually the FLQ grew weary of the lengthy strike and sent in a bomber who handed a shoebox to the first person he met, telling her it was a return from a dissatisfied customer. Within a few minutes, it blew up, killing secretary Thérèse Morin and badly injuring three others.

• • •

The battles over sex and especially over the newly created contraceptive known as The Pill continued through the '60s. In May, after three years of discussion and argument, the Vatican under Pope John XXIII issued a report that finally approved of contraception for Roman Catholics. There were many dissenters within the church against this radical and progressive decision and it would be rescinded three years later by his successor, Pope Paul VI. The church would then return to its role as the primary international institution encouraging over-population and its consequence, global warming.

• • •

On May 22nd, Ugandan Prime Minister promoted Idi Amin Dada to become Commander of the Uganda Army, and demanded that Amin lead troops to oust Mutesa II, the Kabaka (ruler) of Buganda (a kingdom within Uganda). Amin and his soldiers attacked Mutesa's palace the next day, killed his guards, and set it on fire. Mutesa escaped (though he broke his foot jumping from the palace) and sought refuge at the Rubaga Cathedral. Disguised as a priest, he escaped, first to Burundi, then Kenya, then Ethiopia, then England where he lived in exile for the rest of his life. Hundreds of his supporters and guards were killed and buried in mass graves in Kampala. The event increased the power of both Milton Obote, and his military commander Idi Amin, who would, in five years, depose Obote in his own coup and become the most infamous of African leaders—the so-called 'Butcher of Uganda.'

• • •

On May 7th Mao Zedong wrote a letter to his lieutenant Lin Biao projecting a utopian vision of military organization and political indoctrination in which the Chinese people and army would fuse to become indistinct. On June 1st, Mao officially began the Cultural Revolution in China. with an editorial in the *People's Daily* exhorting readers to SWEEP

AWAY ALL MONSTERS AND DEMONS! The editorial urged people to denounce representatives of the bourgeoisie who were out to "deceive, fool and benumb the working people in order to consolidate their reactionary state power." The same day all classes were suspended across China, and Liu Shaoqi and Deng Xiaoping dispatched work teams to high schools and colleges to lead the Cultural Revolution. Almost immediately they got into battles with some of the more outspoken students, who they characterized as 'rightists'.

One and a half million Chinese died in the revolution that lasted until 1976. It was a stunning tableau of extreme violence, killing, torture, and even cannibalism, with the teenage Red Guards, encouraged by the country's leaders, revolting against school teachers, army officers, civic officials, and anyone thought to be bourgeois or intellectual. The Guards also destroyed anything perceived to be old—antiques, artwork, ancient texts, and Buddhist temples. They even almost destroyed entire animal populations like Pekinese dogs, who were associated with the old Imperial regime. The breed nearly went extinct in its own homeland.

· · ·

On June 3rd, two days before a provincial election, René Lévesque was in the middle of a passionate speech before 6,000 people in a political rally inside the Paul-Sauvé Arena in Montréal when a very loud bomb exploded in one of the building's washrooms. The unstoppable Lévesque continued his speech, but reporters covering the event rushed to the washroom to find it destroyed, but fortunately empty of any unzipped users. The bomb was presumed to be FLQ, though why they would be bombing an event featuring separatist Lévesque remains an unsolved mystery.

· · ·

In South Africa, the four million whites who ran the country were at the height of their power, lording it over the 20 million non-whites with viciously repressive and baldly racist policies. The few dissenters were brutally eliminated. The African National Congress was banned. Nelson Mandela was in Robbin Island where he would be imprisoned for 27 years. White students like Ian Robertson, leader of the National Union of South African Students, was also "banned" under the Suppression of Communism Act. Nonetheless, he had the audacity to invite U.S. Senator Robert Kennedy to come to speak to South African students—and Kennedy had the courage to accept the invitation. Kennedy, even though he was a U.S. Senator, did not meet with any officials from the country, but spoke instead only to students and banned Black leaders.

Prior to 1965, Kennedy's attitudes about race had been vague at best, but he had been transformed after seeing the conviction of the SNNC civil rights workers like John Lewis at Selma and around the American south. He was now determined to speak out at an event called the Day of Affirmation of Human and Academic Freedom at the University of Cape Town. He was met by thousands when he arrived at Jan Smuts Airport on June 4 and set the tone of his visit by speaking from the 'Non-Whites' section of the terminal. Before the first event he met with the organizer, Ian Robertson. As a 'banned' person, Robertson was forbidden to meet with more than one person at a time, so Kennedy talked with him alone at his dorm room. Before talking about the event or the situation in South Africa, Kennedy asked him if the student thought the room was bugged. When Robertson allowed that it probably was, the past-Attorney-General of the U.S. recommended a couple of techniques to avoid being audible to the buggers—either play music or tap on the floor while talking.

Kennedy electrified the students in Cape Town by saying, "Each time a man stands up for an ideal or acts to improve the lot of others, or strikes out at injustice, he sends out a tiny ripple of hope. Crossing each other from a million different centers of energy and daring, those ripples build a current which can sweep down the mightiest walls of oppression and resistance."

The foreign press was forbidden from covering Kennedy's visit, but some South Africans did hear his words, transmitted by the extremely brave activist Helen Sussman, and they certainly did get back to the government. John Vorster, then Minister of Justice (soon to become Prime Minister) dismissed Kennedy's visit by calling the student organization "communist" and "a cancer on the life of the society."

Kennedy responded to the taunt at his next speech at Stellenbosch University by asking, "Is anti-communism all we stand for? We stand for human freedom. We stand for human dignity. And we stand for ending discrimination and ending hunger. And we stand for extending freedom and justice all over the globe. And I think that's why we've attracted other people—those who have a difficult time in their own lives to come and follow the banner of the United States, not just because we're anti-communist, but because we stand for something." [16]

In his final stop, Kennedy visited the vast black township of Soweto. His speechwriter, Adam Walinsky, observed that this was "probably the first time ever that a person of authority had gone to this enormous place and said, 'You're human beings. You're okay. I can come and talk to you. I don't have to worry. I'm not armed. I don't have lots of guards around me. It's just you and me.'"

While in Soweto, Kennedy visited with Chief Albert Luthuli, the President of the African National Congress. Luthuli had been awarded the Nobel Peace Prize, which the South African newspaper *Die Transvaler* called "an inexplicable pathological phenomenon". But he, like Robertson, was banned, forbidden from going out, so Kennedy could only have a private one-on-one meeting with him.

"If you can sweep unjust privilege into the dead past," Kennedy told him, "if you can show the dispossessed and the diseased and the hungry and the untaught that there is a better life for them and a fair place in the sun for their children—if you can do all these things, then all of us will take heart from your example, and this continent can take its place in the modern world."

• • •

Back in America a powerful and eloquent new black leader exploded onto the scene. Stokely Carmichael was a veteran of the Freedom Rides of the early 60s, during which he had been beaten and jailed for trying to integrate the bus counters and schools of the deep south. In a dramatic speech on June 16th, he introduced many to his concept of 'Black Power,' questioning the tactic of non-violence in order to end segregation. "In order for non-violence to work," he proclaimed, "your opponent must have a conscience. The United States has none." He claimed that blacks were not fighting for the right to integrate, they were fighting against white supremacy. "In order to understand white supremacy, we must dismiss the fallacious notion that white people can give anybody their freedom. No man can give anybody his freedom. A man is born free. You may enslave a man after he is born free, and that is in fact what this country does. It enslaves black people after they're born, so that the only acts that white people can now do is to stop denying black people their freedom." J. Edgar Hoover was soon convinced that Carmichael might become the thing his twisted mind most feared—a 'Black Messiah'—so he gave the FBI's secret COINTELPRO program full consent to try to destroy him.

• • •

In the mid 1960s women were in many ways even more disadvantaged than Blacks. A married woman could usually not open a bank account, apply for a loan or a credit card, or even get a library card without her husband's permission and signature. In Canada for instance, six times as many women as men were making less than $4,000 a year. For older women, it was even worse. The average annual income for males over 65 was $3,044; for women it was $1,556, which was $200 below the poverty line.

On June 30th, a group of women decided to try to do something about it. Betty Friedan, author of the recently-published *The Feminine Mystique* and 28 others founded the National Organization for Women (NOW). Friedan, elected the first president, believed that "the first step of revolution is consciousness," and it was now time for the second—organization.

NOW and the feminist movement made gains, such as forcing men-only bars and clubs to change their rules and demanding banks give women financial freedom. However, it also got tremendous pushback, not just from powerful males in politics and the press, but also from other women. Phyllis Schlafly was a conservative Republican activist who led a fight against NOW and the women's movement all through the '60s and '70s and was largely responsible for the failure of the U.S. Congress to ratify the Equal Rights Amendment.

• • •

In July, after his 18-month exile in the Congo, Tanzania, and Czechoslovakia, Che Guevara returned to Cuba to consult with Castro, to visit his wife, and to write a last letter to his five children to be read upon his death. It ended with the words, "Above all, always be capable of feeling deeply any injustice committed against anyone, anywhere in the world. This is the most beautiful quality in a revolutionary."

• • •

It is unlikely that young revolutionary Jean Corbo had written a letter to be opened on his death, since he likely saw himself as being invincible. On July 14, the 16-year-old FLQ bomber was killed while placing dynamite beside the Dominion Textile plant in Saint-Henri, a poor neighborhood of Montréal. At his funeral, his father described him as being "a servant of the high priests of separatist terrorism…and the naïve instrument of adult conspirators."

• • •

Two days later, on July 16th, a group of ZAPU guerrillas tried to infiltrate Rhodesia from Zambia by crossing the Zambezi River (itself not a simple task, since it is filled with man-eating hippos and crocodiles). It was another failed mission in the African Bush Wars. The guerrillas were all killed or captured.

• • •

Mao Zedong also picked July 16th to swim across the Yangtze River to signal his determination to carry through the Cultural Revolution. There were no crocodiles to worry about, and Mao used the strong current to float downstream and emerge on the other side of the river an hour later "with ruddy cheeks and buoyant spirit." The Chinese press gushed about the event, saying he "showed no sign of fatigue," and comparing the wind and waves to the black storm kicked up by imperialists, revisionists and reactionaries. Mao penned a new poem to celebrate the event:

> *I care not that the wind blows and the waves beat.*
> *It is better than idly strolling in a courtyard.*

Many of his rabid followers tried to emulate his stunt, but since many of them could not swim, there were many drownings. At the Summer Palace 8,000 people, some soldiers in full uniform, tried to swim across the water. The Xuanwu Lake in Nanjing was suddenly opened for swimming. Several of the newbie bathers drowned every day throughout the summer.

By August, Mao Zedong's fourth wife, ex-Shanghai B-movie star Lang Pin ("Blue Apple"), now restyled as Comrade Jiang Qing, had become the main vindictive crusader of the Cultural Revolution. In her words, she took to "biting whoever Chairman Mao told me to bite." She would soon become the leader of a radical group known as the "Gang of Four". Madame Mao and her gang certainly used the wacky Cultural Revolution to consolidate their power. What Mao himself got out of it is harder to fathom. Perhaps the revolution was all about an old man settling personal scores and reliving the most exciting years of his life, twenty years later. Mao had grandiose ideas of his own historical destiny, and constantly talked of his own greatness. It was not entirely hubris since he had indeed led a quarter of the world's population to liberation in 1949, and then had successfully taken on the two greatest empires in the world, the American and the British, and fought them to a truce in Korea. Now, he knew he had enemies within the Chinese government and might be tossed to the ash-heap of history just as Stalin had been by Khrushchev. Why, then, not take the crazy step of convincing millions of pumped-up teenagers to fight the revolution of '49 all over again, just to try and permanently cement his reputation?

• • •

Meanwhile another bunch of crazy revolutionaries, Ken Kesey's Merry Pranksters, made another trip in their psychedelic bus "Further", this time through the American southwest and Mexico. The driver of the bus would again be Neal Cassady, already lionized as a legend in *On the Road*, Jack Kerouac's opus of the beatnik '50s. Novelist Robert Stone described Cassady as, "the world's greatest driver, who could roll a joint while backing a 1937 Packard onto the lip of the Grand Canyon." Kesey described Cassady's spiritual path as, "the yoga of a man driven to the cliff edge by the grassfire of an entire nation's burning material madness. Rather than be consumed by this, he jumped, choosing to sort things out in the fast-flying but smog-free moments of a life with no retreat."

As they travelled, the Pranksters turned on the people they met to what they called their "acid tests". It took a big leap of faith and a certain amount of courage to ingest the powerful, mysterious drug, and as acid chroniclers Martin Lee and Bruce Shlain wrote, it was "for many young men and women a way of cutting the last umbilical cord to everything the older generation had designated as safe and sanitized. If smoking marijuana turned people into social outlaws, acid led many to see themselves as cosmic fugitives." [17]

•   •   •

Public opinion shifted profoundly in 1966, with more and more people questioning the official words of authorities. Much of this stemmed from what Lyndon Johnson and the U.S. military was now doing in Vietnam, and from increasing suspicions about government involvement in the 1963 assassination of President John F. Kennedy. In 1964, the Warren Commission's conclusion that Lee Harvey Oswald had acted alone was accepted by most of the world, and certainly by the American press, which regurgitated it, as they did most government-produced information, as gospel. Dissenters, however, began to speak up. British philosopher Bertrand Russell published a critical article titled *16 Questions on the Assassination*, and Penn Jones Jr., the publisher of a small Texas newspaper, began printing stories about the many witnesses to the assassination (he claimed 150 in total) who had since died under mysterious circumstances. Neither of these could match the impact of *Rush to Judgement*, Mark Lane's new book about the assassination, when it was published in August. Meticulously researched and highly inflammatory, the book presented numerous arguments that Oswald could not have shot the president on his own; that there had to have been other shooters; and that the Warren Commission was covering up a conspiracy, possibly involving Texan oil interests, right-wing groups, the FBI, the CIA, and conceivably LBJ himself. The book had an enormous influence on the zeitgeist of the era, becoming Number One in the US and sitting on the *New York Times* best seller list for 29 weeks.

•   •   •

John Lennon opened a press conference in Chicago on August 11th by apologizing for his previous comments about Jesus. "I suppose if I had said television was more popular than Jesus, I would have gotten away with it. I'm sorry I opened my mouth. I'm not anti-God, anti-Christ, or anti-religion. I was not knocking it. I was not saying we were greater or better."

• • •

On the 18th, Chairman Mao, wearing a military uniform and a Red Guard armband, welcomed a million students to Tiananmen Square. Over the following months he would review over 12 million Red Guards in Beijing. On the 23rd, the *People's Daily* applauded the violence of the Red Guards and their campaign to destroy all remnants of the old society. The government gave the Red Guards free transportation and accommodation passes, and soon hundreds of thousands of them were travelling to all corners of China to establish revolutionary networks and attack local civic authorities as 'Capitalist Roaders' and 'Bourgeois Reactionaries.'

Schools became hotbeds of revolutionary activity and were soon plastered with posters reading 'Smash the Black Gang', 'Down with the Anti-Socialist Cabal', and 'Carry the Revolution Through to the End!' and accusing various people of being 'Imperialist Running Dogs.' Once the walls of the schools were covered, the students charged out to the streets with their pots of sweet potato paste to stick the giant posters on every available wall. The teenagers egged each other on, trying to outdo each other in demonstrations of revolutionary fervor as the schools descended into chaos. Teachers, and students who were perceived to be 'rightists' were paraded around in dunce caps or forced to wear buckets of heavy rocks around their necks. Some had their heads shaved, others given 'yin and yang' haircuts, in which only half the hair was shorn. In Fujian province, dozens died or committed suicide after being tormented by students. Girls as young as six practiced shouting "Kill!" in shrill, synchronized voices.

The first death happened at a girls' school administered by Beijing Normal University. The girls tortured the Vice-Principal, Bian Zhongyun by spitting on her, filling her mouth with mud, forcing a dunce cap on her head, and then beating her up. They then corralled five more school administrators, splashed them with ink, then pummeled them with nail-spiked clubs. After hours of this torture Bian lost consciousness and was dumped into a garbage can. Once she was eventually examined by doctors, she was pronounced dead. Madame Mao reacted to the news of the killing by asking, "What's so special about beating people anyway? When bad people get beaten by good people, they deserve it."

The Chinese students abandoned their school uniforms and adopted a ragged military look, remarkably like the look adopted by many western hippies and radicals in the '60s—nothing shiny or new, but rather vintage rag-tag military gear, with a leather belt used to whip enemies when needed, and a red and gold armband reading 'Red Guard.'

On August 18th, over a million Red Guards arrived before daybreak at Tiananmen Square to hear speeches from their leaders. Lin Biao told the excited teens to destroy "all the old ideas, old culture, old customs, and old habits of the exploiting classes." Chairman Mao praised one of the students who had weeks earlier killed her Vice-Principal Bian Zhongyun, and re-named the girl Song Yaowu, which means 'Be Martial.'

A new wave of student violence followed. Elementary school kids forced their teachers to eat nails and excrement. At the Beijing Teachers College, a biology teacher was dragged by her legs down a set of steps, and then other teachers, accused of being monsters and demons, were forced to take turns to beat her dead body. The students ripped down everything that symbolized the past—temples, statues, antique shops, architectural cornices and ornamentation. They attacked libraries and lit up the night sky with massive book-burnings. Added to the conflagrations were wooden ancestor tablets, old paper currency, bamboo mah-jongg tiles, western violins, and antique calligraphy scrolls. Flowers, cats, goldfish, and racing pigeons were all deemed to be bourgeois so flower stores were ransacked, and the streets were littered with the bodies of those pet animals.

The Guards also tried to make the cities "redder and purer" by parading people they considered 'class enemies' through the streets. At one point in the summer nearly 80,000 people were jammed into Beijing's railway stations, desperately lined up for trains to take them to exile deep in the countryside. In Shanghai more than 400,000 were exiled, mostly old people stripped of their belongings and forced to wear signs around their necks proclaiming their 'bourgeois crimes.'

• • •

August 31st saw the first release of the film *The Battle of Algiers*, that would become the favorite film of revolutionaries around the world. The film, using the compelling faux-newsreel style known as Italian Neo-Realism, recreated battles in the recent Algerian revolution between Algerians and their colonial masters the French. The film, written and directed by Gillo Pontecorvo with music by famed composer Ennio Morricone, was wildly received everywhere but France. Critic Roger Ebert called it "a great film that exists on this level of bitter reality. It may be a deeper film experience than many audiences can withstand: too cynical, too true, too cruel, and too heartbreaking." It wasn't too much for the Black Panthers, the IRA or the PLO, all of whom claimed it as motivational and instructional for their goals of urban guerrilla warfare. It was definitely too much for the French. *Cahiers du Cinéma* magazine devoted an entire issue to condemning the film, and the French government banned it until 1971.

• • •

The mid-sixties were a period of radical experimentation in the field of art. Fine art was only considered valid if it was extreme, unusual, and preferably controversial. Typically off-beat was Japanese-born artist Yayoi Kusama, who in August was invited to display her work at the prestigious Venice Biennale. Kusama presented a piece titled *Narcissus Garden* comprised of hundreds of mirrored spheres outdoors in what she called a 'kinetic carpet.' To the consternation of the Biennale organizers she walked through the exhibit selling the spheres off to visitors for only 1200 lira ($2) apiece. The curators eventually put an end to that—strange art pieces they could handle but selling them off in the middle of the exhibit at bargain-basement prices they could not countenance.

Kusama returned to New York, where she began to stage 'happenings' through the mid to late '60s. In one, called *Grand Orgy to Awaken the Dead at the MOMA*, she had eight performers step naked into the fountain in the Sculpture Garden of the Museum of Modern Art and adopt poses imitating the sculptures of Picasso and Giacometti. Another had her painting on the bodies of nude models, another was a nude protest outside the New York Stock Exchange, and one an offer from her to have sex with Richard Nixon if he would stop the war in Vietnam. It was an odd proposal, since no one in the Swinging Sixties could imagine Richard Nixon having sex, and Kusama herself has claimed to hate sex and has been virtually celibate her entire life. Her life has been quite strange—she now, for instance, voluntarily lives as a patient in a mental home, but her artworks, very much a product of the '60s, have continued to be popular to this day, exhibited in major public galleries around the world.

Another avant-garde artist of the sixties was Yoko Ono. In her *Cut Piece*, she sat on stage dressed in an expensive suit with a pair of scissors in front of her, and invited members of the audience to slice pieces from the suit until she was close to naked. She was involved with other wildly experimental artists such as the Fluxus Group and composer John Cage in New York. Ono then moved to London, where she famously turned John Lennon on with her coy and inventive artworks. Theirs became the quintessential marriage of this '65 – '75 era—a heady combo of working-class pop success with avant-garde conceptual art with leftwing politics, and all the while being chased by FBI gumshoes.

Kusama and Ono, and in fact all the other artists in the world, were in the minor leagues compared to the one artist who truly revolutionized the artistic zeitgeist of the period—Andy Warhol. "Andy is the first real art celebrity since Picasso and Dali," wrote critic Calvin Tompkins. "From time to time an individual appears, often but not necessarily an artist, who seems to be in phase with certain vibrations—signals not yet receivable by standard equipment. The clairvoyance with which Andy touched the nerve of fashion and commercial art, the energy emanating from God knows where, the inarticulateness and naiveté, the very mystery and empti-ness of his persona—all this suggests the presence of an uncanny intuition. Always somewhat unearthly, Warhol became in the 1960s a speechless and rather terrifying oracle. He made visible what was happening in some part of us all."

By 1966 Warhol had already created many of his most famous and controversial artworks—his Campbell's Soup Can series, and his "Death and Disaster" series of suicide and murder victims, and to some degree had left painting behind him. "I don't paint anymore. Painting is dead," he told filmmaker Emile de Antonio. When asked what he might paint if he did paint in the future, he said, "Well, I like empty walls. As soon as you put something on them, they look terrible." But to photographer David Bailey he denied having stopped: "I haven't stopped painting. I paint my nails. I paint my eyes every day."

In fact, he had (temporarily) stopped painting and had taken up filmmaking. His films were as provocative as his art. One, *Sleep*, was billed as an 'anti-film'. It was five hours and twenty minutes long and consisted of a virtually static shot of his lover at the time, John Giorno, sleeping. He followed this with *Empire*, an eight-hour-long static shot of the Empire State Building. The reaction from audiences to both films was mostly a flurry of demands to get their money back, but their sheer audacity meant they burnished Warhol's ever-growing reputation. In 2004, *Empire* was given the honor of being added to the U.S. National Film Registry, deemed "culturally, historically or aesthetically significant."

On September 15, *Chelsea Girls*, Warhol's most famous and import-ant film, opened in New York. This one was six and a half hours long, but the challenging running time was shortened by playing the film on two projectors running side-by-side, so the audience only had to sit still for a little over three hours. It also had some real stars, including the exotic German singer/actress Nico, who had appeared in Federico Fellini's *La Dolce Vita*, and performed in another of Warhol's creations, the multimedia event *The Exploding Plastic Inevitable.* It was critically acclaimed, with *Newsweek* calling it "the *Iliad* of the Underground", the *Village Voice* claiming it was "a metaphor for burning Vietnam," and the *New York Times* calling it a "grotesque menagerie of lost souls whimpering in a psychedelic moonscape." Of course, being the '60s, not everyone agreed. Catty critic Rex Reed termed it, "a three-and-a-half-hour cesspool of vulgarity and talentless confusion which is about as interesting as the inside of a toilet bowl." Notwithstanding Reed's opinion, the audiences flocked to it and Warhol had his biggest payday in many years.

• • •

Meanwhile, as Warhol was counting his ticket receipts, Kusama was winging back from Italy to New York, and Ono was having her clothes chopped off, FLQ separatists Charles Gagnon and Pierre Vallières were fleeing a police sweep in Québec and heading for the U.S. border. On September 27th, they appeared at the press gallery of the United Nations in Manhattan where they declared they were committed to taking Québec out of Canada and turning it into an independent socialist republic. The next day, the two returned to the UN with protest signs, and were promptly arrested by New York police and sent to the notorious prison known as The Tombs. They began a hunger strike to try to have the jailed FLQ bombers in Québec recognized as political prisoners. While confined, Vallières wrote his revolutionary manifesto, *Nègres Blancs d'Amérique* or *White Niggers of America*, and smuggled it out of jail, a few pages at a time, disguised as letters to his lawyer. Since he and Gagnon refused to return to Montréal, Canada initiated their extradition.

• • •

On the other side of the Atlantic, an equally notorious prison, Wormwood Scrubs, was seeing a much more brazen departure. George Blake was a convicted Russian spy, jailed for 42 years, reportedly for the 42 British agents executed by the Russians due to his revelations. He had begun his secret life as a member of the Dutch resistance fighting against the Nazis. In 1942 he escaped from Holland, made his way to England, and in 1944 was recruited into the Secret Intelligence Service (MI6). After the war he continued to work for the agency, and in 1948 was sent to work under the cover of the British legation to South Korea. He was captured during the Korean War and held in detention in North Korea for three years. While in detention he became a communist and changed sides. Journalists later proposed that he had been brainwashed. He gave his own description:

> It was the relentless bombing of small Korean villages by enormous
> American Flying Fortresses. Women and children and old people,
> because the young men were in the army. We might have been victims ourselves.
> It made me ashamed of belonging to these overpowering,
> technically superior countries fighting against what seemed to me
> defenseless people. I felt I was on the wrong side…that it would be better
> for humanity if the communist system prevailed, that it would put an end to war.

Following his release in 1953, Blake returned to England. Considered a hero, he was sent to Berlin to continue spying for MI6. For six years he was a secret agent for the British, while working even more secretly as a double agent for the Soviet Union. In 1961, he was caught, ultimately confessed, and was sentenced to three consecutive terms of 14 years for a total of 42 years—the longest sentence (excluding life) ever handed out in Britain.

While in Wormwood Scrubs, Blake met two prominent peace activists, Michael Randle and Pat Pottle. Both were serving 18-month sentences for their roles in organizing a demonstration at the USAF nuclear base at Wethersfield, Essex. They conspired, along with Sean Bourke, a recently released Irish petty criminal to attempt to bust Blake out of the prison, because of what they considered to be the "vicious and inhumane" sentence given to him. Blake also managed to link up with Michael Hollingshead, a wild man associate of Timothy Leary, who shared some LSD with Blake, which apparently inspired the spy's next adventure.

A week later, while most of the inmates and guards were watching the weekly movie, Blake broke a window, slid down a porch, then, with a rope ladder thrown to him by Bourke, escaped from the prison. He managed to escape from England, made his way across Europe to East Germany and on to the USSR. He lived in Moscow for the rest of his life, working for Russian Intelligence and stating at one point that spies "have the difficult and critical mission" of saving the world "in a situation when the danger of nuclear war and the resulting self-destruction of humankind again have been put on the agenda by irresponsible politicians. It is a true battle between good and evil." Blake died in Moscow, aged 98, on December 26, 2020.

Sean Bourke, inspired by the revolutionary period, joined Blake in Moscow, and lived there for 18 months under a special Soviet pension. He did not like Russia, though, and eventually returned to Ireland, where he wrote a book titled *The Springing of George Blake*. The British government attempted to have him returned to England to face charges, but Ireland refused to extradite him, stating his actions were political, not criminal. He became both alcoholic and penurious, and died. The coroner ruled his death to be coronary thrombosis aggravated by alcohol abuse, but Russian defector and KGB General Oleg Kalugin later alleged that he had been poisoned by the USSR to prevent him from spilling any details about Russian intelligence.

· · ·

The battle over LSD continued to be fought across America. In the spring a Senate Subcommittee led by a conservative Senator Thomas Dodd of Connecticut went on a rampage against what they called the "scourge" of LSD. The senators were aided by the mainstream press, which ran articles throughout 1966 with headlines like, GIRL 5, EATS LSD AND GOES WILD and THRILL DRUG WARPS MIND, KILLS. The new alternative press begun in '65 and '66, newspapers like the San Francisco *Oracle*, the Los Angeles *Free Press* and New York's *East Village Other* countered with much different news, but their multi-colored inks, psyche-delic graphics, swirly hard-to-read fonts and limited (though not non-exis-tent) distribution meant they were largely preaching to the choir. The lurid stories printed in the mainstream press about LSD frying chromosomes were not refuted by the many Army doctors who knew them to be false, and so the politicians enacted the new Prohibition.

Things came to a head in California on October 6, 1966 when a new law banning LSD took effect. The date reminded some in the com-munity of the number 666, which the Bible claims to be a Satanic number, precursor of the Apocalypse, and so viewed the new law as a demonic act. The San Francisco community, led by the *Oracle*, held a rally in the Panhandle next to Golden Gate Park. It was not a protest, but rather an event designed to show the falsity of the legal system. Rock bands played, and the master of ceremonies read a manifesto entitled, 'A Prophecy of a Declaration of Independence', stating, "We hold these truths to be self-ev-ident, that all is equal, that the creation endows us with certain inalienable rights, that among these are: The freedom of the body, the pursuit of joy, and the expansion of consciousness."

• • •

On the other side of the world, on the same day, October 6th, the Chinese Central Military Commission under Mao's key deputy Lin Biao sent out an urgent direction that all the military institutes and academies in the country were to dismiss their classes so their students could join the Cultural Revolution. The cadets were encouraged to not just leave their classes but to rebel against their officers, which they enthusiastically did, especially targeting the ones who had most harshly disciplined them.

Hundreds of senior army officers were beaten to death or jailed in prisons where they later died. European and American students enjoyed rebelling against their teachers, but none had the license from the very highest level of the government that Chinese students did to "smash those persons in power who are travelling the capitalist road, the bourgeois reactionary authorities, and all royalists of the bourgeoisie, and to forcibly destroy the 'four olds': old culture, old ideas, old customs, and old habits." [18]

There are remarkable parallels between the Red Guards of China and the young baby-boomers and hippies of North America and Europe. In the west, young people flew on standby on American Airlines, Air Canada and other carriers at special half-price rates and hitchhiked in vast numbers for free, travelled down the 'Hippie Trail' from London to Goa and Phuket, and attended massive communal events like huge anti-war demonstrations and rock festivals. In China, millions of Red Guards were allowed to travel by train for free, attended rallies for Chairman Mao, and were encouraged to spread the message of the Cultural Revolution by freeloading to the far corners of the country.

Giant events were held in Tiananmen Square so that the young true believers could see and hear Chairman Mao. By the final event on November 26th, 12 million guards had attended. They arrived on special trains throughout the fall, ballooning by an additional three million the population of Beijing, already a city of seven million. The trains were insanely overpacked, with the latrines completely clogged and the cars reeking of urine mixed with sweat, vomit and excrement. As well as the trains, a fleet of 6,000 trucks brought the starry-eyed cadres to the November event. Hundreds lost their flimsy shoes in the rush to see the big boss, some were even trampled by the crowd, but most seemed mesmerized by the experience. The phrase endlessly quoted in Chinese media was, "I am the happiest person in the world today. I have seen our Great Leader Chairman Mao."

Following the giant rally, the Guards used their free train passes to travel the country. One of their favorite destinations was Jinggang

Mountain, where Mao had set up his first peasant soviet in 1927—one of the cradles of his original revolution. By December more than 30,000 Red Guards were arriving to the wilderness mountain every day, and the holy ground was turning into a disaster area. The People's Liberation Army had to drop food parcels and medicine by helicopter.

Just as hepatitis and gonorrhea plagued western backpackers, so viruses and microbes travelled with the freewheeling Red Guards. The worst infectious disease they developed was meningitis. The U.S. offered help, but China did not respond. Finally, the Chinese government had to put in an order for several hundred tons of medicine from European and Asian drug companies. Over 160,000 people died in the epidemic. Partly to try to put an end to it, the organizing committee of the Cultural Revolution cancelled any new free travel and asked the Red Guards to go home as soon as they could.

• • •

In one of the most notorious examples of the CIA interfering with the politics of other nations, the agency had orchestrated a coup d'état in 1954 overthrowing the elected government of Guatemala and replacing it with the right-wing military dictatorship of Carlos Castillo Armas. The coup was orchestrated primarily on behalf of the United Fruit Company, who were concerned their vast banana profits were threatened by proposed land reforms. Twelve years of unrest followed. On November 2nd, a State of Siege was declared in Guatemala, and thousands of people suspected of leftwing sympathies were 'disappeared'. The largest group fighting the military dictatorship was known as the Guerrilla Army of the Poor, which had 270,000 members. The Guatemalan authorities, backed by the U.S. military, conducted a scorched-earth genocidal campaign against the indigenous Mayan population. Over 200,000 civilians were killed in the war. Piero Gleijeses' *Shattered Hope: The Guatemalan Revolution and the United*

States describes the country as being "ruled by a culture of fear" and hold-ing "a macabre record for human rights violations in Latin America."

• • •

On November 9th, John Lennon entered the Indica Gallery in London, invited by the owner John Dunbar to an advance preview of an exhibit of conceptual art by the Japanese/American artist, Yoko Ono. Lennon was initially unimpressed, especially by pieces such as a bag of nails with an enormous price tag on it. He did, though, climb up a ladder to a telescope aimed at a tiny sign on the other side of the gallery. He expected some sort of negative, "anti" statement, but he instead discov-ered that by looking through the telescope he saw the word "Yes!", which he liked. Ono claimed she had never heard of him, or of the Beatles, but the two did share some banter together in the art gallery. She was smitten and began calling him at his home. When Lennon's wife Cynthia asked him why Ono was constantly calling them, he told her that Ono was just trying to get money for "her avant-garde bullshit."

• • •

Two days after the meeting at the art gallery, the most celebrated rev-olutionary of the Twentieth Century, Che Guevara flew to La Paz, Bolivia, to return to his old business—revolution. After his failure in the Congo and subsequent tropical illness and long treatment in Czechoslovakia, Che had been out of the revolution racket for over a year, but his name and image had never lost their cachet. The famous Alberto Korda photo reminded people that he was the most romantic revolutionary in the world. Even other radical celebrities lusted after him. Jane Fonda was once quoted in a consciousness-raising session saying, "My biggest regret is I never got to fuck Che Guevara." [19]

She might have been less inclined had she seen him as he entered Bolivia on November 11th, dressed in a suit and tie, his long locks shorn, his head shaved, wearing thick spectacles in disguise as a bald, bourgeois Uruguayan agronomist. With him, equally disguised, were a dozen veterans of the Cuban revolution. Castro had told the group they would likely be fighting for ten to fifteen years, and their goal was to liberate all of South America. They began by learning Quechua, the language of the indigenous people of Bolivia. Castro promised them the assistance of both the Bolivian Communist Party and the Soviet Union, but it turned out neither of them had the stomach for a civil war in Bolivia, so Che and his small group had to move alone to set up their guerrilla encampment in the jungle. They ended up in part of the country where the locals gave them no support and didn't even speak the language they had laboriously learned. Nonetheless, they began to skirmish with the Bolivian army, and did enjoy some initial success.

• • •

The rebellious spirit was alive and well around the world. In West Berlin, inspired by Mao's exhortations to the youth of the world to "Bombard the headquarters…Don't be afraid of making trouble. The bigger the trouble we make, the better…There is great chaos under heaven; the situation is excellent," a large group of students wearing Mao badges and calling themselves 'Red Guards' crashed into a meeting being chaired by the president of the Freie Universität and successfully disrupted it and shut it down.

• • •

Later in November, British philosopher Bertrand Russell's War Crimes Tribunal in Stockholm revealed that the US had already dropped four million pounds of bombs in Vietnam that had killed 500,000 civilians. The tribunal, set up in the styles of the Nuremberg Trials, had a panel of several dozen jurors, many well-known intellectuals like Jean-Paul Sartre and James Baldwin. Witnesses to the tribunal included American military personnel and Vietnamese children with severe napalm burns. The jury found the United States and its allies Australia, New Zealand, and South Korea guilty under international law of acts of aggression against Vietnam, guilty of bombardment of purely civilian targets such as hospitals and schools, and guilty of genocide against the people of Vietnam. The findings of the tribunal were largely ignored in the United States.

• • •

On December 1st, the two conservative political parties of Germany combined in what was called the "Grand Coalition" to control 90% of the Bundestag. Ex-Nazi Kurt Georg Kiesinger became Chancellor. Virtually all of the media, including all the mass-circulation tabloids, were owned by conservative Axel Springer. It was a defining moment for the German student movement, who were highly suspicious of the people running Germany and of their parents' generation, and for good reason. The President of the Federal Republic of Germany, Heinrich Lübke had been involved in the anti-Jewish race laws and the concentration camps during the war. Nazi sympathizer Hans Globke had been Director of the German Chancellery from 1953 to 1963. Now there was a man who had actually been a member of the Nazi party in the role.

Students died in the struggle. Benno Ohnesorg was killed by police on June 2nd. Rudi Dutschke's death was directly blamed on an anti-student campaign in Axel Springer's right-wing tabloid *Bild*. Students began coalescing around four leaders: Andreas Baader, Gudrun Ensslin, Horst Mahler and the so-called "Bandit Queen", Ulrike Meinhof. The four would become the founders of the group known by themselves as the Red Army Faction (RAF) and by the press as the Baader-Meinhof Gang.

Gudrun Ensslin, the sultry blonde considered to be the intellectual head of the RAF, radicalized a large part of the German student population with comments like "They'll kill us all. You know what kind of pigs we're up against. This is the Auschwitz generation. You can't argue with people who made Auschwitz. They have weapons and we have not. We must arm ourselves!"

The group claimed as their mentors German philosophers Karl Marx and Herbert Marcuse, world revolutionary leader Mao Zedong, and the black Americans who had rioted in the hot summer of 1965. The group, and their partners in an associated group called the "Revolutionary Cells" were responsible for around 300 bomb attacks and 34 deaths through into the 1970s. In that period 27 members or supporters of the gang were killed.

• • •

Eldridge Cleaver's entry into the penitentiary system was at 18 when he was incarcerated at Soledad State Prison for possession of marijuana. There, he later wrote, "I fell in with a group of young Blacks who were in vociferous rebellion against what we perceived as continuation of slavery on a higher plane. We cursed everything American, including baseball and hot dogs." [20] After an increasingly serious string of convictions and incarcerations, he was released from Folsom Prison on December 12th. He began writing for *Ramparts* Magazine, the glossy journal of revolution. He became romantically involved with radical lawyer Beverly Axelrod and joined the just-formed Black Panther Party as its 'Minister of Information.' He would soon be considered one of the most dangerous men in America.

• • •

On December 17th, the Diggers, an anarchic theatrical collective, staged a happening in the Haight-Ashbury district of San Francisco called "The Death of Money" in which, dressed in animal masks, they carried a coffin full of money (fake, but looking real). It was a follow-up to their lunchtime parade through the business district with a flatbed truck full of topless dancers, encouraging stockbrokers to leave work and jump on board. Hundreds joined in at both events, then inevitably the police tried to break them up, leading to a riot, which was considered all part of the revolutionary fun. "Street events are rituals of release," claimed the Diggers. "Re-claiming of territory (sundown, traffic, public joy) through spirit. No-one can control the single circuit-breaking moment that charges the games with critical reality."

The Diggers (named after a similarly revolutionary group from 17th Century England) moved to create free stores, give away free food, and open free medical clinics. They were credited with creating much of the mythos of hippie San Francisco but were also later accused of acting like male chauvinists who expected the female Diggers to do the work while the male Diggers merely dreamed up new antics. Their actions inspired similar activities around the globe, with active Diggers' outposts in Toronto and London and similar groups called 'Provos' in Amsterdam and Berlin. "Western society has destroyed itself," stated the *Digger Papers*. "The culture is extinct. Politics are as dead as the culture they supported. Ours is the first skirmish of an enormous struggle, infinite in its implications."

•   •   •

Later in that last month of the year, British Prime Minister Harold Wilson met renegade Rhodesian Prime Minister Ian Smith to discuss the extremely contentious Rhodesian issue. Wilson chose to meet Smith aboard the Royal Navy ships HMS *Tiger* and HMS *Fearless*, moored off the British dependency of Gibraltar, to remind him of the still considerable power of the British military. His plan backfired when the Navy piped Smith, a Royal Air Force combat veteran, aboard the ship to a ceremony in the officers' wardroom to which Wilson was not invited—perhaps yet another example of the antagonism of the highly conservative British Armed Forces toward the socialist Prime Minister. When Smith and Wilson did meet, it was clear there was a giant gulf between them, and that the two men loathed each other. The best they could do was agree to disagree, and both departed the negotiations in high dudgeon. Perhaps the Diggers were right. Perhaps politics was dead.

● ● ●

It was very much alive in Beijing, where on December 26th, the occasion of the 73rd birthday of the 'Great Helmsman', Mao Zedong. The Birthday Boy welcomed what he called "the unfolding of a nationwide civil war." It was just another day in the life of one the world's least socially conformist leaders—a graduate, as he constantly reminded people, of what he called "the University of Outlaws." He was a rebellious eccentric who hated his father, who at the age of 34 declared war on the Chinese state, who serially philandered, who wore patched pajamas to state dinners, who caused a famine that cost some 30 million lives, who purged (often to death) many of his former colleagues, who had weird ideas about personal hygiene, like never bathing and never brushing his teeth. He was both a soldier and a poet and now, well into his seventies, was looking forward enthusiastically to a crazy new year of internecine revolutionary strife on a grand scale.

1967

Mao Fashion, Black Panthers Sex Etiquette, Muhammed Ali,
Summer of Love, Detroit Riots, "Vive le Québec Libre"
Bonnie and Clyde Released, British Embassy Burned,
Rochdale Built, Owsley Busted, Che Killed,
Pentagon (Not) Levitated, McNamara Fired.

As the new year dawned, the western world seemed to be going nuts for all things Mao. The latest fashion trend on New York's Fifth Avenue was Mao suits. Brigitte Bardot and Sammy Davis Jr. were two of the many buyers snapping up the $130 garments. *Lui* Magazine, France's answer to *Playboy*, created a special Mao issue they called "The Little Pink Book", with photos of naked young women adopting faux-Red Guard poses. In one, a gorgeous French model, nude except for a rifle, was depicted leaping from a giant white cake. The caption was Mao's famous pronouncement, "Revolution is not a dinner party." There was very little backlash to the idea of using the murderous Cultural Revolution as a theme for popular amusement although, even at this early stage, it had led to the deaths of thousands.

Part of the appeal of Maoism was what the Germans call *Bürgerschreck*—shocking the bourgeoisie. Mao's exhortations to "use our sorcery to turn the old world on its head, crush it to pieces, turn it into dust, create chaos, and great disorder. The bigger the better!" [21] were music to the ears of many young Baby Boomers. One group of Dada-Maoists interrupted a speech by the German Interior Minister by ringing cowbells, throwing painted eggs, stomping around the stage, and having a nine-year-old boy read out Mao quotations including his dubious claim that "Endless terror brings endless fun."

French Maoists 'liberated' twenty cases of caviar, *foie gras*, champagne and fancy cheeses from the luxury food store *Fauchon* and distributed the goods through the *quartier* dominated by poor French Africans. "We aren't thieves, we're Maoists," they claimed. When one of them was caught and incarcerated, Mick Jagger interrupted a Rolling Stones concert to appeal for her release.

The aluminum badges embossed with the image of Mao were so wildly popular around the world that The Great Helmsman himself demanded that China stop production, claiming that the flood of badges meant that China was running out of aluminum to build fighter jets.

Most popular of all was of course The Little Red Book of Mao's thoughts. In the month of January, one single Paris bookstore sold 4,000 copies. European radicals sometimes tried to follow the Maoist revolutionary instructions literally with unintentionally comical results. One cell of German students referred to Lin Biao's theories of "encircling the city from the countryside" in their plan to politicize the countryside around Munich by recruiting cadres in rural Bavarian discotheques. *Turn down the Bee Gees! Turn up the rhetoric!*

French film director Jean-Luc Godard, whose films had been getting wilder and wilder since his debut with *Breathless*, decided that he too was now a Maoist, and so made a very free-form feature called *La Chinoise*. There were no Chinese people in the film but there was a great deal of earnest talk about China, Mao, and revolution. Richard Brody, Godard's biographer, describes the film as being "inchoate, even by Godard's own standards...less a document of Maoist thought, action, or organization than a collage of Maoist graffiti and paraphernalia." He admits the film does have "exhilarating cinematic style," and muses that "It is as if Leonard Bernstein had thrown down his baton for an electric guitar in a three-chord garage band." Genuine French Maoists were not much impressed, and some threatened Godard with a people's tribunal, calling the film "a provocation. A police provocation," because it showed Maoists to be "irresponsible terrorists." [20]

French critics were kinder to the film. Jean de Baroncelli wrote in *Le Monde* that the film was "an avatar—vintage 1967—of the eternal revolt of youth, of that irresistible élan for an ideal of purity, propriety, and nobility, that is the trait of all the adolescents of the world (at least those who have some soul and some heart)."[21] Godard took his revolutionary movie to America, where both it, and he, were received "like a Beatles concert," by his passionate young acolytes, who now included future Hollywood heavy-weights like Francis Ford Coppola, Brian de Palma, and George Lucas. The Maoist epic was shown at various theaters, festivals, and campuses, including Columbia, where it was one of the sparks that ignited the student riots over the university's plans to raze part of a black neighborhood to build a new gymnasium.

The Black Panthers also got into dialectic arguments over the thoughts of Chairman Mao—some of them intertwined with issues of sexual liberation. Panther leader Bobby Seale was nonplussed one day in 1967 to discover lineups of young black men demanding copies of the Little Red Book. He discovered that Black Panther women had told their would-be suitors that "if you want to get next to us, why don't you check out the Red Book?" "The sisters laid the revolutionary ideology right on them," noted Seale approvingly. "We had tried for a long time...to get these brothers motivated, but it took some sisters...to bring (them) in." One concerned female Panther asked Seale for advice. "If a brother doesn't know the ten-point platform and program, I shouldn't give him any, should I? We got into bed, you see, and I asked him if he knew the ten-point platform and program. He said he did, so I sat there grilling him, and he missed about ten words." [22]

Even Jean-Paul Sartre, the existentialist philosopher considered one of the great thinkers of the 20th Century, spent time distributing the Maoist newspaper *La Cause de Peuple* during demonstrations on the streets of Paris. When the baton-wielding *flics* moved in on him, he was protected by students screaming at the police, "You're not going to arrest a Nobel Laureate, are you?" [23]

Not everyone was so enthusiastic about Mao's new revolution. Although the Red Guards took over many of the institutions of China and in January began running the largest city in the country, both the Chinese army and the Communist Party fought back against the young revolutionaries. One of the bloodiest battles took place on Kangping Road in Shanghai, when 20,000 loyalists to the civic administration took on 100,000 rebels armed with iron pipes, clubs, and bamboo poles. After the Red Guards stormed City Hall, newspaper offices, TV and radio stations, there was a run on the banks and a spree of panic-buying for food and supplies. In just the first week of January, 38 million yuan was withdrawn from the banks by the nervous population.

The Chairman encouraged the mob by commanding them to "Seize power! Seize power! Seize power!" On January 22, the parks were all closed by revolutionary decree to prevent them from being used by the "revisionists." Cinemas were shut, museums were closed, and the giant 'Great World' amusement park, recently renamed 'East is Red Park' was shuttered. The rebels renamed themselves the 'Shanghai People's Commune', echoing the name of the Paris Commune, the revolutionary government that had briefly ruled France in 1871. On January 23rd, the army was ordered to support the 'revolutionary masses.' Mao, though still supportive of the new revolutionaries, sometimes erratically flared up against their supporters. He shocked his inner circle by railing not only against his key deputy Chen Boda but also at his wife, telling her, "As for you, Jiang Qing, you have great aspirations but not an ounce of talent, and you look down on everyone else."

• • •

Hippies, though ostensibly non-political, were often seen sporting Mao badges or Mao caps. The counterculture, all wearing their finest, turned out in force for the world's first Human Be-In in San Francisco's Golden Gate Park in January. Somewhere between 20 and 30 thousand participants showed up, to the amazement of the press who gave it major coverage. All of the main psychedelic bands of the day performed. Timothy Leary spoke, as did comedian Dick Gregory, '50s beatnik poet Lawrence Ferlinghetti, and activist Jerry Rubin. Underground chemist Owsley Stanley provided massive amounts of his 'White Lightening' LSD along with 75 large turkeys for distribution by The Diggers. Some were simply there for the communal celebration, others because they saw it as the birth of a new revolution. "A new nation has grown in the robot flesh of the old," claimed the organizers. " Hang your fear at the door and join the future. If you do not believe, please wipe your eyes and see."

The M.C. began the proceedings by saying, "Welcome to the first manifestation of the Brave New World." Some elements of the event were almost a throwback to the tent-show revival meetings of the 19th Century—with an update by Marshall McLuhan. The high priest of the psychedelic movement, the white-pajama-clad pope of dope Timothy Leary urged everyone to start their own religion and he told them the only two commandments of his League of Spiritual Discovery: "Thou shall not alter the consciousness of thy fellow man," and "Thou shall not prevent thy fellow man from altering his own consciousness." The event was a major milestone in the creation of the new counterculture, and a prelude to the upcoming "Summer of Love."

• • •

Elsewhere, things were not as peaceful. In Canada, on January 1, the first of three separatist bombs to be exploded in Canada's centennial year destroyed a Montréal mailbox, a symbol to the separatists of the federal government they were aiming to overthrow. The next day, Ronald Reagan was sworn in as Governor of California. He immediately vowed to "put the welfare bums back to work" and to "clean up the mess at Berkeley", code phrases to indicate to his supporters that he would spend his term as Governor fighting the students, the counterculture, Blacks, and Hispanics.

• • •

On January 17th, accused FLQ terrorists Charles Gagnon and Pierre Vallières were flown from New York back to Montréal under police guard and made their first appearance in a Québec courtroom. The two writers were thus unable to attend the Angry Arts Week, held in New York City. The group "Up Against the Wall, Motherfuckers" grew out of the event. "We are the freaks of an unknown space/time," read their manifesto. "We are the eye of the Revolution." The Anarchist/Dada/ 'street gang with analysis' was loosely run by painter Ben Morea and included radical feminist (and future would-be assassin of Andy Warhol) Valerie Solanas, whose SCUM Manifesto urged women to "overthrow the government, eliminate the money system, institute complete automation, and eliminate the male sex." They were a relatively minor fringe extreme group, but they did later force their way into the Pentagon during an anti-war protest, and they also attacked the U.S. Secretary of State, Dean Rusk, with eggs and blood. Elements of the group morphed into the Bread and Puppet Theater, which continues to this day to create political theater using giant oversized puppets.

At the other end of the protest spectrum was a march in Washington on January 31st led by the National Emergency Committee of Clergy and Laymen Concerned About Vietnam (CALCAV) that included Dr. Martin Luther King, Daniel Berrigan, and Senator Eugene McCarthy.

Others protested the war by leaving the country. In January, twenty-year-old Mark Satin got his long hair cut short "to look nice and square" and split for Toronto to get away from what he later told a *New York Times* reporter was a "godawful, sick, foul country—could anything be worse?" Satin had worked with SNNC, the Student Nonviolent Coordinating Committee, in Mississippi and had been the president of the SDS chapter at the State University of New York at Binghampton, where he had recruited 20% of the student body. He then decided to try to slip across the border. Once in Toronto, he became the most visible leader of the draft dodgers (or 'draft evaders', as most preferred to be called) in Canada. In 1967, there were some 3,000. By 1970, their numbers would swell to more than 25,000. Satin created a 90-page book titled *Manual for Draft Age Immigrants to Canada* that became the bible for young men considering avoiding the war and protesting by moving to Canada. The book, which was described as "the first entirely Canadian-published bestseller in the United States" sold over 100,000 copies.

Satin, like many of his fellow draft evaders, was largely disowned by his family. In an article in the *Ladies Home Journal*, his mother was quoted saying, "I cannot condone what he's done," and then, in a classic condescending remark typifying the generation gap of the time, said "Oh, Mark, my sweet little Mark, why don't you grow up and become a big boy?" As the writer of the piece commented, "Probably no two people understand Mark's decision less than his own parents."

Other members of "The Movement" were not sympathetic to the draft evaders either. Joan Baez, before a concert in Toronto, declared that "these kids can't fight the Vietnamese madness by holing up in Canada. What they're doing is opting out of the struggle at home. That's where they should go, if only to fill the jails." Stokely Carmichael echoed her words during a trip to Toronto, saying, "Those cats can't kick the bastards in Washington from here. They oughta come on back and go to jail with me. If racist McNamara has the guts to draft me, I'll even accept white power to help take over the jails and then we'll see how smug America remains." [24] U.S. General Wayne Clark demanded that the Canadian government arrest and ship all the draft dodgers home to the U.S.

Satin, like most of the draft evaders, was not swayed by the nay-sayers. He became an enthusiastic resident of his adopted country, hitch-hiking across Canada sixteen times and going to university in British Columbia. However, when Jimmy Carter issued an amnesty to American expatriates, he returned to the country he had once described as "godawful, sick, and foul." Most of the ex-pats stayed. Doug Fetherling's mother called him in his new Toronto home in 1967 to tell him he was a disgrace to her family, to his dead father's memory, to the United States, and to the entire white race. By the 1980s he was still in Canada and had become one of the most prominent and acclaimed writers in the country.

Many of the professors at Canadian universities originally arrived in Canada as draft evaders. Andy Barrie became one of Toronto's best known radio personalities. Barrie began his radio career at stations in Baltimore, Hartford, and Washington, D.C. After receiving orders to go to Vietnam, he deserted and went to Canada. He got his first gig in Montréal after a long-time commentator at CJAD resigned in protest during the October FLQ Crisis. He later moved to CFRB, the biggest talk radio station in the country, and then moved again to become the morning host for the CBC's flagship Toronto station. He eventually received an honorary discharge from the U.S. Army, an Honorary Doctor of Laws degree from York University, and the Order of Canada, the highest civilian award in the country.

While Satin, Barrie and the others escaped the war in Canada, south of the border Olympic and now professional boxer Muhammed Ali began to speak out against it. "My conscience won't let me go shoot my brother," said the boxer, "or some darker people, or some poor hungry people in the mud, for big, powerful America. And shoot them for what? They never called me nigger, they never lynched me, didn't put no dogs on me, they didn't rob me of my nationality, rape and kill my mother and father."

Many others, though, accepted their draft call. By 1967 the number of American troops in Vietnam had somehow escalated to 485,000. It would ultimately peak at 535,000, with a total of over 2.7 million Americans serving there over the course of the long war. The American arsenal of weapons now included napalm, cluster bombs, agent orange, and white phosphorus which burned the skin straight through to the bone and caused horrific deaths. All of these would have been considered illegal chemical weapons at the Nuremberg trials. Agent Orange alone is considered to have disabled between one and three million people. [25] Nonetheless, Johnson's generals kept asking for more firepower to kill the Vietnamese, maybe even the Big One. Finally, he had had enough. At one meeting of the Joint Chiefs of Staff, he started screaming obscenities: "Imagine that you're me—you're the President of the United States—and five incompetents come into your office and try to talk you into starting World War III…The risk is just too high. How can you fucking assholes ignore what China might do? You have just contaminated my office, you filthy shitheads. Get the hell out of here right now." [26]

The generals got out. After a pause, Johnson returned to the policy of bombing North Vietnam. He later explained to an aide his thinking on how to increase the bombing without aggravating China: "I'm going up her leg an inch at a time…I'll get to her snatch before they know what's happening." [27]

There was opposition to Johnson on many fronts. On February 22nd a new play titled *Macbird!* opened in New York City. The authorities had pressured the city's theaters not to produce it, but the Village Gate defied the ban. The play superimposed the assassination of John F. Kennedy over the plot of Shakespeare's *Macbeth* with provocative and sometimes hilarious results. The character of 'Macbird' (LBJ), at the urging of his wife 'Lady Macbird' (Lady Bird Johnson) assassinates 'John Ken O'Dunc' (JFK), with the Three Witches, representing students, Blacks and leftists, providing a critique on the action all in iambic pentameter. The writer, Barbara Garson, was often asked if she really thought that Johnson had masterminded the killing of Kennedy, to which she replied, "If he did, it's the least of his crimes."

• • •

The theater on the New York stage could hardly compare with the theater being performed on the streets of Oakland. Black Panthers Bobby Seale and Huey Newton came up with a new plan to deal with the never-ending police violence and the harassment of black motorists. Since California was then an "open-carry" state, the duo would cruise the city streets, and if they observed a black citizen being questioned by police, usually at a traffic stop, they would pull over, climb from their car with their guns fully visible, and remind the citizen of his rights. When the shaken cop would demand to know what they thought they were doing, Newton, who had taken law school classes, would tell him of their Second Amendment right to bear arms.

In February, their radical (some said suicidal) strategy turned on them as the pair were themselves stopped by an Oakland policeman. Newton once claimed he had been stopped by police over 50 times. This time, he at first politely showed his driver's license and answered the questions he was asked. His M1 rifle was in plain view, as was Seale's 9mm. The cop called for backup. Three more squad cars arrived, and a crowd of onlookers began to form. When the officer demanded to see the guns, Newton told him to get away from the car. "We don't want you around the car, and that's all there is to it."

"Who the hell do you think you are?" demanded the cop.

"Who the hell do you think *you* are?" responded Newton, who then climbed from the car and loudly chambered a round in his gun. The police shouted at the growing crowd to go away. Newton shouted at them to stay where they were—they were within their rights to observe what was happening on a public street.

"What are you going to do with that gun?" demanded one of the policemen.

"What are you going to do with *your* gun?" replied Newton, "Because if you shoot at me or try to take this gun, I'm going to shoot back at you, swine." [28]

The angry interplay went back and forth until, amazingly, the police backed away without making any arrests. The incredible standoff sealed the reputation of the Panthers as the baddest motherfuckers on the block. In May, they took their astoundingly brazen attitude to the state capitol, when 30 of them, all openly carrying weapons, marched into the visitors' gallery to observe the lawmakers in action. The Republican-majority body was so shocked that within days they pushed through new legislation ending "open-carry" in the state, and within a week Governor Ronald Reagan signed it into law. It is hard to say which seems more unlikely—that 30 Black revolutionaries could walk into the state assembly chamber carrying semi-automatic rifles, or that a right-wing Republican governor would pass a law championing gun control. That hasn't happened since.

•   •   •

The actions of the Panthers radicalized many people, of all skin colors. Dennis Banks was an Ojibwe from northern Minnesota who was embittered by his youth spent in residential schools. He was shocked while serving with the U.S. Air Force in Japan when he was ordered to 'shoot to kill' Japanese who were protesting having their farms taken from them to expand a U.S. Air Force runway. In 1967 he was serving time in solitary confinement in Minnesota's Stillwater Prison. "It had a tremendous impact on me, what was going on outside of prison that year," he later said. "Sitting in that jail cell I began to understand there was a hell of a movement going on that I wasn't part of—the antiwar movement, the Black Panther movement, the civil rights movement, the Students for a Democratic Society. I began to see that the greatest war was going to go on right here in the United States, and I began to realize that there was a hell of a situation in this country—all these different kinds of people trying so hard to straighten this country out."

Once he got out of prison, Banks started a new organization, the American Indian Movement. AIM became the strongest group representing Natives in this period. Banks was part of the 1969 – 71 occupation of Alcatraz Island, the 1972 Trail of Broken Treaties, and the 1973 takeover and occupation of Wounded Knee, on the Pine Ridge Indian Reservation in South Dakota.

• • •

The madness of the Cultural Revolution continued through the winter. In Beijing, Red Guards imprisoned Soviet diplomats in their embassy and burned effigies of the Soviet premier in the streets. Also in February, the Chinese Cultural Revolution spilled into Africa. Tanzanian President Julius Nyerere rolled out his *ujamaa* dream of Tanzanian socialism. Nyerere organized support from his young "Green Guards" who dressed in green shirts with badges emblazoned with images of Nyerere and Mao and abandoned their schools to imitate Mao's "Long March" with treks around the East-African country. The Green Guard Youth Leaguers proclaimed their hatred of "Playboy and the Beatles; tight trousers and miniskirts; cosmetics and beauty contests," and in the manner of their red-shirted role models in China, burned the houses of those who didn't follow their plans for collectivization.

• • •

Also in that busy month, Régis Debray's book *Revolution in the Revolution?* was published and soon became a new handbook for the world's revolutionaries. Debray was a French Professor of Philosophy who joined Che Guevara in Bolivia. His capture by the Bolivians and the CIA ultimately led them to be able to capture Che.

• • •

In March, Muhammad Ali, the Heavyweight Boxing Champion of the World, was re-classified by the U.S. Army draft board into the 1-A category. Ali responded that he was a conscientious objector and that he would refuse to serve in the army and refuse to fight in Vietnam. "I ain't got no quarrel with them Viet Cong," he announced. "Why should they ask me to put on a uniform and go ten thousand miles from home and drop bombs and bullets on brown people in Vietnam while so-called Negro people in Louisville are treated like dogs and denied simple human rights?" On April 28th he appeared in Houston for his scheduled induction into the U.S. Armed Forces. When his name was called, three times, he refused to step forward. An officer warned him that he was committing a felony punishable by five years in prison and a $10,000 fine. His name was called one final time, and when Ali refused to budge, he was arrested.

Immediately, the New York State Athletic Commission suspended his boxing license and stripped him of his title. Within days, other boxing commissions followed suit. On June 20th, after only 21 minutes of deliberation, a jury found Ali guilty of violating the Selective Service law. He was freed on bail and became one of the most galvanizing and controversial figures in the world. He was hated by much of the white establishment, but he was a hero to the black community, the counterculture and the young anti-war movement.

"I ain't draft dodging," he proclaimed. "I ain't burning no flag. I ain't running to Canada. I'm staying right here. You want to send me to jail? Fine, you go right ahead. I've been in jail for 400 years. I could be there for four or five more, but I ain't going no 10,000 miles to help murder and kill other poor people. If I want to die, I'll die right here, right now, fighting you, if you want to die. My enemy is the white people, not Viet Cong or Chinese or Japanese. You're my opposer when I want freedom. You're my opposer when I want justice. You're my opposer when I want equality. You won't even stand up for me in America for my religious beliefs. You want me to go somewhere and fight for you, but you won't even stand up for me here at home?"

Ali received dozens of death threats, as did the few people who pub-licly supported his position. Newspaper writers who wrote positively about him had their windshields smashed and their offices plagued with bomb threats. Ali was unable to box anywhere in the U.S. for three years. "He was robbed of his best years, his prime years," said his trainer, Angelo Dundee, but Ali did not regret his decision. "Black men would go over there and fight, but when they came home, they couldn't even be served a hamburger," he said. "If America was in trouble, if we had been attacked and real war came, I'd be on the front line. But I could see [the Vietnam War] wasn't right."

His actions and his words had a profound influence on the era. "For the heavyweight champion of the world, who had achieved the highest level of athletic celebrity, to put all that on the line—the money, the ability to get endorsements—to sacrifice all that for a cause, gave a whole sense of legitimacy to the movement and the causes with young people that nothing else could have done," said Reverend Al Sharpton. "Even those who were assassinated, certainly lost their lives, but they didn't voluntarily do that. He knew he was going to jail and did it anyway. That's another level of leadership and sacrifice."

In a top-secret operation code-named *Minaret* the National Security Agency began intercepting the communications of Ali, along with those of Dr. Martin Luther King Jr., and various Democratic senators, journalists, and critics of the U.S. involvement in Vietnam. The NSA itself would later admit its operation was "disreputable, if not outright illegal."

• • •

There was almost no part of the world that escaped the tide of revolution sweeping past every continent. In India, activist leader Charu Majumdar, using as his models the 1949 Chinese Revolution, the 1959 Cuban Revolution, and the Vietnam War, began to organize the pover-ty-stricken peasants of the Naxalbari region of the country. On March 3rd the peasants began seizing land and cultivating crops. The landlords first brought in freelance thugs to fight back, and then the police, who on May 25th opened fire on a group of peasants, killing nine women and one child. A police officer was killed by the peasants in a hail of arrows, likely one of the last uses of bows-and-arrows in the history of world revolution. The revolt, by now characterized as the Naxalbari Uprising, climaxed on July 19th, when paramilitary forces ended it, killing many of the leaders. Charu Majumdar went into hiding but reappeared in Calcutta four years later leading the Naxalite movement, which by then had morphed from a rural peasant uprising to a student revolt, supported by China.

• • •

In April, *TIME* Magazine put The Pill on its cover, dramatizing for its readers the profound effect the new oral contraceptive was having on society. The Pill heralded in the Sexual Revolution and changed women's role in society. It prolonged the age at which women first married, allowed them to invest more in education, and become more career oriented. Soon after the birth control was introduced, there was a sharp increase in college attendance and in graduation rates for women. Of course, there was also a fierce negative response to The Pill by some elements of society, such as the Roman Catholic Church.

• • •

In the spring, there was rumbling from Greece that the population wanted to bring back the liberal democrat George Papandreou to run the country. The United States and President Johnson didn't like the sound of that. Johnson called the Greek Ambassador to his office, and told him, "Listen to me, Mr. Ambassador—fuck your Parliament and your Constitution! America is an elephant. Cyprus is a flea. If these two fleas continue itching the elephant, they may get whacked by the elephant's trunk. And whacked good! We pay a lot of good, American dollars to you Greeks, Mr. Ambassador. If your Prime Minister gives me a talk about democracy, parliaments, and constitutions, then he, his parliament, and his constitution may not last very long."

They didn't. On April 21ˢᵗ, a group of right-wing army colonels overthrew the Greek government. Following the coup, they ruled the country as a hardline dictatorship until July 24, 1974. The coup (which the Colonels preferred to call a "revolution to save the nation") was bankrolled by the Vatican and the dictatorship led by Colonel George Papadopoulos was promoted by the United States. Colonel Papadopoulos had been a captain of a Nazi security battalion tracking down Greek resistance fighters during WWII. He became the first CIA agent to become the premier of a European country. His regime was characterized by extreme xenophobia, anti-Semitism, pro-Nazi sentiment, and especially by virulent opposition to what it termed "consumerism, and degenerate hippie-ism." Within a month of the coup, 8,000 people had been arrested, jailed, or sent to exile on Gyaros Island. There was widespread persecution, with an estimate of 2,000 people violently tortured by the regime. Foreign newspapers, mini-skirts, and long hair were banned; church attendance was made compulsory.

• • •

On April 15ᵗʰ, a crowd of at least 125,000 marched behind Martin Luther King from New York's Central Park to the United Nations, chanting "Hell no! We won't go!" and "Flower Power." Draft cards were set alight and passed like torches from one person to another, then finally dropped into a flaming coffee can.

There was street theater in Germany, too. Fritz Teufel (his last name, appropriately, means "devil" in German) was a provocative self-styled "fun guerrilla", one of the founders of the Kommune 1, a notorious squat on Berlin's Stuttgarter Platz where the hippie squatters plotted revolt against their parents' generation, who they believed had either been complicit or supine in the Nazi era. In April, Teufel was arrested for what the press dubbed the 'Pudding Assassination,' an attempt to douse U.S. Vice

President Hubert Humphrey on his state visit to Germany with 'bombs' of flour, yoghurt, and pudding.

As the era grew more violent, so did Teufel, falling into the orbit of the Red Army Faction and the June 2 Movement. He spent seven years in prison in the 1970s for bombings and kidnappings but didn't entirely lose his mischievous sense of humor. In the '80s he appeared on television with the West German finance minister and sprayed him with a water pistol. In return the minister threw a glass of wine at Teufel. He also ruled that he would only answer questions about his past after interviewers played table tennis with him for an hour.

• • •

On April 27th, Expo 67 opened in Montréal. It was a giant showy exposition of revolutionary new advances in architecture, filmmaking, and other fields. The World's Fair was originally intended to be held in Moscow to celebrate the 50th anniversary of the Russian Revolution, but the Russians backed out and so the fair was held in Canada, celebrating the country's 100th birthday. Expo was wildly successful. On just its third day over half a million people attended, a record for World's Fairs, and the giant attendance continued until October.

Ironically even though Russia was not the host country, the 'far-out', futuristic Russian pavilion was the most popular one of the fair. The favorite hostesses were those from Great Britain who wore Mary Quant-designed miniskirts and radiated a 'Swinging London' vibe. Numerous pavilions had what was considered to be radical, revolutionary architecture. Habitat 67 was an apartment complex that looked like a jumble of Lego-built units. It was designed by architect Moshe Safdie, a young Israeli-Canadian who in the fashion of the era, was merely an architecture student at McGill University in his mid-twenties when he got the gig. It was built in the "Brutalist" architectural style that would revolutionize architecture through the period. It featured poured concrete construction, an absence of decorative features, and no attempt to hide the functional aspect of the building, such as air ducts, plumbing pipes, or heating units. Habitat was a somewhat elegant and fanciful variation on the theme, but many buildings built in the 1965 – 1975 period were considered plain, drab and authoritarian. The Soviets and East Europeans particularly favored brutalist architecture, but there were many examples, such as the Barbican Centre and the National Theater in England; Rochdale College and the Robarts Library, both in Toronto; the Boston City Hall; the University of Illinois in Chicago; and the Al Zaquira Building in Baghdad. The style had many critics, most famously Prince Charles, who railed against the "cold, soul-less" style of the buildings. British commentator Anthony Daniels described the architecture as "a spiritual, intellectual, and moral defor-mity...cold-hearted, inhuman, hideous, and monstrous." The disagree-ments about the new architecture created yet another fractious battle for the period, one that continued even past the '70s, as the concrete buildings began to stain, decay, and crumble, prompting many critics to demand that they be torn down.

A very different and even more revolutionary style of architecture was used by architect and futurist Buckminster Fuller for his design for the U.S. Pavilion at Expo 67. In 1965 he co-founded and inaugurated the 'World Design Science Decade 1965 – 75', an ambitious attempt to spread the resources of the world more evenly among the people of the world. The geodesic dome he designed for Expo was one of the most radical, unique buildings ever, and still stands, now called the Montréal Biosphere. Fuller was one of the most celebrated and original personalities of the period. He considered himself and his work to be "the property of all human-ity", and in 1969 was named the 'Humanist of the Year'. He was wildly popular with the students and hippies of the day, because even though he was himself in his seventies, he considered himself a revolutionary thinker and believed that mankind had arrived at what he called "an entirely new philosophical era on earth."

• • •

One country that was most certainly *not* represented at Expo was China. Not only was the country still largely an international pariah, but it was now deeper than ever engulfed in the Cultural Revolution, which had become virtually a civil war. By the end of 1966 the revolution had appeared to calm down. Students began to go back to school, although more than half the schools were badly damaged and one in five were totally destroyed. By the late spring, though, the violence and fighting returned with a vengeance. Now the students began to construct crude weapons to fight the army. Scissors were attached to the end of staves to create spears, blacksmiths began forging makeshift armor, and giant catapults were constructed to lob bricks against opponents. It was fighting on a medieval scale, but it was still deadly. In Chengdu, the fighting was even more vicious since the large city was the center of China's arms industry and workers were able to access hand grenades, automatic rifles, mortars, and rocket-propelled grenade launchers to fight their bosses.

• • •

On May 26th, *Sgt. Pepper's Lonely Hearts Club Band* was released and became an instant classic—a revolutionary new 'concept album' from The Beatles. The timing was perfect—it heralded in the Summer of Love, which was centered in San Francisco but widely spread across North America and Europe. Of course, as could be expected in this most fractious era, the Blue Meanies immediately denounced the album. Spiro Agnew, then Governor of Maryland, led a crusade to ban the song *With a Little Help from My Friends* because it mentioned getting high. The BBC actually did ban *A Day in the Life* because of the line, "I'd love to turn you on." The ultra-right-wing John Birch Society charged that *Sgt. Pepper* exhibited "an understanding of the principles of brainwashing" and claimed the Beatles were "part of an International Communist Conspiracy."

• • •

The revolutionary spirit of the times even extended to the most remote, quiet, paradisical islands of the Caribbean. The tiny island of Anguilla became independent from Great Britain in the early sixties and become a part of the associated state of Saint Kitts-Nevis-Anguilla. The island resented being lorded over by the larger island of St. Kitts, and after the discovery that money given by Canada to build a pier on Anguilla was instead used to build one on St. Kitts, the Anguillans revolted. On May 30, they forcibly ejected the St. Kitts police force from the island and declared their independence. The island, now calling itself the Republic of Anguilla, began flying a newly designed flag displaying three sharks swimming in a circle. Regrettably the distinctive flag did not fly for long. Their squabbles with the other islands continued. A British gunship and assault troops were sent in 1969 and things did not totally settle down until 1980 when the island was officially allowed to secede from St. Kitts and become what is called a British Overseas Territory.

• • •

On May 26th, a Nigerian Lieutenant-Colonel with the very impressive name of Chukwuemeka Odumegwu Ojukwu, the Military Governor of Eastern Nigeria, announced that he was leading the area out of Nigeria and declaring it to be a new sovereign state to be known as the Republic of Biafra. Since Eastern Nigeria was the location of the country's vast reserves of oil, the central government was not pleased. On July 6th they sent in their troops, beginning a bitter war that would lead to the death of almost two million Biafran civilians, three quarters of them children.

• • •

According to the preaching of the powerful, eccentric preacher and charismatic faith healer Reverend Jim Jones, July 15th was the much-publicized day that the world was going to end. Jones had a large cult following that accompanied him from Indiana to Brazil to California and ultimately to Guyana. He claimed to be the reincarnation of Gandhi, Father Divine, Jesus, Buddha, and Vladimir Lenin. Until he really went crazy, he was politically connected and supported by people like First Lady Rosalyn Carter, Vice-Presidential candidate Walter Mondale, and California Governor Jerry Brown. He was involved in the election campaign of San Francisco mayor George Moscone and in the food giveaway program that was a part of the madness of the kidnapping of Patricia Hearst.

Jones held a powerful sway over his large cult in the 1960s, but only became known to the broader population in 1978, when a United States Congressman, Leo Ryan, flew down to investigate "Jonestown", their compound in the jungle of Guyana. Jones' 'Red Brigade' shot up the plane, killing Ryan and four others, and wounding many more. Jones then convinced his followers to drink cyanide-laced Flavor Aid and Kool Aid. Nine hundred and nine died, including 304 children, the greatest number of American civilians killed in a single event until the events of September 11, 2001. Jones told his followers they weren't committing suicide but rather an act of what he called "revolutionary suicide protesting the conditions of an inhumane world." The world did indeed end for them then, but back on July 15, 1967, to the great surprise of Jones' giant cult, the world did not end.

• • •

During the famous "Summer of Love" there was intense interest in the effects of LSD on society. Not only did thousands flock to San Francisco (with, to quote the song, "flowers in their hair") to partake of the drug and the culture that surrounded it, but dozens of government agencies and think tanks began investigating LSD. The Rand Corporation, primarily focused on designing strategies to counter revolution in Vietnam and the Caribbean, added a new mandate to explore whether acid might be used domestically to counter political activism. The Hudson Institute, another think tank with strong ties to American Intelligence services and the American military, also began investigating the potential use of LSD for social control. Its founder, the rotund, 300-pound Herman Kahn took LSD himself (presumably, a jumbo-sized dose) to try to analyze its potential. Kahn predicted that by the year 2000 there would be an alternative 'dropped out' country within the United States. The ubiquitous Captain Al Hubbard was brought out of semi-retirement in British Columbia to check out the new scene and tell the muckety-mucks in Washington what was going on. The old CIA acidhead was shocked and saddened to discover that the scene in 1967 had descended to a place where what he considered the most precious spiritual substance on earth was being contaminated by lousy bathtub chemists turning out LSD laced with speed and phencyclidine ('angel dust') and being sold by Mafia dealers.

• • •

In the summer of 1967, there was parallel violence exploding across both China and America. On July 20th in Wuhan, the city that in 2019 would give birth to the Covid 19 virus, a violent mutiny broke out between soldiers loyal to Mao's new Cultural Revolution, and others defending the status quo. As the insurrection escalated into what could have begun a full civil war, Mao, who was visiting the city, jumped on an air force jet.

"Which direction are we going?" the pilot asked Mao as he climbed into the plane.

"Just take off first," replied the panicked Chairman.

Once in the air, Mao directed the pilot to fly him to Shanghai. The Chinese press later characterized the Wuhan event as a "counter-revolutionary riot."

• • •

Meanwhile, in the U.S., as cities across the country burned, Rap Brown, the new leader of SNCC, declared "This ain't no riot, Brother. This is a rebellion, and we got 400 years of reasons to tear this town apart!" Whipping angry crowds into a frenzy, he proclaimed, "Violence is necessary! It is as American as apple pie," and called the riots in the exploding cities "a dress rehearsal for revolution."

The most impressive of the dress rehearsals began in Detroit on July 23rd. It was a gruesome riot and rebellion that lasted for five days. Not only did Michigan Governor George Romney send in the National Guard, but President Johnson sent in the 82nd and 101st airborne divisions of the U.S. Army as reinforcements. Many of the veteran soldiers found it a tougher detail than Vietnam. Forty-three people died; over 1,100 were injured; there were over 7,200 arrests and more than 2,000 buildings destroyed. Just across the border, folk singer Gordon Lightfoot wrote and recorded *Black Day in July*, a song that lamented the event, which was subsequently banned by radio stations in 30 states.

• • •

On July 24th, the day after the Detroit Riots began, during a state visit to Canada to witness Expo 67, French President Charles de Gaulle found himself caught up in the delirium of North American rebellion in general and Québec separatism in particular. From the balcony of Montréal City Hall, he impetuously proclaimed, *"Vive Montréal! Vive le Québec! Vive le Québec libre!"* His fiery, undiplomatic words created wildly differing responses in Canada. In Québec, young separatists like 22-year-old Carole de Vault were ecstatic. Feeling that he was avenging the death of Jeanne d'Arc, burned at the stake by the British in 1431, and Louis-Joseph de Montcalm, killed by the British on the Plains of Abraham in 1759, de Vault remembers "seeing those upraised arms, hearing the cry that would go right to the heart of the people of Québec. *"Vive le Québec libre!"* A shiver went down my spine. We threw our arms around each other. We danced and hugged. My friend ran for a bottle of French wine and we drank to the health of the General and to a free Québec." De Vault's life as a Québec separatist would take a very distinct turn when she would go on to play an important and highly controversial role as a police informer in the FLQ October Crisis of 1970.

De Gaulle's speech got a different and very angry reaction from the Canadian government. The French President was forced to cancel his state visit to the capital and fly home from Montréal with his tail between his legs. The RCMP cranked up its intelligence programs against three perceived enemies—students, the FLQ, and France. The Mounties began what was described as "a vast spy operation against a foreign power, France, now elevated to the rank of an 'enemy power' because of its special relationship with Quebec." They also, contrary to specific instructions from Prime Minister Pearson, began carrying out political espionage and surveillance on university campuses, using spies and recruiting informers among students and professors.

• • •

By the summer of 1967 Warren Beatty had completed his radical gangster film *Bonnie and Clyde* but he discovered that Warner Bros, the studio that owned the film, hated it, and had no plans to give it a proper release. It was perhaps no surprise. There have been few other films that have been so loved by the young and so hated by the old. The executives at the studio, including the chief, Jack Warner, were in their late seventies or eighties, and had no interest in going to battle for a picture they despised. Beatty appealed to a young Joe Hyams, then working for Dick Lederer, Head of Warners' Advertising and Publicity department. Hyams recalls, "I remembered that they had a Warren Beatty picture called *Mickey One*, a piece of shit, and the only place in the world it succeeded was in Canada. I said, '*That* picture made it in Canada. *This* picture can make it in Canada.'" Film festivals were rare in 1967, but Montréal had a big one, and Hyams, Lederer, and Beatty managed to get *Bonnie and Clyde* the prestigious opening night slot on August 4th.

"What a reaction. It was incredible!" remembers Lederer. "There were 14 curtain calls for the stars. There was a standing ovation. After it was all over, Warren was in his suite on the bed with a girl on either side. They were dressed but cuddling up to him. There was this nice young

French girl who was the *macher* of the film festival. Warren said to this girl, 'Listen, honey, where is the wildest spot in Montréal? I want to go there tonight.' She said, 'Mr. Beatty, *this* is the wildest spot in Montréal.'"

According to Hollywood historian Peter Biskind, "*Bonnie and Clyde* became a tipping point, to use Malcolm Gladwell's phrase, marking a shift in mass culture of tectonic proportions, away from the proper, morally and aesthetically conservative official culture of the Eisenhower era towards the anything-goes, let-it-all-hang-out counterculture of the 1960s, with its massive antiwar demonstrations and fighting in the streets. After *Bonnie and Clyde*, nothing would be the same." [32]

The film still had lots of enemies. Elderly film critic Bosley Crowther slagged the film so badly in the *New York Times* that he was ultimately fired from his position because the paper thought him out of tune with the new times. The old hated the fact that the film glorified and romanticized the two outlaws and portrayed Texas Ranger Frank Hamer, the lawman who found and killed them, as a vengeful bumbler. That approach ultimately made it a huge hit with the counterculture youth movement and probably was a factor in leading elements of society towards violence. It was a contentious film, loved by the young, hated by the old, making lots of money, nominated for many awards, but tellingly only winning a few.

• • •

The same day *Bonnie and Clyde* opened in New York City, August 13th, a combined force of two hundred guerrillas from ZAPU and the ANC's *Spear of the People* crossed the Zambezi River at the Gwaii Gorge between Victoria Falls and Kazungula and were soon battling units of the Rhodesian African Rifles and the Police Anti-Terrorism Unit. It was much more challenging for the Rhodesians than their previous actions against the guerrillas, and they needed to bring in Hunter strike jets of the Royal Rhodesian Air Force to defeat the insurgents. Recognizing that their days of easy victories against the guerrilla revolutionaries were likely over, the Rhodesians asked for and received 2,000 South African riot police supported by South African helicopters to help them fight the bush wars. For now, though not for long, the white supremacist governments were sticking together.

• • •

On August 22nd, mobs of Chinese Red Guards waving copies of Mao's little red book broke into the British Embassy in Peking and destroyed its radio communication with London. The British Chargé d'Affaires Donald Hobson and his staff were called into the grounds of the embassy by the leaders of the huge milling mob, who demanded he bow his head in shame over troubles in Hong Kong. When he refused to do this the Guards broke through into the embassy, ransacked it and set it ablaze. While the flames burned, Red Guards sexually assaulted some female members of the staff. The British was only the latest foreign embassy the Red Guards had attacked. Others that summer included the Indian, Indonesian, Kenyan, Czech and Russian, with Russian diplomats assaulted in the attack on their embassy. The British Foreign Office reacted sternly to the incident, but not all Britons were upset. Doctrinaire British Maoist Elsie Fairfax-Cholmondeley allegedly danced in jubilation around the burning ruins of the embassy. A compatriot of the woman described her by saying "her background was everything her name suggested. She was a P.G. Wodehouse aunt. If she'd been a spider, she would have had [her husband] for breakfast." The politics of Maoism made for very strange bedfellows. Fairfax-Cholmondeley's enthusiasm for Mao did not help her during the madness of the new Revolution. As a westerner, she was herself later arrested and imprisoned by the Red Guards.

To demonstrate their loyalty to the revolution, members of the Chinese legation in Portland Place, London charged out of their building and battled British bobbies with axes and cricket bats. One of the Chinese diplomats jumped on and then clubbed into submission an abandoned policeman's helmet. Take that, symbol of imperialism!

• • •

If that was a nutty thing to do, two days later saw something much wilder—the craziest stunt yet by the most outrageous, original and inventive revolutionary of the period, Abbie Hoffman. Who was Abbie Hoffman? The introduction to his 1970 book, outlandishly titled *Steal This Book*, describes him as "America's most widely recognized radical, a media personality, an emblem, a symbol, a myth, and still—I may be giving away his secret weapon here—a human being." The writer, Al Giordano continues by saying that before Hoffman, "there was no Bart Simpson. But there was an Abby Hoffman, without whom Bart would not have been possible. And he was a living, breathing person who got clubbed over the head, spied on, infiltrated, outlawed, imprisoned, exiled, forgotten, re-discovered again, forgotten again, and then, as Artaud wrote about Van Gogh, he was suicided by society. And a whole hell of a lot of what we take for granted today as basic "rights" are here and present because real human beings fought for them and were persecuted for waging that fight. His era was full of heroes. But none were as effectively heroic as Abbie." [33] Norman Mailer said, "He has tons of moxie. He is also one of the funniest people I have ever met. Abbie has the charisma that must have come out of an immaculate conception between Fidel Castro and Groucho Marx." [34] On August 22nd Hoffman pulled off a stunt that was Marxist in both the Karl and Groucho senses of the word. Gathering together 15 free-spirited friends, he organized to get on a public tour of the New York Stock Exchange. Once in the visitor's gallery, he led the gang in throwing 300 one-dollar bills to the trading floor below. The wild antic had the expected effect. The excited stockbrokers ran around the floor chasing the bills, causing such pandemonium that the electronic ticker tape stopped cold. Hoffman later described it, saying, "A spark had been ignited. The system cracked a little. Not a drop of blood had been spilled, not a bone broken, but on that day, with that gesture, an image war had begun. In the minds of millions of teenagers the stock market had just crashed." [34]

• • •

Conflicts between the hip and the square were breaking out all over. In Toronto, the leader of the Diggers, David Depoe, acclaimed as SUPER HIPPIE in a cover story on the *Star Weekly* magazine, led battles with the city council and the police over the bohemian Yorkville district. In the much-publicized Summer of Love, Yorkville Avenue had become a circus. Day after day, night after night, hundreds of cars flocked in the area causing traffic gridlock as the suburban occupants rubbernecked to see the drug-crazed, free-loving hippies in action. Depoe and his Diggers petitioned to have the street closed to automobile traffic and turned into a pedestrian mall, but the city traffic czars were not going to be told how to run their roads by a collection of long-haired n'er-do-wells. The stand-off led to a series of sit-ins on the street in late August, which led to multiple arrests.

The situation was complicated by the fact that Depoe was working under a grant from the Company of Young Canadians—a radical organization of young people set up in 1965 by the Federal government. The agency was modelled somewhat on the U.S. Peace Corps, but it was far more extreme. The Peace Corps, still in its heyday, was very much under the control of the Washington establishment. The CYC was run not from above, but by its members—kids in their early twenties, and was designed, to quote one of the revolutionary phrases of the period, to give 'Power to the People.' What that meant, though, was that when the politicians and press learned that Depoe, a paid worker for the CYC, funded by the taxpayers, was being arrested for organizing Yorkville sit-ins (and anti-war demonstrations at the U.S. Consulate), they had a bird.

• • •

The conflicts were much more violent in Asia. The madness in China spilled over into the British colony of Hong Kong. In July, five British policemen were mowed down by machine gun fire in an attack on a police station. The incident set off riots that paralyzed the island through August, and these were followed by a wave of bombings. Bomb-disposal experts defused over 8,000 bombs. Others exploded, one of them killing Wong Yee-man, a seven-year-old girl, and her two-year-old brother.

• • •

The biggest danger to Canada came not from the Diggers or Hippies, but from the Separatists—and not just from bomb-throwing radicals like Pierre Vallières, but from mainstream politicians like René Lévesque. On September 18, Lévesque, a Liberal member of the National Assembly of Québec and a well-respected intellectual light of the province, released a manifesto declaring that, "Québec must become sovereign as soon as possible." *Maîtres chez nous—Masters in our own house.* Three weeks later, the Quebec Liberal Party held their convention, and in a dramatic turn of events Lévesque's ideas were voted down and he walked out of the party. Within months he had begun to set up the *Parti Québeçois*, which soon became the leading separatist organization in the province. He had to walk a fine line, fighting federalists like Pierre Trudeau on the one hand, and on the other, more radical separatists like the bombers of the FLQ, and gadfly essayist Pierre Bourgault, who wanted to sink ships in the St. Lawrence Seaway to stop marine traffic into the continent.

• • •

Four days after the Liberal convention in Québec City, at the university in Madison, Wisconsin, a demonstration against Dow Chemical, the company that produced the gelled incendiary napalm used in Vietnam, turned ugly. The police and riot squad violently intervened resulting in injuries to 65 protestors and three police officers and leading to many arrests. Following the demonstration, a mass rally and student strike closed the university for several days.

• • •

The revolution in education continued to expand. Free schools and Free Universities began to sprout up across North America. Most were modest, privately financed operations. None compared with Rochdale College, a giant 18-story building in mid-town Toronto designed by hippies and paid for by the Government of Canada. In the summer of 1967, a small group led by poet Dennis Lee, (now best known for *Alligator Pie*, his book of children's rhymes), and Howard Adelman, a philosophy student and budding entrepreneur (later Professor Emeritus of Philosophy at York University) came up with the idea of creating an open cooperative commune for living and learning. They named it Rochdale College after the mid-19th Century British experiment, the Rochdale co-operatives.

Amazingly, in a manner that would be inconceivable either before or after this heady period, Adelman convinced the federal government, through its agency, the Canada Housing and Mortgage Corporation, to come up with a $5 million loan (equivalent to $35 million today) to buy the prime real estate and put up the building. Again, in a manner that was unique to the go-go '60s, the building was immediately built. It was a wild, noble experiment, but like so much else in this period, it was ultimately doomed. American science fiction writer Judith Merril, a 'resource person' at Rochdale, described it as being "dedicated to a concept of education that had everything to do with learning and almost nothing to do with teaching." Founder Dennis Lee wrote that that the plan for Rochdale was that it "would provide an idealized *Oxbridge* education…a system flexible enough to fit people, all kinds of people, rather than trying to make people fit a structured system inherited from somewhere and someone else. It is a place where people must create their own environment, make their own decisions, learn to face themselves—because the basic truth everyone must face is about himself—and learn to live as complete, rounded people." It was a nice pitch, but by the '70s, the educational aspects of Rochdale had all but been abandoned. It was being described as the biggest distribution center for illicit drugs in North America. It was trashed, went bankrupt, and closed in 1975.

• • •

In 1967 the best-known distributor of psychedelic drugs was not Rochdale but an eclectic, only-in-California character named Augustus Owsley Stanley III. The grandson of the first A. O. Stanley, Governor of Kentucky and then Senator for the state, and back in the day a crusader against Prohibition, Owsley Stanley III had a varied career. He had worked as an engineer on the Navaho cruise missile. He had been a professional ballet dancer. By 1967 he was both the financier and sound engineer of the Grateful Dead. But he was best known as a chemist who created vast amounts of high-quality LSD and a more powerful variant known as STP. Owsley was, like so many in this era, a driven extremist. He vowed to make the purest LSD in the world, even purer than Sandoz. He also found a way to refine it so that under a fluorescent light it appeared blue-white, and, if shaken, emitted flashes of light. It was *piezoluminescent*—a very rare quality shared by only a few other compounds in the world. However, Owsley finally took a fall. He was busted with a stash of $10 million worth of psychedelics and received a sentence of three years in prison and a $3,000 fine for tax evasion.

His assistant, Tim Scully, vowed to continue the crusade—"Better Living Through Chemistry", as the hippie crowd called it, stealing the slogan from Dupont. Scully was endowed with a reportedly genius-level IQ, but he was not as well financed as his boss had been, so he linked up with Billy Hitchcock, the mysterious sugar-daddy banker to the counterculture. Hitchcock bankrolled Scully and a second chemist named Nick Sand, and the trio, along with Acid Guru Timothy Leary and a large band of other associates became known as the Brotherhood of Eternal Love. They mostly based themselves in the artists' colony and surfer town of

Laguna Beach, California, but their influence spanned the globe. They created a number of pharmaceuticals, some barely known to the scientific community, let alone to narcotics agents. They made ten million hits of their best-known product, which they called 'Orange Sunshine.'

Billy Hitchcock needed a place to stash the vast profits he was accruing from the LSD craze. He headed for the Bahamas, partially to investigate the possibility of buying a remote cay to set up a new laboratory, which led some to accuse him of being "on a *Dr. No* Trip." While there he connected with another colorful character from this era, Bernie Cornfeld, whose 'Investors Overseas Services' was a giant money-laundering pyramid scheme for mobsters, corrupt Third World dictators, wealthy expatriates and international swindlers. This led Hitchcock into a connection with Resorts International, the company that largely developed Paradise Island after re-naming it from its previous moniker Hog Island and building the bridge to it from Nassau. Resorts International had connections with mobster Meyer Lansky; with Richard Nixon's best friend, Florida banker Bebe Rebozo; and with a network of CIA operatives.

Billy Hitchcock connected, through this crowd, to the Castle Bank, a clandestine bank set up by the CIA and used through the 60s and 70s to launder money from the U.S. into Caribbean subversion, coup d'états, and paramilitary operations, including attempts by the Mob to assassinate Fidel Castro. There is also speculation that the CIA used Castle Bank to fund the production of more LSD-25, which operatives in the agency thought could become a powerful tool to neutralize left-wing movements both in America and around the world. Billy Hitchcock and the Brotherhood got involved with the Nassau-based bank, but when the American SEC began investigating transactions in the Bahamas, they moved their money to the Paravicini Bank in Berne, Switzerland, and sloshed $67 million through that "no names, just numbers" bank.

• • •

Che Guevara appeared to have dropped off the face of the earth. The Cuban people had no idea what had happened to their hero. The CIA assumed that he must have been killed in one of his revolutionary activities in the Congo. Only Fidel and Raul Castro and a few others knew that he was still alive, deep in the jungles of Bolivia, trying to light South America ablaze with revolution. For a year, he and his small band had been fighting the Bolivian army in small, somewhat successful skirmishes. They were joined by the French writer Régis Debray, but he was captured by the Bolivians, and through him they learned that the leader of the rag-tag outfit in the jungle was the world's most celebrated revolutionary guerrilla, Che Guevara. René Barrientos, the president of the country, appealed to the Americans for help in killing Che, and the U.S. sent down a group of CIA operatives to assist in tracking him down.

On October 8th, 1,800 soldiers of the Bolivian Army, under the direction of CIA agent Félix Rodriguez, a Cuban exile and veteran of the Bay of Pigs, had a gun battle with the *guerrillas* in which Guevara was wounded and captured. Rodriguez and Barrientos had different agendas. Rodriguez wanted to take Guevara back alive, Barrientos wanted him killed in Bolivia. The CIA man managed to get the Bolivians to untie Guevara's bonds, and the pair had a good mano à mano conversation. Che's last words were to ask the agent to get a message to Castro that one day the revolution would succeed, and another to his wife telling her she should re-marry and try to be happy.

Rodriguez told two of the Bolivian soldiers that the order from their high commander, the President, was that Che was to be executed, so they should shoot him. But, he said, since the story was going to be that Che died of his battle wounds, they should shoot him in the chest, not the head. One of the Bolivian Rangers shot and killed the famous leader. Che's hands were amputated, and sent to the CIA for fingerprint testing, wrapped in a copy of that day's newspaper. It was a military victory for the Bolivian Army and a political victory for Washington, but by displaying his corpse the Bolivians and CIA helped make Che a martyr to the Revolutionary struggle—a *Guerrillero Heroico* to the rebellious youth of the world.

On October 18th, Castro announced the death of Che. In an epic barnburner of a eulogy of his old comrade, Castro told the children of Cuba they should strive to be like Che. In death, Guevara soon became one of the greatest personalities of the 20th Century, one of the greatest revolutionary icons of all time, an archetypal figure who would personally sacrifice everything in the name of the revolution, in search of a fairer world.

• • •

Three days later, on October 21st, 100,000 demonstrators descended on Washington to protest the war, many carrying banners bearing Che's image, others with the flag of the Viet Cong. It was possibly the first protest ever where not just the substance of the protest but the style of it was revolutionary, the first to follow the new dictates of Marshall McLuhan.

"TV time goes to those with the most guts and imagination," declared organizer Jerry Rubin. "I never understood the radical who comes on TV in a suit and tie. Turn off the sound and he could be the mayor! The *words* may be radical, but television is a non-verbal instrument! The way to understand TV is to shut off the sound. No one remembers any words they hear; the mind is a technicolor movie of images, not words. I've never seen "bad" coverage of a demonstration. It makes no difference what they *say* about us. The picture is the story."[35] The anti-war crowd had some pretty good images dreamed up for this one.

Another of the organizers, a Haight-Ashbury Psychedelic Ranger named Michael Bowen announced some cosmic lore gleaned from the Tarot that a five-sided figure is a symbol of power, and that one pointing north, like the Pentagon, represents the forces of evil. Rubin and Bowen announced at a press conference before the event that the plan was that the huge crowd would levitate the Defense Department building 300 feet in the air, whereupon it would vibrate and turn orange, and the Vietnam war would immediately cease. Abbie Hoffman also promised to release a mysterious gas called LACE, allegedly created by Owsley, that "makes you want to take your clothes off, kiss people, and make love."

The giant crowd of acidheads, witches, warlocks, church leaders, and angry Vietnam vets surrounded the mighty fortress and began hissing and shouting their disapproval. They were led by poet Ed Sanders' burlesque rock group the Fugs booming into the sound system "Out, demons, out!". Try as they did, the evening news did not show any images of demons escaping or the Pentagon floating 300 feet above Washington. Instead, though, the event did create unplanned and unexpected images that were almost as iconic and certainly as emblematic of the era. They happened because of a dirty trick of the FBI. Michael Bowen, as part of the planning for the event managed to persuade a millionaire supporter Peggy Hitchcock (sister of Billy Hitchcock) to pay for the charter of a plane and the purchase of 200 pounds of daisies which were to be sky-bombed on the Pentagon during the demonstration. The FBI answered an advertisement in the *East Village Other*, with an operative volunteering his plane for the job. However, on the day of the event he simply never showed up at the airport, and so Bowen was stuck with a huge cache of unused flowers. Rather than throw them out, he drove to the demonstration, and got volunteers to hand them out. Soon, photographers for the world press were taking pictures of the demonstrators pushing the stems of daisies into the muzzles of the guns held by all the soldiers guarding the Pentagon. It became another of the iconic images of the era—stone-faced National Guardsmen standing, startled, as antiwar activists poked flowers past their bayonets.

Jerry Rubin saw the "flower power" images as akin to the old lithographs of the original American revolutionaries hurling cases of tea into Boston harbor. "It made me see that we could build a movement by knocking off symbols," he said. "We had symbolically destroyed the Pentagon, the symbol of the war machine, by throwing blood on it, by pissing on it, dancing on it...painting 'Che Lives' on it. It was a total cultural attack on the Pentagon. The media had communicated this all over the world and lots of people identified with us, the besiegers."

President Johnson, convinced that the Movement was part of a larger communist conspiracy, authorized the CIA to begin *Operation CHAOS*, a massive surveillance program spying on Americans. It is against American law for the CIA to spy on American citizens, but that did not slow them down. Lasting almost seven years, *CHAOS* compiled a computer index of 300,000, and extensive files on more than 7,000, but never proved any communist connection. The organizations the CIA spied on and attacked included not just the likely candidates like SDS, the Black Panthers, and the Puerto Rican Young Lords, but also the Women's Movement, Ramparts Magazine, and the B'nai B'rith.

• • •

The Johnson Administration, concerned that the Cold War might expand into space, worried that the Russians might beat them to the moon, and possibly also influenced by the progressive, utopian tone of one of the new hit TV series of the year, *Star Trek*, proposed what became known as the *Outer Space Treaty*. It was signed at the United Nations in October by the U.S., the Soviet Union, and dozens of other countries, and forbade armed conflict in space, the militarization of space, and the ownership of any celestial bodies. It was a forward-thinking agreement and was adhered to by all until the creation of the U.S. Space Force by President Donald Trump in December, 2019.

• • •

The anti-war movement, to the dismay of the war's supporters, was increasingly attracting mainstream allies. William Sloane Coffin, for instance, had a blueblood pedigree. He was born into the wealthy New York City elite. He had gone to the best private schools, and then to Yale University, where he was initiated into the secret Skull and Bones society by his good friend George H. W. Bush. He worked as a case officer for the CIA through the 50s, and then became the Chaplain of Yale University. However, he, like so many others, was transformed by the Vietnam War. He tried to get Yale to allow him to turn his chapel into a sanctuary for draft resisters. When the administration turned that idea down, he instead gave a Sunday sermon about the need for resistance, invoking the names of Socrates, Gandhi, and St. Peter, and opened the church to 280 young men who all burned their draft cards at the altar. Coffin, along with famed pediatrician Dr. Benjamin Spock was indicted on January 8, 1968 by a Federal grand jury for "conspiracy to counsel, aid and abet draft resistance."

• • •

On November 17th, in Bolivia, Régis Debray was sentenced to 30 years in prison. The same day, 20 people were wounded and 46 arrested when police charged into a crowd in front of the U.S. Consulate in Montréal protesting the bombing of Hanoi. Also the same day, a story appeared in the *Financial Times* of London stating that United States Secretary of Defense Robert McNamara had resigned from the Johnson Administration and was about to become the head of the World Bank. This 'resignation' was news to Robert McNamara, but it did not totally surprise him, since even though he was one of the architects of the Vietnam War, he had over the last year begun to totally lose faith in the American involvement. His visits to Vietnam and his confrontations with angry anti-war demonstrators across America began to convince him that short of annihilating North Vietnam (an option some of his generals were willing to contemplate) the war could not be won. Even his own son hung an American flag upside down in his bedroom, telling his father he was ashamed of America because of him.

Johnson realized that McNamara was starting to question the war and freaked out. Johnson always demanded total fidelity from all his aides and cabinet members. He once shouted, "I don't want loyalty. I want LOYALTY. I want him to kiss my ass in Macy's window at high noon and tell me it smells like roses. I want his pecker in my pocket." Johnson was terrified of the growing anti-war movement. He was worried that McNamara, in questioning the massive but ineffective bombing, was jeopardizing not only the administration but his own mental health. Maybe he would have a mental collapse. Maybe even, as previous Secretary of Defense James Forrestal did, he would commit suicide over his misgivings.

On his last day in office, McNamara got into a heated argument in a cabinet meeting with the hawkish National Security Advisor Walt Whitman Rostow, who urged the President to add 200,000 more troops to the nearly 500,000 already there, and dramatically increase the bombing raids on North Vietnam. McNamara snapped in fury at Rostow, asking, "What then? This goddamned bombing campaign, it's worth nothing. It's done nothing. They've dropped more bombs than in all of World War II and it hasn't done a fucking thing." [36] He then broke down in tears.

•   •   •

A few days later, a gun store in Cap-de-la-Madelaine, Québec was looted of $9,000 worth of heavy caliber guns, revolvers, and ammunition. The burglars left no doubt about who they were. They left a note reading, "Merci. FLQ"

•   •   •

On December 19th, the Neuwirth Law was passed in the French National Assembly. It finally lifted the ban on contraception (both products and information) that had existed in France since the 1920s. Eleven similar bills had been introduced in France between 1958 and 1967 and all had failed, but this bill, introduced by Gaullist lawmaker Lucien Neuwirth passed narrowly, over the objections of elderly politicians such as Charles De Gaulle. It took five years for the law to be enacted, but the famously romantic nation finally joined the rest of the world in this aspect of the Sexual Revolution in 1972.

• • •

The next day, General George Westmoreland warned Washington from Saigon that the North Vietnamese Army and the Viet Cong were about to launch a major attack, but the Pentagon, the government, the press, and the public were all unconvinced. Westmoreland, however, was correct. Eighty-thousand tons of supplies, and 200,000 troops started moving down the just completed Ho Chi Minh Trail, which proved to be one of the greatest achievements of military engineering of the twentieth century. The North Vietnamese began supplying the Viet Cong with equipment such as AK-47 assault rifles and B-40 rocket propelled grenade launchers, to prepare for a new deadly phase of the war that would begin in earnest in 1968.

1968

The Yippies Take Acid, Oliver Stone fights in 'Nam,
Memphis Garbagemen Strike, White Niggers of North America,
My Lai Destroyed, Martin Luther King Killed, Paris Burned,
Sympathy for the Devil Recorded, Daniel Berrigan Arrested,
Robert Kennedy Assassinated, Mexico Olympics Protested.

While 1967 had grim moments, it also had flashes of gaiety and euphoria. The world economy had boomed. The "Summer of Love" had been a largely upbeat experiment. The planet didn't explode on July 16 as Reverend Jim Jones had said it would. Expo '67 brought millions of people together. New music was full of life and originality. The year 1968 would prove to be…a lot more complicated.

On January 1ˢᵗ, Abbie Hoffman and his equally zany and inventive sidekick Jerry Rubin thought they would kick off the new year by dropping LSD and generating some plans for '68. Over the course of their acid-fueled New Year's celebration they fixated on the word "Yippie!", and before the twelve-hour trip was over, they had a new idea—they would become the Yippies. Thousands of other Yippies would join them. The Youth International Party would be a new political party, but a party more in the sense of *Rock on!* than a political movement. There would certainly be no leaders, and no ideology, for they considered ideology 'a brain disease'. They didn't plan to turn this into work. They figured the media would do the heavy lifting. "An event doesn't exist until the media announces it," claimed Rubin. "Once the media announce it, it is an event whether or not it exists." One of their acid insights was that television was just an elaborate mirror game that the authorities used to pacify the public. They figured they would just flip the mirrors around so that the crazy new imagery they created would shock the viewers, blow their minds, and convince them there was an alternative to the old-fashioned straight way of looking at things. Their mad plans perhaps sound nutty today, but the pair, consummate pros in the art of street theatre, would have considerable influence on the zeitgeist of the next two years. Their New Year's Day manifesto included:

- Everyone should do "whatever the fuck they want"

- Bob Dylan songs should replace the National Anthem

- No more jails, courts, or police

- The Pentagon should be replaced by an LSD experimental farm

- The White House should become a crash pad for anyone with no place to stay

• • •

On January 1, the White House, needless to say, was not yet a crash pad. It was, instead the site of a New Year's Day speech by President Johnson who somberly announced that he was no longer able to predict that the war in Southeast Asia would end in 1968. A few weeks later, singer Eartha Kitt, performing at the White House, reduced Johnson's wife Lady Bird to tears by telling her, "You send the best of this country off to be shot and maimed. No wonder the kids rebel and take pot." [37]

In the jargon of the times, 1968 was not a good trip. Instead, it was a bummer—a dark year, not largely characterized by "Yippie!" but rather by war, assassinations, and increasing conflicts between races and generations.

• • •

The same week Eartha Kitt was giving Lady Bird a piece of her mind in the White House, country singer and "Man in Black" Johnny Cash performed in the Big House, behind the bars of the California State Maximum Security Folsom Prison. The prison was one of the most infamous in America, partially because of Cash's song *Folsom Prison Blues*, with its gruesome lines "I shot a man in Reno/Just to watch him die", partially because of its stream of notorious inmates—Charles Manson, Timothy Leary, Eldridge Cleaver, leader of the Hell's Angels Sonny Barger, Eric Menendez, and Mafia enforcer Joseph Barboza. The concept of the prisoner as a heroic figure became trendy in this era, and the idea of performing behind bars became popular, with Cash repeating it at San Quentin Prison in 1969.

• • •

Early in the year, people started dying. On January 11, near Escuintla, Guatemala, the naked body of Rogelia Cruz was found under a bridge. She had been raped, tortured, and murdered. Ten years earlier Cruz had been winner of the Miss Guatemala pageant and the country's entrant in the Miss Universe competition. In the early 60s she became a leader of the guerrilla group *Partido Guatemalterco del Trabajo* (PGT) fighting against the country's military dictatorship. Now, apparently, she was yet another victim of the paramilitaries supported by U.S. operatives who were spreading terror across the country. In retaliation for her murder, the young rebel group attacked American military personnel, killing two men and injuring a third, and then, in retaliation, the Guatemalan military assassinated Cruz' lover Leonardo Castillo Johnson.[38]

• • •

Also in January, two young American soldiers fought in vicious battles in Vietnam. Many of their compatriots were killed, but they survived to tell their tales, which they did, some years later, collaborating on one of the most important memoirs of the brutal war.

Private Oliver Stone, a mixed-up kid from an upper class but dysfunctional family had grown up in New York and Paris, dropped out of Yale, tried his hand at being a novelist, and then volunteered to fight in Vietnam. On January 1, his unit was stationed in a fire zone close to the Ho Chi Minh Trail and the Cambodian border. As darkness fell, the enemy closed in, and a fierce, unimaginably strange all-night battle ensued. There was constant gunfire and explosions with constant confusing mixed radio messages of where the North Vietnamese enemy were or how best to defend against them. At four in the morning, a giant bomb dropped from the sky that knocked Stone out. When he came to...minutes?...hours? later, he found that although he was concussed, he had no apparent injuries. He was alone, but eventually rediscovered his platoon in the tracer-laced night, just as an F-16 jet fighter screamed in above them. The men all dove to the ground to protect themselves from the blast of a 500-pound bomb. Stone survived that terrifying night. The next day he was assigned the task of dragging hundreds of dead NVA soldiers from the jungle, throwing them into a mass grave, dousing them with gasoline and incinerating their bodies. Years later, in 1986, he would turn the events of January 1 into *Platoon*, one of the classic films of the Vietnam war. Three years after that he would collaborate with Ron Kovic, another Vietnam veteran, to make yet another epic film about the war.

Kovic had also volunteered to serve in Vietnam. On January 20, near the village of Mỹ Lộc, he was leading a reconnaissance patrol of scouts of the 1st Amtrac Battalion of Marines when his squad found themselves in a firefight with soldiers from the North Vietnamese Army and the Viet Cong. Kovic found himself deserted by most of his unit. He was shot, first in his foot, then in his shoulder and lung. Another Marine tried to drag him to safety, but in the process his rescuer was shot and killed. A second carried him through heavy enemy fire and out of the combat zone. Kovic's spinal cord was severed. He was paralyzed from the chest down and remains so today.

Within a few years, Kovic became one of the most angry and vocal demonstrators against the war. A leader of the group Vietnam Veterans Against the War, he was arrested 12 times for his wheelchair protests. In 1976 he wrote his passionate memoir, *Born on the Fourth of July*. In 1989, he linked forces with Oliver Stone and Tom Cruise to turn the book about his experience in Vietnam into a powerful movie.

The Tet Offensive began on January 30. Named for the Vietnamese Lunar New Year, Tet was one of the largest military operations of the Vietnam War. More than 100 towns and cities in South Vietnam were attacked by the Viet Cong and the North Vietnamese People's Army of the Republic of Vietnam (PAVN). The operation lasted two months and was ultimately considered a military defeat for North Vietnam. There were over 111,000 casualties to the VC/PAVN forces, and 60,000 to the American and South Vietnamese. It was, though, a Pyrrhic victory for the Americans. The campaign provided an impetus for the growing anti-war movement when the American public began to realize that North Vietnam was a much more formidable enemy than the American Generals had previously claimed, and even more so when they learned from General Westmoreland that the war would require an additional draft call-up of 200,000. The Tet Offensive produced one of most mordantly offensive lines of the war—the comment from an American military commander to Associated Press news correspondent Peter Arnett that "It became necessary to destroy the village in order to save it."

On February 1ˢᵗ, Brigadier-General Nguyēn Ngoc Loan, the chief of the South Vietnamese National Police, summarily executed a handcuffed Nguyēn Vän Lém, a member of the Viet Cong, by shooting him in the head on a Saigon street with a .38 Smith & Wesson revolver. The incident was photographed by AP photographer Eddie Adams and became one of the most iconic and grotesque photos of the war. The photo was seen around the world and served to sow further mistrust in the morality of the South Vietnamese and by association their ally the U.S.A. It also destroyed the reputation of the General, but on his own death 30 years later, Adams, the photographer, defended him, saying "The general killed the Viet Cong. I killed the general with my camera. Still photographs are the most powerful weapon in the world. People believe them, but photographs do lie, even without manipulation. They are only half-truths. What the photograph didn't say was, 'What would you do if you were the general at that time and place on that hot day, and you caught the so-called bad guy after he blew away one, two, or three American soldiers?'" [39] It was a war with very complicated and very mixed moral messages.

• • •

On the same day, February 1, in Memphis, Tennessee two ill-paid garbagemen, forbidden by city rules to shelter from the rain, sat inside the back scoop of their garbage truck trying to stay dry during a downpour. During the storm the malfunctioning machine accidently swallowed both of them and crushed them in with the garbage. The local black community felt the grotesque mishap was caused by a wanton disregard by the city for the lives of its mostly black workers. It was the spark that would lead to the Memphis sanitation strike that would bring Dr. Martin Luther King to Memphis, the city in which he would be assassinated.

• • •

On February 27th, 2,500 people marched to support striking workers at a 7-Up bottling plant in Montréal, chanting *Re-vo-lu-tion! Re-vo-lu-tion!* They threw Molotov cocktails, nearly set the plant on fire, broke dozens of windows in nearby buildings, and battered two police cars and a TV news van.

• • •

In West Germany, 10,000 protestors from across Western Europe converged at the Freie Universität for the International Vietnam Congress. They heard student leader Rudi Dutschke tell them "We will make the Vietnam Congress into an international manifestation of solidarity with the bombed and struggling people." [40]

In France, the demonstrations that would bring the country to a standstill in the spring began at Nanterre University, a hotbed of revolutionary thought and action when students attacked busloads of policemen and chased them away from the school grounds. In March, Paris saw four bombings in a row—two banks on the 17th, Trans World Airways and American Express the next day. On the 22nd, Daniel Cohn-Bendit, the most prominent of Nanterre's student anarchist leaders, led a takeover of the university's administration buildings. The newsletter of the student rebels published an authentic recipe for making Molotov cocktails. The dean of the school, Pierre Grappin, told the Minister of Education, Alain Peyrefitte that most of the professors were now siding with the student militants, and that "We have gone beyond the stage of protest. We have reached the stage of pre-revolution." [41] Young high school students joined in, creating their own revolutionary annex they called the *Comités d'action lycéens*. Romain Goupil, one of their leaders, recalled, "There was an unbelievable political ferment; those who didn't see anything coming were really very cut off from reality. We considered ourselves to be the heirs to 1789, the Commune, the 1917 Russian Revolution. We carried the torch." [42]

. . .

Meanwhile the students of the Chinese Cultural Revolution, encouraged by the leaders of the country, had moved far beyond talk. As just one of thousands of examples, students at the Wuxuan Middle School beat a geography teacher named Wu Shufang to death, then forced another teacher at gunpoint to rip out his heart and liver, which they then barbecued and ate. [43]

On March 1ˢᵗ, at the orders of Jiang Qing (Madame Mao) prominent Chinese theatre director Sun Weishi and her husband Jin Shan were both arrested and imprisoned as part of the Cultural Revolution. Sun was the adopted daughter of Chinese Premiere Zhou Enlai. Even though Zhou held the second highest position in China, he was unable to protect his daughter for fear of angering Mao. Sun was considered one of the preeminent voices of Chinese theater, directing and writing original works since the 1940s, but she had angered Madame Mao, herself originally an actress, by refusing her request to participate with Sun in a 1963 production called *Azalea Mountain*. Madame Mao ordered that Sun be sentenced without trial, and tortured "at leisure", but not killed.

• • •

On March 15ᵗʰ, Pierre Vallières' revolutionary manifesto was published, provocatively titled, *Nègres Blancs d'Amérique* or *White Niggers of America -The Precocious Autobiography of a Quebec 'Terrorist'*. Vallières had written the book while jailed in the infamous Manhattan House of Detention for Men ('The Tombs') in New York after fleeing arrest in Québec on charges related to FLQ bombings. His book, very influential in Québec and the U.S., compared the condition of French Canadians to that of Black Americans, and claimed the parallels between the two peoples as exploited lower classes meant that both should take up arms for liberation against their oppressors. "Only a total revolution," wrote Vallières, "will allow Québeçois, in collaboration with other people of the earth, to build a totally free and totally sovereign Québec. Such a revolution will not come about without war and without violence." He compared French Canadians to the black sharecroppers of the American South but wrote that Québec was "the only place in North America where conditions are ripe for a revolution to break out and succeed."

Vallières wrote the book in pencil, standing up, since neither desks nor pens were allowed in the Tombs. It was also against the rules to write books, so he had to smuggle his work out disguised as letters to his lawyer.

It was not literally written in blood, but it read like it was. Vallières was as much a Marxist as a separatist. He claimed that "we must free ourselves from all the balls and chains that capitalist society attached to our feet as soon as we were born," and that Québecers needed to launch "a total revolution, which will not only overthrow the capitalist state but at the same time abolish everything that has for centuries perverted and poisoned social relations, life in society, private ownership of the means of production and exchange, the accumulation and concentration of capital in the hands of a few." [44]

Ironically, his fiery polemic got as much or more attention in the U.S. as it did in Canada. Québec bookstores shunned the book as being too dangerous, but it sold briskly in the States, after the *New York Times* called it "a revolutionary document that clutches one's throat like a drowning hand."

• • •

On March 16th between 300 and 500 unarmed Vietnamese civilians, many of them women and young children, were slaughtered by U.S. Army soldiers in a rural area known as My Lai. Women were gang raped and their bodies mutilated. The soldiers forced families from their thatched houses by lighting the homes on fire with cigarette lighters, then shooting the people as they ran from the flames. The massacre, one of the most shocking episodes of the Vietnam war, was covered up and whitewashed for many months by the American military, including by Major Colin Powell, then a 31-year-old charged by the Army with the investigation. Powell would go on to become a four-star general and Secretary of State during George W. Bush's Iraq War. When the My Lai massacre was finally publicly revealed by independent investigative reporter Seymour Hersh in November 1969, it prompted global outrage and served to stain America's reputation and to further opposition to the war. In America, though, 65% of people told pollsters they were not bothered by the news of the massacre. Twenty-six soldiers were charged with crimes, but only one, Lieutenant William Calley Jr. was convicted. His defense was that he was "just following orders." Indeed, orders had been given to destroy the village and "close with the enemy and wipe them out for good...burn the houses, kill the livestock, destroy food supplies, and destroy and/or poison the wells." [45] Following the raid, General William Westmoreland, the supreme commander in Vietnam, congratulated the company for "outstanding action", telling them they had "dealt the enemy a heavy blow."[46] Much later, in his memoir of the war, he rescinded those congratulations, describing the event instead as a "conscious massacre of defenseless babies, children, mothers, and old men in a kind of diabolical slow-motion nightmare that went on for the better part of the day, with a cold-blooded break for lunch."

Even though they could not yet know about the massacre (there was of course no social media in 1968), the next day, 80,000 demonstrators protested in Trafalgar Square against the ongoing American involvement in the Vietnam War. The large crowd in London heard speeches from activist/actress Vanessa Redgrave and others, following which a splinter group headed for the American Embassy in Grosvenor Square. They were turned back by the London police, and the event turned into a violent fight with 300 people arrested and 117 policemen and many, many demonstrators injured.

The Vietnam War was increasingly becoming the most contentious and difficult issue of the era. Why was America in Vietnam? Jacqueline Kennedy, widow of the president who sent the first American military 'advisors' to Southeast Asia, had a theory. "The problem with Vietnam," she said, "is that we had three consecutive presidents who all believed their manhood had to be proven in the terrible assertion of military power."

• • •

The other fractious issue of the period, of course, was race. In March, one of the most radical and incendiary books of the era, Eldridge Cleaver's *Soul on Ice* was published and sold more than two million copies.

The *New York Times* called it "brilliant" and "revealing" and named it one of ten best books of the year. The sex-obsessed Cleaver had quite the colorful and profane way with words. He took Mao's dictum that "Political power comes from the barrel of a gun" and turned it into "Power comes out of the lips of a pussy," and sometimes, "Power comes from the barrel of a dick."

• • •

In Africa, also in March, about 200 revolutionary fighters crossed from Zambia into Rhodesia, and set up a compound with Viet Cong-style tunnels in the Chewore hunting reserve. As in the past, supplies proved to be their downfall. Although their camp was hidden from aerial reconnaissance, they made a distinct path to and from their landing site on the Zambezi River, where they were bringing in food and weapons by inflatable boats. A National Parks game scout saw the path, alerted the authorities, and by mid-month the guerrillas were being attacked by ground forces and the Rhodesian Air Force. Forty-eight ZAPU guerrillas were killed and over 50 others were captured. Only a few made it back to Zambia to tell the tale.

With this defeat, the nationalist organizations were forced to reevaluate their strategy, as they began to admit that six years of military operations against Rhodesia had accomplished absolutely nothing. The revolutionaries had all bravely marched into the arms of almost certain annihilation, advancing the cause of noble revolutionary mythology, but not advancing the cause of the liberation of Rhodesia in the slightest. The guerrilla fighters withdrew from the border to reevaluate their strategy, and white Rhodesians began to relax, mistakenly thinking that the battle for Rhodesia was over.

• • •

In this busy month of March, a rift suddenly developed between two previously friendly communist leaders—Mao Zedong and North Korean Premier Kim Il-Sung. Kim told the Soviet president that Mao's unleashing of the Red Guards in the Cultural Revolution was "massive idiocy" and "Chinese wickedness." The Red Guards struck back in their newspapers calling Kim a "fat revisionist, a millionaire, an aristocrat, and a leading bourgeois figure in Korea." Chinese radicals set up massive speakers along the border, pumping insults about the "Dear Leader" into Korea. In the border town of Yambian, freight trains rolled into the DPRK, draped with the bodies of Koreans killed in the Cultural Revolution and painted with graffiti reading, "This will be your fate also, you tiny revisionists." However, China continued to support Korea financially. They postponed building the planned Metro subway system in Beijing so that they could instead build one in Pyongyang for the Koreans. Meanwhile, Korea financed other revolutions around the world—particularly in Africa. Kim Il-Sung supported the insurgents in Angola, and underground fighters like Robert Mugabe in Rhodesia. The President of Guinea declared Kim to be "the leader of the Third World". The Mansudae Art Studio, the branch of the North Korean propaganda department that had built giant godlike statues of Kim Il-Sung across North Korea began to create giant monuments in the familiar socialist-realist style for African countries like Ethiopia, Senegal, and South West Africa (now Namibia).

• • •

The violence in Europe was re-kindled on April 2, as four members of the Red Army Factions lit a department store in Frankfurt on fire, protesting both the Vietnam War and what they perceived to be the authoritarian, neo-Nazi actions of their parents' generation. Founding members of the gang, Andreas Baader and Gudrun Ensslin, and two others were later arrested and in October sentenced to three years in prison. They were released on appeal in June, 1969 and went underground. Baader was subsequently re-arrested on April 3, 1970, and was later sprung from jail by his girlfriend Ensslin and their female supporter Ulrike Meinhof. The press took to calling them the Baader-Meinhof Gang, in imitation of the title of the year's big movie, *Bonnie & Clyde*. Some Germans even began making allusions between the gang and the British heroic outlaw Robin Hood, who famously "took from the rich and gave to the poor."

• • •

In late March, Dr. Martin Luther King Jr. flew to Memphis, Tennessee to campaign on behalf of what he called the Poor People's Campaign. The new campaign was more extreme than his previous work for civil rights. It was revolutionary, not just reformist. He now argued that "reconstruction of society is the real issue to be faced." Dr. King was in Memphis to help support the city sanitation workers who were on strike protesting incidents like the death of the two garbagemen earlier in the year, and the frequent occurrences of discrimination against black workers. On April 3rd, referencing the fact that the plane that brought him to Memphis had been delayed by a bomb threat, King addressed a rally at the Mason Temple. His prescient words would be the last he ever spoke publicly. "What could happen to me from some of our sick white brothers? Well, I don't know what will happen now. We've got some difficult days ahead. But it doesn't matter with me now. Because I've been to the mountaintop. And I don't mind. Like anybody, I would like to live a long life. Longevity has its place. But I'm not concerned about that now. I just want to do God's will. And he's allowed me to go up to the mountain. And I've looked over. And I've seen the Promised Land. I may not get there with you. But I want you to know tonight, that we, as a people, will get to the promised land. And so I'm happy tonight. I'm not worried about anything. I'm not fearing any man. Mine eyes have seen the glory of the coming of the Lord."

The next day, just a few hours after Pierre Vallières was sentenced in a Montréal courtroom to lifetime imprisonment for his role in the FLQ LaGrenade bombing of 1965, Martin Luther King went out on his balcony at the Lorraine Motel in Memphis and was fatally shot by a white gunman named James Earl Ray. King was pronounced dead at a Memphis hospital at 7:05 PM. His death had a profound effect on the world. Stokely Carmichael angrily proclaimed that white America had declared war on black America. President Johnson declared a national day of mourning. There were riots in 120 cities across America. Robert Kennedy, in Indianapolis, Mayor John Lindsay in Harlem, and singer James Brown in Boston managed to cool tempers somewhat in those three cities, but almost every other major city in America was hit with major riots. It was considered the greatest wave of civil unrest since the Civil War. One of the worst hit cities was Washington, DC, where crowds of over 20,000 overwhelmed the 3,100-member police force and nearly 12,000 federal troops called in to protect the capital. By the time the city was considered pacified, 1200 buildings had been burnt, with entire neighborhoods gone and $27 million worth of damage.

In Oakland, two days after the assassination, 15 Black Panthers, led by their 'Minister of Information', Eldridge Cleaver, went out on a deliberate ambush of police officers. After a 90-minute gun battle, Cleaver was wounded, arrested, and charged with attempted murder.

There was reaction to the King murder and the subsequent riots all over the world. In England, a Conservative Member of Parliament named Enoch Powell made a speech condemning the riots and predicting that Great Britain would soon be "overrun" with black people if the immigration policies continued, and the planned Race Relations Act was enacted. He quoted a constituent as saying that "In this country in 15 or 20 years the black man will have the whip hand over the white man." Tory leader Edward Heath promptly expelled Powell from his shadow cabinet and the London *Times* called it an "evil speech…that appealed to racial hatred" but thousands of London 'dockers' went on strike to protest his expulsion, with signs reading DON'T KNOCK ENOCH and BACK BRITAIN, NOT BLACK BRITAIN.

There were many changes to society due to the killing of Dr. King. One was that the Academy Awards presentation was postponed for two days, so as not to conflict with the national day of mourning. When the awards were presented on April 10th, every one of the major awards went to movies that reflected the conflicts of the era. *In the Heat of the Night* was about the racial divide and police bigotry. *Guess Who's Coming to Dinner* was about interracial marriage (and featured a minor comic reference to Dr. King that was cut from all the prints following his death). *The Graduate* was about the generation gap, and *Cool Hand Luke* was, as critic Robert Ebert described it, an "anti-establishment film" featuring Paul Newman battling brutal prison conditions in the Deep South. The most influential of the winning films, *Bonnie and Clyde*, masqueraded as a period gangster film, but spoke to the present. It was cited by many of the revolutionaries of the next few years as having an essential role in influencing their aggressive future rebellion against authority. Typically, though, while it was nominated for nine awards, it only won two secondary ones (Best Cinematography and Best Supporting Actress). The younger generation loved the film, but the older one, the one that dominated the voting of the Motion Picture Academy, mostly hated it. Their disdain didn't affect the box office. By March it had been in the top 12 films in North America for 22 weeks, and by the end of 1968 it was the second highest grossing Warner Brothers film of all time, inspiring everyone from Abbie Hoffman to Andreas Baader.

Meanwhile King's killer, James Earl Ray went on the run. He crossed the border to hide out in Toronto for a month, got a false Canadian passport in the name of Ramon George Sneyd and flew to London. From there, he planned to fly to Rhodesia, where he believed, probably accurately, that the Ian Smith regime would protect him from extradition. At the check-in counter, though, an eagle-eyed ticket agent recognized that the "Ramon George Sneyd" name was one that was on an RCMP watch-list, and Ray was caught. He was extradited back to Tennessee, where he was convicted and received a 99-year jail term.

There was much suspicion that Ray was only a small part of a larger conspiracy, and consequently there were many more investigations and further trials. Following a 1999 trial in which the jury found another man,

Loyd Jowers, guilty of being part of a conspiracy to kill King, his widow, Coretta Scott King said, "The jury was clearly convinced by the extensive evidence that was presented during the trial that, in addition to Mr. Jowers, the conspiracy of the Mafia, local, state, and federal government agencies were deeply involved in the assassination of my husband. The jury also affirmed overwhelming evidence that identified someone else, not James Earl Ray, as the shooter, and that Mr. Ray was set up to take the blame." [47]

The Reverend Jesse Jackson stated, "I will never believe that James Earl Ray had the motive, the money, and the mobility to have done it himself. Our government was very involved in setting the stage for and, I think, the escape route for James Earl Ray." [48]

• • •

American campuses continued to explode. The Students for a Democratic Society (SDS)—still active, though by now thoroughly infiltrated by spies from the FBI's COINTELPRO directive, called for "Ten Days of Resistance" which climaxed on April 18th with over a million students striking across America. Four days later, the SDS, led by activist Mark Rudd occupied Columbia University. School Administrator Henry S. Coleman was taken hostage, and University president Grayson Kirk was warned, "Up against the wall, motherfucker. This is a stick-up." Richard Nixon, Ronald Reagan, and George Wallace reacted with violent law and order statements threatening the students, who in turn reacted by settling in the administration building and declaring Columbia a revolutionary zone.

Of course, there was no unanimity on the college campuses. Right-wing conservative students, often in faculties like engineering, sometimes openly mocked the protesting 'lefties' and took to throwing pails of water on passing protest marchers from the windows of their fraternity houses. At the other extreme were blue collar Maoists like Dennis O'Neil, one of the founding members of the Revolutionary Union, the largest American Maoist party, who described what he had learnt about class in America while on a scholarship to private New England schools. "You can't tell me there's no ruling class in this country because I went to school with the little motherfuckers…We, the scholarship students, were required to do manual labor in the afternoons where everyone could see us, to show gratitude for our scholarships…Obviously it didn't inculcate gratitude in anyone with an IQ above that of peat moss."

The Columbia students began to get support from well-known revolutionaries like punk-anarchist Abbie Hoffman. Hoffman helped them uncover the files identifying Columbia as a center for weapons research and military think tanks. On a more immediate level, he discovered the secret basement passageways that allowed him to get food and supplies to the occupying students and avoid the right-wing students who were surrounding the buildings to try to starve out the protestors.

"Inside," he recalled, "we posted guard around the clock and waited hour-by-hour those five days for the police to come. Bodies sprawled all over; rock music blared. We talked endlessly of issues and strategies, fought boredom, fought fear, got hung up on how decisions were to be made, worked out evacuation routes, laughed, made love, smoked dope, sang, argued, and waited." [49] In solidarity with the Columbia occupation, on Friday, April 26, students all over the world skipped classes as an anti-war protest.

• • •

Three days later, on April 29, *Hair*, an ersatz, quasi-revolutionary, pseudo-hippie musical, opened on Broadway. The musical had semi-legitimate roots, as the two writers, James Rado and Gerome Ragni had some measure of connection to the hippie, draft-dodging community of New York's East Village. The writer of the music, though, Canadian composer Galt MacDermot, confessed to having no real connection to the bohemian scene. "I had short hair, a wife, four children and I lived on Staten Island. I had never even heard of a hippie when I met Rado and Ragni." [50] Many genuine hippies did not warm to *Hair!* (calling it instead a "rip-off") but the critics loved it. Len Harris of CBS called it, "the best musical of the Broadway season…that sloppy, vulgar, terrific tribal love rock musical *Hair!*" The middle-class audiences that attended live musical theatre went in droves. As it played around the globe, it certainly had the effect of informing millions of new people about the aspirations of the hippie/student/anti-war/pacifist/flower-power movement. Nonetheless, the day after the Broadway opening, the NYPD, apparently not getting the message that this was "the dawning of the Age of Aquarius," used clubs to end the Columbia sit-in and arrest all the students.

"This is a ferocious but effective way to be a student—to be educated," said SDS ex-President Carl Oglesby. "The policeman's riot club functions like a magic wand under whose hard caress the banal soul grows vivid and the nameless recover their authenticity—a bestower, this wand, of the lost charisma of the modern self: I bleed, therefore I am."

• • •

Three days later, a similar police action happened in France, beginning the biggest urban revolution of the period. On May 2nd, an 'anti-imperialist' teach-in at the University of Nanterre brought out libertarian anarchists led by Daniel Cohn-Bendit, supported by Maoist shock troops modeling themselves on the Chinese Red Guards, plus right-wing groups aiming to cause trouble. In anticipation of the massive protests, the dean of Nanterre suspended all classes and closed the university. The students took to the streets and ended up fighting police for several hours. The *flics* blocked the downtown streets with tear gas and indiscriminately beat passersby who were in their path.

Four days later there were 15,000 students in the streets around the Sorbonne and St.-Germain-des-Prés. Romain Goupil, then a high school student, recalls that "The university students, our leaders, were there from ten in the morning with their two-by-fours. We high-school students said, "No, we can't be there before 4:30, when school lets out." That's when things got wild. The students were loaded onto buses [by the police], and we threw rocks at the cops. To be 15 years old and be pelting the cops and protected by the crowd, perfect bliss! The cops were dumbfounded. The older student leaders too. They were in the buses and said to themselves, 'Unbelievable, it's catching on!'"

The police threw tear gas canisters into movie theaters and used water cannons to beat back the crowds. Students smashed and overturned cars and dug up and threw paving stones. Trees were cut down to make barricades. The students hurled at the *flics* copies of *The Mass Psychology of Fascism*, the book by one of their heroes, radical Austrian psychoanalyst Wilhelm Reich. There were allegations that the police had participated in the riots as *agents provocateurs*, burning cars and hurling Molotov cocktails themselves. [51]

The next day, 30,000 students marched in Paris, and unions began wildcat strikes in support. Within the week there would be 11 million workers striking—more than 22% of the country's population. Jean-Luc Godard and other filmmakers invaded the Centre du Cinéma, where they were planning, in the anarchist spirit of the revolt, to destroy all the films archived there. They were persuaded that they should leave the films alone and instead liberate movie cameras stored in the Centre, and hand them out to the protesting students so that the kids could document the revolution.

On May 13th almost a million people marched to denounce the government of Charles de Gaulle. The country was nearly paralyzed. Stores were closed, food was running short, the Métro was not running, and most gas stations had run out of fuel. The Renault factory was taken over by the workers, trains stopped running, airports shut down, and the postal service stopped. People were convinced revolution was imminent. Just as in Beijing, it was a revolution of posters and slogans plastered and painted all over Paris, the most famous of which was *Il est interdite d'interdire – It is forbidden to forbid*. On May 22nd the most prominent leader of the revolution, Daniel Cohn-Bendit (nicknamed *Dany le Rouge* for both his politics and his flaming hair) was banished to Germany as a 'seditious alien'.

Throughout the revolution there were dozens of noisy meetings in which often meaningless and unenforceable resolutions were passed. For instance, hundreds of film technicians and professionals declared themselves the *Etats généraux du cinema* and passed a motion demanding that from now on all movie theatres should be free of charge. They also demanded that the Cannes Film Festival be shut down—a demand that did prove to have teeth. The Cannes Festival, one of the biggest annual events in the country, had just begun. The film workers demanded that it should stop, in solidarity with the students. Jean Luc Godard, François Truffaut and other star filmmakers including Roger Vadim and his movie-star wife Jane Fonda headed down to the Riviera to make the demand. The events of May would have a profound effect of politicizing and radicalizing Fonda, who would become one of the most prominent activist leaders of the next four years. Pregnant with her first daughter and living in Paris and St. Tropez with Vadim, she was supposed to be relaxing by spending the spring considering scripts for her next film role. Instead, she was reading *The Autobiography of Malcolm X*, and protesting the Cannes Film Festival.

On arriving in Cannes, the filmmakers found that although the jury that included Monica Vitti, Roman Polanski, and Louis Malle had already resigned in solidarity with the students, the organizers were still trying to keep the festival alive. Some films had been pulled, but others were still scheduled to be shown. A Spanish thriller called *Peppermint Frappé* was expected to be unspooled in an afternoon screening, but the protesting filmmakers took to the stage of the theatre and presented their demand that the festival stop. The organizers and the projectionist pushed forward, the movie began with the images flickering over the protestors, then after a few minutes of argument the house lights came back on, and the film was turned off. The angry audience rushed the stage and a brawl erupted. The following day, the festival was cancelled.

On May 23rd , there was another night of flaming barricades and police violence in Paris' Latin Quarter, and on the 24th the students set fire to the Paris Stock Exchange, and the same day two people were killed on the streets. In Lyon, Police Inspector René Lacroix died when he was crushed by a driverless truck sent careering into police lines by rioters. In Paris, 26-year-old Phillipe Metherion was stabbed to death during an argument among demonstrators.

On the 29th, President De Gaulle suddenly and mysteriously disappeared. France seemed stunned. Not even a mystified Prime Minister George Pompidou knew where he was. It turned out that the President had fled the country. Eventually it was discovered he had absconded to a French military base in Germany, taking with him his personal papers and the family jewels. The next day, 500,000 marched through the streets of Paris, chanting, *"Adieu, de Gaulle."* To their dismay, the old General changed his mind, flew home, and announced that he refused to resign. He instead called a snap election for June. To the great disappointment of the revolutionaries, the Gaullists won a huge majority in the election, and the insurrection was over.

The Second French Revolution largely failed as a political action, but it succeeded as a social and cultural one by transforming French society in a great many ways. It also was the impetus and inspiration for much film, art, literature, and music, including, just for instance, the Rolling Stones' song *Street Fighting Man*. However, many artists found themselves in somewhat of a state of shock over the intensity of the May Revolution. Jean-Luc Godard perceived that he was now living in a changed world and would have to do things very differently. He told a German interviewer, "One must give everything up. One must change one's life...One must completely change oneself, and that is very difficult. Concerning myself, I was also a little afraid; I said to myself, 'Look, maybe it's the end'." Godard had spent several nights in London during the revolution filming the recording of the Rolling Stones' *Sympathy for the Devil* for a commissioned film titled *One Plus One*. Press reports claimed he had his crew lay down a "figure eight track" through the studio to film from. Such a track did not exist then and does not now and would be a technological impossibility except in an Escher drawing, but it made for a good story. In typical Rolling Stones/Jean-Luc Godard 1960s style, the recording studio caught ablaze when a movie light ignited the ceiling. Godard returned to the burning barricades of Paris but came back in August to film additional material for the film—actors portraying black revolutionaries declaiming texts by Eldridge Cleaver and LeRoi Jones, and a scene in a pornographic bookstore featuring long recitations from *Mein Kampf*.

The film premiered at the London Film Festival in November. The producers were unhappy with Godard's cut of the film and re-edited it to include a full version of the Stones' song, which the director had neglected to include. An angry Godard urged the audience to demand their money back and then send it to "black power" leaders. An onstage argument ensued. Godard punched one of the producers in the face and stomach and was ejected from the theater.

His career continued in mad fashion, symbolic of the crazy tumultuous year 1968. He headed for New York, linking up with cinema-verité documentarian D. A. Pennebaker, much celebrated for his recent films about Robert Kennedy and Bob Dylan. The pair, without a permit, filmed the Jefferson Airplane playing on the rooftop of a building on West 54th Street until the police broke up the noisy concert. Godard then went north to Québec to link forces with a group of leftist Canadian filmmakers to make an ill-fated and unfocused documentary about striking workers in the Rouyn-Noranda mining region of northern Québec. Casting about for something to film, Godard tried to stage a sequence in which his girlfriend, Anne Wiazemsky, would wander through a blizzard in her underwear. When she kiboshed that idea, Godard gave up on the film and, without telling either his Québeçois filmmaking partners or the TV station that had bankrolled it, returned to France.

• • •

Across the Channel, in England, there was an equally important revolutionary action happening—not a left-wing student insurrection, but a right-wing attempted coup. Unlike the student revolt in France, the British action was completely clandestine and unknown at the time—only discovered and revealed to the public twenty years later. Kim Philby, the life-long Soviet spy who worked at the very highest levels of British Intelligence (and is considered by many the highest placed spy in all of history) released his memoir *My Silent War* in 1968. It was highly embarrassing to MI6 and to the CIA and helped create an atmosphere of extreme paranoia at both agencies. The brilliant and cadaverous James Jesus Angleton, Head of Counterterrorism at the CIA, became convinced, with little evidence, that Harold Wilson, elected Prime Minister of Britain in 1964, was himself a Soviet agent, and he was not shy about passing on his suspicions to both Britain's counter-intelligence agency MI5, and to sympathetic right-wing British journalists and newspaper owners.

One who was particularly responsive to the notion that Wilson and his Labour cabinet members were all communist agents was Cecil King, the owner of the London tabloid the *Daily Mirror*. King not only plastered his newspaper full of stories with headlines like WILSON MUST GO, but he also began to fantasize about a possible coup d'état of the government. He shocked the army officers at Sandhurst Military Academy by calling for the Army to rise up against the Labour government. He became involved with a plan to use the Shetland Islands, in the far north of Scotland, as a remote prison for interned perceived enemies of the new regime. He partnered in blue-skying about the proposed coup with the retired vice-chief of MI6, George Kennedy Young, who was developing his own theories about the suspected loyalties of people he referred to as Britain's 3.5 million "non-Europeans" (read, Blacks, mostly from the Caribbean) and Jews, who he referred to as "snipcocks" and "cosmopolitans".

On May 5th, King invited the aristocratic second cousin of the Queen, and past Viceroy of India and First Sea-Lord Earl Mountbatten to a private luncheon, in which he described plans for a takeover of the government. He offered Mountbatten the role of Head of State in the new government of national salvation. Although his associate at the meeting, Solly Zuckerman, immediately pronounced the proposal "rank treachery" and walked out, Mountbatten stayed long enough, according to his biographer, to "toy with the idea of becoming head of government in some coup," [52] and told the newspaper publisher that there was also anxiety at Buckingham Palace about the Wilson government. He eventually left the meeting without making a commitment to the conspirators. It is believed that Mountbatten did report the incident to the Queen, who wisely told him in no uncertain terms that he should stay well away from the proposed coup. Wilson's government was never told about the proposed overthrow. Sir Martin Furnival Jones, the head of MI5, excused his inaction at letting the Prime Minister know about the plot against him by saying, "You can't go around to ministers every time there's loose talk by gin-sodden Generals." [53]

• • •

Meanwhile, back in France, Brigitte Bardot began a new movement—the animal rights movement. Along with Black Power, Women's Liberation, the Free Speech movement, the Sexual Revolution, Environmentalism, and Gay Liberation, it became another potent movement that continued from the Sixties right into the 21st Century. The sexy French film star became the figurehead of the movement, battling sealers and furriers until eventually an equally sexy but younger star, Pamela Anderson, became the spokesperson. This was a movement that seemed truly original. After all, Blacks had been fighting for freedom in the U.S. as far back as Dred Scott in 1857, and in the world back to the Haitian Revolution that began in 1791. Women had been fighting for their rights in some manner since the beginning of time, and in the modern era the Suffragette movement, begun in 1903, was an obvious precursor to the Women's movement of the late 60s. Bardot's battle was different. Defending the rights of animals was something truly new.

• • •

There were numerous other new developments in 1968 that had never really been seen before. Yvon Chouinard was a California hippie who took his counter-culture ideals into a field previously only populated by what were referred to in those days as 'straight business creeps.' Chouinard was a self-proclaimed 'dirt-bag rock climber,' and a surfer known for his extreme skill and dedication to outdoor sports, and his willingness to sacrifice personal comfort to pursue them. He spent one summer in the 1960s eating cat food so that he could continue to summit the peaks of Yosemite and the Canadian Bugaboo Mountains. He and his rebel long-haired athletic buddies known as the 'Fun Hogs' were frequently in rows with straight arrow park rangers who were hassling them over park fees, maximum stay regulations, and overnight camping permits.

In 1968 he was stuck in an ice cave on Cerro Fitz Roy in the Andes of Patagonia. Freezing cold in his inadequate outdoor gear, he determined there and then that he wanted to create a company to make better clothing. It was a slow process, but he created Patagonia Inc. and Black Diamond Equipment as much to further the goals of the counterculture as to make a profit. He succeeded on both counts. By the 21st Century he was a billionaire, and along the way he had also created a new model for capitalism. His innovations, using synthetic materials like polypropylene and synchilla® to make lightweight, wicking, warm, waterproof clothing absolutely transformed outdoor sports wear, and thus adventure and exploration (and winter protest marches!). Notably, though, those achievements are eclipsed by his novel long-haired counter-culture approach to capitalism. He ran his company as a form of co-operative and convinced more than two hundred other companies to join him in giving 1% of their profits to environmental organizations. He documented his much-emulated approach to capitalism in a book with the very '60s title *Let My People Go Surfing.* He also used his profits from Patagonia to personally buy 800,000 acres of land *in* Patagonia which he turned into a wilderness park and gave to the people of Chile.

• • •

Violent radical activities continued in May across the United States. On May 17ᵗʰ, Daniel Berrigan, a Catholic Jesuit priest, his brother Phillip, and seven other Catholic activists destroyed 378 Army draft files with homemade napalm at the office of the Catonsville, Maryland draft board. He was arrested and sentenced to three years in prison but jumped bail and went into hiding. He became the first priest ever to be on the FBI's "Most Wanted" list, and he also made it to the cover of *TIME* Magazine. He was finally captured by the FBI in 1970 and spent two years incarcerated in the Federal Correctional Institution in Danbury, Connecticut. His actions inspired thousands of draft-age men to move from protest to civil disobedience, especially the public burning of their draft cards.

• • •

Also in May, the seeds were sown for what would become known as the Sir George Williams Affair of 1969. At Sir George Williams University in Montréal (now a part of Concordia University) six black students from the Caribbean accused biology professor Perry Anderson of racism and claimed he treated them in a demeaning fashion and gave them lower marks than they merited. One of them, Rodney John, described what he called the "farcical" experience of another student named Terrence Ballantyne. "He had a white lab partner. Terrence handed in his lab (report). His lab gets 7 out of 10. His lab partner borrows Terrence's lab and copies it word for word. The guy gets the lab back and guess what? He gets a higher mark and doesn't get any marks deducted for being late. Just imagine you have thirteen students, each with their own stories. This was a pattern." The students presented their case to the administration that Anderson was racially biased, but at a September hearing their complaints were turned down. They did not forget the incident, though, and in January of the next year it would be one of the central causes of the giant student revolt at Sir George Williams that led to fire, destruction and many arrests on the campus.

• • •

The Cultural Revolution in China enjoyed a brief lull in 1968, but not the cult of Mao. The Red Guards actually relaxed from their usual ultra-violence and instead began obsessively studying Mao's Little Red Book. Memorization contests were popular, with one teen winning by reciting all 270 pages without missing a word. Busts of the Dear Leader were ubiquitous in schoolrooms, offices, and factories. In Shanghai alone, 600 new Mao statues went up in 1968, along with hundreds of thousands of paintings and posters. It could be a dangerous business for artists churning out the works, for the slightest deviation from appropriate devotion to the Great Helmsman could bring serious consequences. Zhang Zhenshi, a famous portrait painter, was viciously beaten up because one of his works depicted the Chairman with his face slightly inclined in the wrong direction. Shi Lu was taken to task for portraying Mao standing in front of a cliff, which was interpreted as suggesting he had nowhere to go. The artist was imprisoned for three years.

• • •

In the U.S., things could even be worse for painters. At 9 AM on June 3rd, Valerie Solanas arrived at "The Factory" at 33 Union Square West in Manhattan, the studio of world-famous pop artist and underground filmmaker Andy Warhol. Solanas was a troubled, homeless, radical feminist with a lesbian agenda that she printed up and hawked on the streets of New York. Titled *S.C.U.M.*, she claimed it was the manifesto of the "Society for Cutting Up Men", though it was in fact a society of only one. S.C.U.M's modest aims were threefold:

- *To affect a complete female take-over, to end the production of males*

- *To begin to create a swinging, groovy, out-of-sight female world*

- *To end this hard, grim, static, boring male world and wipe the ugly, leering male face off the map.*

Solanas got on the elevator and went up to the fifth floor to find Paul Morrissey, the real director of the films Warhol was given credit for, and Fred Hughes, Warhol's de facto business manager. The no-nonsense Morrissey was not pleased to see her. In his eyes, she was a pest, always coming around looking for acting work, peddling what he considered to be her idiotic movie script, *Up Your Ass* or, like that morning, looking for Andy. He told her the artist was not in, lied that he would not be in that day, and escorted her back to the elevator. Solanas went back to the main floor, but then hung around, hoping that the artist might show up. As it turns out, he did. Less hard-nosed than his filmmaking partner, Warhol accompanied her back up the elevator to The Factory. When the pair arrived, they now found Morrissey on the lobby phone, talking with one of the "superstars" in Warhol's stable, Viva, who was in an uptown hair salon, telling Morrissey about the dye job she was getting for her role in the film now shooting in New York City, *Midnight Cowboy*. Morrissey handed the phone to Warhol and headed for the washroom. While Warhol listened in his usual detached, bored fashion as Viva nattered at length about the different possible choices of hair dye, Solanas pulled out a Beretta .32 automatic, fired three shots at point blank range at the artist, two more at visiting art critic Mario Amaya, and then tried to shoot Fred Hughes. Her gun jammed on her last shot, so she ran to the elevator and left the building. The lobby of The Factory was of course thrown into pandemonium. Warhol, close to death, was gushing blood and gasping for breath.

The police and ambulance arrived and within 23 minutes Warhol was in the emergency ward of nearby Columbus Hospital. At The Factory, the police pawed through stills of some of Warhol's raunchier movies, ransacked slides of his "death and disaster" paintings, looked with disdain at photographs of naked men, and searched, they claimed, "for evidence." Eventually they took Hughes and Warhol's lover/assistant Jed Johnson to the station house and held them as suspects.

At 4:51 Warhol was declared clinically dead, but through an incredible stroke of good luck there was a doctor in the hospital who decided he would try to save his life. Giuseppe Rossi was an Italian immigrant who had trained as a thoracic surgeon. Because of the rules of American medicine, he could not get a job in any of New York's classier hospitals and so had instead acquired years of experience working in the emergency rooms of Harlem, where he had handled many, many gunshot wounds. He was exactly the man the apparently D.O.A. Warhol needed. The 40-year-old doctor had no idea who this badly wounded patient was—he assumed he was likely a Union Square tramp—but when he saw a flicker of life in Warhol's eye, he threw himself into the task of trying to save his life. Ignoring the usual ritual of five minutes of meticulous hand washing, he immediately sliced open the artist's chest, and attached a giant clamp to the bullet hole in his lung. He then made two more enormous cuts through his torso and ratcheted open his chest to explore the damage. "I've never seen so much blood in my life," said the chief surgical resident, Maurizio Daliana. In the midst of the gruesome emergency operation the operating room was thrown into further turmoil when the hospital's administrators arrived. They told the doctors who their patient was, and that there was already a huge crowd of newsmen and groupies waiting in the lobby. "He cannot die," they said. "He must live."

Ultimately, he did. Rossi left Warhol with a Frankenstein chest of stitches and scar tissue, but he saved his life. The next day, the giant headline in the *New York Post* read, ANDY WARHOL FIGHTS FOR LIFE. The *News'* headline was ACTRESS SHOOTS ANDY WARHOL, CRIES, 'HE CONTROLLED MY LIFE'. Two other actresses from Warhol's stable were quoted. Ultra Violet declared, "Violence is everywhere in the air today. He got hurt in the big game of reality." Ingrid Superstar gave this quote to a reporter: "Andy's shooting was definitely a blow against the cultural revolution. We're constantly being attacked."

"That Warhol was the first artist to be 'assassinated' is a dubious distinction," wrote critic John Perreault. "Nevertheless, it does say something about his importance and his charisma, his penetration into dangerously archetypal zones." Another critic, David Bourdon, summed up the event more pithily. He thought that the shooting might just be the avant-garde artist's greatest work.

By the time Warhol came out of his coma three days later, the world's biggest publicity hound and self-promoter discovered the parade had passed him by. Out of California, pushing the Warhol story to the back pages, came news of another shooting, another assassination. This one would have a profoundly bigger effect on the world.

• • •

With the escalating war in Vietnam and the riots and protests in the campuses and ghettos, President Lyndon Johnson was becoming increasingly unpopular. "Hey, hey, LBJ. How many kids did you kill today?" was the chant heard frequently around the nation. There was mounting pressure on others to run against him in the Presidential primaries. The most natural, in many people's eyes, was Senator Robert Kennedy. The Vietnam War (or "the American War", as the Vietnamese call it) was becoming an increasingly contentious issue around the world, and especially in the U.S.A. Kennedy, even though he had been involved with his brother in getting America into the mess, was in 1968 becoming an outspoken critic of the war, and thus of the Johnson administration. On January 31 he had said on the Senate floor, "If we regard bombing as the answer in Vietnam, we are headed straight for disaster." [54] Many people wanted Kennedy to run in the primaries on an anti-war platform against President Johnson. While there was absolutely no love lost between Kennedy and Johnson, it is very difficult in America to challenge an incumbent. Further, there were many in the Kennedy clan who were terrified Robert might be risking a repeat of the 1963 tragedy by running for the presidency. However, there were winds of change blowing through 1968, and Kennedy did not want to resist them. After an emotional meeting with California farm workers' leader César Chavez, then on a 25-day hunger strike, Kennedy finally decided to throw his hat into the ring. He announced his candidacy on March 16th. Fifteen days later, Johnson stunned the nation by announcing that he "would not seek and would not accept" a nomination for another term as President of the United States. Kennedy, Minnesota Senator Eugene McCarthy and Vice-President Hubert Humphrey were now the contenders in the race. Kennedy, the front-runner, was the most divisive of the three. Many people loved him. Others hated him. FBI Deputy Chief Clyde Tolson was reported saying, "I hope that someone shoots and kills that son of a bitch." [55] Of course, no-one on earth was better placed to orchestrate such an event than Tolson's boss and housemate, J. Edgar Hoover.

It was most important for his run for the White House that Kennedy do well in the California primary of June 4th. Kennedy campaigned vigorously across the state. He spent the day of the election at the Malibu beach house of film director John Frankenheimer. Ironically, Frankenheimer had directed *The Manchurian Candidate*, a highly prescient film about the use of a brainwashed assassin to attempt to kill an American Presidential candidate. To add further to the irony, it was Kennedy's brother, JFK, who had gotten the film made, persuading reluctant studio mogul Arthur Krim to bankroll it as a favor for the President's pal Frank Sinatra, who starred in it.

Kennedy spent the afternoon swimming in the Malibu surf with his kids. When his 12-year-old son David was pulled underwater by a rip tide, it was Kennedy who dove down and pulled him to safety. The incident traumatized Kennedy's boy, and he later blamed it, and the killing of his father, for his descent into drug addiction that eventually killed him. The Presidential candidate cut and bruised his forehead in the accident and Frankenheimer tried to cover the bruise with theatrical make-up before the evening's political festivities at the Ambassador Hotel.

After confirmation of his win of both the California and South Dakota primaries, Kennedy gave his victory speech and exited through the kitchen of the hotel. As he shook the hands of excited kitchen staff, assassin Sirhan Sirhan rushed forward and shot him with an Iver Johnson Cadet revolver. Writer George Plimpton and former football player Rosey Grier wrestled the gun away from Sirhan but it was too late. Kennedy lay mortally wounded on the floor of the kitchen, cradled in the arms of a hotel busboy, Juan Romero, to whom the candidate asked, "Is everybody okay?" Romero responded, "Yes, everybody's okay." A witness reported a woman in a polka-dot dress exclaiming repeatedly, "We killed him!" before running away.

Kennedy was rushed to the Hospital of the Good Samaritan, where he underwent a long, complicated brain operation, but to no avail. He died 26 hours later, at 1:44 on the early morning of June 6th.

The killer, Sirhan Sirhan, was a Palestinian Arab who claimed he had killed Kennedy because of his perception that the Senator was a supporter of Israel who wanted to send bombers to the Middle East to attack the Arabs. In light of the profound effect the assassination had on the world, it can be considered another of the many ramifications of the 1947 decision to create the Jewish state of Israel in the land that had previously been the Arab state of Palestine.

It can also be argued that the death of Robert Kennedy was even more influential than the death of his brother five years earlier. Many, following the killing of Martin Luther King, felt, as civil rights leader and future Congressman John Lewis grimly said, "at least we still have Robert Kennedy." With him gone, all hope was gone, and many turned away from debate and electoral politics, and towards revolutionary violence. Jack Newfield, a reporter covering the Kennedy campaign, wrote in his memoir about Kennedy:

Now I realized what makes our generation unique, what defines us apart from those who came before the hopeful winter of 1961, and those who came after the murderous spring of 1968. We are the first generation that learned from experience, in our innocent twenties, that things were not really getting better, that we shall not overcome. We felt, by the time we reached 30, that we had already glimpsed the most compassionate leaders our nation could produce, and they had all been assassinated. And from this time forward, things would get worse: our best political leaders were part of memory now, not hope. The stone was at the bottom of the hill and we were all alone. [56]

• • •

On June 24th, another political leader—one who was frequently compared with the Kennedys—had a brush with political violence that turned out very differently from theirs. June 24th is St. Jean Baptiste Day, one of the biggest holidays of the year for French Canadians in Québec. The fete originally started as a Roman Catholic religious holiday but by the time of the Quiet Revolution of the 60s, it had become primarily a political and separatist event. In 1968, it was attended by Pierre Trudeau, then on his last day of campaigning for his first term as Prime Minister. Trudeau, though himself a Québecer, was a staunch federalist. As the alcohol-fueled crowd passed his reviewing stand, some violently threw bottles and rocks directly at him. The other politicians and dignitaries around him fled, but Trudeau refused to leave the stand, stood up to the rock-throwing mob, and cemented his image as a fearless leader defying the violent separatists. The next day, Trudeau won a resounding election victory, and would continue to lead the country, with one brief interruption, until 1984.

During the Montréal parade, 43 police officers, 83 spectators and 17 horses were injured. 12 police cruisers were damaged or destroyed, and police made 293 arrests. With many people beaten violently by the police, it went down as a day of infamy among the separatists – *La Lundi de la Matraque* – *the Monday of the Bludgeoning.*

• • •

The young rebellious Québecers were by no means alone. A study in the summer of 1968 found that more than 350,000 young people in the U.S. considered themselves "revolutionaries". One of them, most certainly, was Bernardine Dohrn, who in the summer of 1968 was elected co-leader of the Students for a Democratic Society, one of the first women to be elected to lead an American national organization, something of a first for the radical movement.

• • •

In late June, civil rights activists, including a nationalist MP named Austin Currie squatted in a house in Caledon, Northern Ireland to protest against housing discrimination. The local council had allocated the house to an unmarried 19-year-old Protestant named Emily Beattie, the secretary of a local Ulster Unionist Party official, instead of offering it to either of two large Catholic families with children. RUC officers—one of them Beattie's brother—forcibly removed the activists, and also evicted the two Catholic families from where they were staying. Currie took the grievance of the families to the local council, and to Stormont, the Northern Irish Parliament, but was evicted from both. The incident outraged the civil rights movement, which began organizing for upcoming marches and demonstrations.

• • •

On July 25th, Pope Paul VI issued the *Humanae Vitae* (*Of Human Life*) a papal encyclical that rejected the conclusions of his predecessor Pope John XXIII's 1966 *Pontifical Commission on Birth Control* that had approved contraception for Roman Catholics. The new encyclical forbade all forms of birth control including the newly invented Pill, and abortion, even for therapeutic reasons. It was another sign that some of the liberal changes in society that had occurred only a very few years earlier were starting to be replaced by a conservative and reactionary backlash.

• • •

To underline this, on August 5 – 8 the Republican Party held their Presidential nominating convention in Miami Beach. The moderate wing of the party, led by Nelson Rockefeller, was defeated at the convention and the conservatives took over. Ultra-right-wing Governor of California Ronald Reagan made his first bid for the Presidency at the 1968 convention. He made it clear where he stood on the issues of the day. At the time, Cesar Chavez and Dolores Huerta's National Farm Workers Association was in the midst of its much-publicized attempts to get American supermarkets and consumers to boycott California grapes in order to try get better conditions for farm workers and pickers. When Reagan's plane arrived in Miami for the convention, his white California fat-cat supporters and delegates made a show of descending the ramp and entering the terminal munching on large bunches of table grapes.

Richard Nixon and Spiro Agnew were nominated as the Presidential and Vice-Presidential candidates for the GOP. During the convention Nixon's team created what was known as the "Southern Strategy" that successfully wooed white supremacist and evangelical voters away from the Democratic party and into the Republican fold—a dramatic shift that has transformed American politics to this day.

In tandem with the convention was an event billed as the *Mass Rally of Concerned Black People* in the Miami neighborhood of Liberty City. The event was intended to highlight their frustration with "discrimination, segregation, deplorable housing conditions, economic exploitation, bleak employment prospects, and poor police-community relations." [57] There were certainly poor relations between the police and community. During the event, police fired tear gas, rioters stoned police and looted white-owned shops. Police shot two residents dead and left a 14-year-old boy with a bullet through his chest.

• • •

As the riots erupted in Miami, even more dramatic events began unfolding further south in Uruguay. The *Movimiento de Liberación Nacional*, more commonly known as the MLN, or the 'Tupamaros' (named after the 18th Century Peruvian revolutionary Túpac Amaru II) was an urban guerrilla group started in the mid 60s that exploded into public consciousness in 1968. After President Jorge Pacheco Areco in June enforced a state of emergency, repealed constitutional safeguards, brutally repressing demonstrations and began imprisoning and torturing political dissidents, the Tupamaros began to strike back against the government. The youthful group began bombing buildings connected either to the government or to the U.S.A., broadcasting manifestos on radio stations and robbing banks and casinos. One of them explained, "Tactically, we always characterize the bank robberies as 'taking the money back,'" [58] They soon got the nickname 'Robin Hood' and received a remarkably high degree of support from the general public.

After the police responded with excessive force to a May Day demonstration, teachers and students protested in solidarity, and by June almost all university and high school teachers and students in Montevideo were on strike. The Tupamaros upset President Jorge Pacheco Areco by referring to him as "Paco" Areco because they claimed he did not deserve the beloved three letter word "Che" as part of his name.

On August 7, the guerrillas kidnapped Ulysses Pereira Reverbel, a friend of President Pacheco who was director of the state-owned power and telephone company, and a fierce anti-unionist. Before he was found, unharmed, in a parked Land Rover five days later, the government had deployed more than 3,000 police officers—nearly half of the entire Montevideo police force— to search for him. Pacheco believed that his friend was likely being held in one of what he called the "subversive grottos" of the university. Convinced that the students and professors supported the Tupamaros, the police occupied the Universidad de la República and confronted student protestors in a street battle that lasted over twelve hours. After the police killed several students, the battle escalated until the military occupied all the universities and high schools in Montevideo. The occupation only served to further radicalize students and intensify their support for the Tupamaros—support that would last well into the 1970s.

• • •

On August 13th, half-way around the world on a coastal road running from Lagonisi to Athens, Alexandros Panagoulis attempted to assassinate Greek rightwing dictator George Papadopoulos by throwing a bomb at his limousine. The bomb exploded but did not harm the dictator. Panagoulis escaped to a planned marine rendezvous, but the boat did not show up and he was caught, arrested, tortured, and jailed. After democracy was restored in 1974, he was released, hailed as a hero, and elected to the new Greek parliament.

• • •

August 20th saw the first three of 46 bombs that would be planted in Montréal over the next seven months. The first exploded at 3:30 AM outside Victoria Precision Works, a company making bicycles and children's wagons. Half an hour later, the next blew up a Régie du Québec (RAQ) liquor store. The third demolished a car belonging to an executive of the RAQ. The bombings seemed to be labor related since workers at both the bicycle company and the RAQ had been involved in long, bitter strikes. The bombings carried on through the summer, fall, and into the winter and all had a few things in common. The bombs were virtually the same— sticks of dynamite triggered by a blasting cap timed by a $3.95 Westclox Silver Bell alarm clock. Nearby walls were usually daubed with the letters "FLQ", and the bomb sites were always visited by Robert Côté, the head of the Montréal bomb squad.

Côté had the scariest job in the country. He had just gotten married, just bought his first home, and his new wife was expecting their first child. But he was on call at all times of the day or night to try to defuse ticking bombs or sift through the debris of exploded ones. He carried in his Chevy

Biscayne station wagon a piece of head-to-toe protective armor called a Spooner suit, and a complicated shield with poles for manipulating bombs, but found that neither was of much practical use on the dynamite bombs the FLQ favored. The armor and elaborate gear were good for newspaper photos, but not much else. In reality, the only tool he found useful (apart from his steel nerves) was the nail clipper he had attached to his belt to snip the bombs' wires.

When police received a bomb threat, he would receive a page on his beeper or a call on the phone beside his bed, get the address, respond with "*En route*" *(I'm on my way)* and head for the bomb site". On arrival he would usually find a sea of flashing police cruisers, curious onlookers held back by crime tape, and TV and newspaper reporters. He would step out and ironically announce, *"L'invité d'honneur est arrivé" (The guest of honor has arrived)*. If the bomb had not yet exploded, he would approach it, gingerly try and expose the wiring, and if possible, snip one of the leads running from the ticking alarm clock to the blasting cap with his nail clipper.

One of the most dangerous calls he received was when he was alerted to a bomb in the Eaton's Department Store on St. Catherine Street West. Eaton's was doubly damned—separatists saw the giant chain as a symbol of English-Canadian domination, and the store had ignored the recent entreaties to stop selling bicycles and wagons from the strikebound Victoria Precision Works. A bomb exploded before Côté could get to it, doing $25,000 damage and making the basement of the store, "look like an earthquake had hit." While he was sifting through the rubble and writing up a report on that bomb, a radio station received a threat about a yet another one—this time in the store's jewelry department.

"I went in," Côté recalled, "and somebody yelled, 'It's on the floor' It was between a water fountain and the wall, in a cardboard container about the size of a shoebox. I was all alone and I could hear the *tick, tick, tick*. I got on my knees and lifted the lid and there were four sticks of dynamite, but the clock was face down and there was so much tape around it that I couldn't snip the wires."

"All I could do was push in the alarm button to stop the ticking and deactivate the clock. That neutralized the bomb and I picked it up and walked with it under my arm and all I saw was this huge crowd of people and they all started to applaud. We took the bomb to a big park in Pointe-Saint-Charles and dismantled it. We looked at the clock and realized it had been set to blow five minutes after I neutralized it. That was my closest call." [59]

• • •

The day after the bombs began exploding in Montréal, explosions began going off all over Prague, Czechoslovakia. On January 5, liberal reformer Alexander Dubček had been elected First Secretary of the Communist Party of Czechoslovakia and had initiated numerous reforms of the Warsaw-Bloc country, which had been under the thumb of the Soviet Union since the end of World War II. During what was dubbed the "Prague Spring" there was a flowering of freedom, music, and travel. The Soviets, worried that this liberalization might spread to their other satellite countries behind the Iron Curtain, sent 500,000 troops into the country on August 21. The massive invasion was met with little real resistance, other than hippies and students who reversed dozens of street direction signs to try to confuse the tank commanders. Still, 137 Czech civilians were killed in the invasion, and over 500 were injured. A new leader, Gustáv Husák was installed, replacing Dubček, and the reforms of the Prague Spring were all wiped away. The country returned to being an authoritarian communist state, with a mind-numbing bureaucracy. It is, after all, the home of Franz Kafka, and the next twenty-one years were definitely Kafkaesque. There was some resistance to the state, much of it centered around the Bohemian dissident group Charter 77 and the rock band Plastic People of the Universe. One of the band's songwriters, the activist/playwright

Václav Havel became the first democratic President following the fall of the Eastern Bloc and communist Czechoslovakia in 1989.

• • •

Another bombshell released in August was Tom Wolfe's new book, *The Electric Kool-Aid Acid Test*. Wolfe was quintessentially of the 1960s—one of the most prominent purveyors, along with Norman Mailer and Hunter S. Thompson, of what was called the 'New Journalism'. His writing was wildly original and idiosyncratic, full of piss and vinegar and exclamation marks, acclaimed as being the future of literature. His new book, called "one of the great books of its time" by the *New York Times*, turned thousands on to the adventures of Ken Kesey, Neal Cassady and their Merry Pranksters as they expanded their LSD-fueled transcendental travels from their hippie base in La Honda, California to San Francisco and on across America and Mexico.

• • •

But the story was already transforming. Yesterday's hippies were becoming today's Yippies. As Russian tanks were entering Prague in late August, anarchist provocateur and co-founder of the Yippies, Abbie Hoffman, was flying to Chicago to prepare for the Festival of Life, a wild demonstration that would coincide with the Democratic National Convention from August 25 – 30. Hoffman along with his co-conspirator Jerry Rubin had started the "Youth International Party" – the Yippies – in January and now began making announcements of their plans for a counter-convention in the Windy City. They told the press they were going to put LSD in the water supply. They scattered marijuana seeds in Chicago's vacant lots, timed to be sprouting during the convention. They were going to paint cars taxi-yellow, pick up convention delegates and drive them to Wisconsin. Yippies would dress up as Viet Cong members and greet the delegates. They were going to "fuck on the beaches." They were going to "burn Chicago to the ground." They brought a large hog they named 'Pigasus' that they intended to nominate for President. They did not have any plans for organized violence or rioting, but this was Chicago, run by Mayor Richard Daley, who had recently ordered his police to "shoot to kill any arsonist or anyone with a Molotov cocktail in his hand, and shoot to maim or cripple anyone looting a store in our city."[60] Hoffman and the other organizers tried valiantly but unsuccessfully to get permits for the event from the city, which they believed would seriously reduce the risk of violence, but as they warned the thousands planning to attend, "This is the United States. It is 1968. Remember, if you are afraid of violence, you shouldn't have crossed the border." [61] The Yippies also warned possible attendees that, "People coming to Chicago should begin preparations for five days of energy-exchange. Do not come prepared to sit and watch and be fed and cared for. It just won't happen that way. It is time to be a life-actor. The days of the audience died with the old America. If you don't have a thing to do, stay home, you'll only get in the way." [62] Hoffman was certainly a "life actor" in the drama himself. Soon after arriving in Chicago, he realized he had two police tails. In his typical manner, he responded by either going on elaborate high-speed chases to lose them, or else stopping his borrowed car and going back to theirs to chat with them or ask if they wanted to go to lunch with him. "Over lunch," he says, "we discussed kids, sports, the Beatles, drugs, and the Chicago police hierarchy. I told them all high-level cops were phony liberals and not to be trusted. They nodded and picked up the tab for lunch. I made their job easier for them, giving them lots of useless information for the reports they had to file. In turn, they kept me informed on their orders, giving me advance warning of their actions."

Relations were not as friendly with other Chicago cops. Hoffman, and the other organizers and participants were arrested and beaten-up dozens of times during the week. One cop told Hoffman that they were "wiping the streets up with you hippie fuckers." After being told he would be arrested the following day, Hoffman asked, "Why?" "We'll think of something," said the officer.

"I had figured after I was processed at the precinct I would be back on the streets in a few hours. Instead, the police moved me from precinct to precinct, cell to cell, for thirteen hours, without food, phone calls, or lawyers, while cops beat the shit out of me. I laughed hysterically through all the beatings. I was so winged-out from not sleeping and all the tension. One of the cops shoved a bullet in my face and said, "See this? It's got your name on it. I'm going to get you tonight.""

"I've got a silver bullet with your name on it. I'm the Lone Ranger!" replied Hoffman, who says he never let the cops get the last word. "Every time I got in these situations, I played it like I was in my own private movie." [63]

The movie became a very dark one. On August 28th, a giant battle erupted outside the Conrad Hilton Hotel, in which police pushed protestors through plate-glass windows into a high-end bar full of delegates, then pursued them inside and beat them against the broken glass. The melee, which the investigating report described as a "police riot", was broadcast live on television around the world, with the bloodied protestors chanting, "The whole world's watching!" Inside the convention, Connecticut Senator Abraham Ribicoff, in his nominating speech for George McGovern, went off-script by saying, "And with George McGovern as President of the United States, we wouldn't have Gestapo-like tactics in the streets of Chicago." The delegates broke into ecstatic applause. One of the television cameras panned to a reaction shot of Mayor Daley. He was not miked, but lip-readers later quoted his angry response as, "You motherfucker Jew bastard, get your ass out of Chicago."

Dozens of bystanders were beaten in the 'police riot.' Magazine publisher Hugh Hefner left his Playboy Mansion with one of his favorite contributors, cartoonist Jules Feiffer, to investigate what was happening in Grant Park. Both he and Feiffer were beaten by baton-wielding cops.

He got back by writing indignantly in *Playboy* about civil rights and police over-reach.

Over 500 civilians and 152 police officers were injured during the convention, and 600 protestors were arrested. The most serious charges were given to the organizers—Abbie Hoffman, Jerry Rubin, David Dellinger, Tom Hayden, Rennie Davis, John Froines and Lee Weiner— now known as the Chicago Seven. They were charged with conspiracy and crossing state lines to incite a riot.

The government added Bobby Seale's name to the list, even though he was not an organizer, barely knew any of the others, and had been in Chicago for less than twenty-four hours. It was felt by many that Seale was added to the group by the prosecutors since he was a Black Panther and would thus make the group look more threatening to the jury that would judge them. His presence was only one of the many contentious issues of the "Trial of the Chicago Eight (later Seven)" that would be held in Chicago in the fall of 1969.

An Army intelligence report into the Chicago demonstration determined that one in every six of the demonstrators was in fact an undercover operative. George Demmerle, Abbie Hoffman's bodyguard, was an FBI agent who had hung around the Yippies all summer, encouraging them to do things like blow up the Brooklyn Bridge. Bob Pierson was a Chicago cop disguised as a biker who latched on to Jerry Rubin and became his bodyguard. His testimony at the trial would put Rubin behind bars for 66 days, before the sentence was overturned on appeal.

Was the action in Chicago a success or a failure? Who, ultimately, was changed by what happened there—the demonstrators, or the 'silent majority', who sat at home, disapprovingly watching them on TV? Perhaps everybody. "Chicago, I think, was the place where all America was radicalized," wrote Tom Wicker in the *New York Times*. "The miracle of television made it visible to all—pierced, at last, the isolation of one America from the other, exposed to each the power it faced. Everything since Chicago has had a new intensity—that of polarization, of confrontation, of antagonism and fear." America was probably in the most violent and intemperate mood it had been since a hundred years earlier, in the Civil War.

• • •

Days after the events in Chicago, Huey Newton, who had founded the Black Panther Party back in 1966 with Bobby Seale, was convicted of manslaughter for the death of Oakland police officer John Frey a year earlier. Newton was sentenced to two to fifteen years. He claimed, in his autobiography *Revolutionary Suicide* that Frey had actually been killed from friendly fire—bullets from another policeman. Newton became some-what of a living martyr, symbol of a cause promoted not just by the Black Panthers but also the white-majority Peace and Freedom Party. The command "Free Huey!", printed on buttons, posters, and t-shirts, became one of the slogans of the era. Newton's conviction went through two appeals. Ultimately the charges were overturned, and he was released on August 5, 1970.

• • •

On September 1ˢᵗ, in the continuing madness of the Cultural Revolution, there was a meeting of the Committee of Revolution Killing Conference at Pingshan Square in Shangsi County in the province of Guangxi, China. Ten officials at the conference were beaten to death, then their hearts and livers were removed, sautéed, and served to the other representatives of the conference. It was one of dozens of incidents throughout Guangxi of cannibalism and killings by "beheading, beating, live burial, stoning, drowning, boiling, group slaughters, disemboweling, digging out hearts, livers, genitals, slicing off flesh, blowing up with dyna-mite, and more." [64] There were hundreds of instances of mass rapes fol-lowed by cannibalism. Estimates of the death toll during the revolution in Quangxi run between 70,000 and 500,000. The deputy director of the school where the butchery had taken place later defended his actions, saying, "Cannibalism? It was the landlord's flesh! The spy's flesh!"

The news from Guangxi was too much even for Chairman Mao, and so on September 7 he had Zhou Enlai announce to the country that the Cultural Revolution was over. "Now the whole country is red," announced Zhou, "Now we can declare that through repeated struggles during the past twenty months we have finally smashed the plot of the handful of top party persons in authority taking the capitalist road—counter-revolutionaries, revisionists, renegades, enemy agents and traitors."

• • •

On the same day, September 7, in an effort to publicize the burgeoning Women's Liberation Movement, demonstrators protested the Miss America contest by throwing symbols of female oppression including girdles, makeup, mops, and containers of false eyelashes into a "Freedom Trash Can" on the Atlantic City boardwalk. The most memorable image was that of a burning brassiere, which soon became a provocative symbol of Women's Liberation. Feminism became one of the most important legacies of the revolutionary times. In the 60s and 70s "women's libbers" got extreme pushback, not just from conservatives, but from other revolutionaries. When asked what the position of women was in the Black Power movement, Stokely Carmichael replied "Prone." He later claimed to have been joking. The most important revolutionary of the period, Mao Zedong, had promoted feminist ideals as early as 1910, and earlier in 1968 had famously proclaimed that "women can hold up half the sky." However, he was also treating the many young women he consorted with contemptuously, sleeping with many though never ever bathing (and never brushing his teeth) instead knowingly infecting many with venereal disease and creepily claiming, "I wash myself inside the bodies of my women."

Things were not much better in the West. Women's opinions were generally thought useless. When New York State legislators held a hearing to discuss proposed changes to the state's abortion laws, they invited 13 witnesses—12 men and only one woman—a nun. Women made a fraction of the money that men did. In 1968, women made up only eight per cent of the graduating classes in American medical schools and only four per cent in law schools.[65] There was not a single woman in the cabinet of the U.S. administration, and hardly any women were executives in major corporations. The Women's Liberation Movement was determined to try to change that.

• • •

On September 27, after Portugal's aging dictator António Salazar had a stroke, Marcelo Caetano became the new authoritarian Prime Minister of Portugal. Salazar, who had been ruling Portugal with an iron fist since 1932, lived until July 1970, reportedly under the delusion that he was still leader of the country. Caetano continued the right-wing internal policies and the fight against the independence of Portugal's African colonies until he was ousted in the Carnation Revolution of April 1974.

• • •

After a hot summer of student protests in Mexico, the nation's capital exploded on October 2nd in an orgy of state violence known as the Tlatelolco Massacre. *Dissent* Magazine described 1968 in Mexico as being "a time of expansiveness and the breaking down of barriers: a time for forging alliances among students, workers, and the marginal urban poor and challenging the political regime. It was a time of great hope, seemingly on the verge of transformation. Students were out in the streets, in the plazas, on the buses, forming brigades, going to the people. A revolution was happening—not Che's revolution—but a revolution from within the system, nonviolent, driven by euphoria, conviction, and the excitement of experimentation on the ground."

As the Mexican President and especially his Minister of the Interior Luis Echeverria continued to alternately ignore or violently push back against the very active people's movement, a giant peaceful march was planned for October 2nd. Over 10,000 university and high school students assembled in the Plaza de las Tres Culturas, surrounded by hundreds of bystanders and spectators, including many families and children. With the much-disputed Olympics that were costing economically beleaguered Mexico $175 million only two weeks away, one of the chants heard booming around the square was *No queremos olimpiadas, queremos revolución!* (We don't want Olympics, we want revolution!). Shortly after 6 PM, 5,000 soldiers and 200 tankettes surrounded the square, closed off the entrances and exits, and began firing into the crowd—first into the students, then into the hundreds of onlookers. The death toll has never been accurately confirmed, but it is generally believed that nearly 400 were killed, and many hundreds more were seriously wounded. More than 1,500 were arrested. The state controlled Mexican media blamed the massacre on what they called "criminal provocation" by the students, but later investigations showed that in fact teams of snipers from a secret branch of the government called the 'Olympia Battalion' fired on both the students and the soldiers to get the carnage going. In 2006 Luis Echeverria, the government minister accused of masterminding the slaughter, (and from 1970 to 1976 President of Mexico) was arrested and charged with genocide. In 2003 Freedom of Information requests in the U.S. revealed that the Pentagon and the CIA had been heavily involved in providing military equipment and training in 1968 to the secret "Olympia Battalion" that had caused the massacre.

The drama continued at the Olympics itself. The next day the International Olympic Committee held a secret emergency meeting to decide whether to call off the Olympics. The committee at the time was run by Avery Brundage, a man typical of the old dinosaurs still running much of the world in the 1960s, who the young Turks and revolutionaries were rebelling against. The *Independent* dubbed Brundage, "the ancient IOC emperor, anti-Semite, and Nazi sympathizer bent on insulating the Games from the meddlesome tentacles of the real world." Brundage's views won the day, and the IOC decision, by only one vote, was that the games should continue. Tommie Smith, the star of the U.S. track and field team, announced at a press conference that "I don't want Brundage presenting me any medals."

•   •   •

At 1 AM the next morning, a squadron of tanks rumbled through the streets of Lima, Peru, heading for the Presidential Palace. After a little gunfire, the palace guards surrendered, and the soldiers entered the palace and woke up President Fernando Belaúnde from a deep sleep induced earlier, it is believed, by drugs given by treasonous elements within the palace. As an officer tried to arrest him, the democratically elected Belaúnde shouted at him, "Identify yourself, you miserable traitor. You are talking to the Constitutional President of the Republic!" The officer did identify himself as Colonel Enrique Gallegos and told the President he had orders for his deportation. "You sons of…traitors…unworthy of the uniform that the country has entrusted to you!" cursed Belaúnde. "You are dismissed! Bringing so many tanks and guns just to detain an unarmed man! Shoot me then, damn it!" [66] Belaúnde attempted to get away but was grabbed by four officers who dragged him out of the palace and forced him to the airport and on to a plane, which deported him to Argentina. General Juan Velasco Alvarado, the leader of the coup, was sworn in as the new president the same day. Unlike most of the military dictatorships of Latin America, which were usually right-wing and supported by the rich and by the United States, Alvarado's was leftist and egalitarian. He nationalized many industries, created the second biggest (after Cuba's) agrarian reform in Latin America, created an education system for the large Indigenous population, and created close ties with Cuba and the USSR, which naturally meant the American government was hostile to his regime. He ruled until 1975, when another group of military commanders staged a coup against him, this time, more conventionally, from the right.

• • •

In Mexico, on October 16th, black American runner Tommie Smith won the gold medal for the 200 meters event, and his fellow black American runner John Carlos won the bronze. When being presented with their medals (not by Brundage) as the *Star-Spangled Banner* played, the pair, each wearing a single black glove, bowed their heads and raised their fists in the Black Power salute. Carlos also wore a necklace of beads which he announced were "for those individuals that were lynched, or killed and that no one said a prayer for, that were hung and tarred. It was for those who were thrown from boats in the Middle Passage." The image of their protest became the most memorable image of the Mexico Olympics. Brundage, calling it "a nasty demonstration against the American flag by negroes," ordered Smith and Carlos suspended from the US team and banned from the Olympic Village. When the U.S. Olympic Committee refused to do that, he threatened to ban the entire U.S. track team. This threat did lead to the two dissenting athletes being expelled from the Games. On their return to the U.S., they were ostracized by most of the U.S. sports establishment and vilified by the press. Brent Musberger of the *Chicago American* called them "a couple of juvenile black-skinned storm troopers."

The silver medalist, Australian Peter Norman, who sympathized with the pair's protest, joined them in wearing a human rights medal on his uniform for the ceremony. As a result, he too was ostracized by the Australian press, government, and Olympic Committee. In spite of qualifying, he was not allowed to compete in the 1972 Olympics, nor to participate in the 2000 Olympics that were hosted by Australia. Years later, the trio saw some measure of the tide turning in their favor. Carlos and Smith were presented with the Arthur Ashe Courage Awards in 2008, and Norman received a formal apology from the Australian Parliament in 2012.

The questions and recriminations over the '68 Olympics continued. Philip Agee, attached at the time to the US embassy in Mexico City as an undercover CIA officer, blamed Echeverria for the unrest that had led to the Olympic protest. He asked, "whether this two-week circus was really worth all the bloodshed, and whether Mexico lost more prestige by killing protestors than it gained by putting on the Games." [67] The Tlatelolco Massacre, along with other actions of the U.S. he had witnessed in Latin America, such as the invasion of the Dominican Republic and the support of extreme police actions in Uruguay, was the reason he left the agency in 1966, exposed its activities and became one of its harshest critics.

• • •

The Chinese Cultural Revolution may have been declared officially over, but the insane excesses continued. On October 15th, after being tortured and raped in prison for seven months on the orders of Madame Mao, theater director (and stepdaughter of Premiere Zhou Enlai) Sun Weishi was discovered dead in her cell, naked and shackled to the wall. Unable to prevent the death of his stepdaughter and to prevent many of the other excesses of the Cultural Revolution, Zhou continued to implement most of Mao's commands, calling it his "private inferno." He did manage to prevent some of Mao's more eccentric orders, such as changing the name of Beijing to 'East is Red City', replacing the famous guardian lions in front of Tiananmen Square with statues of Mao, and destroying other traditional Chinese artefacts.

A campaign to cleanse the party was in full operation from the summer of 1968 until the fall of 1969. Just as Stalin had done in the Soviet Union, Kim in Korea and Castro in Cuba, Mao turned China from a communist state to a cult of personality. Karl Marx thought his philosophy would be instituted by intellectuals and industrial workers, but all these leaders attempted to have it instituted by rural peasants, and all of them felt that the complexities of Marx's dialectic would not be understood by the mostly illiterate farmers, and instead what the peasants would rally behind was the notion of a powerful, messianic leader. In Mao's case, hero-worship also appealed to his massive ego. "He worships himself; he has blind faith in himself," reported his deputy Lin Biao. "He will take credit for every achievement but blame others for his failures." The cult of personality (also Lin's turn of phrase) was instituted by a campaign of intense poster and statue making titled "Three Loyalties and Four Boundless Loves" meant that the Chinese were bombarded with images of Mao everywhere they went.

Any hint of disloyalty to Mao meant persecution. Over 170,000 people were harassed in some way or another. More than 5,000 committed suicide, were beaten to death, or were executed.

• • •

Inspired by the more positive propaganda coming from China and ignoring the negative news, on October 4th, Aldo Brandirali started the Union of Italian Communists (Marxist-Leninist). It soon became more a cult than a political movement, with his acolytes shouting worshipfully, "Sta-lin! Ma-o! Bran-di-rali!" Brandirali called his young followers "Pioneers"; the press dubbed them *I Balilli di Mao* (Mao's altar boys). The leader, decked out in a green Mao suit, policed his followers' sex lives, decreeing that "orgasm must be simultaneous" and banning masturbation, oral, and anal sex because they were "manifestations of a petty-bourgeois mentality." He also demanded they sell off all the luxury goods they owned—Vespas, record players, hair dryers—to generate money for the movement. He was ultimately disgraced when it was revealed he spent most of the money on a high-end condo and an Alfa Romeo Giulia for himself.

• • •

In October, there were over 40 campus bombings in the U.S. by student radicals, mostly by Molotov cocktails, of ROTC (Reserve Officer

Training Corps) offices. The same month, Pierre Vallières and Charles Gagnon, jailed in Québec for their role in deaths of Thérèse Morin, who was killed in the 1966 Lagrenade bombing, and Jean Corbo, the sixteen-year-old FLQ member who died while placing a bomb in the Dominion Textile plant, led a hunger strike in their Quebec prison. A large percentage of the prisoners in their jail joined them, and the event became a *cause-célèbre*, with inmates fainting from hunger at their court appearances, huge press coverage, and the FLQ exploding 14 new bombs in sympathy with their incarcerated brothers. As usual the bombers politicized their actions with notes found later in the destroyed buildings such as "The FLQ has shown today the only way to abolish the regime of justice for the rich. This is directed at a representative of a rotten society." [68]

• • •

From the 8th to the 13th of October, battling Prime Ministers Ian Smith and Harold Wilson met once again aboard the British warship HMS *Fearless* to try to deal with Rhodesia's rebellious departure from the Commonwealth and the country's demands that it remain an all-white government. It became clear that the two men loathed each other, and the talks went nowhere. The British approach to the talks was summed up in the acronym NIBMAR—No Independence Before Majority Rule. Smith countered with his infamous comment, "Let me say it again. I don't believe in black majority rule ever in Rhodesia, not now, not in a thousand years." The situation on the ship was maritime apartheid, with the British and Rhodesian delegations staying completely apart from each other, except during the testy conference room meetings. Following the totally unsuccessful negotiations, the British government banned the Rhodesian delegation from attendance at the November 11th Armistice Day ceremonies in London, a snub that became a major factor in Rhodesia's decision to cut all ties with the British crown and become a republic, which they did in March of the next year.

• • •

In November, Richard Nixon defeated Hubert Humphrey and was elected President of the U.S. Years later, it was discovered that in the waning days of the campaign, knowing that the election was going to be very tight, and that President Lyndon Johnson was working hard to secure an end to the Vietnam War at the peace talks being held in Paris, Nixon secretly masterminded one of the most cynical and Machiavellian moves in the history of electoral politics. Through a powerful Taiwan lobbyist and Washington insider/socialite named Anna Chennault, Nixon, to quote his right-hand man H.R. Haldeman, "threw a monkey wrench" into the Paris Peace Talks by getting Chennault to secretly tell South Vietnamese leader General Nguyën Văn Thiệu that if he backed away from the talks, Nixon, if elected, would later secure him more favorable terms. Thiệu agreed. With the South Vietnamese out, the talks fell apart. As a consequence, the war continued and thousands more died. President Johnson learned from the FBI, CIA and NSA of Chennault's efforts to sabotage the Paris peace talks and said "the bitch" was guilty of treason.

Johnson's national security advisor Walt Rostow urged him to "blow the whistle" and "destroy Nixon", but the President demurred, arguing that it would cause too big a scandal if the public learned that the United States had been spying on its ally South Vietnam. Johnson's failure to respond to Nixon's scandalous action begs the question of who Johnson wanted to see follow him as the new President. Did he want his moderately liberal, anti-war Vice President Hubert Humphrey to succeed, or did he actually favor Humphrey's Republican opponent, Richard Nixon, a famously hawkish conservative who shared Johnson's antipathy towards the young, student, black, left-wing crowd who had caused Johnson not to run again for office himself?

Nixon claimed in the campaign he was going to end the war and create 'law and order' in the country. Instead, the war continued for seven more years, and his reign was defined by disorder and chaos. His strategy, such as it was, was to systematically and ruthlessly increase the bombing of North Vietnam, Laos, and Cambodia, with another plan in his back pocket. "I call it the madman theory," he told an aide. "I want the North Vietnamese to believe I've reached the point where I might do anything to stop the war. We'll just slip the word to them that 'Nixon is obsessed about communists. We can't restrain him when he's angry—and he has his hand on the nuclear button'—and Ho Chi Minh himself will be in Paris in two days begging for peace." [69]

Lê Duân, who took over the leadership after the death of Ho Chi Minh, once told a visiting journalist that on 13 different occasions the U.S. had threatened to use nuclear weapons on Vietnam. In one incident Nixon recklessly put the military on secret alert, flying 18 nuclear-armed B-52s over the polar ice cap toward the USSR, trying to force Soviet leaders (unsuccessfully) to pressure the North Vietnamese to accept U.S. peace terms.[79]

On the domestic front Nixon quickly instituted new "no-knock" laws so that heavily armed policemen could smash down doors, usually so they could search for drugs in order to bust perceived enemies. Examples are legion. John Sinclair, leader of Michigan's White Panther party and manager of the MC5 got nine and a half years for giving two joints to an undercover cop. Lee Otis Johnson, a black militant and anti-war organizer at Texas Southern University was given 30 years for sharing a joint with a narc. The fight was led by the FBI but they often got local police to do the dirty work. Police in Buffalo planted dope in a bookstore run by Martin Sostre, a Black anarchist who served six years in prison before Amnesty International interceded on his behalf.

• • •

Roman Catholics continued to be persecuted in Northern Ireland. After the very first civil rights march, on August 24ᵗʰ, another was planned for October 5ᵗʰ, but the march was banned by the Northern Ireland government. When the marchers ignored the ban, the Royal Ulster Constabulary (RUC) surrounded the Catholic protestors and beat them indiscriminately. More than 100 were injured, including a number of nationalist politicians. The incident, captured by news cameramen and telecast around the world, caused outrage among Catholics and nationalists, and sparked two days of rioting between nationalists and the RUC. The October march is one of the incidents that is considered to have officially initiated "The Troubles" that would last until the late 1990s.

• • •

Meanwhile, another revolution continued on another front. In November, *Newsweek* Magazine ran a cover story featuring a half-naked Jane Fonda titled ANYTHING GOES: THE PERMISSIVE SOCIETY. Fonda was presented as the young sex-symbol of the sixties, but she was starting to see herself differently, after being politically radicalized by her Malibu neighbors Donald Sutherland and his wife Shirley Douglas, daughter of Tommy Douglas, leader of Canada's socialist New Democratic Party, and by Marlon Brando, who had become a supporter of both the Black Panthers and the American Indian Movement. Jane Fonda, symbol of the Sexual Revolution, would soon become Jane Fonda, prominent leader of the anti-war movement, and then, in the 1980s, Jane Fonda, the most visible pioneer of the Fitness Revolution. It might be argued that all three revolutions failed. The Sexual Revolution ran into the AIDS virus. The anti-war movement did stop the Vietnam War, but it did not stop the U.S. from getting into other dumb wars. As for the Fitness Revolution, America today has by far the highest rate of obesity in the world. (The American rate is 36%; the Vietnamese is 2%)

• • •

On November 27th, Eldridge Cleaver, after campaigning unsuccessfully for President under the banner of the Peace and Freedom Party,
jumped bail and vanished, heading first to Canada, then Cuba, and then
Algeria, where he set up an international office for the Black Panthers.

• • •

The premiere performance of *Das Flot der Medusa*, an oratorio written as a Requiem to Che Guevara by Hans Werner Henze was scheduled
for December 9th at the Planten un Biomen Hall in Hamburg, Germany.
The event was disrupted by students, first by one who hung a large poster
of Che Guevara on the rostrum rail, then got into a scuffle with an official
from NDR Radio trying to tear it down, then by others hoisting red and
black anarchist flags. The choir, onstage ready to perform, began chanting
"Under the Red Flag we sing not", while composer Henze led the audience
in chants of "Ho, Ho, Ho Chi Minh". The police arrived in force, arrested
the students and the event was closed down—the premiere cancelled.

• • •

On Christmas Eve, the three astronauts of Apollo 8, Frank Borman,
James Lovell, and Bill Anders became the first three humans to ever reach
an extra-terrestrial object—the Moon. As they circled it and emerged
from the dark side, they saw something no-one had seen before—an earthrise. They immediately responded with awe. "Oh my God!" said Anders.
"Look at that picture over there! There's the Earth coming up. Wow, that's
pretty." Commander Borman responded, joking, "Don't take that, it's not
scheduled." Anders, laughing, replied, "You got a color film, Jim? Hand
me that roll of color film quick, would you?" Lovell continued to marvel
at the sight, saying "Oh man, that's great," as Anders loaded and fired the
camera to take one of the most famous and influential photos of all time.
Lovell, ever the nerdy astronaut, noted down the aperture and shutter
speed of the shot—f-11, 1/250th/second.[70] Titled *Earthrise*, the picture has

been called "the most influential environmental photograph ever taken." It was later instrumental in changing people's view of their planet, and their place in it. The photographer himself remembers, "It really undercut my religious beliefs. The idea that things rotate around the Pope and up there is a big supercomputer wondering whether Billy was a good boy yesterday? It doesn't make any sense. I became a big buddy of [atheist scientist] Richard Dawkins." [71]

Notwithstanding Anders' newly-minted atheism, the most memorable moment for the millions watching the event on television was when the three astronauts on Christmas Eve took turns reading the first ten verses describing the Bible's version of the creation of the earth from the Book of Genesis. This being the contentious '60s, though, NASA was sued by Madalyn Murray O'Hair, leader of the American Atheists organization, alleging the religious reading violated the First Amendment.

Anders, the most eloquent of all the Apollo astronauts, would later describe the importance and meaning of the mission: "We came all this way to explore the Moon, and the most important thing is that we discovered the Earth…We're all astronauts on this spaceship Earth, and we have to learn to work and live together." The photo has been credited with helping create the modern environmental movement.

The photo was not initially consecrated by Anders or by NASA, but rather by a counter-culture California hippie named Steward Brand. In the mid-60s Brand was a serious enthusiast of LSD, connected in San Francisco with the Grateful Dead and with Ken Kesey's Merry Pranksters. In 1966, on an acid trip on the roof of his house in North Beach, California, Brand became convinced that if the world could see an image of the whole earth, it would change people's attitude towards the planet. He created buttons that he sold for twenty-five cents in Haight-Ashbury that read, "Why haven't we seen a photograph of the whole Earth yet?" Now, two years later, with Anders' photo, he had the image. He placed it on the cover of a new book that he published called *The Whole Earth Catalogue*. The oversized book with its motto, "Stay hungry. Stay foolish." became the wildly popular bible of the counterculture, especially of the do-it-yourself, back-to-the-land, communal-living wing of it. The big book, which sold as many as 1.5 million copies a year served as what he called an 'access to tools'—a sixties version of Google and Wikipedia full of information about how to create an alternate reality—information about camping, building, climbing, carpentry, gardening, mapping and the brand-new field of personal computing. Brand was definitely a pioneer in that field as well, making a presentation in late 1968 to the Fall Joint Computer Conference on the revolutionary and still theoretical new technologies of hypertext, email and the mouse.

So did 1968 end on a positive, upbeat note? Not entirely. In late December, as Apollo 8 sped back to earth, a new, more ominous phase of the Cultural Revolution started, as thousands of Red Guards began to be shipped out of the cities to be "re-educated" by the peasants. Many would die in the process. Between 1968 and 1980 some 18 million students would be banished from the cities.

Two days after Christmas a narc named Neal Purcell busted Timothy Leary for marijuana possession in Laguna Beach, California. It was only for two roaches, but when combined with other charges it led to the possibility of an almost lifetime prison sentence for the psychedelic crusader.

On the last day of the year, two major bombs were placed in Montréal. One, at the City Hall, was discovered and de-fused by the cool master bomb disposal expert Michael Côté. The second, at one of the city's federal buildings, exploded, blowing out between 800 and 1000 windows. The bomb blast brought in 1969, a year that would be even more violent and divisive than the last.

1969

Castro Celebrates, Growing Up Absurd,
Elvis In the Ghetto, Santa Barbara Oil Spills,
The Concorde Flies, Norman Rockwell Outdated,
Girls Get Witchy, Bernadette Devlin Gets Elected,
I am Curious (Yellow), Stonewall Gays Fight Back,
Easy Rider, Ted Kennedy, Men on the Moon,
Alcatraz, Altamont, Cops Kill Fred Hampton.

The new year began in Cuba with major celebrations marking the tenth anniversary of the Cuban Revolution. In many ways, the revolution that had begun in 1959 was still a success. Even though the US blockade had caused severe economic problems (which wouldn't be helped when Hurricane Camille wiped out most of the country's sugar harvest), the Cuban people largely supported the achievements of the revolution in education, health care, agriculture, road construction, and housing. Castro himself survived a reported 638 assassination attempts by the CIA, the Mafia (in employ of the American government), and Cuban counter-revolutionary dissidents. An almost unimaginably wide array of techniques were used, including exploding cigars, a poisoned skin-diving wetsuit, a ballpoint hypodermic syringe, and an aerosol can filled with LSD. In one of the wilder scenarios, Marita Lorenz, an ex-lover of El Commandante, was sent to his suite at the Havana Hilton to murder him with poison pills. Castro suspected something was up and asked her if she was there to try to kill him. When she confessed that she was, Castro, according to her, handed her his revolver and told her to shoot him. She did not. Instead, they made love, and after which she ran off to America, leaving Castro, and her CIA minders in Cuba.

Castro continued not only to run Cuba, but also to support revolutionaries around the world. He created the Latin American Solidarity Organization which adopted the motto, 'The duty of the revolutionary is to make revolution.' He supported revolutionary movements throughout South America, and he invited everyone from the Viet Cong to the Black Panthers to train in Cuba. The American political establishment found him terrifying. "The greatest threat presented by Castro's Cuba is as an example to other Latin American states which are beset by poverty, corruption, feudalism, and plutocratic exploitation," wrote Walter Lippmann in *Newsweek* Magazine. "His influence in Latin America might be overwhelming and irresistible if, with Soviet help, he could establish in Cuba a communist utopia."

• • •

The student movement began to heat up around the world. In early January, 800 members of the Students for a Democratic Society met in Ann Arbor, Michigan to create a new wing called the Revolutionary Youth Movement. There, they heard leader Bernardine Dohrn proclaim, "There's no way to be committed to nonviolence in the middle of the most violent society that history has ever created. I'm not committed to nonviolence in any way." Her followers chanted "Ho-Ho-Ho Chi Minh" and "Two-Four-Six-Eight. Organize and Smash the State."

• • •

On January 4, Irish 'loyalists', including 100 off-duty members of the B-Specials Protestant militia ambushed and attacked a march by the People's Democracy students' movement at Burntollet Bridge in County Derry. The Royal Ulster Constabulary, plainly antagonistic to the students, looked on and did little to prevent the violent attack. The Protestants attacked the marchers with iron bars, stones brought in from a nearby quarry, and sticks spiked with nails. The massacre, and the lame reaction from the police and the British government caused a new crisis in Ireland. One of the students, who later became Professor Lord Bew of Queen's University, Belfast, considered it "the spark that lit the prairie fire" that would start The Troubles that continued in Northern Ireland for the next 30 years.

• • •

Five days later, 40 members of the Swarthmore Afro-American Student Society occupied the admissions office of the small Quaker college outside Philadelphia. They demanded that the school increase its enrollment of black students, and that they hire black administrators and a black counselor to advance a black perspective on campus. The students continued their occupation for a week. On January 16, the beleaguered president of the college, Courtney Smith, troubled over his inability to negotiate a resolution, suffered a heart attack while crossing the campus. He was one of the first fatalities of what would be an extremely violent year.

On the other side of the country, members of the Third World Liberation Front picketed San Francisco State, seeking the establishment of a 'Third World College' and the hiring of more minority faculty. The violent protest led to 25 incidents of arson, three bomb explosions, and 150 arrests. Across the bay in Berkeley, student protestors who two years earlier were only carrying flowers and signs, were now armed with billy-clubs with which they battled campus police.

The education revolution advanced on a variety of fronts. Radical philosopher Paul Goodman continued to speak across North America,

promoting his belief that the ills of western society meant that young people were *Growing Up Absurd* (the title of his bestselling book). At Stanford
University, Dr. Bruce Joyce promoted new *Models of Teaching*, new theories
of skill-based, not fact-based schooling. A mantra of *No math! No spelling!
No textbooks!* was embraced by many young teachers and rejected by older,
traditionalist educators.

The model of the Summerhill School in England was adopted by
hundreds of new 'free schools' that opened around North America. The
biggest and grandest of these, Rochdale College in Toronto, opened in
October but there were big problems right from the start. Strikes were a
recurring reality in this 1965 – 1975 period, and the construction of the
18-story high rise was slowed by the labor unrest. A strike by the con-
crete-pouring union delayed the planned opening enough that many of
the adventurous communards who had signed on to the experimental new
college were forced to give up on it and find other places to live. At the
same time, the city refused to give the college a tax exemption as an educational institution so there was suddenly no money to run any of the
planned programs. Also, the city's bohemian enclave, Yorkville Village,
had just seen three scourges. First there was an influx of 'speed freaks'
(methamphetamine users). Then there was an infectious outbreak of hepatitis. Finally, there was a brutal police crackdown on the residents. This
repressive action was supported both by developers who wanted to get rid
of the kids and gentrify Yorkville into a chic upscale shopping and dining
area, and by local politicians like Syd Apps, ex-captain and star of the
Toronto Maple Leafs, now a Member of the Provincial Parliament and
anti-hippie crusader.

The Yorkville hippies, many wired on speed, most penniless,
descended on Rochdale. Through 1969 and 1970 a building designed to
accommodate 800 in communal, experimental, but not anarchic conditions was now home to 1,500, many of whom were semi-transient. The
longhaired crowd surfed on couches, took no responsibility for the place,
and largely turned it into a disintegrating crash pad. The strike by the

construction workers meant that much of the building was not working properly. Cement dust made the elevators inoperable and many doors and windows in the high-rise had not even been installed. Nonetheless, adventurous programs got underway—everything from science fiction workshops to large-scale sculpture endeavors to lectures on the airy-fairy branch of philosophy called phenomenology, to filmmaking and film screening. One local hipster impresario began screenings of the wildest films of the era, which brought down the wrath of the Ontario Censor Board, especially when he offered free admission to anyone who would attend his screenings nude.

The free college was also a magnet for U.S. draft dodgers. In fact, young draft age men showing up at Canadian Immigration at the Buffalo/Fort Erie or Detroit/Windsor border stations were often directed by guards to head to Rochdale to find a place to stay. The college was also soon attracting drug dealers. The 15th floor in particular was, by the end of 1969, reputed to house 60 dealers, a substantial number of whom were undercover narcs working for either the Toronto Police or the Royal Canadian Mounted Police.

Students had changed profoundly in the last five years of the 1960s. Even the radical thinkers who had proposed change in the early 60s were now shocked. Paul Goodman, once in the vanguard of educational change, was flabbergasted by the students of 1969. "There was no knowledge," he wrote, "only the sociology of knowledge. They had so well learned that research is subsidized and conducted for the benefit of the ruling class that they did not believe there was such a thing as simple truth."

• • •

The radical student movement still had lots of life, but there was no doubt that there was also now a very powerful backlash. On January 20, Richard Nixon and Spiro Agnew were sworn in as President and Vice-President of the U.S. They surrounded themselves with a coterie of hard-line right-wingers, almost all of whom would be removed, fired, or jailed in disgrace within the next three years. Nixon was elected with the pledge that he would bring the now more than 500,000 American soldiers back from Vietnam. Instead, he began to escalate the war.

Nixon appointed his campaign chairman, John N. Mitchell, as Attorney General. Breaking all standard protocol, he told FBI chief J. Edgar Hoover that the usual background check for an AG did not need to be conducted. Mitchell promptly instituted wiretapping, preventive detention, the use of 'no-knock' warrants for police, frisking suspects without a warrant, a restructured Supreme Court, and a slowdown in school desegregation and civil rights cases. "This country is going so far to the right," he gloated, "you won't even recognize it." [72]

· · ·

On January 28th, *The Georgian,* the student newspaper of Sir George Williams University in Montréal ran a special edition investigating what they called the administration cover-up of the accusations of racism by black Caribbean students against biology professor Perry Anderson. The articles galvanized the school and the next day more than 400 students occupied the university computer lab where they remained until February 11th when negotiations with the administration broke down. The faculty of the school sided with Anderson and vetoed a proposal by the administration to examine the allegations of racial bias against black students. The situation escalated and the Montréal riot police were called in to evict the students. As the students and police fought in the halls of the university, other students threw thousands of computer punch cards out into the streets below. A fire broke out in the computer lab. It was blamed on the students at the time, though later investigations suggested that it was set by the police as a way of forcing the students out of the building. "The violence was perpetuated—I have no hesitation saying this—by the police and administration," claimed one of the students, Rodney John. "Are students going to start a fire when they're locked in?"

As the fire burned, the crowds watching the fire from below were heard chanting "Let the niggers burn," and "Burn, niggers, burn!". As they tried to escape the burning building, 87 students were arrested, subjected to racist taunts, and ultimately charged with 1,044 counts of rioting, arson and other crimes. The man considered to be the leader, Kennedy Frederick of Dominica, was brought into court inside a cage like a wild animal. Ultimately, though, almost all the charges were dropped by the Crown or thrown out by the judge.

Similar protests by black students took place in high schools, colleges, and universities across the United States. Black students, according to Charles Hamilton, the department chair of political science at Roosevelt University, would no longer allow themselves "to be made into little middle-class black Sambos." One of the most disorderly schools was Franklin Lane High School on the border of Queens and Brooklyn. One police officer reported, "Every day there is a riot on the subway or a fight in the bathroom or an arrest in the halls or a brawl in the cafeteria or a suspension of more black students. Lane is a time bomb and everyone—blacks, whites, teachers, Board of Ed—admits it could explode any day." On January 20th, it did explode when three students attacked a teacher named Frank Siracusa and set him on fire. The school was closed down for several days, and, when it reopened, it was with 50 New York policemen stationed on the school grounds.

A wave of trouble continued through the term in other Brooklyn schools including Bushwick, Samuel Tilden, and Erasmus Hall. At the City College of New York, 200 black and Latino students occupied the administration building, broke into President Buell Gallagher's office, and emptied his private stock of liquor. In Durham, North Carolina, over 60 members of the Afro-American Society seized the Administration Building and laid out their demands—a black studies program comparable to the ones now being offered at Ivy League colleges, and a ban on the school's use of the old blackface minstrel song, *I Wish I Was in Dixie*. The outcome of the protests often depended on the reaction of the school administrations. When the school officials reacted mildly, as they did at the City College of New York and the University of Chicago, the protests ended peacefully. When the officials freaked out, to use the argot of the day, things got out of hand. San Francisco State University President S.I. Hayakawa fanned the flames with his speech calling the students a "wealthy arrogant elite with a mission to improve the lot of poverty-stricken and illiterate peasants by rebelling against the system and overthrowing it." Ronald Reagan, then Governor of California, chimed in calling student protest "guerrilla warfare."

February 7th saw the biggest escalation of the continuing campus protest, when Chancellor Edwin Young of the University of Wisconsin at Madison refused to respond to demands from 500 black students. His refusal provoked hundreds of white students to join the protest which led Madison's mayor to ask Governor Warren Knowles to send in the National Guard. When a phalanx of soldiers appeared on campus, it galvanized the students against the authorities. The protest grew to include nearly 5,000 students, which provoked the Governor to call in another 1,000 guards- men, who began teargassing and attacking the students. The protests cli- maxed with 10,000 students marching on the state capitol.

• • •

In the first six months of 1969 there were at least 84 bombings, attempted bombings, or incidents of arson on American campuses. Few could avoid the angry zeitgeist of the era. Even Elvis Presley, who had pre- viously steered well clear of politics, went into the studio on January 23rd to record *In the Ghetto*. Others, once pivotal to "the movement", couldn't stand the heat so they got out of the kitchen. "I was anointed the Big Bubba of Rebellion, High Priest of Protest, the Czar of Dissent, the Duke of Disobedience, Leader of the Freeloaders, Kaiser of Apostasy, Archbishop of Anarchy," wrote Bob Dylan. "All code words for *Outlaw*." While previ- ously apolitical Elvis was recording *In the Ghetto*, Dylan was recording his new country album *Nashville Skyline*, on which there was nary a peep of protest.

Dylan had handed the reins of protest music to others like the Detroit band MC5, who while less musically gifted, were profoundly more committed to the revolution. To quote their chronicler Don McLeese, "The MC5 weren't just a band; they were a movement, the musical vanguard of the militant White Panther Party. In order to embrace the music, you apparently had to commit to the destruction of Western civilization as we knew it." John Sinclair, their manager (and founder of the White Panther Party) claimed his band was "totally committed to revolution, as the revolution is totally committed to driving people out of the separate shells and into each other's arms." The Man took note. Sinclair was arrested for offering two joints to an undercover policewoman and sentenced to ten years in prison.

• • •

There were other crises, revolutions and protests going on in early 1969. On January 28th, a well drilled by Union Oil off the coast of Santa Barbara, California blew out and spewed more than three million gallons of oil into the Pacific. The devastating event that killed more than 10,000 seabirds, seals, dolphins, and sea lions, did much to energize the new burgeoning environmental movement. There was a wildly differing response to the disaster from the young and the old. Teenage high school student Kathy Morales was quoted in the *Santa Barbara News-Press* crying out with tears streaming down her face, as she watched the final convulsions of a dying loon, "You want to talk about The Establishment? This is my life out here. I come out here all the time to watch the sea and the birds and the animals. I can't think of coming down here again. I don't know now if it will ever be the same again and no-one can tell me." [73]

In contrast, in an appearance before a U.S. Senate Subcommittee, Fred Hartley, the president of Union Oil, dismissed the event, saying "I don't like to call it a disaster. I am amazed at the publicity for the loss of a few birds." [74] There were massive protests against Union Oil and the Department of the Interior which was approving new drilling even as oil continued to bubble up from the sea floor. The event reached new levels of absurdity when in full view of hundreds of people on boats protesting the disaster, a new drilling rig, that had been brought in to replace the previous one, flipped upside down. That nuttiness finally did get sorted out and to this day oil drilling continues in the Santa Barbara Channel. The 1969 oil spill was an unmitigated disaster, but the blackened beaches did have a slight silver lining. Wisconsin Senator Gaylord Nelson was inspired by the ghastly site of the 800-square-mile oil slick to create Earth Day, which began the following year.

• • •

Lots of fuel was needed for the gas-guzzling autos and airplanes of the era. There was a revolution of sorts in aviation as the world embraced what was proudly called the Jet Age. On February 9th, Boeing flew the first test flight of the radical and enormous 747. On March 21st, the supersonic *Concorde*, built by a consortium of Air France and British Airways, made its first flight. The speed and ease of trans-oceanic travel meant ideas, including revolutionary ideas, could travel faster to all parts of the globe.

• • •

At a conference of the PLO in Cairo, Yasser Arafat was elected Chairman of the Palestine Liberation Organization. Arafat had already become the face of Palestinian resistance after his successful defense of the Jordanian town of Karameh against the Israeli Army in 1968. Arafat would be the highest profile military and political leader of the Palestinians for the next 30 years.

• • •

On February 8th, the last issue ever of the *Saturday Evening Post* was published. The magazine, in publication since 1897 was a bastion of conservative, middle class, small-town American values, but increasingly was

finding it hard to hang on to its readers. For years it had been well represented by illustrator Norman Rockwell who painted over 300 covers of the
magazine, mirroring its conservative, middle-class audience. Now, both he
and the magazine seemed to have lost their way. "I used to reflect the country's mood in my work," he said, "but now the questions are so bitter—and
nothing is clear-cut."

• • •

There was a new wrinkle in the convoluted tapestry of the world's
military misadventures when in February the Chinese Army launched an
ambush on soldiers stationed on Damansky/Zhenbao Island, disputed territory on the northeastern border between China and the Soviet Union.
Hundreds of Chinese and 31 Russian soldiers lost their lives fighting over
this meaningless scrap of land. When Russian Premier Alexei Kosygin
tried to telephone Mao to resolve the issue, the Chinese operator cursed
him, in typical Cultural Revolution manner, as a "revisionist element",
and cut him off. The Russian Premier got so angry about the nasty border
incident that he proposed "wiping out this modern adventurer" with a
nuclear attack, until allies refused to endorse the plan. "We are now iso-
lated," whined Mao plaintively, "No one wants to make friends with us." [75]

The Chinese Cultural Revolution was technically over, but in
reality, the battles continued, especially in outlying areas of the country
such as Mongolia. Suspected of being spies and traitors to the cause of
Chairman Mao, over 800,000 Mongols were incarcerated, interrogated,
and denounced in mass meetings. The torture used in Mongolia was grotesque even by the low standards of the Cultural Revolution. Teeth were
pulled out, tongues sliced off, eyes gouged out of sockets, flesh branded
with hot irons. After 20,000 had died, it became too much even for Mao,
who told General Teng Haiqing, the administrator of the torture, to end it.

• • •

On February 13th, the FLQ bombing of the Montréal Stock Exchange inflicted a million dollars of damage and sent 27 people to hospital. On March 7th, Pierre-Paul Geoffroy plead guilty to 124 offenses in connection with 31 Montréal bombings. He was sentenced to life in prison for each of the charges—the harshest sentence ever handed out in the British Commonwealth to that time.

• • •

Upon learning that the Ho Chi Minh Trail was now looping through northern Cambodia, Richard Nixon decided, on March 15th, to escalate the war. He and his friends were at his Key Biscayne 'Winter White House' when they heard the news. A source in the Secret Service described Nixon's drunken reaction: "They were half in the tank, sitting around the pool drinking. And Nixon got on the phone and said, 'Bomb the shit out of them!'" [76]

Knowing that he would likely not have the support for an attack on Cambodia from either Secretary of Defense Melvin Laird or Secretary of State William Rogers, and certainly not the support of Congress or much of the public, Nixon told his Security Advisor Henry Kissinger that "State is to be notified only after the point of no return. This order is not appealable." He added that there was to be "No comment, no warnings, no complaints, no protest...I mean it, not one thing to be said to anyone publicly or privately without my prior approval." Two days later, sixty B-52 bombers rained down hundreds of bombs three miles inside the Cambodian border. The reported successful mission had Nixon and Kissinger "really beaming" according to Haldeman, but the reports suggesting that the enemy had been routed proved to be highly inaccurate. A 'Daniel Boone' Special Forces unit was sent in for mop-up duty and was massacred by the NVA. A second unit was ordered in but the American soldiers mutinied and refused to walk into what they felt would be a slaughter.

• • •

On March 28th, students burst into hearings of the Senate and the Board of Governors of McGill University, shouting *"Revolution! Vive le Québec socialiste! Vive le Québec libre"*, then 9,000 marched on the streets. Under the spotlights of a hovering police helicopter, they broke windows and damaged police vehicles. Their main demand was that the giant university that had been operating in English since 1821 transform itself into a French institution.

• • •

In the heady years of the late '60s, witchcraft was one of the most puissant spin-offs of the counterculture. Many women began to identify themselves with the ancient cult, and it was cited in popular music in songs like Donovan's *Season of the Witch*, and Fleetwood Mac's (and later Santana's) *Black Magic Woman*. Women, either singly or in small groups, developed an interest in the pagan rites and began exploring the use of spells, tarot cards, and other medieval rituals. A group calling themselves WITCH (The Women's International Terrorist Conspiracy from Hell) loudly demonstrated on Wall Street, and to their delight the market promptly fell by five points. They went on to show up at the Bridal Fair in New York's Madison Square Garden, wearing black bridal veils, carrying signs reading "Confront the Whore-makers" and "Here Comes the Bribe", and releasing white mice amongst the audience of brides-to-be, their mothers, and the sellers of bridal gowns, kitchen appliances, and packaged honeymoon trips.

Gloria Steinem even included the witchcraft phenomenon in her seminal article in the April 4th issue of *New York* magazine, titled *After Black Power, Women's Liberation*. The article was highly influential in bringing the new Women's Liberation Movement to the attention of the world and establishing Steinem as one of its most prominent leaders. The main goals of the 'Women's Libbers', as Steinem laid them out, were equal rights, equal pay, and reproductive rights for women. In 1969, the average pay for women with a college education was less than that of men with only grade eight. Women wanting to enroll in medical school were regularly told they should instead become nurses. Forty-three American states still had 'protective legislation' limiting the hours and places where women could work, legislation that New York Governor Nelson Rockefeller admitted was really designed to protect men's jobs, not women's safety.

• • •

The student revolt that had raged through the winter picked up steam again in the spring semester. On the morning of April 9th, five hundred SDS protesters marched past the home of Harvard president Nathan Pusey chanting "Smash ROTC", and then proceeded to take over the school's administration building. They didn't mince words. When Robert Watson, the Dean of Students told them, "You have no right to be in this building. I am ordering you to leave or face discipline," he was told, "We've taken the building; now get the fuck out of here."

The students announced that they were there to protest the Harvard Administration's connection to the Vietnam War. A Boston underground newspaper published files liberated by the students that revealed ties between the Harvard faculty (including future Nixon Security Advisor Henry Kissinger) and the CIA, the State Department and the Defense Department. Under the headline READING THE MAIL OF THE RULING CLASS, the article read, "The common style of corporate chieftains, warmakers, and Harvard's elite is no accident: many prestigious Harvard professors and administrators are deacons of the church of American empire. Their hands are bloody. The work they do ends in the murder of millions and the looting of the resources of the world. Official Harvard is a dynamo of the imperialist machine."

The imperialist machine fought back. In the early morning of April 10th, three buses pulled into Harvard Square and disgorged 400 local and state policemen in riot gear. The police attacked the building with a battering ram and attacked the occupiers with clubs and mace. Ultimately 196 students, including 50 women from the university's sister school Radcliff, were hauled off to jail. As had happened earlier in the year in San Francisco and at Madison, the police brutality rallied support for the students and turned them into martyrs. Five days later 10,000 students turned out at Soldier Field and voted to strike against the university. Their bold manifesto read:

> *Strike for the eight demands. Strike because you hate cops. Strike because your roommate was clubbed. Strike to stop expansion. Strike to seize control of your life. Strike to become more human. Strike to return Paine Hall scholarships. Strike because there's no poetry in your lecture.*
> *Strike because classes are a bore. Strike for power. Strike to smash the Corporation. Strike to make yourself free. Strike to abolish ROTC. Strike because they are trying to squeeze the life out of you. Strike.*

· · ·

While these skirmishes, generational battles, and culture wars were flaring up all over the world, there was also still the very real threat of a Cold War nuclear Armageddon between the United States and the U.S.S.R., China, and North Korea. On April 15th, North Korean MIG-21 jets shot down an American Lockheed Super Constellation spy plane off the Korean coast, killing all 31 sailors, cryptographers, and marines onboard. The reasons why the incident escalated into a shooting are complicated, and the American response was indecisive and unclear. What is clear is how close the world came to nuclear war. It is arguable that there were certifiable mad men running all four of these countries, and one of them, Richard Nixon was also a drunk. Reportedly he was well in his cups when he ordered a pilot at the Kunsun Air Base in South Korea to load a B61 nuclear bomb onto an F-4 fighter jet and prepare for a nuclear strike against North Korea. An urgent order to stand down was given on the advice of Secretary of State Henry Kissinger who asked the Joint Chiefs not to do anything until Nixon sobered up the next morning. It was neither the first nor the last time that Nixon was prepared to use his nuclear arsenal. "If the president had his way," Kissinger once growled to his staff, "there'd be a nuclear war every week." [77]

• • •

On April 17th, the 21-year-old firebrand Bernadette Devlin was elected to the British Parliament. She was the youngest MP in Westminster at the time, and until 2015 held the distinction of being the youngest woman ever elected to Parliament. In a sense she represented youth as well as Ireland and as well as women. It was unheard of to have 21-year-olds running for political office before this period, and it remains extremely rare today. But everything about this 1965 – 75 period was about youth. At the time, many of the revolutionaries described in this book were barely able to vote. Chronicler of the Chinese revolution Edgar Snow mused that he "often had a queer feeling among the Reds that I was in the midst of a host of schoolboys, engaged in a life of violence because some strange design of history had made this seem infinitely more important to them than football games, textbooks, love, or the main concerns of youth in other countries." Many of the Weathermen, the Tupamaros, and the FLQ were teenagers or in their early twenties. In Cambodia, or, as they re-named it, Kampuchea, the Khmer Rouge took the cult of youth to its farthest extremes. Children as young as nine became AK-47-carrying soldiers for the revolution. The Khmer Rouge murdered all the educated professionals and turned the country over to children and teenagers. The Kampong Son oil refinery was run by a management team who were between the ages of eight and 18. They called the Chinese advisors at the plant who were in their thirties and forties "grandfather." When one of the Chinese technicians was offered a flight to visit Angkor Wat, he nervously refused because his pilot was only 17. A popular rhyming ditty of the period ran:

> *You are old*
> *We are young*
> *Mao Zedong*

Both the media and the advertising world embraced the cult of youth. *TIME* Magazine awarded its 'Man of the Year' award in 1966 to 'Anyone Under 25'. Pepsi-Cola's famous slogan from the period was "Now it's Pepsi – For Those Who Think Young." The quintessential car of the era, the Ford Mustang, was primarily targeted at young male baby boomers. Mao's Little Red Book proclaimed, "The world is yours. You young people are full of vigor and vitality like the eight or nine o'clock sun in the morning. You are our hope."

Though Mao was always praising the energy of young people, he sent millions from their homes in the cities out to the country starting in late 1968 in 're-education programs' to learn from the great proletarian masses. In the period of 1965 to 1975 as many as 18 to 20 million young students were banished to the countryside. For most, it was a disastrous, horrible part of their lives. Vast areas of China were still experiencing famine, and the students were often hungry or barely subsisting on pickled cabbage or thin broth infested with maggots and flies. Intellectuals, scientists, and engineers were also frequently sent off to the cadre camps and delegated to jobs like emptying buckets of urine and manure. In northern China the winter temperatures often fell to minus 40 degrees, and the students were forced to live in caves or in mud and straw shacks with little heating They worked long hours slogging through mud and snow. Camp leaders were vindictive, ordering their charges to do things like moving thousands of bricks from one spot to another for no reason other than to keep them busy. Girls were especially vulnerable. There were hundreds of reports of rape and molestation by the locals. So many died that Mao and Zhou abandoned the re-education program in 1970 and ordered the students who were left to return home.

• • •

Teenagers also suffered during the Troubles in Ireland. On April 19, 16-year-old Catherine Devenny was laying on a sofa in the small house at 69 William Street in Derry, Northern Ireland, recovering from surgery. From the front door of the house, Catherine's father, Samuel, and her 21-year-old brother watched a street battle between the Royal Ulster Constabulary and Catholic protestors. Two of the rioters ran into and through the house into the backyard. Samuel Devenny closed the door, but police forced it open and began clubbing him. They broke his glasses and dentures and left him bleeding from numerous head wounds.

The police then attacked Catherine. They smashed her with batons, pulled her off the sofa and kicked her until she lost consciousness. Her 18-year-old sister Ann attempted to protect both her father and sister, but she too was kicked and thrown across the room. She struggled to get back to her father and sister, but officers lifted her by the hair and forced her away.

Two other men in the house were also attacked by the police and one of them was left unconscious in the front hallway. Samuel Devenny was sent to hospital, where he died of a heart attack. Thousands attended his funeral, and he became one of the first martyrs of the Troubles.

The Metropolitan Police Chief Superintendent Kenneth Drury later reported that, "Whilst it is appreciated that the officers…on duty in the riot area on the day in question were under extreme provocation, being constantly attacked and sorely tried, there is no evidence that their action could be justified in any way and this code of conduct can never be condoned in any force responsible for the preservation of law and order." [78]

The assault on the two girls and the death of their father was part of a battle that started when police charged into the Bogside, the Catholic ghetto of Derry, and began throwing their weight around. The cops had already been condemned in an inquiry led by Lord Cameron which concluded that "a number of policemen were guilty of misconduct, which involved assault and battery, malicious damage to property…and the use of provocative sectarian and political slogans." [79a] Now the people of the Bogside were fighting back to try to prevent the police from repeating these kinds of actions.

The Bogsiders were led by an extraordinary young woman who had just burst upon the scene. Bernadette Devlin was a psychology student at Queen's University, who on April 17th in a most unlikely turn of events had been elected as a British Member of Parliament in a by-election in Northern Ireland. Now, only two days later, she was running through the streets of Bogside in jeans, leading the protestors in setting up barricades and preparing missiles to fight back against the police. The cops, plainly biased against the Catholics, would occasionally retreat to the Protestant side of Derry, where they were fed tea and sandwiches by the locals, and where they could rest and regroup for a new attack.

A young boy was the first to notice them and shouted, "My God, they're coming!" Everyone stopped dead. Devlin remembered, "It was one of the most horrific sights I have ever seen. High above us, the city wall was lined with a great silent mass of black figures. Slowly the mass started to move, down through the walls, into the two roads still not barricaded, and when the two battalions of police met, they joined forces and started a stomp towards us, beating their shields with their batons and howling dreadfully in the manner of savages trying to intimidate their foes. Everybody just fled. Trapped in our own barricades, the nearest place we could flee to was a recently built high block of flats. Through megaphones we screamed to the people to open their doors to everyone but the police, and to the crowd not to panic but walk to safety as quickly and calmly as possible. I took refuge, along with some pressmen, in one of the flats, and once we were in, the tenant put all his furniture against the door. Then the police trucks came, dozens and dozens of them, smashing down the barricades, and wailing on through the Bogside like an invading army."

Numerous witnesses reported the police shouting, "If you see Bernadette Devlin, get her!" The next day, the young activist was summoned to appear in court on four charges of inciting a mob to violence. Two days later, on her 22nd birthday, she was in London, taking her seat in Parliament. Defying tradition, which requires a new MP to wait a few respectful weeks before making a non-contentious speech, Devlin made her maiden speech within an hour. She became instantly famous for her penetrating fiery dissection of Northern Ireland and its Unionist regime. The speech was printed in papers all over England and Ireland, and was called, by a Conservative MP, Norman St. John-Stevas, "the most electrifying maiden speech for 40 years." Irish historian Brian Feeney pronounced that, "Tiny, waif-like, quick-witted, alert, superb on TV, a child of the 1960s, Bernadette Devlin was a nightmare for unionists, who appeared like clodhoppers compared to her."

She was swamped with 10,000 letters and telegrams and dozens of offers to appear on television talk shows around the world. Of course, not all were complimentary. Unionist Christopher Bland called her. "Ireland's greatest national disaster since the potato famine." One letter read, "You Fenian scum! You and all your kind should be held under water till the bubbles come up!" A group of witches wrote her saying, "Dear madam, you are so beautifully evil that myself and my fellow witches in the South Down coven have decided to make you one of us." The Reverend Ian Paisley slagged her with the phrase, "International Socialist Playgirl of the Year."

• • •

The Sexual Revolution, which began three or four years earlier, exploded in 1969 with numerous new films, magazines, and books that exploited the new liberation. In April, the Swedish art film *I am Curious (Yellow)* opened across North America. The distributor, Barney Rosset, who had recently been able to finally import Henry Miller's *Tropic of Cancer,* D.H. Lawrence's *Lady Chatterley's Lover*, and William Burroughs' *Naked Lunch* into the US, benefited again from the publicity garnered when American customs officials seized the film. Once the U.S. Court of Appeals finally overturned the customs decision, he had theaters lining up to play the film, and customers lining up to see it. Though it did provide many with their first sight of cinematic full-frontal nudity, it also disappointed, as the exciting illicit glimpses of pubic hair were interrupted by long diatribes about American imperialism, Spanish fascism, and Chinese communism. Nonetheless it made a great deal of money and became the highest grossing foreign language film of all time in the U.S. and Canada.

It didn't escape attention that there was lots of money to be made out of this sexual revolution. As *I am Curious (Yellow)* played around North America and Europe, another Scandinavian sex romp, *Quiet Days in Clichy*, based on the Henry Miller novel, was filming in Denmark. When it played the next year in Montréal, the FLQ decided to rob the stuffed box office to finance their terrorist activities. They had their planned robbery ready to go, but when they arrived at the theater, they discovered that the police morality squad had shut down the screening and seized the print. Instead, the theater was showing a Western. It was virtually empty, and certainly, the separatists felt, not worth robbing.

Hollywood got into the business, too. *Midnight Cowboy*, while a serious, mainstream film, had scenes in it unimaginable only a few years earlier—a group rape, nude sex scenes, and a quasi-homosexual relationship between an aspiring gigolo (Jon Voight) and a disabled pimp (Dustin Hoffman). It was the first X-rated film to win the Oscar for Best Picture.

Books like Philip Roth's *Portnoy's Complaint*, Dr. David Reuben's *Everything You Wanted to Know About Sex...But Were Afraid to Ask*, and *The Sensuous Woman* by "J" (the anonymous nom de plume of author Joan Teresa Garrity) all pushed the boundaries of what had previously been the *verboten* subject of sex.

Onstage, British theater critic enlisted the help of luminaries Samuel Beckett, Sam Shepard, Jules Feiffer, and John Lennon to create a hit play titled *Oh Calcutta!*. The play had nothing to do with the Indian city. The title was a play on the French expression *O quell cul t'as (What an ass you have!)*. It featured non-stop full nudity and sexually charged scenes that had never before been seen in playhouses.

Lennon got into the act again with his album *Two Virgins*, in which he and Yoko Ono appear full-frontal nude on the front cover, and full-backtal (to coin a phrase) on the rear. The sight of Ono's rather enormous bush and Lennon's uncircumcised penis were too much for various authorities. The city of Cleveland declared the album obscene, and the state of New Jersey seized and destroyed 30,000 copies of the record.

Magazines were probably the biggest beneficiary of the sexual revolution and the place where images of naked women and articles about politics could sometimes co-exist. On May 2nd, *Screw* Magazine, a radical weekly pornographic magazine founded in 1968 published an article titled, "Is J. Edgar Hoover a Fag?" It was the first public reference to the Washington rumor that the director of the FBI was a cross-dressing homosexual in a relationship with his live-in partner and FBI assistant Clyde Tolson.

In September, Bob Guccione published the first North American edition of *Penthouse* magazine, which he had begun in England in 1965. To some degree it followed the model of *Playboy* but it was much more risqué. It also took on the revolutionary political issues of the time—investigating Latin American military torture, the assassination of John F. Kennedy, and the plight of neglected Vietnam war veterans. The provocative articles along with explicit photography by Suze Randall and even more explicit advice by Xaviera Hollander ('The Happy Hooker') made Bob Guccione one of the richest men in America. His sex empire led by *Penthouse* earned him $3.5 to $4 billion.

Not all forms of popular culture had yet entered into the revolutionary spirit of the times. Television was still heavily controlled and censored by internal "Standards and Practices" departments of the three American networks. Virtually the only show that recognized the vast changes sweeping through society, at least in the U.S., was *The Smothers Brothers Comedy Hour* on CBS. The network had battled with the brothers and their producer for several years over the mildly leftwing slant of the show, tame sexual references, and appearances by Pete Seeger, Joan Baez and comedian David Steinberg. Eventually, CBS CEO and president William S. Paley abruptly and angrily cancelled it, causing yet another rift between the show's demographic of 15 to 35-year-olds and the establishment.

Possibly the most revolutionary move in television in the year 1969, though little recognized at the time, was the creation by Ted Turner of the so-called 'Super-Station' WTBS in Atlanta. It took a few years, but ultimately the WTBS platform inspired Turner to start CNN, the cable news network that would transform the way the world received the news. In 1969 Turner was known as the 'Mouth from the South' and 'Captain Outrageous'. He was a brash, politically conservative owner of a large billboard advertising company, and a sailor who would go on to win the America's Cup. Ted Turner transformed television, his politics, and his net worth. He would ultimately marry Jane Fonda, one of the revolutionary icons of the 1965 – 75 era, and give a gift of one billion dollars to the United Nations to help the UN fight issues like overpopulation, poverty, and nuclear proliferation.

• • •

Not even the hidebound world of sports was immune to the revolutionary winds of change blowing through 1969. To the shock of the mostly very conservative owners of baseball teams (though not Ted Turner, who in the 1970s was owner of the Atlanta Braves), their players began wearing long hair, earrings and (while off the field) sandals. Even more shocking was that, like workers in so many other industries, the players had begun to organize. In 1966, Marvin Miller had been elected executive director of the new Major League Players Association, and in 1968 he negotiated the first collective bargaining agreement in professional sports. Until then, the minimum salary for a starting player was (unbelievably, by today's standards), only $6,000 per year. In 1969, the players threatened to go on strike unless they got a dental plan, a proper pension plan, and a life insurance program. A players' boycott of the season was averted just prior to the start of spring training.

There was also a feeling that 'America's pastime' was too slow-moving and low-scoring and that sports fans were turning away from the sport, finding it boring compared to football, basketball, and auto racing. Baseball was getting too dull for the youthful, fast-paced zeitgeist of the late sixties. In large part this was because offensive skill (pitching) had advanced far beyond defense (hitting).

To counter this, the men who ran Major League Baseball, notwithstanding numerous dinosaurs in their ranks, agreed to two new rules—they lowered the height of the pitching mound from 15 to 10 inches to reduce the pitcher's advantage, and they introduced the new position of 'Designated Hitter'—a hard-hitting specialist who could replace the pitcher at the plate and thus jazz up the game with more hitting and more scoring. They also invited the first non-American team ever, the Montréal Expos, into the league, giving the grandiose name of the MLB championship, the World Series, (slightly) more credibility.

• • •

Two Montréalers who were not as welcome in America were FLQ revolutionaries Alain Allard and Jean-Pierre Charette. Both were wanted as accomplices in the bombings that had sent Pierre-Paul Geoffroy to jail. The pair crossed the border to hide out in New York, first with Black Panthers and then with East Village radicals Sam Melville and Jane Alpert. Melville had grown up poor in Buffalo and drifted around until, at the age of 35, he met the two Québecers who suddenly gave new meaning to his life. His 22-year-old lover, Alpert, was a recent Swarthmore graduate now working for an underground paper called the *Rat Subterranean News.* "This country's about to go through a revolution," Melville told Alpert. "I expect it to happen before the decade is over, and I intend to be part of it."

Through the spring, Melville and Alpert holed up in their apartment with the two FLQ activists picking their brains about the minutiae of bombing and violent revolution—where to get dynamite, how to wire the timers, how to insert bombs into briefcases, how to write communiqués, and how to phone in bomb threats. In short, how to import the Québeçois model for violent insurrection into the U.S. In return, Melville found the

Canadians a gun, and Alpert found them tickets for a good plane to hijack. On May 5, the foursome drove to LaGuardia Airport, and said goodbye.

"How can we ever thank you?" asked Jean-Pierre Charette.

"We're all fighting for the same cause," replied Jane Alpert.

That night the two Americans huddled over a radio until they heard the announcer on the radical New York station WBAI read a news bulletin, "National Airlines flight number 91 has been diverted from Miami to Havana, where it has now landed." The pair jumped for joy, with Melville crowing over and over, "Those little bastards. They did it! They really did it!" [80] Charette and Allard remained in exile in Cuba for ten years, but eventually returned to Montréal, where they were promptly arrested, found guilty, and jailed.

• • •

On May 19th, the U.S. Supreme Court concurred with Timothy Leary in the case *Leary vs United States*, declaring the Marihuana Tax Act unconstitutional and overturning his 1965 conviction. To celebrate, Leary announced, the same day, his candidacy for the Governor of California against the Republican incumbent, Ronald Reagan. His campaign slogan was, "Come together. Join the party."

• • •

Ten days later Bruce Mayrock, a student at Columbia University, set himself ablaze outside the United Nations headquarters in New York, to protest the continuing genocide against the nation and people of Biafra.

• • •

Confirming what Sam Melville and Tim Leary and everyone else thought was going on around them, The Who's Pete Townsend put together a band called Thunderclap Newman to record the song *Something in the Air*. It became the Number One song in Great Britain for three weeks in July. "Lock up the streets and houses," sang Speedy Keen, "Because there's something in the air." Lest there be any confusion, the hit song exhorted listeners to "Hand out the guns and ammo…Because the revolution's here. And you know it's right."

• • •

On May 26th, John Lennon and Yoko Ono began their week-long Bed-In for Peace at the Queen Elizabeth Hotel in Montréal. On June 1st, they were joined by Timothy Leary, who joined in a discussion about peace and participated in the hotel-room recording of the new anti-war anthem, *Give Peace a Chance*. Lennon later wrote *Come Together* as a theme song for Leary's California gubernatorial campaign. It became the first song on *Abbey Road*, and a Number One single in the U.S., but it did not prevent Reagan from handily defeating Leary in the election.

• • •

Hearing from his spies that the CIA had infiltrated the Black Panther Party, Fidel Castro ejected Eldridge Cleaver from Cuba. Cleaver headed for Algiers, the city a London newspaper called "the headquarters of world revolution." Also in June, Brazilian professor and guerrilla fighter Carlos Marighella published his *Mini-Manual of the Urban Guerrilla*. The book became the handbook of revolutionaries around the world. In November, Sao Paulo undercover police ambushed Marighella and shot him to death.

• • •

St. Jean Baptiste Day, the June 24th statutory holiday in Quebec, was not as contentious in 1969 as it had been the previous year when the Prime Minister was attacked with rocks and bottles, but an incident occurred that symbolized another major radical change happening in the world in this period—the decline of religion. All over the western world organized religion saw a steep fall in the late '60s and early '70s, but nowhere more so than in Québec. In 1960, Québec was considered the most religious jurisdiction on the planet but by 1970 it was one of the least. Not only did people stop going to the Roman Catholic churches that had dominated Québeçois society for 300 years, but people began actively battling the power of the church. At the June 24ᵗʰ parade, a group of protestors attacked the float carrying the statue of St. Jean, the patron saint of French Canadians, and knocked it to the ground sending its head and halo rolling down the street.

Many of the monasteries, nunneries, and churches that had dotted the province closed, some of them transformed, of all things, into locations to shoot action, horror, and even soft-core sex films for the province's exploding new film industry. Sexual liberty was in, the repressive religion of the past was out. Québec became one of the few places on earth where the worst swear-words have religious, not sexual or scatological meaning: *Tabarnak! Câlice! Baptême! Esti! Viarge! (Tabernacle, Chalice, Baptism, Host, Virgin Mary)*.

• • •

At the SDS National Convention in Chicago in June, the student group broke apart into factions. One of them, the Revolutionary Youth Movement, transformed itself into the Weathermen, effectively destroying SDS. They took their name from the line, "You don't need a weatherman to know which way the wind blows", from Bob Dylan's *Subterranean Homesick Blues*. The Weathermen, as led by Bernardine Dohrn, were truly fringe extremists. They took a lot of acid and played a lot with guns and bombs. They believed that all white youth, themselves included, were guilty of crimes against third world people that had to be purged by spilling white blood to prove to Blacks, Vietnamese, and other victims of American imperialism that white revolutionaries were serious. They broke into small cells of eight to ten for security and had group "acid-tests" to try to weed out any potential police infiltrators. They believed, just as the CIA did, that LSD could be used as a truth serum. Their Cincinnati cell thought they had found an agent provocateur when one of their members, Larry Grathwohl, an ex-Green Beret who had fought in Vietnam, announced during an acid trip, "You're right, I am a Pig." The Weathermen were shocked, but they liked Grathwohl and especially liked his ability to get them drugs and guns and teach them how to make bombs. They debated his confession, and eventually decided he was merely expressing his guilt for having fought in 'Nam, so they let him stay. Two months later, Grathwohl fingered two New York Weathermen for the FBI.

• • •

There was one group of society that had not, so far, tried to assert itself. Both public sentiment and laws were so extremely prejudiced against homosexuals that members of the LGBT community throughout the 50s and 60s did everything they could to remain underground and hidden. Police generally had an open ticket to persecute gays, and seldom got any pushback either from the gays themselves or from civil rights protection organizations. The American Psychiatric Association listed homosexuality as a mental disorder. The U.S. Post Office reported to law enforcement any addresses that received material they thought might have a queer bent, and the FBI and local police forces kept lists of known homosexuals and when possible 'outed' them to their employers or to newspapers.

The few establishments that catered to homosexuals were usually run by the Mafia. When one of them, the Stonewall Inn in New York's Greenwich Village, was raided on the night of June 28th, the cops expected that the gays would submit to the raid in the way they had always responded in the past. Instead, the event turned into a major street riot. Hundreds of Greenwich Village residents appeared on the street in front of the bar and began shouting encouragement to the gays, drag queens, and transves-tites who the police were attempting to arrest. The Stonewall Riots, which continued for several more days, were every bit as intense as the student, Black, Irish, or anti-war riots of the time, but somewhat more entertaining. There was the usual breaking of glass and smashing of police equipment, but there were also impromptu kick-lines, with the demonstrators singing, to the tune of *Ta-Ra-Ra Boom-de-ay*: "We are the Stonewall girls / We wear our hair in curls / We don't wear underwear / We show our pubic hair." Police responded with night sticks and arrests.

Beat poet and Greenwich Village resident Allan Ginsberg, observing the mayhem, responded by saying, "Gay Power! Isn't that great! It's about time we did something to assert ourselves." All historians of Gay Power agree the movement began that night on Christopher Street. Within a year it had spread across North America, and eventually, it would spread around the world.

• • •

Meanwhile, in Ireland, the situation continued to deteriorate. July 12th is the annual day of Protestant celebration of King Billy's 1690 Battle of the Boyne victory over James II and what the Protestants referred to as "his Fenian hordes." It is frequently an excuse for drinking and fighting. The 1969 event was no exception and proved to be a curtain-raiser for the violence that would soon come. Royal Ulster Constabulary police force officers beat up a Catholic citizen, Francis McCloskey who died the next day becoming one of the first fatalities of The Troubles. The residents of the Bogside in Derry began stockpiling stones and materials for barricades and missiles, in anticipation of another provocative Protestant march coming soon on August 12th.

• • •

On July 14th, a new Hollywood film celebrating the frayed edges of youth culture premiered in New York City. *Easy Rider* turned thousands on to the freewheeling adventures of *Captain America* and *Billy*, two long-haired, pot-smoking, motorcycle-riding characters portrayed by Peter Fonda and Dennis Hopper. It also transformed Hollywood because the low-budget film, produced by Fonda and directed by Hopper, out-grossed all the big, old-fashioned pictures made with bloated budgets by the major studios. Suddenly 'old Hollywood' was convinced it had totally lost touch with the new young audiences, and basically gave up and retired. Along with the *Nouvelle Vague* pictures coming out of France and the 'underground' film movement based in New York, San Francisco, and Canada, *Easy Rider* helped change society and create a renaissance that produced in the early '70s one of the most creative periods in the history of Hollywood.

• • •

On July 19, Senator Ted Kennedy, during the annual Edgartown Yacht Club Regatta, hosted a party attended by the crew of his sailboat, and a group of young unattached women who had worked on Robert Kennedy's 1968 presidential campaign. The venue was a cottage on Chappaquiddick Island, a small islet off Martha's Vineyard in Massachusetts. Following the party Kennedy drove one of the young women, Mary Jo Kopechne, to catch the final midnight ferry for Martha's Vineyard. En route his car skidded off the road and into the tidal passage that runs between the two islands. Kennedy escaped from the car, but his companion did not. He dove repeatedly to try and save her, but he failed and eventually gave up. He swam across the channel and returned to his hotel room on the main island. It was not until 10:00 AM the next morning that he contacted the authorities, by which time the submerged car and Kopechne's body had been discovered and retrieved by a police diver. The event was not just a tragedy but also a huge political scandal. Kennedy received a two-month suspended sentence for leaving the scene of an accident and lost his driver's license for 16 months. More importantly, it cost him the presidency. He had been considered a front-runner, but with his reputation so blemished, he did not run in either 1972 or 1976, and when he did run in 1980, he lost the primaries to incumbent Jimmy Carter. Had he not crashed off the road into Katama Bay, many believe he would have won the nomination and defeated Nixon in the 1972 election. Certainly, if he had done so the history of this period would have been very different.

• • •

The very next day the attention shifted back from this tragic incident to the moment the world had been looking forward to for months, and one of the most important milestones in the history of the world. NASA, inspired by Ted Kennedy's older brother JFK's 1962 goal of getting a man to the moon by the end of the decade, launched astronauts Buzz Aldrin, Neil Armstrong, and Michael Collins just six months shy of Kennedy's deadline. On July 20th, Aldrin and Armstrong successfully navigated the Lunar Module *Eagle* around a boulder field and with less than a minute's worth of fuel left in the tank, landed it safely on the Moon in the Sea of Tranquility. A few hours later, Armstrong descended to make the first footprint on the moon and spoke the first words heard from the surface— words that were heard by the millions of people watching the event on live black and white television from around the world. "That's one small step for man," said Armstrong, "One giant leap for mankind." No-one seemed to object that he blew the first part of the line (he meant to say, *"a* man") or that the second part seemed to ignore the fifty per cent of humanity that are not 'man'.

In a period in which America's reputation was being battered by race relations, the Vietnam War, and generational battles, Apollo 11 was the exceptional event that made the country feel good about itself and made the world feel good about America. However, before the spacemen were even back on earth, another crazy accident indicated yet another problem that would become more and more evident over the coming years.

• • •

The late '60s and early '70s were certainly the most polluted and dirty period in human history. The issue had been ignored for years, but now activists moved from other causes into the cause of trying to clean up the mess. One seminal event that helped start the environmental movement was when the Cuyahoga River, running through Cleveland, Ohio, caught on fire, on July 22th. "Burn on, big river, burn on!" sang satirist Randy Newman. It was actually the fourteenth time that the Cuyahoga had caught ablaze, but this was the biggest fire. Mayor Carl Stokes invited the national media to witness the absurdity of a river being a fire hazard. The conflagration caught the attention of the public and some politicians, and the event helped spur battles with polluting industries and eventually the passage of the Clean Water Act of 1972. Thousands of activists began to adopt environmentalism as their cause, battling for a clean world through organizations like Greenpeace, the Sierra Club and Pollution Probe.

• • •

In Derry, Northern Ireland, August 12th was the beginning of one of the fiercest battles in this violent period. The authorities were asked to cancel the annual 'Apprentice Boys' parade that celebrates an ancient Protestant victory over Catholics. because of the smoldering tensions of the summer. However, they refused to do so, citing 'tradition.' Consequently, a large number of loyalist Protestants, ready for battle, were allowed to march along the edge of the Catholic area of the Bogside. After the Catholics and the unionists hurled insults back and forth, the Royal Ulster Constabulary (RUC) began encouraging the unionists to use slingshots to fire rocks at the Catholics, while they attacked a different opening into the Bogside with CS gas, armored vehicles, and water cannons.

Bernadette Devlin was again a leader of the Catholic defenders of the Bogside. "We threw up barricades of rubble, pipe, and paving stones," she recalled. "Anything we could get our hands on to prevent the police coming straight into the area and, in their own words, 'settling the Bogside once and for all.'" Devlin led the manufacture of Molotov cocktails, or what the Irish call 'petrol bombs.'

"They were made, literally, by pregnant women and children. Kids of seven or eight who couldn't fight, made the petrol bombs, and they made them pretty well. Kids of nine or ten carried them in crates to the front lines. The young girls collected stones and built the barricades, and the girls, the boys, and the men fought on the front line with the police. The police answered our stones and petrol bombs with stones of their own, and with ever increasing supplies of tear gas."

The Derry fighting expanded into Belfast, where the RUC began attacking the Catholic areas with armored cars equipped with high-velocity .50 caliber Browning machine-guns mounted on turrets. They began firing in bursts that tore through the walls of the row houses, one of them killing Patrick Rooney, a sleeping nine-year-old boy.

On August 13th, Jack Lynch, the leader of the Republic of Ireland, gave an impassioned speech condemning the actions of the RUC and suggesting that the United Nations should send a peacekeeping force to Northern Ireland. He also secretly consulted his cabinet about sending Irish forces into Northern Ireland for a humanitarian effort. The next day, beating Ireland and the UN to the punch, the British deployed their troops to Derry and Belfast, beginning an occupation that would last 30 years. The British troops put an end to the immediate fighting but would soon become considered by many to be the worst villains in "The Troubles".

The Battle of the Bogside lasted for three days and nights. Ten people were killed, 154 were wounded by gunfire, and 745 others injured. More than 1,800 families (75% of them Catholic) were displaced from their damaged or burnt homes. Bernadette Devlin was arrested. There was a possibility she might have been charged with the extremely serious crime of sedition (treason) for encouraging British soldiers and Irish soldiers to desert and come to aid of the community, but she was ultimately jailed for only a short term in December for 'inciting to riot.'

The bloom was off the rose as far as the British were concerned. "To begin with, I was the greatest publicity gimmick since Kraft cheese slices," says Devlin, "but it wasn't long before people discovered the final horrors of letting an urchin into Parliament. The British had shown what grand democrats they were: anybody, even a Northern Ireland brat of 22 was allowed to sit in their House of Commons. And what did these ungrateful Irish peasants do, when you made them Members of Parliament and gave them 3,200 pounds a year? They simply went home and threw stones at you." [81]

The Irish Catholics unexpectedly found themselves touted as the new masters of urban revolution. "We had an influx of foreign revolutionary journalists searching for illumination on the Theory of Petrol Bomb Fighting," remembers Devlin. "The people of the Bogside thought it was fantastic: they didn't know how to spell revolution, never mind work it out, but they were really delighted with themselves that people should come from the Sorbonne to ask the unemployed of Bogside where they learned to fight so well."

Soon after her arrest at the Battle of the Bogside, Devlin headed to the U.S. to try to get support from Irish-Americans. She met with Black Panthers in Watts and gave them her support, and she was introduced to America on The Tonight Show with Johnny Carson. Johnny was receptive, but she found Irish Americans conservative and unsupportive. She refused to speak at an event in Detroit when she found that blacks were not allowed in. She was to be presented the key to New York City by Mayor John Lindsay but frustrated by the Irish community in the U.S., she left the country before the ceremony. The man she sent in her stead, fellow organizer Eamonn McCann, gifted the key, in a witty display of revolutionary solidarity, to the Harlem chapter of the Black Panthers.

• • •

Just to remind people of Mother Nature's power, another storm, even more powerful than Bernadette Devlin, was also crossing the Atlantic. Hurricane Camille did more damage to Cuba than ten years of the American embargo. After clobbering Cuba, Camille roared across the Gulf of Mexico where it strengthened to a Category Five storm packing

175 mph (280 km/h) winds. One of the most powerful hurricanes ever, it crossed into Mississippi on August 18 and headed north, destroying or damaging thousands of homes and trailers, doing $1.42 billion damage, causing 256 deaths, and reaching as far as Newfoundland.

• • •

Another storm was blowing at the same time that would turn the most celebrated rock festival ever into a mud bath. The Woodstock Festival of August 15 – 18 was formally billed as "An Aquarian Exposition of Peace & Music." Whether the thousands of attendees were revolutionaries or simply music-loving hedonists is debatable, but they certainly thought they were part of a counterculture revolution. Not even the torrential rain of the weekend could dampen the spirits of the music-loving hippies. The establishment felt differently. On the Sunday of the festival, Nelson Rockefeller, Governor of New York State, called one of the organizers, John P. Roberts, and told him he was thinking of ordering 10,000 National Guard troops to control or shut down the festival. Max Yasgur, the farmer who owned the land that was the site of the event (and who was vilified by his neighbors for allowing it), spoke of how nearly half a million people had peacefully spent three days on his farm, saying, "If we join them, we can turn those adversaries that are the problems of today into a hope for a brighter and more peaceful future." Indicative of the culture wars of the period, the *New York Times* ran an editorial titled NIGHTMARE IN THE CATSKILLS which read in part, "The dreams of marijuana and rock music that drew 300,000 fans and hippies to the Catskills had little more sanity than the impulses that drive the lemmings to march to their deaths in the sea. They ended in a nightmare of mud and stagnation…What kind of culture is it that can produce so colossal a mess?" There was, though, considerable push-back to this frenzied negativity from both the newspaper's reporters and from readers and eventually the *Times* recanted with articles describing the largely successful, peaceful festival.

"Yeah, it's far out, man," folk singer Arlo Guthrie blathered to the huge crowd. "I don't know if you…I don't know, uh—like how many of you can dig how many people there are, man. Like, I was rappin' to the fuzz—right? Can you dig it? Man, there's supposed to be a million and a half people here by tonight. Can you dig that? Thruway's closed, man. Yeah! Lotta freaks." There were certainly never a million and half people there, but it was a gigantic crowd—probably over 400,000, plus at least three brand new babies who were born at the festival.

The Saturday night concert ran until 9:30 AM Sunday morning. Yippie activist Abbie Hoffman interrupted The Who's 5 AM performance with a revolutionary diatribe, reminding the giant crowd that "The revolution is more than digging rock and roll or turning on. The revolution is about coming together in a struggle for change. It's about the destruction of a system based on bosses and competition and the building of a system based on people and cooperation." The Who, though, owned the stage at that point in the proceedings, and bandleader Pete Townsend wasn't about to share it with some acidhead anarchist, however big a name he might be. Townsend ignominiously shoved Hoffman out of the spotlight.

The Jefferson Airplane was the final band to perform that day, ending their set with their song, *Revolution*. The climactic Sunday concert began at 2 PM and ended at 11 AM Monday morning. At 7 PM Country Joe and the Fish performed their hit song condemning the Vietnam War, *I Feel Like I'm Fixin' to Die Rag.* Jimi Hendrix closed the festival with an electric, psychedelic version of *The Star-Spangled Banner.*

• • •

Not everyone, of course, was enamored with the longhaired counterculture hippie lifestyle. On September 29, Merle Haggard's counter-counterculture anthem *Okie From Muskogee* was released, and soon rose to #1 on the country music charts and #41 on the *Billboard* Hot 100 chart. Haggard claims he wrote the song to support the troops fighting in Vietnam. "We were in a wonderful place in America and music was in a wonderful place.

America was at its peak, and what the hell did these kids have to complain about? These soldiers were giving up their freedom and their lives to make sure that others could stay free. I wrote the song to support those soldiers." Within a few years, the songwriter began to have misgivings about the hippie-knocking song. While he continued to perform it, he began to treat it ironically, like a quaint outdated museum piece. Like so many people in this era, his position changed as the years rolled on. "I sing the song now with a different attitude…I've become educated…I play it now with a different projection. It's a different song now. I'm different now."

• • •

On September 1, military officers led by Colonel Muammar Gaddafi overthrew King Idris I in the el-Fateh Revolution in Libya. Gaddafi had been born in the desert to a family of nomadic, illiterate, Bedouin camel-herders. He was a real revolutionary and a highly divisive figure. He was loved by much of the Libyan population and hated by the rest. French students claimed he was "the only Third World leader with any real stomach for struggle." Ronald Reagan referred to him as "the mad dog of the Middle East," even though Libya is not in fact in the Middle East but instead in North Africa. Regardless, Reagan's air force pilots knew where it was and attacked it on April 15, 1986. Gaddafi held on to power until October 20, 2011, when he was brutally killed during the Libyan Civil War.

• • •

The day after Gaddafi's revolutionary coup, September 2, was the last day on earth for the 79-year-old leader of North Vietnam, Ho Chi Minh. Ho was a revered figure, considered one of the most influential leaders in the world, an intellectual and poet as well as a political and military leader. In his youth, he had widely travelled the world as a sailor and chef, and he spoke fluently in English, French, Mandarin, Cantonese,

Russian, and Esperanto as well as his native Vietnamese. He began his political education in the U.S., England, France, and Russia. He lived in exile from Vietnam from 1911 until 1941. While in England, he was particularly influenced by the battles of the Irish against the British, especially by Terence MacSwiney, who during his 74-day hunger strike in Brixton Prison famously said, "It is not those who can inflict the most but those who can suffer the most who will conquer." Ho followed this maxim while leading his country on its long wars against the French and then the Americans. Over two million Vietnamese died in the 'American War' as well as 58,200 Americans. Still, even though Ho did not live to see it, the Americans withdrew; the Viet Cong and North Vietnam won, and Saigon is now Ho Chi Minh City. Although the Vietnamese paid a terrible price for their independence, they understood a basic truth that did not seem evident to the Americans. As Ho's foreign minister later said, "We knew that they could not stay in Vietnam forever, but Vietnam must stay in Vietnam forever."

• • •

With a similar kind of thinking to Donald Trump's idea that nuclear bombs might be able to destroy hurricanes, the U.S. Atomic Energy Commission came up with the concept that atomic bombs might be exploded underground to release natural gas. When environmentalists learned that the AEC planned to explode a 33-kiloton bomb under a Colorado mountain in order to 'frack' the shale bed below, they determined to use some 'people power' to try to stop it. Activist Chester McQueary recalls, "We scattered over the mountain in twos and threes, so that we could not all be removed by the authorities in one fell swoop. At 30 minutes before blast time, we set off smoke flares to confirm for AEC officials that we were still on the mountain and inside the quarantine zone." [82] Most of the protestors were yanked off the mountain at gunpoint, but McQueary and his fellow protestor Margaret Puls were on a slope that was too steep for the Air Force helicopters to land so they were left alone. "There was a mighty WHUMP and a long rumble moved through the earth, lifting us eight inches or more in the air" he says. "We felt aftershocks as we lay there looking at each other, grateful that we were still breathing and all in one piece."

The nuclear experiment appeared to work. The bomb vaporized enough rock to open up a 300-foot-high, 150-foot-wide underground cavern, and the miners were able to start extracting gas. There were only three problems. First, the gas was discovered to now be highly radioactive. Second, the value of the extracted gas was only about 40% of the high cost of extracting it (atom bombs aren't cheap). Third, the brave protestors like McQueary and Puls turned the American public off the whole idea. By 1973 the AEC gave up on its grand scheme of digging for natural gas with atomic bombs.[83]

• • •

On September 10, a riot broke out regarding the ongoing battle over the use of French in Québec schools. More than 1500 nationalists and separatists, including the radical *Chevaliers de l'Indépendence* battled a group of recent Italian immigrants and other new Canadians, who were defending the right to use English in the classroom. Hundreds of police got involved, tear gas canisters and Molotov cocktails were thrown, and 118 businesses had their windows smashed. The mayor of Saint-Léonard read the Riot Act. Thirty-seven were arrested. The event led to the passage of a new law in the Québec legislature regarding minority language rights that led to more street protests and the bombing of an English language educational institution, Loyola College.

• • •

September 23 saw the premiere of *Butch Cassidy and the Sundance Kid*—a big, glossy glorification of two outlaws from the Wild West era of the 1890s. In an unintentional manner, the story mirrored that of Che

Guevara. Like Che, the pair, played by Paul Newman and Robert Redford, went on the run to Bolivia, where, again like Che, their lives were ended by a hail of bullets from the military. The movie became one of the favorite films of the Weathermen and other militant revolutionaries. The writer, William Goldman, won an Academy Award for the film. Goldman also coined the famous phrase, "Nobody knows anything," which although written to describe the uncertainty of success in the film business, is also perhaps an appropriate maxim for this very fractious era.

• • •

On the next day, September 24, one of the wildest and most infamous trials in history began in Chicago. The defendants—Abbie Hoffman, Jerry Rubin, Tom Hayden, David Dellinger, Bobby Seale, Rennie Davis, John Froines, and Lee Weiner were defended by celebrity radical lawyer William Kunstler. They were up against an almost cartoonishly antagonistic, elderly judge, Julius Hoffman. Abbie Hoffman and Jerry Rubin turned the trial into political theatre. On one day, the pair arrived in court dressed in judicial robes. When the judge ordered them to take them off, they did—to reveal that underneath they were wearing uniforms of the Cook County police. Abbie Hoffman made much of the fact that he and the judge shared the same name, and at one point blew the judge a good morning kiss, an action which his honor angrily told the jury to disregard. On another occasion the younger Hoffman told the judge in Yiddish that he was a *shande fur de goyim* (a disgrace in front of the gentiles). The circus continued.

The Cook County Jail gave six of the defendants forced haircuts while they were incarcerated. The *New York Times* reported that Cook County Sheriff Joseph I. Woods displayed pictures of the shorn defendants at his speaking engagements, in one case "to about 100 laughing and applauding members of the Elk Grove Township Republican organization at a meeting in the suburban Mount Prospect Country Club."

The prosecution had only added Bobby Seale to the conspiracy trial because they felt that as a Black Panther, he would make the group look more dangerous. In fact, he barely knew any of the other 'conspirators' and had been in Chicago for less than 24 hours. Further, since his lawyer was ill, he was not represented at the trial. Seale objected to the proceedings on dozens of occasions because they were proceeding without his lawyer. Finally, the judge ordered that Seale be bound and gagged, and chained to a chair. This sight caused such an uproar that on November 5th the judge declared a mistrial for Seale. The Chicago Eight became the Chicago Seven, and their trial continued into 1970.

In solidarity with the defendants, the Weathermen planted their first bomb, blowing up a statue in Chicago that commemorated the policemen killed in the 1886 Haymarket Riot. In an unrelated but equally dramatic explosion on the same day, the FLQ ignited a bomb at the home of Montréal mayor Jean Drapeau.

• • •

On the other side of the continent, 7,000 activists blocked the Peace Arch land crossing from the US into Canada to protest a proposed U.S. explosion of a nuclear bomb at Amchitka Island in the Aleutian chain of islands off Alaska. The island is on the tectonically unstable 'Ring of Fire', so apart from all the other issues involved with nuclear testing, scientists warned of the possibility of the large nuclear explosion triggering earthquakes and tsunamis. The protestors held signs reading 'Don't Make a Wave' and 'It's Your Fault if our Fault Goes.' The Peace Arch protest was the first action of the movement that would within a year become Greenpeace, the biggest environmental activist group ever.

• • •

On October 7th, Jim Duncan exploded a bomb at the Selective Service Induction Center on Whitehall Street in Manhattan, and the same day the police went out on a wildcat strike in Montréal. This led to rioting, a death, an attack on the Murray Hill Limousine Service by the FLQ, dozens of robberies of banks and homes, radicalized taxi drivers, and the theft of hundreds of firearms by the FLQ.

The next day, there was an equally violent event in Chicago. October 8th was the second anniversary of the death of Che Guevara, and the Weathermen wanted to not just honor their hero but "bring the war back home" with some revolutionary violence to the Mother Country. They called it the 'Days of Rage' but it turned out to be only one day, because within hours of the start of the event, in which hundreds of hard-core militants took to the streets armed with poles, clubs, helmets, gas masks and flak jackets, smashing dozens of windows and whooping *Battle of Algiers* war chants, they were beaten and shot at by the police and more than half the Weather Brigade was arrested.

• • •

The militants of New York, Montréal, and Chicago were drunk on confrontation and an overblown confidence in their ability to make revolutionary change. While they were smashing things on the streets, a far more transformational experiment was taking place in computer labs. On October 29th, probably the most revolutionary action of this period or indeed of the last half of the 20th century took place, with the creation of the Internet. Four computers, one each at UCLA, UC Santa Barbara, the University of Utah, and the Stanford Research Institute were linked together and then began to communicate. It was an ignominious beginning since it was only a one-word message – LOGIN – and the overloaded computer system crashed after the first two letters were typed, but it was a start, and proof that it might be possible for the world to communicate instantaneously with words and eventually images using computers and satellites.

• • •

October and November were the climactic months of the battle in America over the Vietnam War. In the autumn of 1969, over two million people in America marched to protest the war. The new president Richard Nixon claimed he was trying to bring the war to an end, but he continued to hammer North Vietnam with bombing. Another 10,000 U.S. soldiers had already been killed under his command. Many Americans suspected he had plans for increased warfare, and they were right. He and Henry Kissinger planned a savage attack for the end of the year, one that would possibly involve nuclear weapons. It was only the massive demonstrations on the streets of Washington that stopped them from carrying it out.

Nixon claimed that "Under no circumstances will I be affected, as policy made in the streets equals anarchy." Comedian Dick Gregory, responded by saying, "The President says nothing you kids do will have any effect on him. Well, I suggest he make one long-distance call to the LBJ ranch."

Nixon's Vice-President Spiro Agnew was sent out to fight back, which he did with his characteristically inflammatory rhetoric. "A spirit of national masochism prevails," he claimed, "encouraged by an effete corps of impudent snobs who characterize themselves as intellectuals." He added that he believed the upcoming Moratorium March would be controlled by "hardcore dissidents and professional anarchists" who would plan "wilder, more violent" demonstrations.

There seemed to be some possible truth to that when just days before the giant November protest, bombers Sam Melville and Jane Alpert set off explosives at the New York offices of Standard Oil, the Chase Manhattan Bank, General Motors, and the New York Criminal Courts building where the Panther 21 trial was being held. The following day, November 12th, the pair were fingered by an FBI informant and arrested while setting more dynamite in National Guard trucks outside a New York armory.

The bombings got the President more support from what he called the "Silent Majority," but on the same day, November 12th, the New York

Times revealed the details of the My Lai Massacre in a bombshell report by Seymour Hersh that turned thousands more Americans against the war.

Three days later, well over half a million people marched against the war in front of the White House. Another quarter million marched in San Francisco. High school students there were forbidden from participating by the school board, who claimed it was "unpatriotic," so instead over 50% of them struck from school and had their own march.

Nixon seethed about the marches, obsessively watching television coverage and peering from the windows of the White House to see how many people were participating. He proposed sending helicopters to blow out the candles that the marchers were carrying. Instead, police arrived with tear gas. The massive, peaceful rallies featured music by Leonard Bernstein, John Denver, and Pete Seeger who led the crowd singing John Lennon's new anthem *Give Peace a Chance*. Speeches by Coretta Scott King, Averell Harriman, and Dr. Benjamin Spock attracted thousands more people to the anti-war movement.

Nixon publicly claimed the massive demonstrations had no effect on his policymaking, but privately he worried that he was going to lose the war. He could easily have persuaded the North Vietnamese to a ceasefire, but he would not agree to stop bombing Hanoi. The first demand of the North Vietnamese was that they would not agree to any settlement until the U.S. stopped bombing their country.

• • •

While this was happening, few people were aware that a possibly even bigger threat of nuclear war was developing between China and the U.S.S.R. In the summer, in retaliation for the February Chinese attack on Damansky Island, 300 Soviet soldiers backed by helicopters and armored vehicles had launched a surprise attack across the Chinese border at Xinjiang. Now, hardliners in Moscow began arguing for the need to remove the 'China threat' with a nuclear attack. In Washington, the Soviet embassy asked the Americans how they would react to a Russian attack on a Chinese nuclear facility. The Americans ignored the query.

The Chinese went into a frenzy constructing underground bunkers to protect themselves for the upcoming predicted nuclear war. Shanghai ultimately had an elaborate honeycomb of tunnels that could reportedly hold two and a half million people. The new underground city beneath Beijing covered an area of 85 square kilometers. The mud from all this digging was just piled up in the streets, an estimated 30,000 tons of debris and putrefying waste. Then the government got the idea that the people should all build small mud kilns in their yards to use the dirt to bake bricks to reinforce the underground bunkers. Molds, embossed with anti-Soviet slogans, were distributed for the creation of the bricks.

Small children were enlisted as tunnel rats to dig out the shelters. There were many collapses and hundreds of kids suffocated to death. Other young children paraded in formation on the streets, carrying wooden dummy rifles and diving to the ground to cover their eyes at the blast of a whistle. Once the second "Nuclear All Clear" whistle was given, the kids would jump up and continue marching.

One young teenager named Zhai Zhenhua remembered her feelings about the build-up to the expected nuclear holocaust: "War brings disaster but also opportunity. I would rather die heroically on the battlefield than live the hopeless life I had been given. And if I didn't die, things in China would definitely change for the better after the war, I thought. This was crazy, of course, but I was living in a crazy time." [84]

Mao, Zhou Enlai and Lin Biao became convinced that the Soviets were going to drop the big one on them on October 20. Mao hightailed it for Wuhan. Lin split for his bunker in Suzhou, then put all military units on high alert. One million soldiers, 4,000 planes and 600 ships took up strategic positions across the country. The Chinese held their breath. October 20th came and…no bombs were dropped.

• • •

On November 7th, a Montréal demonstration called *Opération Libération* in support of releasing Pierre Vallières and Charles Gagnon from jail led to five bombs being set at City Hall, the police headquarters, and several banks.

• • •

A week later, on November 14th, the Saturn rocket carrying Apollo 12 blasted off from Cape Canaveral. It was the second attempt to land men on the moon. It was remarkable how much had changed since Apollo 11. The feat had been done before, so the world's attention was no longer rapt. The event was just as monumental, just as difficult, and just as dangerous but it was not treated as seriously by either the public or the astronauts. Instead, the spacemen handled their duties with a degree of the cocksure flippancy that characterized much of life in this period. Instead of the deadly serious words spoken by Neil Armstrong when he arrived on the moon, the diminutive Alan Bean jocularly noted, after jumping from the ladder, "Whoopie! Man, that may have been a small one for Neil, but that's a long one for me!" Bean said the words to try to collect a $500 bet that celebrated Italian journalist Oriana Fallaci made with him that he didn't have the nerve to be so cheeky. Bean and his partner Charles 'Pete' Conrad smuggled a camera timer aboard, without telling Mission Control, so they could take a selfie of themselves together on the moon. (Of course, they did not refer to it as a 'selfie' since the expression would not be coined until 2002.) Once they arrived on the moon, they began using a series of flip-cards designed to guide them through all the operations they were to make. They discovered that their fellow astronauts, knowing the pair slightly resented the tedious nature of the geological experiments the scientists wanted them to perform, had inserted, again without the knowledge of the Mission Control brass, images of *Playboy* playmate centerfolds in amongst the directions.

• • •

On November 20th, their Lunar Module *Intrepid* lifted off from the moon, reconnected with the command module, and successfully returned to earth. The same day, there was a very different voyage being made in San Francisco Bay. Richard Oakes was a Mohawk native from the Akwesasne reserve that straddles the U.S. and Canada on the St. Lawrence River. He had worked in the traditional profession of the Mohawks for some years as a high steel worker but left the skyscrapers of Manhattan to live in San Francisco where he became an activist for Native rights. On November 9th he was one of a number of natives who sailed from Fisherman's Wharf to Alcatraz Island.

From 1910 to 1963, Alcatraz had been first a military and then a maximum-security prison. It was now abandoned. Native groups in the 1960s were determined to find a way to protest years of discrimination and abuse. After discovering provisions of the old treaties that promised Natives the use of federal property abandoned or unused by the government, the United Indians of All Tribes decided to attempt to occupy Alcatraz. They claimed it under the terms of the 1868 Treaty of Fort Laramie and demanded that it be turned into an Indian education and cultural center.

The first event was meant to be only a symbolic circling of the island that was designed to draw the attention of the press to their plans. However, when the Canadian schooner they chartered for the short voyage drew close, Richard Oakes impetuously leapt into the water and struck out for the island. The panicked skipper ordered everyone else to stay on board, but three others joined Oakes in the water. Oakes was shocked at the frigid water and strong currents but used his St. Lawrence River swimming skills to get to the island. He and the others were ultimately returned to the mainland by the Coast Guard but his rash action had cemented his position as leader and spokesperson for the occupation when it began in earnest.

On November 20th, seventy-eight Indians landed—men, women, and children from all over the country, including battle-hardened Vietnam veterans who took on the role of a security force. The Coast Guard immediately blockaded the island making it hard for them to get food or supplies but various yachts and fishing boats broke through the cordon, bringing donations from supporters. The authorities attempted to land, but the hardened and experienced Vietnam vets held them at bay. The radical protest got the Natives considerable attention and sympathy. Creedence Clearwater Revival bought them a boat, renamed the *Clearwater.* A film company bought them 28 teepees. Someone donated a generator, and Native plumbers located needed supplies to repair the toilets in the old prison.

Oakes, with his wife and five children beside him, announced to the press corps, "This is actually a move, not so much to liberate the island, but to liberate ourselves for the sake of cultural survival. We're only young people concerned about our future. And we might—might—wake up the conscience of America." [85]

The natives offered to purchase Alcatraz Island from the government for "$24 in glass beads and red cloth, a precedent set by the white man's purchase of a similar island [Manhattan] about 300 years ago." In deeply sarcastic manner they suggested that Alcatraz was "more than suitable for an Indian reservation, as determined by the white man's own standards," as "it has no fresh running water, inadequate sanitation facilities, no educational facilities, no health care facilities, and the population has always been held as prisoners and kept dependent on others."

Unfortunately, the Alcatraz occupation worked better symbolically than practically. It continued into the new year, but degenerated into anarchy, and would witness a grim tragedy at the beginning of 1970.

• • •

The vicious fighting continued in Biafra, with France, Spain, South Africa and other countries supporting Biafra while England, the U.S., and others supported Nigeria. The greatest toll was on the children of Biafra, hundreds of thousands of whom suffered from extreme malnutrition from Nigeria's blockade. Thousands of Britons protested England's support of

Nigeria. One of them was John Lennon, who sent the MBE honor given to him in 1965 back to the Queen with a note reading, "Your Majesty, I am returning this MBE in protest against Britain's involvement in the Nigeria-Biafra thing, against our support of America in Vietnam, and against *Cold Turkey* slipping down the charts. With love, John Lennon."

• • •

The language battles in Québec continued with the bombing and destruction of a greenhouse at McGill University on November 30th. The bombers left their calling card but no explanation of what exactly an experimental botany greenhouse had to do with the issues or the struggle. Of course, the bomb broke a lot of glass, which was always popular.

Two of the FLQ bombers, Normand Roy and Michel Lambert, fled Québec and headed first for Paris, then Algeria, then Jordan, where they joined a Palestinian terrorist training camp and were schooled, along with 60 other commandos, the rest all Arab, in Marxist thought and the use of AK-47's.

• • •

The wild trial in Chicago continued through the fall. Bobby Seale, unsupported by any legal counsel, was given advice throughout the trial by Fred Hampton, the Chairman of the Illinois chapter of the Black Panther Party. This irritated Judge Julius Hoffman and increased the already intense attention of the authorities on Hampton. The FBI had infiltrated an informer named Bill O'Neal into Hampton's circle. On the evening of December 3rd, Hampton taught a course on political education at a Chicago church after which a number of Panthers, including agent O'Neal, returned for a dinner at Hampton's apartment. During the meal O'Neal slipped a sedative, Secobarbital, into Hampton's drink, and a few minutes later the Chairman fell asleep in the midst of a telephone call with his mother.

At 4 AM the next morning, 14 heavily armed members of the Special Prosecutions Unit of the FBI, provided with warrants by Cook County State's Attorney Edward Hanrahan, broke down the door to the apartment and shot the one person who was awake, a guard named Mark Clark. The shotgun he was holding discharged into the ceiling; the only shot fired by the Panthers. The police fired over 90 shots, ripping the apartment apart with the gunfire. Hampton was hit twice in the shoulder by bullets, and then, according to Panther Harold Bell, a cop identified Hampton and then was asked by another in the squad whether he was dead. He was told, "He's alive. He'll make it." Bell then heard two more shots ring out and then the words from one of the cops, "He's good and dead now." [86]

Seven other Panthers were all shot and wounded while sleeping, then beaten up and arrested on charges of aggravated assault and attempted murder of the officers. The police proclaimed the 'bravery' and 'restraint' of their Tact Squad, and released photos to the press, later shown to be fake, of the holes in walls supposedly made by Panther gunfire.

Two days after the murder, on Saturday, December 6th, members of the Weather Underground demonstrated their solidarity with Hampton and the Panthers and their outrage over the murder by blowing up numerous Chicago police vehicles in a retaliatory bombing spree. The group's leader, Bernardine Dohrn, announced, "We've known that our job is to lead white kids into armed revolution...Kids know the lines are drawn; revolution is touching all of our lives. Tens of thousands have learned that protest and marches don't do it. Revolutionary violence is the only way." William Sullivan, Deputy Director of the FBI, announced that the Weathermen organization, "has the potential to be far more damaging to the security of this nation than the Communist Party ever was, even at the height of its strength in the 1930s."

The Hampton murder case went through many trials and inquests. In 1992, a group of nine plaintiffs including the mothers of Hampton and Clark received a $1.85 million settlement for the killing, the largest ever for a civil rights case. Their attorney described it as "an admission of the conspiracy that existed between the FBI and Hanrahan's men to murder Fred Hampton." Twelve years later the city of Chicago declared December 4, 2004 as Fred Hampton Day, and three years after that unveiled a sculpted bust of Hampton outside the newly named Fred Hampton Family Aquatic Center.

• • •

On the same Saturday as the Hampton murder, one of the most notorious and deadly musical events of all time took place in California. Following accusations that the ticket prices had been too high ($8! Shocking!) on their recent North American tour, the Rolling Stones agreed to do a free concert at the Altamont Speedway near San Francisco. The disastrous concert ended with four deaths, one of them the murder by the Hells Angels of a black man in front of the stage, as the Stones sang their rock anthems *Gimme Shelter* and *Sympathy for the Devil*. One of the Angels was charged with the murder but was ultimately acquitted. Three days after the Altamont murder, the Los Angeles District Attorney's office announced the arrest of Charles Manson and his followers for the murders of Sharon Tate and four others in August. Many conflated Altamont and the Manson murders together as symbolizing the end of the hippie era of 'peace and love.'

• • •

As if to confirm this, on December 12th, a bomb exploded at the headquarters of the *Banca Nazionale dell' Agricoltura* at the Piazza Fontana in Milan, Italy, killing 17 people and wounding 88. The same afternoon three more bombs exploded in Rome and Milan and another was found undetonated. The bombings were attributed to Italian anarchists and 80 people were arrested. The main suspect, Giuseppe Pinelli supposedly committed suicide while in custody by jumping out of a window, but three police officers were later put under investigation for his death. One of them was later murdered by left-wing militants in retaliation.

In fact, the bombings were 'false-flag' operations by the extreme right wing neo-Fascist organization *Ondine Nuevo*, that were designed to discredit the Italian left. The group had received training and advice from the Greek dictatorship led by George Papandopolous. A U.S. Navy officer, David Carrett, was also indicted for his participation in the bombings, and the head of the Italian secret service SID and a member of the highly secret pseudo-Masonic society P2 (*Propaganda Duo*) were implicated in the cover-up of the right-wing bombing plot.

• • •

In another court case, Bernadette Devlin was found guilty of incitement to riot in the Battle of the Bogside incident and was jailed. Soon after her release, she was re-elected to the British House of Commons and declared she would sit as an independent socialist.

• • •

From December 26 – 30, the similarly named Bernardine Dohrn led the Weathermen in their 'Wargasm' National War Council in Flint, Michigan. Suspecting that they might be infiltrated by FBI agents, they demanded that everyone at the meeting take LSD, as they felt that no-one could stay undercover while under the influence of acid. Perhaps the drug can be blamed for the more idiotic statements that came out of the meeting, including a paean to the Manson gang. "Dig it!" exclaimed Dohrn. "First, they killed those pigs, then they ate dinner in the same room with them, then they even shoved a fork into the victim's stomach. Wild!" Another Weatherman proposed attacking the Strategic Air Command's base in nearby Dayton, Ohio, to destroy the hydrogen bombs that were stored there. "It's time to get down," declared the 'Weather Bureau.' "Any kind of action that fucks up the pig's war and helps the people win is a good kind of action." They ended the event with what one of them later called "a collective puberty rite"— some heavy dancing and fucking until the early morning, then broke up to go totally underground to make war on America.

• • •

So ended one of the most colorful and unique decades in history. Let Abbie Hoffman have the last word on it: "The '60s are gone—dope will never be as cheap, sex never as free, and the rock and roll never as great."

1970

Native Accident, Acid is Groovy / Kill the Pigs,
Weathermen Townhouse Explodes, Earth Day Begins,
Kent State Killings, Angela Davis On The Run,
Juan Peron In Exile, Gay Pride, Timothy Leary Escapes,
Phone Phreaking, Canada in Crisis, Pierre Laporte Killed,
Germaine Greer Gets Radical, The Beatles Implode.

On New Year's Day, three Wisconsin activists from a group calling themselves the 'Vanguard of the Revolution' brought in the new decade by stealing an ROTC plane and dropping bombs on an army ammunition plant outside Madison. It made the news but was not terribly shocking. By a conservative count, there were some 250 bombings in America between September 1969 and May 1970—an average of about one a day. The government claimed the number was as much as six times higher.[87] Of course, even that would only be a tiny fraction of the number being dropped on Vietnam in the same period.

• • •

On January 3rd, Yvonne Oakes, the 12-year-old stepdaughter of Native organizer Richard Oakes, fell through a broken railing and down a stairwell in Alcatraz Prison. There was so much acrimony by this point towards her father that there were even rumors that she had been pushed. Oakes left the island with his badly injured stepdaughter and never returned. It was the end of his role as leader of the protest. Yvonne died from her injuries in San Francisco on the 8th.

A few days later, Jane Fonda visited Alcatraz, inspired by the Native protest, and concerned about the tragic death of the young girl. It was really the beginning of Fonda's new life. She soon became one of the leading activists of the era and certainly the one with the highest profile. While on the island, Fonda met with some of the most militant of the Natives— LaNada Means, the sister of leader Russell Means, Vietnam vet Sid Mills, and the leaders of the Sioux tribe, who encouraged her to visit reservations around the country to see for herself what Natives were up against. Fonda not only agreed to do that but soon began to make big changes in her personal life. She left playboy French director Roger Vadim and became involved with political activist Fred Gardner, one of the writers of Michaelangelo Antonioni's revolutionary new film, *Zabriskie Point*. Gardner turned her on to the G.I. coffeehouses that were sprouting up near military bases and acting as hubs for disaffected soldiers. Through him she met activist lawyer Mark Lane and film publicist Steve Jaffe, and soon the foursome were visiting the coffeehouses near Ford Ord and Fort Lewis and skillfully using Fonda's huge celebrity to bring attention to the movement.

The death of the 12-year-old, the national press attention that Fonda's visits engendered, and some draconian plans by the local authorities to forcefully remove the natives from the island all led to President Richard Nixon to assign some of his senior staff to try to find a solution to the impasse. Nixon had little empathy for Blacks, students, or women's libbers. He did, though, have a certain amount for Natives, largely because of his respect for his high-school football coach, an Indian, who had gone on to become a big political supporter of his former player. By the summer,

Nixon's team had come up with a few constructive solutions to the many issues facing Natives in America, and the occupation ended, if not amicably, at least peacefully.

The amount of time Nixon's team spent thinking about Native issues was miniscule compared to the time they spent conspiring to defeat anyone they perceived as liberal, progressive, or a potential political enemy. One of the many people on Nixon's ever-growing 'enemies list' was William O. Douglas, a justice on the U.S. Supreme Court. Douglas had served on the Court since 1939—the longest term in its history. His many records as a judge still stand. He gave more speeches, was more widely travelled, wrote more books (over 30) and had more marriages (four). He is considered the most committed civil libertarian ever on the court. Republicans hated that as well as his passing judgement on numerous cases in favor of the disadvantaged, he was also a fierce environmentalist and strong opponent of the war in Vietnam. Through 1970, Gerald Ford, then Republican House Minority Leader, later, of course, Nixon's Vice-President and the man who replaced him as President, led the charge against Douglas. Ford attempted to impeach the judge, accusing him of embracing "a hippy-yippie-style revolution", and mocking him for his support of environmentalism, his "liberal opinions," and "his defense of that filthy film, *I Am Curious (Yellow)*". As part of the government's efforts to take down Douglas (which ultimately failed), the judge revealed that the FBI had conducted a sting operation against him in which they planted marijuana on his property.

• • •

On January 11th Timothy Leary entered an Orange County courtroom to face charges for the Laguna bust over the two marijuana 'roaches'. On the day the trial went to the jury, newspaper headlines in Orange County read DRUG CRAZED HIPPIES SLAY MOTHER AND CHILDREN. An army medical officer reported that a gang of longhairs had invaded his home, killed his wife and kids, and scrawled "Acid is Groovy. Kill the Pigs" in blood on the wall. Years later, the officer was himself convicted of the crime. At the time, though, the reporting in the press made it look like a repeat of the Manson insanity. It was a very bad omen for Timothy Leary, the world's most famous proselytizer of LSD-25. The jury returned a guilty verdict, and Leary spent five weeks in solitary confinement awaiting sentence. While in prison, the court in Houston gave him ten years for the 1965 bust in Laredo. The Orange County judge, calling Leary a "nuisance to society", then added another ten years to run consecutively, meaning that Leary, aged 49, was facing a virtual life sentence for two roaches and a bag of marijuana so small it could be hidden in his wife's underwear.

• • •

Two days later, a fistfight between black prisoners and members of the (white) Aryan Brotherhood broke out in the yard of California's Soledad Prison. From a tower, a white guard named Opie G. Miller shot and killed three black inmates. A supervisor later freely admitted that Miller was shooting to try to protect the white convicts. After the deaths were ruled "justifiable homicide", George Jackson and two others retaliated by killing a prison guard named John V. Mills. The trio were charged with murder.

Jackson's prison life had begun in 1960. He was charged with robbing a gas station of $70. His court-appointed lawyer convinced him he should plead guilty in order to get a light sentence that would be served in the county jail. He did, and instead received an indeterminant sentence of one year to life. He spent the next ten years in Soledad maximum security prison, seven and half of them in solitary confinement. While in Soledad, he co-founded the Black Guerrilla Family. He once said, "I met Marx, Lenin, Trotsky, Engels, and Mao in prison, and they redeemed me." He also met Fay Stender, a brilliant radical lawyer (and concert pianist). She began to represent him, and she also fell for him. On one occasion, at least according to the revisionist history *Destructive Generation: Second Thoughts About the Sixties,* prison guards "had to separate her physically from Jackson and drag her out of the visiting area with her clothes half off."

[88] Stender organized to get his writing published and got French intellectual (and ex-con) Jean Genet to write the foreword. Once released, *Soledad Brother: The Prison Letters of George Jackson* became a critical and commercial sensation.

• • •

Along with his many other sins, Richard Nixon can largely be blamed for shutting down the Apollo space program. In January, his administration cancelled Apollo 20, and in September it cancelled Apollo 18 and 19. Apollo 17 in 1972 would be the last mission to the moon. The Apollo program was of course instigated by John F. Kennedy, and so it was no great surprise that the ever-vindictive Nixon did not climb aboard. Money was another issue. The Vietnam War had already cost America $850 billion, and taxes had to be raised by 10% just to pay for it. As an alternative, NASA proposed creating Apollo X—a habitat on the Moon that might become a springboard to other planets, but Nixon wasn't interested in that either. According to space experts Alastair Storm Browne and Maryann Karinch, had Nixon not killed the Apollo program, we would likely have been on Mars by the 1980s. [89]

• • •

After the two-and-a-half-year war and the death from starvation of almost two million people (most of them young children), the break-away state of Biafra surrendered on January 15th. President Chukwuemeka Odumegwu Ojukwu fled to Côte d'Ivoire. The Igbos of Biafra suffered enormously from the defeat, losing most of their property and assets, and being extorted to the tune of $100 million a year by illegal roadblocks and other measures of the Nigerian security forces. Nigeria grew to become the richest country in Africa.

• • •

The censorship battles continued in England. On January 16th, John Lennon's art gallery exhibit *Bag One* was shut down by Scotland Yard for displaying "erotic lithographs". A week later a screening of Andy Warhol's film *Trash* was raided by the police, who not only confiscated the print but took the unprecedented action of arresting the entire audience of 200 people. Britain's official film censor, John Trevelyan later exonerated the film saying that "This is an intellectual film for a specialized audience. I have seen it, and while it is not my cup of tea, there is nothing at all corrupting about it." Neither filmmakers, film censors, nor the police knew what to expect in this heady, volatile period.

• • •

The Pentagon reported in January that there had been 73,121 deserters in 1969. There would be 89,088 more in 1970. By comparison there were approximately 20,000 deserters from the U.S. forces in all of World War II.

• • •

On January 26th, Simon & Garfunkle released *Bridge Over Troubled Waters*, a song that tried to sooth the beating heart of the period. It won "Song of the Year" and "Record of the Year" at the Grammys and became one of the best-selling hits of the 1970s.

• • •

Five days later, Mao Zedong, Zhou Enlai and the Central Committee of the Chinese Communist Party, ignoring the mellow message of *Bridge Over Troubled Waters*, re-opened the Cultural Revolution by calling for a strike against all 'counter-revolutionary activities' in order to eliminate all 'corruption, speculation, and waste.' This new campaign, termed "One Strike and Three Antis", was supposed to last for just ten months, but it was revived in 1971 when hundreds of thousands more people were found to be insufficiently loyal to the Cultural Revolution and were charged with crimes. In the city of Wuwei, so many doctors were arrested that the hospital was almost forced to close down. One was charged with the crime of "liking freedom." Another was accused of having listened to a foreign radio station way back in 1963. The victims were sent to jail, banished to one of the gulags, enlisted in local "re-education classes" denounced and paraded through the streets, or simply shot. Thousands, unable to handle the harassment, committed suicide.

• • •

There were 17 significant bombings in a two-week period between February 6 – 21 across America, including two bombs set by the Weathermen on February 12th outside the Berkeley Police complex that wounded a policeman, broke many windows, and destroyed some police cars.

• • •

On February 26th, during Québec-Palestine Solidarity Week, Jacques Lanctôt and Pierre Marcil were stopped for a faulty tail light. The police found a sawed-off rifle in their van, plus a wicker basket large enough to carry a body and a news release announcing the kidnapping of Moise Golan, the Israeli consul and trade attaché. Lanctôt was released on bail and went underground for six months. He would re-emerge in October as the instigator of the biggest internal crisis in Canada since the Riel Rebellion of 1885.

• • •

The cultural wars continued. On February 27th, the Jefferson Airplane was fined $1,000 for profanity in Oklahoma City, and five days later Janis Joplin was fined $200 for using obscene language in Tampa,

Florida. On March 6th, an album of Charles Manson's recorded songs, *Lie: The Love and Terror Cult* was released. Virtually no stores would stock it.

• • •

Also on March 6th, a gigantic explosion destroyed a townhouse at 18 West 11th Street in Greenwich Village in New York City. At first it was thought to be a simple gas explosion, but two women who survived the blast suspiciously disappeared. This led detectives to investigate further and to eventually discover that the elegant townhouse was being used by the Weathermen as a bomb factory. Three members of the leftwing paramilitary group were killed in the blast. The two who escaped, Kathy Boudin and Cathy Wilkerson, went on the lam. They continued their terrorist activities for ten more years. Wilkerson finally surrendered in 1980 and Boudin was captured after masterminding a deadly Brinks truck robbery in 1981.

There was an enormous amount of dynamite in the house. Had it all exploded, bomb experts believed the entire block would have been destroyed. As it was, the explosion completely destroyed the house and severely damaged the buildings on either side of it, one of which included the apartment of actor Dustin Hoffman, who was badly shaken but not injured by the event. The accident was very disruptive to the Weathermen organization; many left because of it, but those who remained coalesced under the leadership of Bernardine Dohrn and Bill Ayers and continued their war on America until the mid '70s. Two days after the explosion, on March 8th, Richard Nixon and Attorney General John Mitchell demanded that J. Edgar Hoover make the Weathermen and the Black Panthers his top priority. The FBI formed Squad 47—'the Weathermen Squad'.

• • •

Also on March 8th, 150 protestors from the United Indian People's Council, along with activists Jane Fonda and Mark Lane, marched on

Fort Lawton, Washington, in an attempt to take back land that Native Americans believed was rightfully theirs. Fonda became the star of the event. There were so many military guards ogling her and taking Polaroids that dozens of the native protestors were unnoticed as they made their way into the compound. Eventually, though, the event turned ugly. Trucks were overturned, Fonda and others roughed up, tear gas was fired and there were ten arrests. Still, it was ultimately a somewhat successful protest, as eventually the army did agree to turn over a section of the land for a native cultural center. But it also caused a schism in the Indian movement because some of the natives were angry that celebrity movie star Jane Fonda was getting the attention for their cause. The situation was exacerbated when Fonda went on *The Dick Cavett Show* to talk about her passion for their movement. She took native activist LaNada Means with her, but it was of course Fonda who got most of the attention. Some natives argued, inaccurately, that Fonda's activism was a hypocritical attempt at personal publicity. With these issues growing, Fonda began to shift her attention more from the Indian Movement toward the war in Vietnam.

• • •

Since the mid-60s, the North Vietnamese army, in order to give themselves a route into South Vietnam, had been infiltrating the northeastern third of Cambodia. Prince Sihanouk, the leader of Cambodia, at first tolerated the foreign presence in his country, but when the North Vietnamese began to support the anti-Sihanouk Khmer Rouge, he went to Moscow to ask them to rein in the North Vietnamese. When they did not, he lost power, and the country fell into a level of anarchy. On March 29, an enraged crowd fell upon the brother of Prime Minister Lon Nil, tore out his liver and cooked and ate it. Prince Sihanouk was deposed.

The new pro-American government demanded that the North Vietnamese leave. Instead, in support of the Khmer Rouge, the North Vietnamese army invaded, and began fighting against the Cambodian army. On March 29th the People's Army of Vietnam launched a major offensive into the northeast of Cambodia, and on the very same day the South Vietnamese and the Americans invaded the country in the south. Henry Kissinger tried to contain the war. He advised the American forces based in the capital Phnom Penh, "Don't think of victory; just keep it alive," but the American forces in Cambodia, under command of Admiral John S. McCain, Jr., who proprietarily called it "my war", kept demanding more troops, and arms. All across the Cambodian countryside, peasants began attacking the Vietnamese. Some were Viet Cong; many were civilians. On April 15th, the bodies of 500 Vietnamese floated down the Mekong River back into South Vietnam.

• • •

On April 4th, a man was stopped for speeding in Germany. He presented identification claiming to be German author Peter Chotjewitz, but police soon realized that he was in fact Andreas Baader, one of the founders of the Red Army Factions, wanted on charges connected to the fire-bombing of a department store in Frankfurt in 1968. He was jailed but within a few weeks he was sprung in an elaborate prison break masterminded by fellow RAF founder Ulrike Meinhof. Armed with pistols, she, Gundrun Ensslin, two other women and a masked man smuggled themselves into a meeting with Baader in the prison library for a phony 'interview'. He and his saviors all escaped. The group, which became known as the Baader-Meinhof Gang (despite the fact that the real leader of the group was really Ensslin), escaped to Jordan where they spent time in a Fatah training camp until they were expelled because of a "difference in attitudes."

The gang returned to terrorize Germany, and also to capture the imagination of the country with bombings and bank robberies from 1970 to 1972. Germany was still guilt-ridden because of their country's role in WWII, and a segment of the population felt some measure of sympathy with the group's anti-Nazi, anti-authoritarian, anti-capitalist stance. When they began robbing banks, journalists began comparing the gang to Bonnie and Clyde. Baader encouraged this allusion, announcing that his favorite movies were *Bonnie and Clyde* and *The Battle of Algiers*. A poll showed that a quarter of West Germans under the age of 40 were sympathetic toward the gang, and a tenth said they would hide a gang member from the police. Prominent intellectuals like Jean-Paul Sartre and Simone de Beauvoir stood up for the group, although when they actually met, Sartre described Baader as a twat (*"Quel con!"* were his actual words).[90] Baader's achilles heel proved to be the flashy stolen sports cars he liked to drive. An exotic Iso Rivolta IR 300 led to his downfall. The gang was captured after a lengthy shootout in Frankfurt in June, 1972.

• • •

On April 7th, Jane Fonda arrived at the Dorothy Chandler Pavilion for the Academy Awards. She was dressed like a movie star but gave the Black Panther clenched fist salute to the screaming fans, many of whom responded with boos. As expected, given her new polarizing activism, she lost the "Best Actress" award so did not get to make a speech, political or otherwise. However, later at Elizabeth Taylor's 'Oscar Losers Party' she rustled up some hefty checks for the Black Panthers from the Hollywood crowd following which she moved on to a Panther party to deliver the money. Two days later she left for Denver to participate in a 36 hour 'Fast for Peace' and afterwards made a stop at the Home Front Coffee Shop outside the Fort Carson military base in Colorado Springs. As the press now considered her the most interesting and colorful new personality of the anti-war movement since Abbie Hoffman, she was trailed by dozens of reporters and photographers. She was at Fort Carson to support a group of one hundred soldiers who had been thrown in the stockade for flashing peace signs reading 'We're Sick of the War' outside the army infirmary. After being kicked out of Fort Carson, Fonda and her partners, including lawyer Mark Lane, moved on to other army bases, where typically they were enthusiastically greeted by disaffected soldiers, then arrested, finger-printed, sometimes teargassed, and escorted away by military police.

• • •

On April 22nd, largely due to the response from activists and politicians to the grotesque Santa Barbara oil spill of the previous year, the world saw the first Earth Day. The event has grown to be recognized in 192 countries and is now considered the largest secular holiday in the world. It is celebrated by more than a billion people every year.

• • •

Two days later, Tricia Nixon invited Grace Slick to the White House for tea. The Jefferson Airplane singer arrived with Abbie Hoffman who was planning to spike Nixon's tea with LSD. She was turned away by the guards, who told her she was not on the FBI approved list.

• • •

Both francophones and anglophones were convinced there would be separation if the Parti *Québecoise* won the Québec election of April 29th. A few days before the vote, the Royal Trust Company loaded eight armored trucks with all the cash, securities and valuables from their Montréal bank vaults and shipped them to Toronto for safekeeping. When the big day came, the *PQ* won 25% of the vote but only six seats, which resulted in an increased demand for revolutionary rather than electoral action.

• • •

The next day, April 30th, Nixon announced that the U.S. had invaded Cambodia. American college campuses exploded with protest.

• • •

The following day, the Puerto Rican group nationalist group MIRA set off a bomb in the Loew's Paradise in the Bronx during a screening of *The Liberation of L. B. Jones*, a potboiler about Southern racism and Southern cops. Indicative of the increasingly cavalier attitude of people toward bombings, the police tried to clear the theater, but the audience refused to leave and demanded to see the rest of the movie.

• • •

Jane Fonda moved on from meeting with small groups of disaffected and angry soldiers to speaking in front of large student assemblies. On May 4th, she spoke to an overflow crowd at the University of New Mexico. "Suddenly I feel the flood gates are opening," she cried. "You have to express what you feel. What I feel is rage, rage at being lied to—rage because I am a woman." As she was beginning to wrap up her talk, the famed poet Gregory Corso unexpectedly stumbled onto the stage. Corso is the beatnik poet acclaimed for his writing and credited with introducing the beat expressions like 'man', 'cool', 'dig', 'chick' and 'hung up' into the popular idiom. Now he grabbed Fonda's mike and demanded to know "why in the fuck" she hadn't mentioned the four students who had just been shot by the National Guard at Kent State University in Ohio. This was news to both Fonda and the students. Once the news was confirmed, they rapidly massed to demand that the New Mexico university shut down in protest.

The same thing happened across the country, with more than four million students striking at over 100 universities and colleges, and rampaging at Princeton, Stanford, Yale and the University of Kansas. Naturally, there was widespread revulsion and outrage over the government murders at Kent State University. However, not from the so-called 'Silent Majority.' A Gallup Poll showed that 58% of respondents blamed the student protestors for the deaths. The response to Kent State widened the already huge gulf between the generations. Historian Howard Means chronicled the stories of many students from Kent and other universities who returned home after the killings to be told by their parents that more students should have been killed to teach the student protestors a lesson. The subsequent angry family rows meant that students ended up being disowned by their families over the pivotally contentious event.[91]

The callousness of President Nixon's response to the Kent State massacre was not known until years later, when reporter Bob Woodward uncovered a White House recording of Nixon reacting to the Attica prison killings. "This might have one hell of a salutary effect," Nixon mused to his Chief of Staff H. R. Haldeman. "They can talk all they want about the radicals. You know what stops them? Kill a few."

As Haldeman grunted his agreement, Nixon continued, "Remember Kent State? Didn't it have a hell of an effect, the Kent State thing?"

"Sure did," replied Haldeman. "Gave 'em second thoughts." [92]

Publicly, Nixon was slightly more circumspect, merely calling the students, "bums", and the protesting G.I.'s "alleged soldiers and veterans."

A few days later, Fonda was the keynote speaker at an anti-war rally in Washington DC with 100,000 in attendance. She began her speech with, "Greetings, fellow bums." She continued across the country as a leader of the GI's Against the War movement. The FBI had her under full surveillance. G-men followed her, trying to find violations of the 1917 Espionage Act in her speeches. She was also constantly being stopped by highway patrols, which she interpreted as a form of government harassment. "There was a tightening in my stomach," she reported. "I never knew what would happen next…but I also felt a deepening resolve not to turn back."

• • •

Eleven days after the massacre at Kent State, police fired a barrage of 460 shots at a dormitory at Jackson State College in Jackson, Mississippi, killing two students and injuring 12 others. There was again deep revulsion about the killings, but nowhere near as massive a response as there had been to Kent State. Why not? This was America, and this time the students were all black. Fifty-one years later, on May 15, 2021, a formal apology for the police action was finally issued by the State of Mississippi.

• • •

Membership in the Black Panther Party peaked in the spring of 1970, when the party had thousands of members and offices in 68 cities. The Panthers' social programs, such as their free breakfast and ghetto school initiatives were running at full capacity, but violent interactions with the police were also frequent and intense. On May 19th, there was a shootout between Panthers and police in New York City, in which two officers were killed. Also in May, Algeria allowed Eldridge Cleaver to set up a 'Black Panther Embassy' in Algiers. He began to style himself as the leader of a global revolutionary movement, and he led Black Panther delegations to the Soviet Union, China, North Vietnam, and North Korea. Panthers Donald Cox and Sekou Odinga fled the US to become the #2 and #3 men to Eldridge Cleaver in Algeria. The FBI continued its infiltration and set out to destroy the party by sowing a rift between the revolutionary wing led by Cleaver, and the reformist wing, led by Huey Newton.

Bernardine Dohrn released her Weathermen Declaration of War on May 21st, confirming solidarity with the Black Panthers. The most eloquent intellectual in the Black Movement, Angela Davis, was a witness to the attack on the Los Angeles Panther headquarters by the TACT squad of the LAPD, with backup from the National Guard and the Army. It was a full-blown assault, with helicopters, bombs, gunfire, and tear gas directed at the building. Davis was involved in another personal battle at the time. Because of her involvement with the Panthers and her membership in the Communist Party USA, the Board of Regents of the University of California (with the support of Governor of California Ronald Reagan) were trying to remove her from her position as an Assistant Professor in the Philosophy Department at UCLA. Now, she was also involved in organizing the demonstrations and the strike over the police raid on the Panther offices. Support for the Panthers was welling up in Los Angeles from high school students led by the afro-coifed Davis chanting on the steps of City Hall, "I want to be a Mau Mau, like Malcolm X. I want to be a Mau Mau, like Martin Luther King."

• • •

On May 24th, which was Queen Victoria's birthday, a statutory holiday in Canada, the FLQ showed their feelings about British royalty by exploding a giant bomb outside the Montréal Board of Trade that shattered hundreds of windows. Four days later, they simultaneously exploded bombs in Montréal at the Canadian General Electric building and the Queen Mary Veterans Hospital. They staged an armed robbery of the *caisse-populaire* at the Université de Montréal and made off with $58,775. Three days after that, on the last day of the month, they set seven bombs, five of which exploded. One was at a financial collection agency, another at the home of billionaire businessman Peter Bronfman, the owner of the Montréal Canadiens, Labatt's Brewing, and later the Toronto Blue Jays. Yet another of the bombs, containing 31 sticks of dynamite was placed outside a Westmount home where it was discovered by a ten-year-old boy and dismantled by MPD bomb disposal chief Michael Côté.

• • •

Meanwhile across the ocean, the Irish Republic was thrown into turmoil after Prime Minister Jack Lynch fired two cabinet ministers because of allegations that they were importing weapons for northern nationalists from America. The trial and subsequent acquittal of the two ministers created what was considered the biggest political crisis since the foundation of the state.

• • •

On June 1st, in Argentina, the Montoneros, a far-left Catholic revolutionary group supporting ex-President Juan Peron, kidnapped and assassinated former anti-Peronist President Pedro Aramburu. The killing was in retaliation for a mass execution staged by the military junta that had ruled the country since ousting Juan Peron in a coup d'êtat in 1955. Juan Peron had ruled the country from 1946 to 1952, with his wife Eva Peron by his side. Both were enormously powerful personalities. "Evita" as she was known, had been born in extreme poverty in a tiny village on the Pampas, and had moved to Buenos Aires to become a film actress. After meeting and marrying Peron, she became an important, fiery, feminist member of the government, loved by the people of Argentina and referred to as the "spiritual leader of the nation" until she died of cancer in 1952.

After her death Juan Peron was re-elected and served until 1955. He led the most advanced economy in South America, which boomed in the early 50s, but he lost the support of both the right-wingers running the U.S. State Department, and of the Argentine Catholic Church. The country's reputation was also damaged by the vast number of German ex-Nazis who Peron had allowed into the country. His political fortunes were not helped by the underage girl, Nelly Rivas, with whom Peron became intimately involved. Her age was never officially confirmed, but when a magazine reporter asked if she was in fact only 13, the 59-year-old Peron merely responded that he "wasn't superstitious." Peron was excommunicated by the Sacred Consistorial Congregation of the Catholic Church. This action led to a mass rally for Peron at which 364 people were killed, mostly by Argentine Navy jets initiating a military coup d'êtat. Peron barely escaped, leaving his paramour Nelly Rivas behind and jumping on a gunboat provided to him by Paraguay's dictator, Alfredo Stroessner.

Peron spent his years of exile in Venezuela, Panama, and eventually, at the invitation of dictator Francisco Franco, Madrid. The junta in Argentina did what they could to erase the legacy of Juan and Eva Peron. They outlawed the mere mention of their names and removed the corpse of Eva that had been on display in Buenos Aires and ordered that it to be secretly re-buried in Milan, Italy. However, the people of Argentina did not forget the Perons. Juan Peron in exile led a very complicated political life. He was often called a fascist, he consorted with ex-Nazis, but he was also a big supporter of the Jewish cause and of Israel, and he was frequently considered not a fascist but instead its opposite—a progressive revolutionary. He supported the work of the radical Argentine film collective the *Grupo Cine Liberación*, and while in exile in Madrid secretly met with both Salvadore Allende and Che Guevara, whom he called, "an immature utopian—but one of us—I am happy for it to be so because he is giving the Yankees a real headache." He promised Guevara that if he ever got back in power he would help the Argentinian-born Cuban revolutionary get back to his homeland. He tried to dissuade Guevara of his plans to foment revolution in Bolivia, telling him, "You will not survive in Bolivia. Suspend that plan. Search for alternatives. Do not commit suicide." Guevara did not take his advice. Peron remained in exile in Madrid until 1973 when he returned to Argentina for his third term as President.

• • •

The first week of June was a very busy week in worldwide revolutionary activity. On June 2nd, the Québec government announced a $50,000 reward for information leading to their home-grown terrorists. On the 6th, a bomb exploded at the Club Canadien in Montréal. Three days later, the Weathermen exploded a bomb at the New York City Police Headquarters, and two days after that, in a record-breaking deal, the Brazil government exchanged 40 jailed political prisoners to secure the release of the West German ambassador to their country and allowed his kidnappers to fly to Algeria.

• • •

On June 14th, President Nixon ratified a 43-page outline of proposed security operations known as the 'Huston Plan' to fight the anti-war movement, the Weathermen, Panthers, the Puerto Rican FALN, and celebrity activists like Jane Fonda and Dr. Benjamin Spock. It involved the same sort of illegal burglaries that would lead to the Watergate scandal, and the creation of prison camps in western states where anti-war protestors would be detained. It was so extreme that it got push-back from both J. Edgar Hoover and Attorney-General John Mitchell who later described it as being a part of what Mitchell termed the "White House Horrors."

The team followed up, though, doing things like sending a memo to the FBI's Subversive Activities chief in Los Angeles. The order directed him to send a phony letter to *Variety* columnist Amy Archerd, maintaining that at a fundraising affair, Jane Fonda and a Black Panther had led a refrain of "We will kill Richard Nixon and any other motherfucker who stands in our way." Investigative reporter Jack Anderson later described it as "a clear-cut frame-up of a private citizen by a high government official." Anderson wrote that Nixon considered people like Jane Fonda and baby doctor Spock to be much more dangerous than terrorists, because they were trusted, establishment figures who were also idealistic and outspoken. Both were high on Nixon's 'Enemies List', along with TV talk show host Dick Cavett, and actor Paul Newman (who claimed he considered being listed on it "his greatest accomplishment.")

• • •

In Northern Ireland, following the violent events of 1969, the country was more polarized than ever. On the one side were the Catholics and Republicans, now supported by a re-invigorated Irish Republican Army; on the other the Protestants, Unionists, supported by the local police, the UDF, and the undisciplined B-Specials militia. The British Army were theoretically neutral, but were increasingly perceived to be anti-Catholic, and pro-Unionist. The situation was exacerbated by the shift from a Labour to a Conservative government in Britain. The new Home Secretary, Reggie Maudling, described as a "clever, lazy, corrupt politician" made a few fruitless visits to Northern Ireland. When his plane took off from Belfast after one visit he was reported saying to the flight attendant, "What a bloody awful country. For God's sake bring me a large Scotch." Two hardline, blatantly anti-Catholic churchmen, Reverend Ian Paisley and Reverend William Beattie were elected to the Northern Irish government, and Paisley later represented Northern Ireland in the British parliament. In June there were fierce gun battles on the streets of Belfast and the British Army shot and killed five men. By September, over 100 explosions were detonated by the IRA and its Protestant counterpart, the Ulster Volunteer Force, resulting in 21 fatalities.

• • •

Four days after the bombing of the Outremount residence of businessman Jean-Louis Lévesque on June 18th, thirty plainclothes police raided a summer cottage in the Laurentian Mountains. They discovered 350 pounds of dynamite, a copy of Carlos Marighella's *Manuel de la Guerilla Urbaine*, 250 copies of a communiqué that began, "The sickening representative of the U.S.A. in Québec, Consul Harrison W. Burgess, is in the hands of the Front de Libération Québeçois." They arrested Francois Lanctôt, who would become a player in the kidnapping of James Cross in October that led to the Québec Crisis. A writer in the Montréal weekly *Le Petit Journal* wrote, "As soon as one FLQ cell has been dismantled, another takes its place." Proving this, two days after the Laurentians bust, a bomb exploded at the Department of National Defense in Ottawa, killing a French-Canadian office employee named Jeanne d'Arc Saint-Germain.

• • •

Four days later, on the one-year anniversary of the Stonewall Rebellion, the world's first Gay Pride parades were held in New York, Los Angeles, and San Francisco. The New York parade grew from about 3,000 people attending in 1970 to four million in 2019—the largest parade of any kind in the city's history.

• • •

On July 3rd, the British Army imposed an illegal curfew on 20,000 people in the Lower Falls area of West Belfast, Northern Ireland. They claimed to be on a hunt for some IRA members. They wantonly looted many houses and killed four men, none of whom were connected to the IRA.

• • •

Nine days later. Robert Côté of the Montréal Police Department dismantled a "super bomb" containing 130 pounds of dynamite that was designed to explode beside the headquarters of the Bank of Montréal.

• • •

On July 17, the Canadian rock band The Guess Who performed at the White House for Richard Nixon and Prince Charles. Were there two less likely rock and roll fans on earth at the time? At the request of Pat Nixon, the band did not play their biggest hit, *American Woman*, because of its allegedly anti-American lyrics.

• • •

Ramirez Illich Sánchez, the young Venezuelan terrorist in training, not yet known by his *nom de guerre* Carlos the Jackal, was expelled in July from the Patrice Lumumba University in Moscow, and so he travelled to Beirut to volunteer for the PFLP – the Popular Front for the Liberation of Palestine. He gained a reputation as a fighter in the Black September battles of 1970 between the PFLP and King Hussein of Jordan. After the fedayeen were expelled from Jordan, Sánchez, now 'Carlos,' ended up in Beirut and then London, where he had been sent as an agent by the PFLP.

• • •

On July 21st, a letter threatening the life of Montréal Police Department bomb squad leader Robert Côté was sent from the Anarchist

Front of Québec after he was presented with the Order of Canada, the first member of a municipal police force to receive the distinction.

• • •

Soledad Brother: The Prison Letters of George Jackson, made Jackson a *cause célèbre* and a hero to much of the black community. He was certainly a hero to his 17-year-old brother, Jonathon, who got Angela Davis to purchase a shotgun for him from a San Francisco pawnshop on August 6th. The next day, he entered the Marin County courthouse where the trial of Black Panther James McLain was taking place. Jackson pulled it and two other guns registered to Davis from his coat, tossed McLain a revolver and the pair of them proceeded to free three prisoners from the holding cells. Young Jackson and the prisoners then took the Judge, the Deputy District Attorney, and three jurors hostage, and announced their goal was to free George Jackson from custody. They taped the muzzle of the shotgun to the judge's jaw and made their way out of the courthouse. On the way out they passed a newspaper photographer and shouted at him, "You can take all the pictures you want. We are the revolutionaries."

While driving away from the courthouse, a gun battle erupted between the hostage-takers and the police. Jackson, the Judge, and two of the prisoners were all killed in the shoot-out, one of the jurors was injured, and the District Attorney was paralyzed for life. A warrant was issued for Angela Davis, on charges of being an accomplice to conspiracy, kidnapping, and murder. She went on the run. She changed her appearance by chopping off her massive afro and plucking her eyebrows. She travelled to Chicago, then Miami, then New York City, where she was eventually captured two months later on October 13th.

• • •

Italy was a bit late to the crazy party of extremist revolutionary violence, but it made up for its tardiness by continuing long after most others had left the field. The *Brigate Rosse* (Red Brigades) carried out some 14,000 acts of violence and caused 75 deaths between 1970 and 2003. The group was formed in August by academics from the University of Trento led by Renato Curcio and Margherita Cagol, two lovers who eventually married. The group's tactics and philosophy were developed from the Italian partisans (mostly communist) who fought against Mussolini's fascists in the Second World War, and the Tupamaros of Uruguay. At first, their targets were mainly large corporations. Throughout 1970 and 1971 they were involved in the sabotage of Milan-based companies like Sit-Siemens, Pirelli and Magneti Marelli. In 1972, they undertook their first kidnapping.

• • •

On September 4, Salvadore Allende was elected President of Chile even though his opposition had serious financial support from the CIA. He was the first socialist ever to be elected as national leader in the Americas.

• • •

In the U.S., a newly formed group called the Vietnam Veterans Against the War became one of the most powerful organizations fighting against the war. On Labor Day, they staged a big event in which they marched between two Revolutionary sites, Morristown, New Jersey and Valley Forge, Pennsylvania. En route they engaged in mock guerrilla warfare and reenacted some of the techniques used by the U.S. troops against the Vietnamese. Mark Lane, Donald Sutherland, and Jane Fonda spoke at the event, with Fonda calling the Nixon administration "a beehive of cold-blooded killers." The VVAW assigned her a bodyguard who unbeknownst to them or to her was an LAPD plant who fed information about her activism schedule to the FBI.

• • •

Since his 20-year incarceration in San Luis Obisbo prison began in the winter, Timothy Leary had done everything he could to make himself appear a docile, contented convict. He was given a standard prison personality test, but since he himself had helped develop the test (named after him – it was called the "Leary Interpersonal Behavior Inventory") years earlier while a research psychologist at the Kaiser Foundation, he knew how to answer the questions to best appeal to the prison authorities. He was equipped with a stash of LSD so was able to stay high while maintaining a low profile. That all changed on September 12, when he slipped across the prison yard while most of the inmates were eating dinner. He climbed a tree, scaled a wall, removed his sneakers and padded barefoot along the roof, then donned a pair of handball gloves and grabbed a telephone cable and, kicking his legs like a monkey, shinnied along the wire. He was in full view had any guards looked in that direction, and he was exhausted from the exertion, but he eventually made it to a splintery pole, slid down to the ground, and ran to the roadside. After a few minutes a pickup truck pulled up. A woman called out the password: "Nino." Leary replied, "Kelly" and jumped into the truck with the two young strangers. They handed him a new set of clothes and new ID papers that identified him as 'William McNellis' They headed south, dropped his old clothes in a gas station to mislead the police, switched to another car and then headed north to San Francisco. Only then did they reveal to him who they were—two comrades from the Weather Underground.

In the bay city, Leary was introduced to Bernardine Dohrn and other leaders of the revolutionary gang, who proudly announced to the press that they were responsible for liberating Leary. They put out a release describing him as a political prisoner who was "captured for the work he did in helping all of us begin the task of creating a new culture on the barren wasteland that has been imposed by Democrats, Republicans, Capitalists and creeps." They said one day LSD and marijuana would make a better future world, but for now, "we are at war…we know that peace is only possible in the destruction of U.S. imperialism. We are outlaws. We are free."

Leary shaved much of his head, grew a moustache and dyed his hair. He also put out a manifesto, declaring himself to now be a 'psychedelic revolutionary.' "To shoot a genocidal robot policeman in defense of life is a sacred act," he proclaimed. "World War III is now being waged by short-haired robots whose deliberate aim is to destroy the complex web of free wild life by the imposition of mechanical order…Blow the mechanical mind with Holy Acid…dose them…dose them…stay high and wage the revolutionary war." Then, to the shock of those who thought of him as a gentle pacifist, he warned, "I am armed and should be considered danger-ous to anyone who threatens my life and freedom."

Ken Kesey wrote him a letter that eloquently said what many others were thinking: "In this battle, Timothy, we need every mind and every soul, but oh my doctor we don't need one more nut with a gun. I know what jail makes you feel, but don't let them get your head in their Cowboys and Indians script…And keep in mind what somebody, some Harvard holy man I think it was, used to tell us years ago: 'The revolution is over, and we have won.' The poor country still may not survive and even if it does survive and comes again to its feet, there's still years of work and suffering and atonement before we can expect it to walk straight and healthy once more, but the truth is already in the records: the revolution is over, and we have won."

That's all very well, thought Leary, but meanwhile I have the FBI on my tail and if they catch me, I'll be going back to prison. So instead of listening to his old acid comrade, he boarded a TWA jet with his new disguise and new identity and flew with his also-disguised wife to Paris, and then on to Algiers. There, he connected with Eldridge Cleaver, who at first welcomed him to his revolutionary nirvana. Leary smuggled 20,000 hits of acid into Algeria, and said he planned to turn on all of Africa. He praised the Black Panthers, calling them, "the hope of the world."

"How perfect that we were received here and protected by young Blacks," he wrote to Allen Ginsberg. "Algeria is perfect. Great political satori! Socialism works here…Eldridge is a genial genius. Brilliant! Turned on, too!"

The CIA, though, had infiltrated Cleaver's Algerian HQ, and managed to stir up tensions between Cleaver and Leary (in fact, between Cleaver and all the other revolutionaries of the era, including his old partner Huey Newton). A CIA document stated that "Panther activities have taken some interesting turns. Eldridge Cleaver and his Algiers contingent have apparently become disenchanted with the antics of Tim Leary… Electing to call their action protective custody, Cleaver and company, on their own authority, have put Tim and Rosemary under house arrest due most probably to Leary's continued use of hallucinogenic drugs." [93]

Cleaver confirmed this in a communiqué to the underground press, saying, "We want people to gather their wits, sober up, and get down to the serious business of destroying the Babylonian empire," and telling them, "To all those of you who look to Dr. Leary for inspiration and leadership, we want to tell you that your god is dead because his mind is blown on acid."

Leary had to split. He almost unbelievably found a renegade CIA operative in Algiers who could get him exit visas, and he and his wife fled for the original birthplace of lysergic acid, Switzerland.

• • •

Nowhere on earth were the conflicts as complicated as in the Middle East. After the Kingdom of Jordan lost control of the West Bank of the Dead Sea to Israel in 1967, Palestinian fighters known as fedayeen moved their bases to Jordan and stepped up their attacks on Israel. They began to act like a state within a state, disregarded Jordanian laws and regulations (even things like traffic lights and stop signs), and twice attempted to assassinate their host, Jordan's King Hussein. By September Jordan had had enough, and on the 16th, the Jordanian Army attacked the fedayeen. The conflict, which continued until September 27, was known as "Black September", and the name stuck. When the Jordanians forced the PLO fedayeen to leave the country for Lebanon, Black September became an underground terrorist organization, first mounting attacks on Jordan (including a 1971 assassination of the Prime Minister), then focusing on terrorist attacks on Israel, the most notorious of which was at the 1972 Munich Olympics.

• • •

On September 19th, in Matteotti Square in Genoa, Italy, a geology student named Kosta Georgakis set himself ablaze to protest the dictatorship of George Papadopoulos, another extreme example of the growing resistance to the Greek regime.

• • •

September 26th saw the first publication of *The Greening of America*, for some time the Number One best-selling book in America. It proposed that the coming revolution would be personal and cultural, not political, and not violent. It also predicted the Women's Liberation Movement and the Environmental Movement, and the new social changes that would be created by advances in science and technology.

• • •

It was already beginning to be clear that technological changes would transform all corners of life just as much as political change would. New changes in telephone technology, especially regarding long-distance and satellites meant a big change in how people began to communicate. In this era, though, the telephone system was very much run by giant money-grubbing monopolies that people frequently hated and fought back against whenever they could. The 'Blue Box' was an illegal, home-brew invention that created a way to "stick it to The Man" and make free long distance phone calls anywhere in the world. The boxes were developed by a number of counterculture electronic tinkerers known as 'phone phreaks'.

One of them, John Draper, who went by the underground name 'Captain Crunch' was named after his discovery that Captain Crunch breakfast cereal offered free toy whistles inside their boxes that conveniently happened to blow at exactly the needed 2600 Hz tone required to access the telephone companies' internal routing service. Once inside the phone monoliths' internal systems, the boxes allowed the user to dial any number on earth (or even at sea) without being charged.

The most celebrated underground builders of Blue Boxes were Steve Jobs and Steve Wozniak. Just as they eventually would with their creation of the Apple computer, they transformed what had previously been a somewhat clunky, awkward device used by hobbyists into a compact, svelte (albeit illegal) device that Jobs could market to the California underground for pranking and political calls.

Wozniak famously tested their devices by using them to call, for instance, the Vatican. Adopting a thick German accent and claiming to be Henry Kissinger, he asked to speak to the Pope. According to Steve Jobs, if it weren't for Wozniak's blue boxes, "there wouldn't have been an Apple." Building and selling the 'Blue Boxes' convinced Jobs that electronics could be both fun and profitable, and also showed the pair that they could take on the large companies and beat them. It was a perfect manifestation of the attitude of the young anti-corporate counterculture. For Jobs in 1970 it was Bell and AT&T. In the future, he would take on Big Blue—IBM. Then in the 21st Century, he would utterly transform the telephone itself.

• • •

On September 24th, Paul and Jacques Rose (leaders of the so-called 'Chenier Cell' of the FLQ) along with their mother and eleven-year-old sister left Québec in Mrs. Rose's Plymouth Valiant for a planned travelers-check kiting scheme though the U.S. to finance their planned terrorist activities, and to attempt to buy guns.

On the morning of Monday, October 5th, four members of the 'Liberation' cell of the FLQ appeared at the front door of the house of

James Cross, the British Trade Commissioner in Montréal. They took him hostage and hid him in an apartment at 10945 Rue des Récollets, thus setting in motion one of the most devastating events in Canadian history. The gang had their communiqués and manifesto prepared, and they quickly got their demands to the authorities. They expected the release of 23 *felquistes* currently in prison, the publication of their manifesto, a 'voluntary tax' of $500,000 in gold ingots, the re-hiring of mail truck drivers recently replaced by the Federal government, and passage to Cuba for themselves and the political prisoners. If this didn't happen, they said, Cross would die.

They picked a busy time for their kidnapping. The Québec government was in the midst of the complicated task of introducing universal health care; the city government was in the midst of a civic election; the Montréal police were swamped with bank robberies, labor unrest and other FLQ activity; and the Federal government was just about to open a new Parliament and to officially recognize China. At first, though, the police thought they could quickly resolve the crisis. They identified the two ringleaders as Jacques Lanctôt and Marc Carbonneau, and mistakenly thought it might be relatively easy to capture them and end the kidnapping.

The next day the Rose gang, now in Dallas, heard about the Cross kidnapping on the radio and immediately began to drive back to Canada. They didn't want to miss out on this big moment for their movement. As they were driving back, on October 8th the Weathermen exploded a bomb in the Marin County Courthouse, and 90 minutes later the Seattle Weathermen bombed the ROTC building at the University of Washington. In Québec, with James Cross still held hostage, the Canadian government made one concession they thought might diffuse the crisis. They allowed Radio-Canada to broadcast the manifesto of the FLQ.

"Workers of Québec, start to take back what belongs to you, take for yourself what is yours," read the Radio-Canada announcer. "Make your own revolution in your neighborhoods, in your workplaces. Let those who have been contemptuously called the "lousy French" and "alcoholics" vigorously undertake the fight against the bludgeoners of liberty and justice and render harmless all the professional robbers and swindlers: the bankers, the businessmen, the judges, and the sold-out politicians. We are the workers of Québec and we will struggle on to the bitter end. Together with all the people, we want to replace this slave society with a free society. Our struggle can only lead to victory. An awakening people cannot long be kept in misery and contempt."

The announcer continued, in the well-modulated voice of a media professional, but obviously without any of the fire that a true believer would convey:

"Long live free Québec!
Long live our political prisoner comrades!
Long live the Québec revolution!
Long live the Front de Libération du Québec!"

The next day of this busy week, the Weathermen bombed a courthouse in Queens in support of an inmate riot at the Queens House of Detention.

The day after that, Paul and Jacques Rose, now back in Montréal, along with their accomplices Francis Simard and Bernard Lortie, waited in a safe-house they had prepared for another action, listening to a radio report of Québec Justice Minister Jérôme Choquette's response to the demands of the Cross kidnappers. Once it was clear Choquette was not going to back down and submit to all the other demands, the foursome put on disguises and balaclavas, grabbed M1 semi-automatic rifles, piled into a '68 Chevy Biscayne and headed for the house of the Québec Deputy Premier, Pierre Laporte.

When they arrived on the sunny Saturday autumn afternoon, Laporte was tossing a football with his nephew, his wife Françoise watching from the porch. "I saw two men behind the vehicle pointing sub-machines at my husband's stomach," she later recalled. "One of them said, 'This isn't a joke. We're not fooling. Get in. Right now.' Pierre bent over and got in. I didn't wait for the car to leave. I immediately went in and called police."

With two senior political figures now held hostage, the Federal government accepted that they were in the midst of a dangerous crisis. On October 12th, they called out the Canadian Army to protect politicians and property and to assist the police in Montréal. Meanwhile, other revolutions continued.

• • •

Also on October 12th, radical Australian feminist Germaine Greer's book *The Female Eunuch* was published in London and soon became an international bestseller and *cause-célèbre*. Greer argued that men hated women and that women should end their status as eunuchs by getting to know and accept their own bodies, taste their menstrual blood, and give up celibacy and monogamy, and that change had to come by revolution, not evolution.

The following day the Weathermen's new 'Women's Brigade' got into the feminist revolutionary spirit by bombing Henry Kissinger's alma mater, the Harvard University Center for International Affairs.

• • •

Also on October 13th, in a famously combative interview with CBC reporter Tim Ralfe, Canadian Prime Minister Pierre Trudeau was asked about all the soldiers now in the streets of Ottawa and Montréal. Asked how far he would go with the police and military, Trudeau famously replied, "Just watch me." He went on to tell Ralfe that only "bleeding hearts" and "weak-kneed people" would be concerned about soldiers in the streets when there was an attempt being made by a "parallel power" to take over the country.

On the same day, Canada became one of the first Western nations to recognize what was then known as 'Red China'. It was upsetting news to

Richard Nixon. His National Security Advisor Henry Kissinger reported, "Giving vent to his dislike of Pierre Trudeau, Nixon remarked that future contacts or channels with the Chinese could take place anywhere *except* Ottawa." Kissinger continued, "It cannot be said that Nixon and Trudeau were ideally suited for each other…Trudeau was bound to evoke all of Nixon's resentments against 'swells' who in his view had always looked down on him. He disdained Trudeau's clear enjoyment of social life; he tended to consider him soft on defense and in his general attitude toward the east." [94] Kissinger was of course being diplomatic. Nixon simply despised Trudeau, and the feeling was mutual. In 1973, Trudeau would make his first state visit to the PRC, but it was not his first visit to China. In 1948 he had toured through the country as a bearded student backpacker during Mao's revolution. In October of 1970, though, Trudeau was certainly not thinking about touring China. Instead, he was facing the crisis of the biggest domestic threat to the country since Confederation.

On October 14th, a group of 'eminent personalities' signed a petition and held a press conference to urge the beleaguered government of Québec to release 'political prisoners'—the term they used to describe FLQ members who were being held in jail for over 200 terrorist crimes. Both Federal and Provincial governments were furious that these influential Québecers appeared to be wanting them to give in to the kidnappers. The following day 6,000 University of Montréal students struck in support of the FLQ, and that evening a large crowd of over 4,000 separatist supporters filled the Paul Sauvé Arena in Montréal to hear speeches by Pierre Vallières and others, and to raise their fists and shout "FLQ! FLQ! FLQ!" It appeared both to many Canadians and to the Canadian government that much of Québec was actually sympathetic to the kidnappers who had taken Cross and Laporte hostage.

Two days later, at 4 am on the 16th, the Canadian cabinet declared that a state of 'apprehended insurrection' existed in Canada and they proclaimed the War Measures Act. The Bill of Rights was suspended. Within hours hundreds of FLQ members, supporters, and sympathizers were pulled from their beds and arrested by Montréal police. Meanwhile Pierre Laporte attempted to make an escape by breaking free of his restraints of a dog chain and handcuffs and tried to break through a window. The kidnappers heard the commotion and rushed to pull him back in. He was badly cut in the incident. They roughly patched him up but refused to get him any medical attention.

• • •

The same night, on the other side of the country, there was a five-hour concert for Greenpeace at Vancouver's massive Pacific Coliseum. It starred Phil Ochs (billed at the concert as "the vanguard of the revolution"), James Taylor, Chilliwack, and Joni Mitchell. Supported and organized by Joan Baez, the concert raised over $30,000, which was deemed sufficient to keep the new group afloat and to help finance chartering the ship that would sail to the Amchitka nuclear test zone in 1971.

• • •

The following evening Pierre Laporte made another attempt to escape through the broken window. He was caught again and this time one of the kidnappers strangled him to death with the dog chain. They put his dead body into their car, parked it beside a nearby military base, and left a message with a radio station announcing that "Pierre Laporte, Minister of Unemployment and Assimilation, was executed at 6:18 p.m. this evening by the Dieppe cell (Royal 22nd.) *Nous vaincrons* FLQ. P.S. The exploiters of Quebec had better watch out." It would be an understatement to say that the country was stunned to hear that the Deputy Premier of Québec had been murdered.

James Cross, still very much alive, was ultimately held for a total of 59 days. He spent his time watching television and playing solitaire, being careful to never catch sight of his captors, since he was convinced that they would kill him if they thought he had seen their faces. Unlike most hostages of the era, he never fell victim to the 'Stockholm Syndrome' by sympathizing with them. "I hated the lot of them and would have cheerfully killed them if the opportunity arose," he told history researchers at Cambridge University in 1995.

In the first week of November, a young separatist activist named Carole de Vault, a volunteer for the Parti Québécois, and the mistress of the leader of the PQ, Jacques Parizeau, was approached by Robert Comeau, a university professor and active member of the FLQ. Comeau wanted de Vault to hide a mimeograph machine used for printing FLQ manifestos, and to participate in a robbery to raise funds for the Laporte and Cross kidnappers. De Vault was torn. She sympathized with the goals of the FLQ, but not their violent methods. She consulted with Parizeau's wife (of all people), who told her she should go to the police. De Vault was conflicted—knowing that if she didn't tell the police, James Cross might die, but if she did, she might. Comeau had already told her his thoughts after the FLQ suspected an informer had ratted on their plans to kidnap American consul Harrison Burgess:

"Informers. One day we will pay them a visit. We will put a bullet through their heart and pin a note to their body saying, 'This is what happens to those who betray the FLQ.'"

On November 6th, after a sleepless night, de Vault finally made up her mind, went to a Montréal police station and gave a detailed statement that included specific information about Cross' kidnapper Marc Carbonneau. The information was passed to one of the lead detectives in the kidnapping investigation, Julien Giguère, but he did not take it seriously and stuck the report at the bottom his growing 'crackpots' pile.

That evening, working from a separate lead, the Montréal police raided the hiding place of the Laporte kidnappers. They captured one of the kidnappers, Bernard Lortie, and two women who had been helping the gang, but three of the four members of the cell were not discovered. With the help of the two women, who had bought them plywood, wallpaper and building supplies, they had earlier built a secret crawl space in a closet.

They now rushed and hid in it when the police showed up. After the cops left with Lortie, the three kidnappers/killers snuck away, and headed for a country farmhouse where they managed to hide for the next two months.

• • •

Throughout the fall, Jane Fonda made a tour of 54 colleges, churches, and meeting halls across North America, speaking out against the war. In late November, the FBI arranged to have her stopped at customs as she returned from Vancouver. The guards found drugs such as Valium, Dexedrine and vitamin supplements. She was handcuffed, arrested for drug smuggling, and held overnight in a cell with a woman who had been charged with murdering a man and dismembering his body. The next day, headlines across the country read JANE FONDA CAUGHT SMUGGLING DRUGS and JANE FONDA ARRESTED FOR ASSAULTING A POLICE OFFICER. After she was released on $5,000 bail, she held a press conference and announced in fury that she was not a smuggler, saying, "I am a health food freak. I was never hassled until I started speaking out against the war. This was a political arrest!" She continued to tour America, getting sacks of hate mail and several death threats. Backstage at an event in Bakersfield, California a man was caught stalking her while brandishing a handgun.

• • •

A week after her first approach to the Montréal police, Carole de Vault's life as an informer kicked into high gear. The company she worked for was robbed by the FLQ, and Robert Comeau returned to her apartment to get her to collaborate on writing a new FLQ communiqué, in which the group would tweak the police by revealing that the three Laporte kidnappers had successfully hidden from the police during the November 6th raid. De Vault told her detective contact Julien Giguère the news, which certainly got his attention. He pulled her file out of his 'crackpots' pile and made her his main priority.

De Vault continued to play the role of an FLQ sympathizer, even loaning Comeau money so that he could pay the rent on the house where Cross was being held, and trying, for now unsuccessfully, to get the address of it from Comeau. Her life became a dangerous cat-and-mouse game, with the police secretly tapping her phone, Comeau discovering the police surveillance technicians, and then de Vault secretly getting Comeau's fingerprints to the cops on a beer glass. De Vault hints that she and Comeau were lovers in this period but does not confirm it. He did stay overnight at her place. She does say they kissed and "exchanged caresses", but that he was so wound up by the crisis that "it didn't go any further." He was right to be nervous. Due to what she was telling the police, he was now being tailed by five unmarked police cars wherever he went.[95] Through the information the cops got from de Vault, they were able to identify and begin to follow three other members of the Viger cell's support team.

De Vault kept supplying the police with information that could have led them to Cross and his kidnappers, but to the frustration of their informer the police tailing team frequently lost Comeau and the other FLQ supporters in the dense downtown Montréal traffic. Eventually, though, her tips lead the police to the house at 10945 Rue Des Récollets. On December 3rd, the army cordoned off the block surrounding the house, and had the utilities companies turn off the power and water. The kidnappers discovered they had been found, so threw out a message saying they would release Cross in return for safe passage to Cuba. They demanded that a local communist lawyer, Bernard Mergler handle the negotiations. Mergler refused, saying he had no sympathy for the FLQ, but he was willing to act on behalf of the Cuban government, if they wanted him. He and the chief government negotiator, Robert Demers, went to the Cuban consulate to talk to the Cubans. It took some time, since the consular officials had to call Havana and get approval from Raul Castro, but eventually they got the go-ahead and went to the Rue des Récollets address, which by then was surrounded by 500 soldiers, with snipers on all the surrounding buildings, and a big sign reading "FLQ" that the kidnappers now painted on the window.

Mergler went to the door, met Carbonneau and his accomplice Jacques Lanctôt, and asked Cross if he was alright. "Oh, I'm fine," replied the phlegmatic Brit, "considering the circumstances." Mergler explained the plan. Île Sainte-Hélène, the site of Expo 67, had been declared temporary Cuban territory. The four men would drive there, their wives and children would join them, Cross would be turned over to Cuban officials, a military helicopter would fly them to the airport, and then a military aircraft would fly them to Cuba.

The kidnappers agreed, then got into a prolonged discussion about whether they should take their television set with them. "We can't take it with us," said one of them. "Think how terribly bourgeois it would be to arrive in Cuba carrying a TV set." However, they wanted it, so they bundled Cross, Mergler, and the TV set into the back of Carbonneau's battered 1962 Chrysler and took off for the old Expo site in a giant cavalcade of police motorcycles.

Within hours, they were in the air, heading for Cuba. Once they were in flight, they realized they had forgotten their TV set. "There was a lot of crying on the flight," Lanctôt later wrote. "Everyone had a heavy heart. It was the first time we had left our beloved Québec, which we had plunged into a deep crisis." [96]

"Let them go," said Prime Minister Trudeau, dismissively. "They'll be back." He was right. The separatists hated their new lives in exile in Cuba, and later France, and all of them returned eventually to face trials in Montréal.

While the Cross kidnappers were safely in Cuba, and the hostage victim safely back in Britain, the three remaining kidnappers/killers of Pierre Laporte were still on the lam and struggling to stay alive. With the help of some FLQ sympathizers they found first an unheated barn, then an old farmhouse to hide out in north of Montréal. Suspecting the cops were on their trail, they dug an 18-foot tunnel and a six-by-six cave in the frozen ground under the old house. By December 28th the police had figured out where the kidnappers were. They had the basement tunnel surrounded and commanded the gang to come out. Paul Rose shouted back, demanding a neutral negotiator be present and asking, "Is Lisacek there?" He was referring to Detective Albert Lisacek, a man with a reputation as 'the toughest cop in Canada' and for breaking down doors and beating up suspects. In another raid only a few weeks earlier he had grabbed Rose's mother by the hair, called her a bitch and threatened to kill her. And now, he was indeed standing outside the secret tunnel. Only once the negotiator arrived and Lisacek left did the gang push open the tunnel entrance and give themselves up.

• • •

Three days later, on the last day of the year, Paul McCartney filed a lawsuit against the other three Beatles in London's High Court of Justice to officially end the band's contractual partnership. If anything indicated "the end of an era," this was it. The band had been struggling for two years, over creative differences and difficulties between McCartney and Yoko Ono, producer Phil Spector, and especially financial advisor Allan Klein. McCartney's feelings were exacerbated by unpleasant public comments by John Lennon, and resentment from George Harrison about perceived slights from John and Paul. It all added up to tension and grief within the group that had begun as the 'Fab Four', and who had, in a major way, symbolized the era. The trial, which was eventually resolved by the judge in favor of McCartney, was dubbed *Beatledämmerung* by *TIME* Magazine, referencing Wagner's opera about a war among the gods.

1971

Paul Rose Found Guilty, Idi Amin Seizes Power,
Female Revolutionaries, New Foods, Panther Breakfasts,
Ping Pong Diplomacy, Baby Doc, Mexican Massacre,
Pentagon Papers Released, Oz Magazine On Trial,
Tupac Shakur Born, Concert for Bangladesh, Attica,
Greenpeace, Belfast Bombed, Ms. Magazine Published.

With the Laporte killers now in prison and the Cross kidnappers in Cuba, the October Crisis was over. In the first weeks of the new year, the Canadian army pulled from the streets of Montréal most of its 7,000 troops and their tanks and armored carriers, thus ending what the sovereigntists called 'the occupation of Québec'. Life in the city and the rest of the province began to return to normal.

• • •

In early January, on the other side of the Atlantic, young Bobby Sands, age 17, was forced by gun-toting Protestant Ulster 'loyalists' out of his job as an apprentice coach-builder. His crime was that he was Catholic, or in their words "Fenian scum". His family was later ejected from their home by a unionist mob. The two events radicalized him into militancy and caused him to join the Provisional IRA. He would ultimately become the most famous of Republican martyrs in the Troubles, after he died from his hunger strike in Her Majesty's Prison Maze in Northern Ireland in 1981.

• • •

Unlike other trials of the era, which were usually delayed for years, the trial of Paul Rose proceeded with extraordinary haste. He had been captured less than a month earlier, and now, on January 25th, his trial began. Rose turned the trial into something of a re-play of the anarchic trial of the Chicago Seven, except that the stakes were much higher. His charges were murder and kidnapping. Dressed very casually in an untucked work shirt and a baggy sweater with holes in the sleeves, he began by claiming that he could not get a fair trial. First, like Bobby Seale, his lawyer was not available to represent him. Robert Lemieux was being held in a cell in the same courthouse, facing charges of seditious conspiracy, obstructing justice, and being a member of the outlawed FLQ. Second, Rose contended, he would not be tried by a jury of his peers, since there would be no poor people, no students, and no women. Quebec law at the time allowed on juries only men who owned $5,000 worth of property or paid over $500 a year in rent. No women were permitted.

Faced with Rose's arguments about the jury selection process, the judge snapped at him, "Don't abuse my patience."

"Mine is even more abused," replied Rose. "You're a lackey—no—a whore of the establishment. No, you're worse. At least whores earn their money. They work for it."

Again, like Bobby Seale, Rose was hauled out of the courtroom. He was allowed back in for his final address to the jury but then was expelled again for calling the judge a hypocrite.

After 25 minutes of deliberation, the jury found Rose guilty of murder. The judge immediately sentenced him to life, with no possibility of parole for ten years. He left the courtroom with his arm raised and fist clenched, shouting, "*Vive le Québec Libre! Vive le pouvoir du people! Nous vaincrons!*

•   •   •

The same day that Rose's trial began, Colonel Idi Amin Dada seized power. He had heard that Ugandan President Milton Obote was about to arrest him for misappropriating army funds, so he took control of Obote's residence, the city of Kampala, and Entebbe Airport. At first Amin claimed he was a soldier, not a politician, and his coup was only designed to create an interim government. Within a week he changed his mind (not the first time, nor the last) and declared himself to be President of Uganda, Commander-in-Chief of the Armed Forces, Uganda Army Chief of Staff, and Chief of Air Staff. Amin began a policy of political repression and ethnic persecution, and more than 20,000 refugees fled the country. Over the next eight years of Amin's reign in Uganda, somewhere between 100,000 and 500,000 would be killed.

•   •   •

In January, Jane Fonda moved to Detroit. She was there to work with the Vietnam Veterans Against the War (VVAW), the many Vietnamese refugees living in Michigan and the 65,000 draft resistors living across the border in Ontario. She was still being tailed by the police. At one point her car was broken into and all her records and VVAW membership lists were stolen. On the last day of January, the group held an event in which many vets testified about their experiences in Vietnam. They told about killing the gooks for sport, shoving North Vietnamese out of helicopters, cutting off their ears for souvenirs, gang-raping the women (sometimes with entrenching tools), shooting dogs and cattle for fun, and setting villages on fire.

While working the Detroit conference, Fonda met two of the young stars of the New Left, John Kerry and Tom Hayden. Kerry, the spokesman of the VVAW was a decorated and wounded veteran of the war. He would go on to become Lieutenant Governor and Senator for Massachusetts, Democratic Presidential candidate, Secretary of State, and then Presidential Climate Envoy. Tom Hayden was one of the founders of the Students for a Democratic Society and would go on to become a California Senator and the husband of Jane Fonda.

• • •

Women were a remarkably large part of the revolutionary activities of this ten-year period. In Japan, Fusako Shingenobu created and led the Japanese Red Army (*Sekigun-ha*), an underground organization with the modest goals of overthrowing the Japanese government and monarchy, destroying Japan by "extinguishing Japanese ethnicity", and starting a world revolution. Battles with the Japanese police sent over 200 *Sekigun-ha* members to jail. Shigenobu eluded capture and with about 40 followers escaped to the Middle East, where she linked forces with the People's Front for the Liberation of Palestine and led several major terrorist incidents in the early '70s.

Shigenobu was just one of the many women who had central important roles in the most radical political organizations of the era. Others included Ulrike Meinhof and Gudrun Ensslin of the Red Army Faction / Baader-Meinhof Gang; Angela Davis of the Communist Party USA; Afeni Shafur of the Black Panthers; Bernardine Dohrn and Kathy Boudin of the Weathermen; Diane Nash, early Freedom Rider and co-founder of the Student Nonviolent Coordinating Committee; Magdalena Kopp, a founder of the Frankfurt Revolutionary Cells and later lover and co-conspirator of Carlos the Jackal; Gabriele Kröcher-Tiedemann, another associate of Carlos and key member of the German anarchist group the June 2 Movement; Irish civil rights leader and politician Bernadette Devlin; Dolores Huerta, the co-leader with Cesar Chavez of the United Farm Workers of America; Assata Shakur of the Black Liberation Army, who to this day is still a fugitive, with a two million dollar bounty on her head; Carole de Vault of the Front de Libération du Québec; American Indian

Movement leader Anna Mae Aquash and of course (in a different manner) Patricia Hearst of the Symbionese Liberation Army; and media activists Joan Baez and Jane Fonda.

The first of the female revolutionaries of this period, foiled Statue of Liberty bomber Michele Duclos, later confessed in a Québec television interview that while she personally hated terror and violence, she had felt back in 1965 that she needed to make some noise. "We were 25, we were dumb, we did stupid things."

At one minute before one o'clock on March 1st, the switchboard of the Capitol building in Washington D.C. received a phone call alerting them that in 30 minutes a bomb would go off—and right on time, it did. A committee room, a washroom, the Senate restaurant, and a barbershop were destroyed. There were hundreds of thousands of dollars of damage. Bernardine Dohrn's Weather Underground—the new gender-neutral name for the Weathermen—sent a letter to the Associated Press claiming responsibility for the bombing and saying it was done in protest against the Nixon bombing of Laos, and to "freak out the warmongers." The bombing was the first attack on the Capitol since the British torched it in 1814 in retaliation for the American looting and bombing of the Ontario legislature by American sailors and soldiers in Toronto (then called York) the year before.

• • •

In early March, 2,500 women, including feminist writer Germaine Greer, dressed in a nun's outfit, marched through central London in a Women's Liberation March.

• • •

This was a period of new invention in many fields, including food. It seemed to come to a peak in 1971. The first Starbucks opened in March. A cup of coffee cost all of…nothing, as it was offered free as a 'come-on' to buy their coffee beans for the then-expensive price of $1.25 a pound. Restaurants were promoting their novel introduction of salad bars. McDonalds released their new Quarter Pounder. Brand new arrivals in supermarkets included Hamburger Helper, Franken Berry sugar-filled cereal, and Cup O'Noodles soup. The trendy new cocktail, the Bloody Caesar, invented by a bartender in Calgary in 1969, was taking the 70s by storm.

Coca-Cola didn't change its formula. They had removed the cocaine long ago, and each can still contained ten teaspoons of sugar (which some said was much worse for you than cocaine). They did, though, come up with a brilliant new jingle and TV spot in 1971, in which a groovy-looking, multi-racial group of smiling teenagers sang, "I'd like to buy the world a Coke," implying that if they did that, all the world's problems would be solved, and we'd all live "in perfect harmony." South Africa objected to the black faces in the ad, and asked Coke to edit them out. The company not only refused, but decided, because of the controversy, to sell off all its bottling plants and other investments in the country. Elsewhere in the world, the spot was highly successful, resulting in the sales of many thousands of cans and bottles of the famous beverage.

At the other end of the food spectrum, Ballantine Books published Frances Moore Lappé's *Diet for a Small Planet*, and it sold three million copies. Warren Belasco, the academic credited with creating the discipline of Food Studies, described in his *Appetite for Change: How the Counterculture Took on the Food Industry* how *Small Planet*'s "mix of recipes and analysis typified radicals' faith in the ability to combine personal therapy with political activism." People reading the *Small Planet* book were likely also the ones boycotting the use of Saran Wrap because it was produced by Dow Chemical, the same company that produced the deadly Napalm jellied gasoline used to bomb Vietnam.

Lappé defied the common belief of the time, which was that the world was so over-populated that it could no longer feed itself, and instead argued that if the world grew crops for humans instead of for livestock, ethanol, or high-fructose corn syrup, there would be enough food to feed every famine-afflicted person on earth. The book did not turn everyone on earth into a vegan, but it did jumpstart the vegetarian movement, and soon large numbers of people were rejecting Quarter Pounders and instead developing a taste for a macrobiotic diet, brown rice, yoghurt, and granola—foods that were barely known and seldom eaten before this period, but had now become popular, at least within the counterculture.

Another radical attempt to battle hunger was the Black Panthers' Free Breakfast program. Begun in 1969, the program really got going once Huey Newton championed it after his release from jail in 1970. By 1971 it was at its peak, with over 45 Panthers' chapters serving 10,000 children in deprived neighborhoods every school day. American federal authorities attempted to discredit and derail the program and police frequently raided program locations while children were eating. The food program was only one of what the Panthers called their "Survival Pending Revolution" programs—others being their free ambulance, free busing to prisons, and free housing cooperative programs.

• • •

The 'Fight of the Century' between Muhammed Ali and Joe Frazier on March 8th was used as cover by the activist group the Citizens Committee to Investigate the FBI to pull off a burglary of an FBI office in Pennsylvania. The group rightly expected that all eyes would be on the fight that night. The hundreds of files they stole from the FBI office exposed the agency's COINTELPRO operations that used postal workers, telephone switchboard operators, and illegal break-ins to spy on black organizations, college students, civil rights workers, and anti-war activists. Some of the files they uncovered were on Ali himself. The FBI had gained access to files on Ali going back to his elementary school report cards.

On March 24th the *Washington Post* ran a front-page story describing the hundreds of files that the group had liberated. Although the FBI put 200 agents on the case, it was never solved. The media coverage of the liberated material was one of the factors that led to the creation of the Church Committee of the U.S. Senate into the many intelligence abuses of the FBI, CIA, NSA and IRS in this period.

• • •

On March 11th, the theatrical show FTA (Army slang for 'Fuck the Army') opened outside Fort Bragg, California. It starred Jane Fonda, Donald Sutherland, Country Joe and the Fish, Peter Boyle, and Dick Gregory. The show attracted a huge audience of both disaffected soldiers and undercover FBI agents who were taking notes and using infrared cameras to photograph the G.I.'s. It was well reviewed. The *Los Angeles Times* reported that, "Jane Fonda's anti-war show scored a hit playing outside an Army base—the soldiers roared time and time again in their decision to see the end of war." Although the show was followed by dozens of FBI agents in an effort to close it down, the show continued to 15 more venues near military bases across the US, and eventually played off-Broadway, where it won an Obie award.

• • •

On the night of March 25th, the Pakistani military junta attacked East Pakistan, annulled the 1970 election, arrested the Prime Minister, and systematically eliminated nationalist Bengalis, students, the intelligentsia, and soldiers. The nine-month-long Bangladesh Liberation War is now considered to have been genocide, as the West Pakistani forces engaged in mass rape and mass murder. Between 300,000 and 3 million civilians were killed and between 200,000 and 400,000 Bangladeshi women were raped. Ten million refugees fled for India, and 30 million were internally displaced. Most of the world supported the Bangladeshi people but U.S. President Richard Nixon, along with China and many Arab nations continued to support West Pakistan Dictator Yahya Khan, despite the reports of genocide and forced starvation. The war spawned George Harrison's

Concert for Bangladesh, the world's first large scale benefit concert that would take place in August. In December India attacked and defeated the occupying West Pakistani Army thus ending the war. The surrender of Pakistan on December 16th led to the creation of what would be the seventh-largest nation in the world.

• • •

The U.S. had imposed an economic and political embargo on China from 1950 until 1971. The two countries perceived each other as enemies and were on the brink of nuclear war. This began to change in a most unusual manner when a self-styled American "hippie athlete" named Glenn Cowan began an unlikely friendship with Chinese athlete Zhuang Zedong at the World Table Tennis Championship in Japan. The two practiced together and gave each other small gifts (a silkscreen landscape from Zedong, a T-shirt with a peace symbol and the words 'Let it Be' from Cowan). For years, few Americans other than some members of the Black Panthers had been allowed into China but after Cowan broke the ice, the American Table Tennis team applied to visit. They were initially turned down, but then Mao read about the Chinese player's connection with the American and after stating, "This Zuang Zedong not only plays table tennis well, but is good at foreign affairs, and has a mind for politics," Mao authorized the visit. On April 10th, the team with their coaches and spouses crossed into China to begin a series of games with expert Chinese players. This so-called 'Ping-Pong Diplomacy' had a remarkable effect on thawing over 20 years of extremely frosty relations between the two countries. Only two months later, on June 10th, the U.S. lifted the embargo on China, and on February 28, 1972, during Richard Nixon and Henry Kissinger's visit to Shanghai, the two countries, to the shock of most of their citizens, signed an agreement normalizing relations with each other.

• • •

On April 21st, the long-time dictator of Haiti, François 'Papa Doc' Duvalier died. His 19-year-old son, Jean-Claude ('Baby Doc') was installed as the new president. To give the transition some legitimacy, a referendum was duly held. Exactly 2,391,916 votes were cast and exactly 2,391,915 voted in favor of the new young leader. As a certain sign of electoral authenticity, exactly one was opposed.

Jean-Claude did not really want the job. He preferred the role of playboy to that of dictator. The United States, always central to Haitian politics, didn't think much of him, but since he toed their favored anti-communist line, they let him stay in the job until 1986, when they finally had enough and forced him into exile in France. Baby Doc married one of his many sexy girlfriends, Michèle Bennett in a grandiose two-million-dollar wedding befitting the leader of the poorest country in the Americas. Michèle took over much of work of running the dictatorship while he dozed through cabinet meetings or drove his Ferrari around the palace grounds. While serving as First Lady, she and her family used her position, and Air Haiti planes, to smuggle cocaine from Colombia through Haiti to the U.S. Her brother served three years in jail in Puerto Rico for the operation.

• • •

The day after Papa Doc's death, April 22nd, more than 1,000 angry veterans of the Vietnam war threw their medals, ribbons, hats, jackets, and military papers over a fence erected to keep them away from the U.S. Capitol building. A few of their leaders, including future Presidential candidate and Secretary of State John Kerry appeared before a Congressional hearing, where they denounced the war.

• • •

The battle over Women's Liberation continued, with an April 30th debate at the Town Hall, New York, between combative novelist Norman

Mailer and feminists Germaine Greer, Jill Johnston, Diana Trilling and Jacqueline Ceballos. The event, called a 'Battle of the Sexes', was a wild, free-spirited event on the subject of feminism with, at one point, two women joining the panelists onstage and kissing and groping each other on the floor, to the apparent shock of Mailer. It was considered one of the great societal and activist influences on the growing women's liberation movement. Greer was later voted the "Woman of the Year" in Great Britain, and the "Journalist of the Year" by Playboy Magazine.

• • •

Student battles continued in Mexico's 'Dirty War' of the 1970s. On June 10th, Corpus Christi Day, after the state government angrily slashed the budget of the University of Nuevo León, students from several large universities staged a major protest in downtown Mexico City. The march was surrounded by riot police and tankettes, and by a special secret shock group known as *Los Halcones (The Hawks)* that had been trained by the CIA and the Federal Security Directorate. *Los Halcones* shot indiscriminately into the student protest, killing dozens. Many of the wounded students were taken to the Hospital Rubén Leñero and were followed by the paramilitary *Halcones* who proceeded to kill many more in the emergency operating rooms. The death toll was nearly 120, with the youngest being 14. In 2018, the massacre was featured in *Roma*, the Oscar-winning Mexican film.

Following the Corpus Christi massacre and other clashes with students, President Echeverria enacted draconian new laws to attempt to neutralize the politicized youth. Most famously, he banned all rock music played by Mexican bands. From 1971 until well into the 1980s, live rock concerts and all radio airplay of rock songs was banned by the Mexican government.

• • •

On June 13th, the *New York Times* printed the first excerpt of the *Pentagon Papers*, which RAND Corporation military analyst Daniel Ellsberg had secretly copied from U.S. government documents. The *Papers* documented the lies perpetrated by the Johnson and Nixon administrations and the Pentagon about the Vietnam War. A court order from the Nixon government prevented the printing of further excerpts. It was the first time that the U.S. government had restrained the publication of a newspaper since the Civil War. Ellsberg immediately had to go into hiding to elude an FBI manhunt.

Simultaneously, another censorship battle erupted, this time in England. The counterculture underground *Oz* Magazine was begun in Australia by young publisher Richard Neville, described there as "a pioneer in the war on deference." After raids by Sydney police, charges of obscenity and a sentence of three to six months in prison with hard labor (later overturned on appeal), Neville left Australia and travelled up the so-called 'hippie trail' through Asia and Europe to England. In 1967 he started a new London edition of the magazine that featured psychedelic design and political commentary on the Vietnam War, the Greek military junta and activities of the British police.

In 1971, at the ripe old age of 29 he was feeling that he and his magazine had lost touch with youth. He offered a group of young students the opportunity to create a special edition that he called the "Schoolkids' *Oz.*" The kids produced some wild material, including an X-rated version of the beloved Rupert Bear comic character that had been a British institution since the 1920s. The name of the edition was misinterpreted as being *for* school kids, instead of being created *by* school kids, and so once again Neville, along with two associates, was charged, this time for "conspiring with certain other young persons to produce a magazine containing obscene, lewd, indecent, and sexually perverted articles, cartoons and drawings with intent to debauch and corrupt the morals of children and other young persons, and to arouse and implant in their minds lustful and perverted ideas."

It became the longest obscenity trial in British history and received a huge amount of attention from the press and public. There were massive, noisy protests outside the courtroom with celebrity picketers like John Lennon and Yoko Ono and the burning of effigies of the judge. The publishing trio were found guilty and jailed. On their first day in prison their jailers forcibly shaved off their long hair. The three appealed. At their new trial, it was determined that the plainly biased judge of the first trial had grossly misdirected the jury. They were acquitted and continued (until 1973) to publish the magazine, which had now, due to its new notoriety, massively increased its circulation.

There was an even more incendiary publishing event in 1971 when controversial publisher, writer and gambler Lyle Stuart published a book titled *The Anarchist Cookbook*. Written by teenage writer William Powell, it included 'recipes' for the construction of bombs, instructions on how to create and use Molotov cocktails; and insanely complicated instructions on the home manufacture of LSD, mescaline, tear gas, and the phone phreaking devices that Steve Wozniak, Steve Jobs, and 'Captain Crunch' were building. The young author had a very ambivalent attitude towards his own book, claiming rather unconvincingly that it was not designed for violent revolutionary groups like the Weathermen or Black Panthers, but rather to educate the 'silent majority.' After converting to Anglicanism in 1976, Powell attempted to have the book taken out of circulation, but because the publisher owned the copyright, this was not possible. Over the years, more than two million copies have been sold.

The FBI bad-mouthed the book, calling it "one of the crudest, lowbrow, paranoiac writing efforts ever attempted," and it was investigated by both John Dean at the Nixon White House and by Mark Felt, the Associate Director of the FBI (also, famously, 'Deep Throat' in the Watergate scandal). However, both concluded that since the book "did not incite forcible resistance to any law of the United States", it was free speech and protected by the First Amendment. There were a thousand bombings a year in the period 1970 – 1975 in the U.S., with many of the bombs built using instructions in *The Anarchist Cookbook.* The book was found in the possession of extremists including the right-wing Minutemen, the Puerto Rican Young Lords, Patricia Hearst's kidnapper Bill Harris, and later the Oklahoma City bombers, the Columbine High School shooters, anti-abortion bombers, and the London public-transport bombers.

• • •

On June 11th, in San Francisco Bay, a large force of government officers removed the last of the Natives, without much resistance, from their 18-month-long occupation of Alcatraz Island. In part the occupation ended reasonably peacefully because the Natives realized it had actually been somewhat successful, and that the Nixon administration had responded slightly positively towards it. Perhaps Nixon was just glad it was Natives occupying Alcatraz, and not him.

• • •

On June 16th, Black Panther Afeni Shakur gave birth to a baby boy. She named him after Tupac Amaru, the eighteenth century Incan revolutionary leader who fought against the Spaniards (and for whom the Tupamaros are also named). The boy grew up to become the rap megastar Tupac Shakur.

• • •

Twelve days later, June 28th, by a unanimous decision the Supreme Court of the United States overturned Muhammed Ali's conviction for refusing the draft. On the same day Daniel Ellsberg surrendered to the U.S. Attorney's Office for the District of Massachusetts in Boston and was arrested under the Espionage Act of 1917. He faced a possible 115 years in jail. Two days later the Supreme Court cleared the *New York Times* to resume printing of the *Pentagon Papers*.

• • •

On July 1ˢᵗ, the 26ᵗʰ Amendment to the U.S. Constitution was ratified. It dropped the voting age in America from 21 to 18. It had been a long battle, beginning way back in WWII, and it was brought to a head during the Vietnam War, with the slogan, 'Old enough to fight, old enough to vote.' The change had been fought by conservatives like Representative (and Chair of the House Judiciary Committee) Emanuel Celler who argued that youth "lacked the good judgement" needed to make appropriate decisions, and that the qualities that made 18-year-olds good soldiers did not translate into making them good voters—or at least not the type who would likely vote for people like him. Nonetheless, President Nixon approved the change and the Supreme Court narrowly passed it. England had already made the change in 1970. West Germany and Canada followed in 1972, and Australia and France in 1974.

• • •

The Women's Movement began to get organized on July 10ᵗʰ when 300 women came together to create the National Women's Political Caucus. The leaders included Gloria Steinem, Betty Friedan, Bella Abzug, and Shirley Chisholm. At the opening convention Gloria Steinem declared, "This is no simple reform. It really is a revolution."

On the other side of the world another woman was fighting *against* an attempted revolution in her country. Prime Minister Indira Gandhi (virtually the only female senior statesperson in the world) was fighting back against Calcutta students who had organized under the Naxalite movement begun by Charu Majumbar in 1967 during the peasant uprising in central India. The Prime Minister organized a colossal police and army counter-insurgency operation named *Operation Steeplechase* during which 20,000 suspects and cadres were arrested. Majumbar himself was rounded up and later died in prison, presumably from torture. The movement did not die out but instead returned in the 21st Century, and indeed is still very active today. In 2006 Prime Minister Manmohan Singh declared the Naxalites the most serious internal threat to India's national security. There have been violent encounters between police and Naxals as recently as 2020.

• • •

On August 1st, George Harrison and Ravi Shankar presented their Concert for Bangladesh at Madison Square Garden in New York. The event brought the conflict and genocide in Bangladesh into the public eye and helped reveal that both the Nixon government and Red China were providing arms to the West Pakistani dictatorship. More than $250,000 was raised for the displaced people of Bangladesh, but as was typical of events of this period, millions more dollars were held up in escrow over tax battles regarding the gate receipts.

Harrison invited his former bandmates to perform with him at the concert. Ringo Starr accepted, but Lennon and McCartney did not. McCartney refused because he was wary that promoter Allan Klein would potentially take the credit for having organized a Beatles reunion. Lennon agreed on the condition that his soul-mate Yoko Ono could also participate but Harrison refused to invite her on the grounds that the concert was intended as an exclusive gathering of rock stars, not a festival of avant-garde music.

• • •

In the early hours of August 9th, the British government began what it called *Operation Demetrius*, a violent round-up of 342 men suspected of being members of the Irish Republican Army. All but one were Catholic and had been fingered by the Royal Ulster Constabulary Special Branch and MI5. Using batons and smashing through doors and windows, the army forced their way into the homes of the suspects. In what became known as the Ballymurphy Massacre, the 1st Battalion, Parachute Regiment of the British Army killed 11 citizens in the Ballymurphy section of Belfast. One was a Catholic priest who was waving a white cloth while going to the aid of a wounded man. Others were shot in the back while lying injured on the ground.

The British Army began interning the men in giant camps where they were subjected to beatings, sleep deprivation, white noise, starvation, and other forms of torture. A popular technique was to tie a sack around the internee's head, strip him of his clothes, take him up in a helicopter and threaten that he would be thrown out unless he confessed. Frequently the helicopters would be brought to within a few feet of the ground and then the internees, still thinking they were high in the sky, would be pushed out.

Hundreds of homes were burned. More than 7,000 people, most of them Catholics, were left homeless and 2,500 Catholics fled south of the border to refugee camps. *Operation Demetrius* completely turned the Catholic population against the British and the government of Northern Ireland. In Derry, 8,000 workers went on strike, 16,000 households began withholding their rent and utility payments in protest, and there was a surge of new volunteers seeking to join the Provisional IRA. In 1970, 29 people were killed in The Troubles. In 1971, a shocking 180 died, including 94 civilians. The worst was yet to come.

• • •

George Jackson's brother was now dead and Jackson himself was in San Quentin prison with a murder charge hanging over him. He somehow managed to acquire a Spanish Astra 9mm pistol, and on August 21st pulled it from under a wig and announced, referencing Ho Chi Minh, "Gentlemen, the Dragon has arrived." He proceeded to kill five prison guards and two white prisoners and wounded three other officers. As he attempted to escape the prison, he was shot dead.

• • •

On September 3rd, the Nixon Administration put Daniel Ellsberg on Nixon's 'Enemies List' and organized a covert group of CIA agents and ex-agents known as 'The Plumbers'. Their first mission was to break into the offices of Ellsberg's psychiatrist to try to find information that would discredit the former U.S. military analyst. Their experience with this burglary would lead to the break-in at the Watergate Hotel that would ultimately lead to the forced resignation of President Nixon. The Plumbers also organized a plot to have a group of Cuban American waiters "totally incapacitate" Ellsberg at a public dinner/rally in Washington. Some interpreted this as a planned assassination, others as a plan to try to render him incoherent by putting a massive dose of LSD in his soup. Ultimately the plan was unsuccessful.

• • •

The Prisoners' Rights movement that had been growing for the past ten years climaxed on September 9, when over 1,200 prisoners rioted in Attica State Prison east of Buffalo, taking 42 staff hostage and holding the prison until September 13. The prisoners were protesting against physical abuse by prison guards, and rules that allowed them only one shower a week, one roll of toilet paper a month, no access to books or newspapers, and poor medical treatment. They were also reacting to the August killing of George Jackson in California. Their manifesto read, "We are men! We are not beasts and do not intend to be beaten or driven as such."

It was a wildly dangerous and violent five days. When negotiations seemed to break down, Correctional Services Commissioner Russell Oswald begged New York Governor Nelson Rockefeller to accede to one of the demands and come to the prison to help find a peaceful solution.

When he would not, the pair agreed that New York State Troopers would take back the prison by force. During the attack, the Troopers killed ten hostages and 29 inmates. After the re-capture of the prison, hundreds of inmates were stripped naked, forced to crawl on broken glass, and were violently beaten by rows of troopers and prison officials. The New York State Special Commission on Attica wrote, "With the exception of the Indian massacres in the late 19th century, the State Police assault which ended the four-day prison uprising was the bloodiest one-day encounter between Americans since the Civil War."

In retaliation, on September 17th the Weathermen exploded a bomb beside Commissioner Oswald's office at the New York Department of Corrections. The communiqué they left with the bomb claimed that the prison system was an example of "how a society run by white racists maintains its control."

• • •

During the same week, on the other side of the globe a plane carrying Chairman Mao's key deputy Lin Biao and members of his family crashed in Mongolia under mysterious circumstances. A huge rift had grown between Mao and Lin over negative comments Lin had made about Mao's wife, Jiang Qing. According to the official Chinese reports, Lin had conspired to assassinate Mao and take over in a coup, but when the assassination and coup attempt were foiled, Lin commandeered a plane to escape and defect to Russia. According to the official story, the plane ran out of fuel and crashed into the Mongolian wilderness. There are other theories about what happened, but regardless, Lin was definitely dead, and Mao and his scheming wife consolidated even more power. Within a month, over 1,000 senior military officials suspected of being supporters of Lin were purged from the Armed Forces. Zhou Enlai replaced Lin as the second most powerful man in China.

• • •

On September 15th, the fishing vessel *Phyllis Cormack*, re-named the *Greenpeace*, sailed from Vancouver on the initial mission of the newly formed Greenpeace organization. Their plan was to intercept a U.S. nuclear test explosion off the Alaskan island of Amchitka. A combination of interference by the American Coast Guard ship *Confidence* and horrifically bad weather in the Gulf of Alaska forced the *Greenpeace* to turn back, but news about the voyage had caught the attention of the press and the public. Although the U.S. did detonate one bomb, the pressure from Greenpeace resulted in a decision by the American military to end nuclear weapons testing in the Alaskan islands.

Aboard the *Greenpeace* that year and skippering another vessel for the organization in 1972 was Paul Watson. He would go on to become one of the most important eco-warriors of the next 50 years. His revolutionary and activist zeal led him to be ousted from Greenpeace in 1977. He began a new organization, the Sea Shepherd Conservation Society, which now has a fleet of ships working to preserve whales and other wildlife around the world. His tactics have involved actively ramming rogue whaling ships and have resulted in serious legal battles in the United States, Canada, Germany, Costa Rica, and Japan. Back in the '70s he was accused of being an eco-terrorist. He responded to the charge by saying, "There's nothing wrong with being a terrorist, as long as you win. Then you write the history." He also quoted the famous aphorism of British writer Gerald Seymour, "One man's terrorist is another man's freedom fighter."

• • •

The Weathermen exploded a bomb on October 15th at the Massachusetts Institute of Technology outside the office of White House aide William Bundy who they blamed for his crafting of the war in Vietnam. The next day, the FBI financed, armed, and controlled an extreme right-wing group of former members of the Minutemen anti-communist organization. This support transformed the Minutemen into a para-military group they called the 'Secret Army Organization' that targeted groups, activists, and leaders involved in the Anti-War Movement. The Secret Army Organization promptly adopted the sort of intimidation and violent acts the police force itself was constitutionally restrained from using.

• • •

China's support of African countries was based partially on idealism and revolutionary zeal. "Among the independent countries in Africa," speculated one Chinese document, "if only one or two of them complete a real national revolution…the revolutionary wave will be able to swallow the whole African continent, and the 200 million or more Africans will advance to the forefront of the world."

It was also, though, based on the hope that the votes of the many African nations would get them a coveted seat at the United Nations, something they had been blocked from acquiring by the United States and Taiwan for more than 20 years. Finally, on October 25th, Albania's motion to admit the People's Republic of China to the United Nations was passed, with the support of the Soviet Bloc, Britain, France, and Canada, and that of many of the unaligned countries, especially the African countries that had been receiving vast amounts of medical, engineering, and military aid from China for the past five years.

• • •

Carole de Vault's career as an informer for the Montréal police did not end with the capture of the FLQ kidnappers in 1970. She continued to be active through 1971 in what was left of the FLQ, and continued working as an agent for the police, passing on information about proposed bombings, hijackings, and even another kidnapping. On November 19th, she passed on information about a planned attempt to extort $200,000 out of the federal government with a false threat of a bomb aboard an airliner. The FLQ had De Vault write the communiqué, which read, in part, "The FLQ will use this money to advance the cause of the liberation of the

Quebec people. The people of Québec will not be truly free until power is in the hands of the workers. *Vive le FLQ. Nous vaincrons!"* The FLQ also enlisted her to organize getting the communiqué to radio stations. What they did not know was that she secretly let the police know the threat was a hoax. Both Air Canada and KLM took the threat very seriously, but they learned from the Montréal police and the Mounties that their passengers were totally safe, and there was no need to ground the flights.

As the FLQ fell apart in 1971, it was replaced with two new groups with pretensions to terrorist activity—the Front Nationale and the Parti Communiste du Québec (PCQML). De Vault became involved with both. She was even offered $200 a week to spy on the Parti Québecois by the PCQML, an offer she reported to the police. Her detective contacts were most interested but mystified by the offer. They knew the penurious outfit didn't have $800 a month to throw around, and so they became convinced that the new organization must be a front for a foreign actor—likely either the KGB or the CIA. It was *Spy vs Spy*, as the monthly *MAD* Magazine comic feature had it in those days. The times were complicated, and Carole de Vault was playing high stakes poker from both sides of the table.

• • •

In November, Argentina's Montoneros revolutionary group, in association with militant auto workers took over a Fiat manufacturing plant, sprayed 38 cars with gasoline and lit them on fire. On December 4th, another fire broke out, this one in Switzerland. While avant-garde rock musician Frank Zappa and his group the Mothers of Invention were performing at the Montreux Jazz Festival, a fan fired a flare into the rafters of the Montreux Casino, which then caught fire and burned to the ground. Deep Purple, who were preparing to record in the casino the next day, watched the fire from their hotel across Lake Geneva, and later immortalized the event in their song *Smoke Across the Water*, and their album, *Burn*. There was yet another infamous fire in 1971, when England's largest hippie commune, a rock music venue that had hosted all the major bands of the era called the Eel Pie Island Hotel, burned down under mysterious and suspicious circumstances.

• • •

On December 4th, the Ulster Volunteer Force exploded a bomb in McGurk's Bar in Belfast, a place frequented by Irish Catholic Nationalists. Fifteen people were killed, including two children, and 17 more were injured. The British security forces falsely announced that it was a prematurely detonated IRA bomb.

• • •

In December, the first issue of Ms. Magazine was published. Within eight days its initial test run of 300,000 copies sold out. The magazine rapidly became the voice of the Women's Liberation Movement. By the end of the year, it had generated 26,000 subscriptions and more than 20,000 letters from readers. The common theme of the response, said founder Gloria Steinem, was "At least I know I'm not alone. And I'm not crazy. The system is crazy."

1972

Bernadette Devlin in Parliament, Nixon in China,
Nuclear Bombs in the South Pacific, Japanese Red Army,
Deep Throat Released, Watergate Burglarized,
George McGovern Slaughtered, Jane Fonda Vilified,
Black September in Munich, Steve Jobs in India,
Cold War Hockey in Russia, Last Tango in Paris,
The Joy of Sex, The Trail of Broken Dreams,
Nixon Re-elected, Mozambique Massacre, Baez Bombed.

The Year of Our Lord 1972 would be the worst year of the Troubles and the most violent year in Ireland since 1921. There would be 10,000 shooting incidents and nearly 500 killed in bombing explosions. The year began badly when on January 30th, a day that would be remembered as Bloody Sunday, British soldiers shot 26 Catholic civil rights demonstrators in The Bogside, Derry, killing 14 and seriously wounding 12. An inquiry into the incident, considered by many to be a whitewash, cleared the British soldiers and authorities of all blame. However, a second inquiry, completed in 2010, declared that the killings were "unjustified" and "unjustifiable", that none of the victims were armed and that none posed a serious threat. Bloody Sunday is considered one of the most significant incidents in the

Troubles, as it intensely increased the hostility of the Irish towards the British army and the authorities.

The next day, infuriated that she was not allowed to speak about the killings by the British Army in Ireland even though she had personally witnessed them, firebrand M.P. Bernadette Devlin crossed the floor of the House of Commons and lunged for British Prime Minister Edward Heath. Since the diminutive Devlin could not quite reach the Prime Minister, she instead slapped Conservative Home Secretary Reginald Maulding, a politician who had once publicly described Ireland as "a bloody awful country." After she was ejected from the House, Devlin told the press that she had struck the Home Secretary because his comments about Bloody Sunday had been "untrue and perfunctory and lacking in any compassion" for the people who had been killed and injured.

The following day was declared a national day of mourning in Ireland. Thirty-five thousand people marched to the British Embassy in Dublin and burned it to the ground. The IRA could barely keep up with the flood of recruits as young people of both sexes queued up to join. Paul McCartney, Black Sabbath, John Lennon, and U2 all recorded songs commemorating the victims of the event. McCartney's song, *Give Ireland Back to the Irish*, was banned by the BBC.

• • •

In Canada, the second of the Pierre Laporte murder trials began on February 7th. Radical separatist lawyer Robert Lemieux had himself been behind bars the year before when Paul Rose was tried for his role in the kidnapping, but the lawyer was now out and was therefore able to defend Rose's brother, Jacques. The trial began with a protest by the defendant, who claimed he would not cross the picket-lines of the striking guards of his prison. Still wearing pajamas, slippers, and a bathrobe, he had to be forcibly dragged by police from his cell and into court. Lemieux began by introducing a motion challenging the legitimacy of the court. He declared that the Court of Queen's Bench was a "colonial court which cannot by law judge Mr. Rose, who is fighting *against* colonialism and *for* the installation of an authentic, popular and democratic regime in Quebec." He also objected to the law that had created an all-male jury.

When the judge threw out both of Lemieux' motions, Rose angrily shouted from the prisoner's box, "You reject our motion and I reject your decision!" Rose brandished an abridged version of the British North America Act with him that he ripped in half and hurled at the judge, shouting, "This is what I think of your constitution and your decision." The document sailed over Judge Eugène Marquis, who ignored it, responding, "I'm an old pacifist."

Ultimately, the jury was deadlocked. Rose's many supporters in court noisily celebrated the outcome. However, the prisoner remained behind bars until he was re-tried in the fall of '72. A collection of Quebec celebrities, including singer Pauline Julien and sculptor Armand Vaillancourt (both themselves separatists) attempted without success to get him freed on bail. In his second trial Rose was acquitted. Afterwards Lemieux told the jury, "This verdict is not the verdict of the establishment, but a popular verdict, an authentic Québec verdict. You will be proud of it for a long time."

However, Rose still had to face yet another trial, this one on the charge of murder. That trial began January 9th, 1973, with three women on the jury, as the 'No Women' law had finally been revoked. Québec was not independent or as the péquistes would say, *libre*, but it was changing. The month-long trial ended with the jury foreman stating, "After studying all the evidence, we have arrived at the unanimous conclusion that the accused is not guilty."

The courtroom broke into applause and tears. Rose announced to the media assembled on the courthouse steps, "I am going to fight for the liberation of my brother Paul and all the political prisoners who have been tried by the iniquitous and scandalous justice of the establishment."

However, the establishment was not yet done. Jacques Rose *still* had one more court appearance to make.

• • •

Meanwhile…in China, whatever remained of the Cultural Revolution ended with the visit to China of Richard Nixon on February 21st. For months leading up to the visit both Shanghai and Beijing were scrubbed clean and much of the detritus of the Revolution was removed. The thousands of statues of Chairman Mao were junked. Enormous posters that proclaimed (in red) "Long Live the Invincible Thoughts of Chairman Mao" were painted over (in newly approved colors of sky blue, cream, and apple green) with signs welcoming Nixon with "Great Unity of the Peoples of the World." To add a touch of the bizarre to the event, Nixon was greeted by the People's Liberation Army Band playing *Home on the Range*.

The meeting between Nixon and Mao, scheduled to be 15 minutes in length, went on for an hour. In the U.S., it was acclaimed by politicians of both stripes. Republicans were not about to knock an initiative of Richard Nixon, and Democrats were not about to knock an attempt at rapprochement with China. Nixon, though, did not get what he came for—a compromise over Vietnam, and much of the third world saw the event as Korea's Kim Il-sung described it: "Nixon went to Beijing waving the white flag."

• • •

On March 24th, British Prime Minister Edward Heath abolished Stormont (the ruling body of Northern Ireland) and announced direct rule of Northern Ireland by Westminster. It was a major blow to the Unionist (Protestant) forces in the country. Irish Prime Minister Brian Faulkner defiantly told a crowd of 100,000 that "Northern Ireland is not a coconut colony," but nonetheless he and his cohorts had to resign. The combination of this dismissal of the Irish government and the ever-increasing strength of the IRA meant that working-class loyalists in the country formed the Ulster Defense Association, an armed paramilitary force that would soon be staging fascist-style marches through Catholic areas of Belfast dressed in motley army-surplus camouflage outfits and triggering street fights with the Catholics. By the end of the year, they would claim to have 40,000 members.

• • •

One of the very few places on earth where there was no dissent or apparent strife (at least on display) was the autocratic communist dictatorship of North Korea. The country's leader, Kim Il-Sung, was publicly presented as the *"peerless patriot, national hero, ever-victorious iron-willed brilliant commander, outstanding leader of the International Communist Movement, ingenious thinker, sun of the nation, red sun of the oppressed people of the world, greatest leader of our time."* Had they wanted, they could have included in that long list of accomplishments the fact that he was the sole ruler of North Korea during the period of six South Korean Presidents, ten U.S. Presidents, and two British monarchs—George VI and Elizabeth II. On April 15th, his 60th birthday, a 240,000 square meter monument was opened overlooking Pyongyang, crowned by a 20-meter-tall bronze-and-gold statue of the Dear Leader.

• • •

In 1971, France began testing nuclear bombs in the coral archipelago of Tuamotu in the South Pacific. When the recently created Greenpeace organization learned that France planned more explosions for 1972, they placed notices in New Zealand newspapers looking for a sailor with a yacht who was willing to sail into the test zone to protest the event in a similar manner to what they had done with the fishing boat during the Amchitka nuclear tests.

David McTaggart had a long career as a builder/developer in Toronto and San Francisco until a gas explosion destroyed a ski-lodge he was building in the Sierra Mountains. With his life in tatters, he retired and began sailing the South Seas. He, like Greenpeace, was from Vancouver. He took this as a sign, and so, after learning of the organization's interest, he volunteered to sail his boat into the nuclear zone. When New Zealand authorities learned of his plans, they mercilessly hassled him and his small crew—likely at the behest of the French government. McTaggart was finally able to get away and sail for the test site. It was a wildly difficult and dangerous protest. It is one thing to march around for a few hours outside an army base or a consulate, but quite another to secretly sail the vast distances of the Pacific into a zone where the French military planned to explode nuclear bombs.

Many other people were also protesting the French nuclear tests. Dock workers all around the Pacific refused to service French ships. In Stockholm, the protests led eight nations to sign a treaty banning nuclear tests. Noticeably absent were France and China.

It was a cat-and-mouse battle in the South Pacific between French naval frigates and McTaggart's 38-foot sailboat. With a Canadian as skipper and an Australian as part of the small crew, questions were raised about the situation in the parliaments of both Canada and Australia. Both nations, along with many others, continued to protest and to alert France about the presence of *Greenpeace III* in the test zone.

Three large French warships began harassing the sailboat. They motored at close quarters to force McTaggart to violently tack or gybe to avoid collisions. Two of the big cruisers then fell in on either side of the small yacht. "I still do not know how we survived," said McTaggart. "The minesweeper *Hippotame* flanked us on our starboard. *La Bayonnaise* came in parallel to our port side, a scant fifteen yards from us. With her huge grey hull rising up and down, the force of her displacement churned the small space of water between us into a maelstrom. They were probably under orders from the Admiral to scare the hell out of us, but they got carried away and were vying with one another in recklessness."

The French did not scare the *Greenpeace III* out of the test zone, and so McTaggart and his crew of two continued to bounce around in the rough seas. There was no GPS or other electronic navigation in 1972. They had to use traditional sextant sightings of the sun and stars to keep themselves within the test zone but outside of the 12-mile French territorial waters, where they could have been arrested. Radio communication with the world was sketchy but they did learn that supporters around the world were staging protests in sympathy. The craziest of these was a group of Australians who proposed that they would join the Greenpeace protest by flying into the zone, bailing out of the plane with scuba gear and an inflatable boat, then somehow linking up with the sailboat.

On June 29th, the sailing crew, and the world, heard that the first of the French bombs had been exploded. A flood of official protests were lodged with the French government, one by Canadian Prime Minister Pierre Trudeau, others by all the South American countries who were downwind of the potential radiation. The French barely responded. The following day, the *Greenpeace III* was rammed by the French warship *La Paimpolaise.* The collision entangled the ketch with the warship and lifted it out of the water. It finally broke free but there was considerable damage to the mast and rigging. After some heated dialogue between McTaggart and the captain of the minesweeper, a tug was sent out from the French base of Mururoa Atoll to tow in the disabled yacht and the French Navy agreed to attempt to repair the damage. Once in the atoll, McTaggart and his crew had a wary relationship with the French. The navy was upset with the Greenpeace protestors for having disrupted their nuclear testing and for having publicized it to the world. At the same time, they were impressed by their seamanship and bravery. The Admiral offered them several formal lunches, the naval shipyard repaired the damage, and hundreds of French sailors cheered and saluted them when they left the harbor. However, the

French sent out deliberately inaccurate reports about the incident that were designed to besmirch the protest.

The French did not stop. When they resumed nuclear testing in 1973 McTaggart and *Greenpeace III* would be back sailing in the exclusion zone—with much graver results.

• • •

On May 5th, the trial began in Montréal for separatist Georges Dubreuil, who had confessed to police to 15 politically motivated bomb-ings. A psychiatrist convinced the judge that Dubreuil had a schizophrenic "divine mission to change the world" and the charges were dropped. The next day, the RCMP Security Services burned down a barn in Sainte-Anne-de-la-Rochelle, Québec, after the Mounties failed to convince a judge to allow them to wiretap the building, where they suspected separat-ists were planning to meet with members of the Black Panthers. In a later hearing about the many incidents of policing excesses by the Mounties, Assistant Commissioner Rod Stamler admitted that the barn-burning was "morally wrong and unlawful". The Director of the RCMP criminal oper-ations branch confessed that the force entered over 400 premises without warrants in the early '70s and illegally entered and stole more than 1,000 files from the *Agence de Presse Libre de Québec* and the *Mouvement pour la Défense des Prisonniers Politique Québécois.*

• • •

In honor of Ho Chi Minh's birthday on May 19th, the Weather Underground exploded a bomb in the Air Force wing of the Pentagon. The bomb, presumably placed by one of the female members of the group, destroyed the women's washroom and broke pipes that flooded the computer rooms below. The event was enthusiastically applauded by radi-cal groups around the world.

• • •

At 10 PM on May 30th, three members of the Japanese Red Army carrying violin cases containing Czech VZ-58 assault rifles boarded an Air France flight in Rome. On landing at Lod Airport (now Ben Gurion Airport) outside Tel Aviv, they opened fire indiscriminately and threw grenades at passengers. Twenty-six people were killed. Among the dead were 17 Christian pilgrims from Puerto Rico, one Canadian woman, and eight Israelis, including the head of the Israeli National Academy of Sciences, who was running for the Presidency of Israel in the upcoming election. Two of the Japanese were killed and the third arrested in the massacre. They had been recruited for the job by the Popular Front for the Liberation of Palestine who seemed remarkably adept at finding volunteers from such diverse counties as Japan, Canada, and Germany. One of their most high-profile recruits, Fusako Shigenobu, described the mission's purpose as being "to consolidate the international revolutionary alliance against the imperialists of the world." [97]

• • •

June 12th saw the release of *Deep Throat,* the most infamous film of the so-called "Golden Age of Porn" (1969 to 1984). The film received mainstream attention and ushered in a trend known as 'porn chic' with political and entertainment celebrities and middle-class suburban couples across North America openly admitting they had attended screenings of the film. It was wildly successful, bankrolled with $50,000 by a member of the Colombo crime family, and grossing (in both senses of the word) an enormous figure which some claim was $600 million. The film also became famous when 'Deep Throat' was chosen by the managing editor of the *Washington Post* as the code name for the deeply guarded secret government informant who was providing reporter Bob Woodward with shattering information about the Watergate political scandal.

The Watergate incident began on June 17th when security guards discovered a break-in of the Democratic Party Headquarters at Washington's Watergate Hotel. The invasion by five burglars led by ex-CIA operative

Howard Hunt had been authorized and organized by President Nixon and his Attorney-General John N. Mitchell, and their Committee to Re-elect the President (CREEP). A few days later, Mitchell hired a former FBI agent named Steve King to try to prevent Mitchell's wife, a notoriously loose cannon, from learning about his connection with the break-in, or from contacting reporters. In fact, Martha Mitchell did discover the news and did call well-known Washington reporter Helen Thomas about it. During that call, King pulled the phone from the wall, and then five men beat Mrs. Mitchell 'black and blue', kidnapped her in a violent scuffle, and had her tranquilized by a psychiatrist.

Years later, in his interview with David Frost, Nixon claimed that "if it hadn't been for Martha Mitchell, there'd have been no Watergate." When the Washington Post was about to publish one of its many articles about John Mitchell's role in organizing the slush fund for CREEP, Mitchell threatened reporter Carl Bernstein, telling him, "Katie Graham [publisher of the *Washington Post]* is going to get her tit caught in a big fat wringer if that's published."[98] Dogged, relentless investigation by young reporters Carl Bernstein and Bob Woodward at the *Post* resulted in the exposure of the massive scandal.

• • •

On July 10th, the U.S. Democratic Convention began in Miami Beach, Florida. It was one of the most unusual conventions ever, beginning every night in the early evening and running through until daybreak. The nominee, George McGovern was possibly the most liberal, radical candidate for the Presidency since Henry Wallace in 1948. The rules were changed so that issues such as feminism, abortion, and gay rights could be addressed on the convention floor. It was so loosely run, in the spirit of the era, that McGovern's eloquent acceptance speech, which he considered the best speech he gave in his life, did not start until 2:48 AM, by which point, of course, most of the country had gone to bed.

Warren Beatty was one of the celebrity delegates of the convention. After filming *McCabe & Mrs. Miller* for renegade director Robert Altman 18 months earlier, he had grown disillusioned with (or fatigued by) the film business. He had turned down the opportunity to star in *The Godfather, The Great Gatsby, Last Tango in Paris, The Sting* and *Butch Cassidy and the Sundance Kid.* Instead, he plunged into working full time on the presidential campaign of George McGovern.

"The McGovern campaign was at the center of the '70s," says Beatty. "It laid the foundation of everything that happened in the Democratic Party afterwards. The Democratic Party was at its lowest point, and the establishment guys said, 'Oh, fuck it, we're just giving up.' That's when the real interesting guys moved in, and they were all young, because McGovern couldn't tolerate anybody who was older. Gary Hart happened because of the McGovern campaign. Same with Bill Clinton."

Beatty, in a manner that could only have happened in the freewheeling 1970s, became one of the three or four most important people working on the campaign. He travelled throughout the primaries on the tour bus, door-knocked, spoke to women's Tupperware parties, assembly-line workers on factory floors, and marijuana-fueled student rallies. He advised the candidate, contributed to his speeches, brought in star power that helped inject life into the campaign and virtually invented the political benefit rock concert, that since 1972 has become a feature of virtually every presidential campaign.

Future President Bill Clinton, then a long-haired McGovern volunteer, remembers asking a recalcitrant female whether there was anything in the world he could do to get her to vote with the McGovern team. Clinton recalls, "She said, 'Yeah, if you can get Warren Beatty to walk on the beach with me.' As God is my witness, 30 minutes later I get on an elevator and there he is. I explained the deal to him. He said, 'Sure, I'll do it.' He walked 100 yards on the beach. That woman voted with us on every single thing."

The McGovern campaign wondered whether Beatty's reputation as one of the greatest Lotharios of all time might bite them, especially in middle America, but, in the free-spirited '70s, it didn't seem to have any negative effect. His celebrity status certainly helped with their ability to raise campaign funds. In Cleveland, one starstruck contributor wrote out a check for $50,000. Beatty told the man, "I won't take that money. People of your standing—if you can't give six figures, we want nothing from you." The chastened man tore up the check and wrote another for $125,000.

In the end, according to McGovern, Beatty raised over a million dollars. Beatty began to think to himself that if he could raise a million dollars for McGovern, maybe he might be able to raise 30 or 40 times that from one of the Hollywood studios to make his pet-project movie about the communist revolutionary John Reed. Once the grueling convention ended, Beatty holed up for four days in his Miami hotel room and turned out a 25-page outline of what he had in mind for his adaptation of Reed's *Ten Days That Shook the World.*

Meanwhile, his sister Shirley MacLaine, also a movie star, became the latest proponent of Maoist communism. After spending two months touring China with a group of American women, she described her experiences in a book she titled *You Can Get There From Here.* She felt the Chinese people were "so open and vital," and wrote that "In China we saw low food prices and streets free of crime and dope peddling. Mao Zedong was a leader who seemed genuinely loved, people had great hopes for the future, women had little need or even desire for such superficial things as frilly clothes and make-up, children loved work. Relationships seemed free of jealousy and infidelity because monogamy was the law of the land and hardly anyone strayed. I had a growing feeling that the Chinese way might be the way of the future."

MacLaine even praised the obviously strict authoritarianism of the Chinese state. "I, one who aspired to art and the supreme importance of the individual, was changing my point of view as to just how important individualism really was. I was seeing that it was possible somehow to reform human beings, and here they were being educated toward a loving communal spirit through a kind of totalitarian benevolence…maybe the individual was simply not as important as the group." [99]

On returning from Beijing, MacLaine went through a period of self-examination, and concluded that Mao's dictum that one should "serve the people" meant that she should return to the stage. She proceeded to open a new cabaret style show in Las Vegas, claiming, to somewhat mystified reporters on opening night that "Mao Zedong is probably responsible for my being here."

While Beatty was scriptwriting in Miami and MacLaine was high-kicking in Las Vegas, yet another Hollywood movie star, Jane Fonda, was arriving in Hanoi. She had been invited by several film and cultural organizations to see with her own eyes what the bombing was doing to the country. She did not have to wait long. On her first night she was escorted into an underground bunker to avoid the bombs being dropped by American B-52's. She spent much of her time filming the damage to the country's dyke system, and being interviewed by Hanoi radio, for direct broadcast to American airmen and soldiers. There is some argument about these interviews. One POW claimed that "We heard Jane Fonda yakking till we almost went fucking crazy." Anti-Fonda press reports claimed that her interviews were heard by thousands of U.S. soldiers, but this was likely not true, because Radio Hanoi was constantly being jammed by the Americans.

There is no doubt that the most contentious moment of the trip occurred when Fonda was photographed wearing a North Vietnamese helmet while sitting at the controls of an anti-aircraft gun. Fonda had immediate regrets and pleaded with the North Vietnamese not to publish the pictures. "It was a two-minute lapse of sanity that will haunt me till the day I die," says Fonda. "I simply wasn't *thinking* about what I was doing, only about what I was *feeling*—innocent of what the photo implies."

She returned to America, landing at JFK airport dressed in Vietnamese black pajamas and a coolie hat. She was greeted by some cheering supporters and others who shouted "Hanoi Jane" and "Pinko Slut." The White House tried to have her found guilty of treason. Most of the press were against her. Reporter David Halberstam (himself a critic of the war) called her a "stupid fucking actress." William Manchester, editor of the right-wing *New Hampshire Union Leader*, called for her to be charged with sedition and if convicted, shot. A U.S. congressman said her tongue should be cut out. One of the many assassination threats she received read, "Someday, sometime, somehow—whenever you are in the right place at the right time a shot will ring out ending your life." Gloria Emerson, the only female reporter covering the war for the *New York Times*, was one of the very few who defended her, saying she had terrific impact and "spoke out against the war with great courage and eloquence."

• • •

Perhaps ultimately more influential than Fonda's Vietnam visit, MacLaine's book, or Beatty's movie script was an article written by Stewart Brand that appeared in the July issue of *Rolling Stone* magazine. Brand had moved on from his days experimenting with LSD, creating the Trips Festivals, hanging with the Merry Pranksters, and editing the *Whole Earth Catalogue*. He was now deep into the new world of personal computers. He wrote his article not on a personal computer, as they barely existed at the time, but in longhand on a table in his Sausalito houseboat on which, it is claimed, Otis Redding wrote *Sittin' on the Dock of the Bay*. The visionary *Rolling Stone* article, (later turned into a book called *Two Cybernetic Frontiers*) described the new work being done with computers so they and their users could communicate with each other. More importantly, he proposed the counterculture concept that information shared on these linked computers should be free. Extraordinarily, it worked out that way.

• • •

The dreary situation in Northern Ireland continued to deteriorate. Weeks of ferocious bombing and shooting through the summer culminated in Belfast on July 21ˢᵗ, which came to be called Bloody Friday. Within an 80-minute period the IRA exploded 20 bombs that killed nine people and wounded 130. Many were horribly mutilated. "For much of the afternoon," wrote *The Observer*, "Belfast was reduced to near total chaos and panic. Thousands streamed out of the stricken city and huge traffic jams built up. All bus service was cancelled, and on some roads, hitch-hikers frantically trying to get away lined the pavements." The bombing campaign backfired. It did not bring the British back to the bargaining table. It caused a backlash against the IRA, and it encouraged a wave of retaliatory sectarian revenge attacks by the UDA against Catholic civilians.

• • •

Two weeks later, on August 4, Idi Amin Dada issued a decree expelling the 60,000 Asians living in Uganda. In one of the largest mass migrations ever, about 30,000 moved to live in England, and the rest went to Australia, Canada, South Africa, and Fiji.

• • •

More protests erupted at the August Republican National Convention in Miami Beach, Florida. The Vietnam Veterans Against the War marched to the convention to hear Ron Kovic, a paralyzed veteran in a wheelchair, angrily tell the delegates, "You have lied to us too long. You may have taken our bodies but you haven't taken our minds." The following day 3,000 protestors led by Tom Hayden and Jane Fonda circled the convention hall shouting, "Murderers—delegates kill!"

On September 4, Jane Fonda ceremoniously cut off her new partner Tom Hayden's long hair, decked him out in a new suit and tie, and exchanged her T-shirt and jeans for a wrinkle-proof conservative outfit. The pair, with their new approach to winning over middle-America, then began a 90-city Indochina Peace Campaign, starting at the Ohio State Fair.

• • •

The next day, at the Munich Olympics, eight members of the Black September faction of the PLO took 11 members of the Israeli Team hostage in an operation they called *Iqrit and Biram*, named after two Palestinian Christian villages whose inhabitants were expelled by the Israel Defense Forces as part of the creation of Israel in 1948. Their demand was the release of 234 Palestinians and non-Arabs held in Israeli jails, and the release of Andreas Baader and Ulrike Meinhof, the two leaders of the Red Army Faction held in West German penitentiaries. Israel completely refused to negotiate. Germany offered what they called 'an unlimited amount of money' for the release of the hostages, but the terrorists responded saying they neither cared about money nor their own lives.

In a rescue attempt generally perceived to have been bungled, West German police snipers fired on the terrorists while they were being transported with their hostages by helicopter to an airfield. All the hostages died at the hands of the terrorists. A West German policeman was caught in the crossfire. Five of the eight Black September members were shot and the other three were captured and arrested.

Israel responded with *Operation Wrath of God*, an attempt to find and kill all those involved in the Munich massacre. The hunt lasted 20 years, with numerous Arabs who the Israelis believed were connected to the hostage-taking killed in targeted assassinations across Europe and the Middle East.

• • •

Richard Oakes, the organizer of the Native occupation of Alcatraz Island, left the occupation after the accidental death in 1970 of his stepdaughter but continued to work as an activist for Native rights. On

September 20th he was shot and killed at a YMCA camp in Sonoma, California by Michael Morgan, an avowed white supremacist,. Morgan was charged with voluntary manslaughter but was acquitted. Oakes' supporters claimed the shooting was an act of murder and that the jury and district attorney were racially prejudiced against the native leader.[100]

• • •

Also in Northern California, Steve Jobs began taking LSD in his final year at Homestead High School. He mixed psychedelics with his other interest—electronics—and continued to work with his pal Steve Wozniak to create illegal telephone 'Blue Boxes.' In September, he enrolled in what was considered one of the coolest universities on the west coast, Reed College in Portland, Oregon. "When you say Reed," said the college's president, Colin Diver, "two words come to mind. One is brains. The other is drugs."

"I was interested in Eastern mysticism which hit the shores about then," recalled Jobs. "At Reed there was a constant flow of people stopping by—from Timothy Leary and Richard Alpert to Gary Snyder. There was a constant flow of intellectual questioning about the truth of life." After just one semester, the future computer whiz and business tycoon dropped out of Reed without telling his parents, because, he said, he didn't want to spend their money on an education that seemed meaningless to him. He continued to experiment with drugs, slept on the floor of other students' dorm rooms, returned soft drink bottles for money, and ate free meals at a local Hare Krishna temple. In the early '70s, the computer represented everything students—especially students like Steve Jobs—hated about the regimentation of America. It was just another massive tool of big corporations, government, the military, and bloated universities. The most common feeling towards the computer was the disdain for the instruction that was printed on all computer punchcards: "Do Not Bend, Fold, Staple, or Mutilate."

Although Jobs was, like so many others in the '60s and '70s, technically a student drop-out, he did continue to audit a class in calligraphy that interested him. "If I had never dropped in on that single calligraphy course in college," he said much later in a Stanford University commencement speech, "the Mac would have never had multiple typefaces or proportionally spaced fonts." But apart from the course in calligraphy, he mostly took LSD at Reed.

• • •

Oregon's Reed College was tame by comparison with Ontario's Rochdale College, which by '72 had mostly become, as one resident described it, "a flophouse for the international drug trade." Totally experimental and largely anarchic in structure, it had tried all manner of administrative models, even crowning a playwright and theater director, Jim Garrard, King James I for a year. Ambulances delivered 58 drug overdose victims to Toronto hospitals, three of whom were dead on arrival. There were several unfortunate incidents of residents throwing themselves out of 17th story windows.

Police, armed with crowbars and axes, raided the college at one point, and were met with 1,500 angry residents throwing furniture into a massive bonfire on the sidewalk in front of the building. Toronto alderman Tony O'Donohue called on the federal government to "put an end to the madness" and convert the building into a police college or a home for the aged. The group of tenants running the finances of the college (known by others as 'the sleazes') stopped mortgage payments in 1972, and on September 13, the Canada Mortgage and Housing Corporation appointed Clarkson and Company as receiver of the building. Over a thousand people continued to squat in the crazy college and the crisis continued for another three years.

• • •

Canada was also the site of one of the most bitter sporting contests fought during the Cold War—an ice hockey series between the Soviet Union and the West. Canada's players, widely felt to be the best in the world, were not allowed to play in international, or Olympic hockey, since the top tier were all playing professionally in the NHL. Russian players, though ostensibly 'amateur', were in fact mostly secretly employed by either the KGB or the Russian Army and were paid by the armed services to practice and play hockey full-time, year-round.

This series was designed to pit the best Canadian players against the best Russian players without any rules about amateur or professional status. The Canadian government wanted to call the series the 'Friendship Series' but the key organizer, Allan Eagleson, would have none of that, and it ended up being called the 'Summit Series.' Played at the height of the Cold War, there was very little friendship on display between the teams or their fans.

The series began in Montréal and continued to three other Canadian cities and then moved on for four games in Moscow. In this era the Russians were paranoid about their sportsmen and performers defecting while in the west, so the Soviet team was accompanied by a large number of KGB minders to control the activities of the players. They had reason to be paranoid. For instance, one of Russia's most acclaimed male ballet dancers, Rudolf Nureyev, had defected in Paris in 1961, and another, Mikhail Baryshnikov, would defect in Toronto on June 29, 1974.

The hockey cognoscenti were almost unanimous in their opinion that the Canadians would sweep the series 8-0, so it was a complete shock to the country when Russia won two and tied one of the first four games. At that point, the gloves came off and the Canadians began playing the rough, dirty game that typified NHL hockey in the 1970s. The lowest point came when Bobby Clarke, leader of the brawling 'Broad Street Bullies', as the Philadelphia Flyers were then known, viciously slashed Russian star Valeri Kharlamov, sending him to the dressing room with a fractured ankle. Commentator Brian Conacher said that "from the broadcast booth I was shocked and disgusted when I saw Clarke viciously chop at Kharlamov's left ankle," and observed that "emotionally these games had clearly gone beyond sport for Team Canada and had truly become unrestricted war on ice." [101]

The war continued when organizer Alan Eagleson (later disgraced and jailed for other activities in the hockey world) physically attacked one of the Russian scoring officials; Pete Mahovlich confronted police with his stick; and Canadian players and fans aggressively gave Russian officials the finger. Even Canadian mega-star Bobby Hull criticized the behavior of Team Canada, saying that the fighting and gestures of the Canadian players "were a bad example to young players and diplomatically harmful." The event provided lots of rock 'em, sock 'em entertainment, but did nothing to thaw the Cold War between Russia and the West. Canada won the icy contest 4-3.

• • •

"October 14, 1972," wrote Pauline Kael, the most important movie critic in America, "should become a landmark in movie history comparable to May 29, 1913—the night *Le Sacre du Printemps* was first performed—in music history. *Last Tango in Paris* has the same kind of hypnotic excitement as the *Sacre*, the same primitive force, and the same thrusting, jabbing eroticism. The movie breakthrough has finally come."

The film was directed by Bernardo Bertolucci and starred Marlon Brando and 19-year-old French ingenue Maria Schneider. Both the production and the response to the film typify the excesses of the early '70s. The film cost $1.7 million to make and grossed $96.3 million at the box office. It opened at the New York Film Festival and then played to millions all over the world. In countries where it was banned (like Spain), moviegoers travelled hundreds of kilometers to see the film in other jurisdictions. Maria Schneider, though, announced that she felt she had been violated by Brando and Bertolucci, who had forced her to do an unscripted scene involving anal sex that she felt was humiliating. The director and star nearly went to jail because of it.

There was a media frenzy over the film, with newspaper reports that people were offering up to $100 to get into the packed theaters, while "well-dressed wives" vomited in response to the scandalous production.[102] In Montclair, New Jersey, theatergoers had to push through a mob of outraged residents hurling epithets like "homos!" and "perverts!" A bomb threat halted the screening. The film was banned in various jurisdictions including Nova Scotia, Brazil, Chile, and Portugal. In Italy, the film grossed a record-breaking $100,000 in six days, but then all prints were seized by the police, and destroyed. Director Bertolucci, Brando, Producer Alberto Grimaldi, and Screenwriter Franco Arcalli were charged with "aggravated, gratuitous pansexualism" and received suspended sentences of two-to-four months. Bertolucci also had his civil rights revoked for five years, depriving him of his right to vote. Meanwhile, Pauline Kael insisted "it may turn out to be the most liberating movie ever made...a film people will be arguing about as long as there are movies."

The public in the 1970s was definitely interested in the new liberated attitudes towards sex. Alex Comfort, a British scientist and physician, published a how-to manual in 1972 called *The Joy of Sex—A Gourmet Guide to Lovemaking*. The illustrated book described numerous sex positions and opened the eyes of readers to practices such as oral sex, bondage, and swinging. Of course, there was pushback. Religious groups fought with some success to keep it out of public libraries, especially in the United States. What did the publishers care about a few libraries? The book sat for *eleven* weeks at the top of the *New York Times* bestseller list, and for *seventy* weeks from 1972 to 1974 in the top five.

• • •

On October 17th, a very powerful bomb was detonated by the Montoneros and the Revolutionary Armed Forces in the Sheraton Hotel in Buenos Aires. Six hundred guests were terrorized, and one was killed—Lois Crozier, a travel agent from West Vancouver, with her husband Gerry gravely wounded.

• • •

Seven men broke out of 'The Tombs' prison on October 23rd to unite as the Black Liberation Army under the leadership of Joanne Chesimard (aka Assata Shakur). She was described by the New York *Daily News* as "the high priestess of the cop-hating BLA" and "a black Joan of Arc". They began a string of cop-killings, bombings, and bank robberies across New York. In Ireland, on the same day, the Ulster Volunteer Force raided a British Territorial Army weapons depot in Lurgan, procuring a cache of L1A1 rifles, Browning pistols, and Sterling submachine guns. They also stole several tons of ammonium nitrate from the Belfast docks.

• • •

On the first day of November, about seven hundred Native Americans arrived in Washington as part of a protest they called the *Trail of Broken Dreams*. The trail had begun on the west coast in Los Angeles and Seattle. The natives, driving campers, trucks, and cars had picked up additional protestors as they crossed the country. Led by activists including Dennis Banks, the group hoped to meet with Richard Nixon and present him with their list of proposals about changes they hoped to see in the relationship between Natives and the American government. They learned on their arrival in the capital that not only would Nixon not meet with them or receive their proposals, but that Harrison Loesch, the official in the Interior Department that oversaw the Bureau of Indian Affairs, instructed the BIA, contrary to the usual protocol with visiting Indian groups, to not provide any assistance to the Trail.

The Trail group already considered Loesch to be an old-guard reactionary and a symbol of everything many Indian people despised about the Interior Department and the BIA.[103] With their plans disrupted, members of the Trail entered the BIA headquarters. While the natives were in negotiations with Nixon's domestic affairs advisor John Ehrlichman, Washington riot police attacked the building. Eventually the natives forced the police out of the building and barricaded themselves inside. After being double-crossed by the government on a proposed alternative solution, the Indians donned traditional warpaint, erected a teepee in front and put a sign on the government building reading NATIVE AMERICAN EMBASSY. Press reports warned about the possibility of "Another Wounded Knee." Counterculture celebrities like Dr. Benjamin Spock and Stokely Carmichael showed up to lend support, as did a seventh-grade class studying Indians.

The occupying natives began fashioning makeshift spears out of broom handles and scissors, assembling Molotov cocktails, and also trashing much of the artwork and the records in the building. Finally, on November 7th, the day of the U.S. federal election, the protestors came to a grudging agreement with the government and abandoned the building. They left behind a sign that read: "Gentlemen: we do not apologize for the ruin nor for the so-called destruction of this mausoleum. For in building anew, one must first destroy the old. This is the beginning of a new era for the Native American people. When history recalls our efforts here, our descendants will stand with pride knowing their people were the ones responsible for the stand taken against tyranny, injustice, and the gross inefficiency of this branch of a corrupt and decadent government."

As is frequently the case in America when it comes to native issues, very little attention was paid to the protest. Instead, all eyes were on the presidential election, in which Richard Nixon slaughtered liberal Democrat George McGovern, winning, in the arcane Electoral College voting system, every state except Massachusetts. (Popular bumper stickers in 1973 read "Don't Blame Me! I'm from Massachusetts"). Even though his second term would ultimately prove to be the most disastrous Presidential term in American history, for now right-wingers were elated and the left was devastated. The gloom was best expressed by the always entertainingly overheated Hunter S. Thompson, who wrote that Nixon "represents that dark, venal and incurably violent side of the American character." Nixon, Thompson said, was "America's answer to…the Werewolf in all of us…At the stroke of midnight in Washington, a drooling red-eyed beast with the legs of a man and the head of a giant hyena crawls out its bedroom window in the South Wing of the White House and leaps 50 feet down to the lawn…pauses briefly to strangle the Chow watchdog, then races off into the darkness…towards the Watergate, snarling with lust, loping through the alleys behind Pennsylvania Avenue."

• • •

Also in November, China's Premier Zhou Enlai was diagnosed with bladder cancer. His doctors reported that he had about a 90% chance of recovery, but medical treatment for the highest-ranking party members had to be approved by Mao. The always-unpredictable Chairman ordered that Zhou and his wife should not be told of the diagnosis, that no surgery should be done, and that no further examinations should be given. Henry Kissinger learned of the issue and offered to send cancer specialists from the U.S., but the offer was turned down. Finally in 1974, after continuing medical issues and pressure from other party members, Mao approved the surgery, but it was too late. Zhou was mostly hospitalized until his death on January 8th, 1977.

• • •

In New York, super-star artist Andy Warhol, like so many other people, jumped on the Mao bandwagon. After his near death in 1968 Warhol's artistic output had shrunk, but in '72 he came up with a new idea for a series of paintings. "Since fashion is art right now and Chinese is in fashion, should I do some Mao portraits?" he asked his friend David Bourdon. "I could make a lot of money. Mao would be really nutty…not to believe in it—it'd just be fashion. And still a portrait is not considered a painting. Fashion is art right now...Don't do anything creative, just print it up on canvas." [104]

Warhol and his team of assistants got to work, ultimately turning out over 2700 versions, mostly using simple silkscreen techniques, some with additional painterly squiggles, in an assortment of color combinations that could accessorize any living room. While real Maoists were roaming the jungles of Sri Lanka and preparing a violent insurgency in Peru, Warhol was preparing another assault on the art world with his versions of Mao's smiling face. In November, he launched the series at the Castelli Gallery in Manhattan, then through the venerable Knoedler Gallery of New York and dealer Bruno Bischofberger in Switzerland. He sold many more at galleries in Basel, Turin, and across Mao-crazy and Warhol-crazy Europe, with the largest of them going for $30,000. In total they raked in nearly $2 million, and garnered Warhol the best reviews he'd had in years. The London *Times* hailed Andy Warhol as "the most serious artist to have emerged anywhere since the war, and the most important American artist...Warhol is in some ways like Oscar Wilde. He hides a deep seriousness and commitment behind a front of frivolity."

Not everyone was so smitten. One New York reader wrote a letter to his newspaper reminding people, "Mao Zedong murdered about 60 million Chinese and caused poverty and starvation in all of China...To put prints of such a person on the wall is equal to putting Satan in New York to replace the Statue of Liberty."

In 2015, one of Warhol's 1972 Mao paintings sold for 47.5 million dollars.

• • •

The Rhodesian Bush War began to escalate between the white renegade Rhodesian government and the guerrilla forces of ZANLA. On the 4th of December, Ian Smith made a sobering radio address to his white Rhodesian supporters, telling them, "The security situation is far more serious than it appears on the surface, and if the man in the street could have access to the security information which I and my colleagues have, then I think he would be a lot more worried that he is today." Indeed, almost at the same time he was saying this, a party of 21 armed men under command of a tough guerrilla leader named Rex Nhongo slipped into Rhodesia from Mozambique and began attacking remote farms and seeding the roads with mines. As expected, this brought a draconian response from the Rhodesian government that began burning villages and confiscating cattle in order to remove the guerrillas' support systems. The African fighters had been trained in China with Mao's maxim that "The guerrilla must move amongst the people as a fish swims in the ocean." Rhodesian forces, desperate to hold on to power, were attempting to remove and destroy the guerrillas' 'ocean'. Ian Smith was plainly on the wrong side of history, but he refused to admit it. On the one hand he was being confronted by a huge black population who were being told by their leader Robert Mugabe, "Let us hammer the white man to defeat. Let us blow up his citadel. Let us give him no time to rest. Let us chase him in every corner. Let us rid our home of this settler vermin." On the other hand, he was being told by B.J. Vorster, the leader of Rhodesia's only friend in the world, South Africa, that in his opinion white minority rule was unsustainable in a country where blacks outnumbered whites 22:1.

On December 16th, the Portuguese 6th company of Mozambique Commandos entered the village of Wiriyamu in the district of Tete in Mozambique and slaughtered between 150 and 300 civilians, many of them children, because the settlement was suspected of harboring Frelimo guerrillas. Later reports smuggled out by priests such as Father Adrian Hastings quoted agents saying that the orders given to the Portuguese commandos were that they were to "kill them all."

• • •

As the Christmas season and the end of the year approached, activist singer Joan Baez and three others were invited to fly to Hanoi to witness what was happening to the North Vietnamese capital. It seemed as if it would be a relatively safe time to visit, but it was not. Knowing that members of his 'enemies list' would be in Hanoi, President Nixon decided to put his air force crews to work over the holiday season and authorized what was later described as the heaviest bombing in the history of the world. Baez and the three other observers were hustled from their hotel rooms to underground bomb shelters up to eight times a night. Baez took her guitar down to calm people's nerves with song, but she found she could not stand up to sing in the basement shelters. Since the concussion blasts to the city were so extreme, she had to sit on the ground. During the days, Baez and the team toured the city and nearby countryside, viewing the damage, and marveling, as all visitors did, how quickly restoration teams, mostly made up of women, old men, and young boys and girls, got to work making repairs.

Hanoi was an appropriate metaphor for the pattern of the early '70s: Build, Destroy, Re-build.

1973

Timothy Leary Jailed, Peace in Paris,
Roe vs Wade, Wounded Knee, Symbionese Liberation
Army, Juan Peron Back in Argentina, Marlon Brando,
Sacheen Littlefeather, David McTaggart Sails Again,
Stockholm Syndrome, Coup in Chile, Sexist Tennis in Texas,
Greece in Crisis, Gang of Four, Gulag Archipelago.

On January 3rd, as Joan Baez was flying back from North Vietnam, the trial of another member of the Nixon 'enemies list' began in Los Angeles. Daniel Ellsberg had been charged under the Espionage Act of 1917 with theft and conspiracy for his release of the *Pentagon Papers* to the *New York Times*. The trial judge effectively denied Ellsberg an opportunity to defend himself. His exasperated lawyer said that he "had never heard of a case where the defendant was not permitted to tell the jury what he did." The judge responded, "Well, you're hearing one now."

• • •

Also in Los Angeles, on January 17th, Timothy Leary, in shackles, was ushered off a plane, greeted by 50 helmeted police with riot guns lining the path to a Volkswagen van, and driven off to prison. He had had quite a journey since escaping from the California prison back in 1970. After Eldridge Cleaver effectively banished him from Algeria, Leary went to Switzerland. Nixon's Attorney General John Mitchell convinced the Swiss to jail him and attempted to get him extradited back to the U.S. The Swiss refused. Leary found a mysterious benefactor, high-flying arms dealer Michel-Gustave Hauchard, who got Leary out of jail and into a high-end penthouse in Lausanne. Leary connected with Dr. Albert Hofmann, the man who had discovered LSD 30 years earlier, who reassured Leary that regardless of what press and politicians were saying, his tests all proved that LSD did not cause brain damage.

Leary's jangled lifestyle meant that his marriage blew up and he finally lost his wife in Switzerland. However, he soon found a new girl-friend, an adventurous European heiress named Joanna Harcourt-Smith. There is some suspicion that the exotic woman was working as an under-cover agent for the American authorities, or possibly that she was even a double- or triple-agent involved with the mysterious, wealthy, drug-smuggling ring that called itself the Brotherhood of Eternal Love. Harcourt-Smith convinced Leary that they should fly to Sri Lanka, charter a yacht, and sail away into the sunset. First though, she wanted them to stop in Kabul, Afghanistan, ostensibly to meet a crown prince, which they did. While there, American narcotics agents nabbed Leary, and even though Afghanistan had no extradition treaty with the U.S., a CIA man named Terrance Burke twisted the arms of Afghan authorities who agreed to ship him back to America.

Leary was now in deep trouble. Orange County D.A. Cecil Hicks claimed that "Leary is responsible for destroying more lives than any other human being." President Nixon called him, "the most dangerous man in America." The judge at his hearing claimed, "if he is allowed to travel freely, he will speak publicly and spread his ideas," and bail was set at an impossible $5 million. Leary was found guilty and received an additional five years for his prison escape on top of the existing 20. He was sent to Folsom Prison and put in solitary confinement in a cell next to Charles

Manson. They could not see each other but they could talk. Manson at one point cryptically told Leary, "They took you off the streets so that I could continue your work." [105]

•   •   •

The Paris Peace Accords, an attempt to find an end to the war in Vietnam, had been dragging on for months. There were many road-blocks—for example, the shape of the negotiating table. The North Vietnamese demanded a circular table, to indicate that all parties to the accords were equal. The South Vietnamese demanded a rectangular table, to indicate that there were four distinct sides to the conflict. Remarkably, and despite the drama over the shape of the table, a cease-fire agreement was signed in Paris between North and South Vietnam, the Viet Cong, and the U.S.A.

Within days, Hanoi released more than a hundred POWs. The Nixon Administration and the Pentagon begin *Operation Homecoming*, later described as "a carefully prepared TV commercial on behalf of the White House." Hardline American officers were chosen as the heroes, Jane Fonda as the villain. The U.S. agreed to pay North Vietnam $3.25 billion in war reparations, but later reneged, using the questionable claims of extensive North Vietnamese torture of P.O.W.'s as an excuse.[106] There was no appearance of a cease-fire. In fact, to try to buy time for the South Vietnamese to take over the fight, Nixon ordered a new intense bombing of both North and South Vietnam. Due to the rapid escalation of the Watergate scandal, though, he had to rescind the order.

Henry Kissinger and North Vietnamese leader Le Duc Tho were jointly awarded the 1973 Noble Peace Prize for signing the Peace Accords. The awards were greeted with derision. The *New York Times* dubbed it the 'Nobel War Prize'. Diplomat George Ball commented that "the Norwegians must have a sense of humor", and comedian Tom Lehrer mordantly said, "Political satire became obsolete when Henry Kissinger was awarded the Nobel Peace Prize." Tho declined the prize, saying that such "bourgeois sentimentalities" were not for him, and that regardless of the signed paper, there was no peace. Both Saigon and America continued their acts of war.

• • •

There was false hope that the Vietnam Peace Accords might also end the vicious fighting in Cambodia. Prime Minister Lon Nol proclaimed a unilateral cease-fire throughout the nation in January and the United States temporarily stopped their massive bombing. The Khmer Rouge, though, ignored the cease-fire and advanced to the suburbs of the capital, Phnom Penh. The U.S. Seventh Air Force resumed bombing, dropping another 82,000 tons of bombs and, they claimed, killing 16,000 of the 25,000 Khmer Rouge who were besieging the city. From the commencement of *Operation Menu* in 1969 until they finally abandoned the Cambodian conflict, the American Air Force dropped an astounding 539,129 tons of explosives on Cambodia.

With both the Americans and the North Vietnamese gone, and the Lon Nol government in retreat, the Cambodian people soon began to witness the utter horror of the Khmer Rouge. The genocide inflicted on Cambodia by Pol Pot and the Khmer Rouge was on a level of the worst in history—including the extermination of Indians by the Spanish conquistadors in South America and by the American cavalry in the U.S., Hitler's holocaust, Stalin's purges, the ethnic cleansings in Rwanda and Bosnia. Pol Pot became possessed by the most extremist Maoist thought, demanding that the country be utterly transformed. Everything that had preceded it was to be destroyed. Even Mao was frightened by Pol Pot's murderous revolutionary zeal.

• • •

Worldwide, China had become by far the biggest donor of foreign aid. In its quest to foment revolution and assist the Third World, mostly in Africa, China now assigned 6.92% of its national budget to foreign aid, at huge cost to the Chinese people, many of whom were starving. By comparison, the United Kingdom was giving .7% of its budget to foreign aid, the USSR about .9%, and the United States about 1.5%. Meanwhile, China was building railroads across Africa, providing medicine and guns, supporting the expensive Bush Wars against colonialist regimes and renegade states in Southern Africa, and bringing hundreds of Africans to China to educate them in the revolutionary teachings of Chairman Mao.

• • •

One of the most significant court cases in American history, known as 'Roe vs Wade' was decided on January 23rd in the U.S. Supreme Court. The case, about protecting a woman's right to an abortion started small but became monumental when it pitted abortion-rights groups against anti-abortion groups, and divided U.S. opinion into 'pro-choice' and 'pro-life' camps. The trial was named for 'Jane Roe', the pseudonym for Norma McCorvey, a young, abused, poverty-stricken Texan woman, who was used by both sides of the abortion debate. The prosecution was headed by Henry Wade, the District Attorney responsible for enforcing Texas' anti-abortion statute. Ironically McCorvey, the woman at the center of it all, was a lesbian. She had nevertheless become pregnant, and after her first attempt to try to procure an abortion failed (she fictitiously claimed she had been raped by a group of black men), she approached a pair of activist female lawyers who took her case right up the U.S. Supreme Court and won. The verdict drastically changed many aspects of life in America, not least the crime rate, which shrank dramatically in the years after the decision, because there were so many fewer unwanted children.

• • •

On February 27th, two hundred Oglala Lakota activists and followers of the American Indian Movement seized and occupied the town of Wounded Knee on the Pine Ridge Indian Reservation in South Dakota.

They demanded the reopening of treaty negotiations to attempt to redress grievances and right the wrongs that affected the lives of their people. The choice of their protest was both deliberate and symbolic as it was the site of the 1890 Wounded Knee Massacre in which 250 Lakota were slaughtered by the U.S. Cavalry.

The protestors were soon surrounded by more than 1,000 FBI agents, U.S. Marshalls, and National Guards equipped with Armored Patrol Carriers, helicopters, .50 caliber machine guns, and over 130,000 rounds of ammunition. The mood of the event was well described by one of the protestors, Annie Mae Aquash, a Mi'kmaq activist from Nova Scotia. In her words "these white people think this country belongs to them. The whole country changed with only a handful of raggedy-ass Pilgrims that came over here in the 1500s. Now, a handful of raggedy-ass Indians can do the same and I intend to be one of those raggedy-ass Indians."

The gunfire during the 71-day siege resulted in three deaths and 14 badly wounded Lakota. The event captured the imagination of the world and was closely followed by the international press and by Americans, who, polls said, were largely supportive. The blockade of the town meant it was very difficult to get goods in. People from across the country began driving to Pine Ridge with supplies for the natives. The government invoked the 1967 H. Rap Brown Law, named after the Black Power activist, that allowed them to stop and arrest anyone believed to be crossing state lines to take part in a civil disorder. Those who made it as far as the reservation then had to lug supplies in 50-pound backpacks and dodge the flares and searchlights of the government authorities to get to the besieged protestors. A group of anti-war activists from Chicago sent three Cessna planes over the reserve to drop large containers of food. The FBI sent its helicopter, nicknamed 'Snoopy', to investigate. In one instance snipers from the chopper fired at a family carrying the food back to the town.

Several protestors were killed by government snipers during the siege and two U.S. Marshals were wounded from gunfire from the Natives. The conflict dragged on through the cold South Dakota winter. It became more difficult for the protestors to continue after Kent Frizell, a hardliner from the Department of Justice, took over the management of the government's response, and tried to end the stand-off by cutting off electricity, water, and food supplies, and forbidding entry by the media.

• • •

Meanwhile in Africa, Idi Amin Dada broke off diplomatic ties with India and Israel, and eventually also with the U.K. (even though he declared himself the King of Scotland). He began plans for a war with Israel, using paratroops, bombers, and suicide squadrons. He became aligned with Colonel Gaddafi's Libya, the USSR, and East Germany, all of whom supplied arms and military assistance. The American Ambassador, Thomas Patrick Malady, recommended that the U.S. reduce its presence in Uganda, calling Amin "racist, erratic and unpredictable, brutal, inept, bellicose, irrational, ridiculous and militaristic." His rogue regime became so dark and violent that British Foreign Secretary David Owen proposed having him assassinated. Amin boasted that he kept the decapitated heads of political enemies in his freezer. There was a widespread belief that he was a cannibal, although he claimed that human flesh was "too salty" for his taste.

• • •

As things were getting crazier in Uganda, they were also getting crazy around San Francisco Bay. The area was under the grip of both the Zodiac Killer and a group of black militants known as the Zebra Killers. The "Zebra Killers" was the name the police gave the group. They actually referred to themselves as the "Death Angels". Once finally apprehended in 1974, they were charged with killing 15 people and wounding eight others. The Zodiac Killer is believed to have been a single, white, serial killer. He began his killing spree in 1968, and in his many mysterious letters and cryptograms to the two San Francisco newspapers and to the *Vallejo Times*

Herald, he claimed to be responsible for 37 deaths between 1968 and 1974. The case has never been solved.

The next criminal to be roaming *The Streets of San Francisco* (a popular new TV show of the era) would grab the attention of the world like no other. On March 5th, Donald Defreeze, a convicted bank robber full of revolutionary rhetoric, broke out of Soledad Prison by climbing over a fence. He then headed north to Berkeley, located a radical commune and according to lore, opened the door and announced, "I'm here. Let's start the revolution." Within a day he had made his way into the bed of his first recruit, an attractive 22-year-old sometime student, sometime janitor, sometime lesbian, and fulltime self-avowed revolutionary feminist named Patricia Soltysik, who preferred to go by the name 'Mizmoon'. The pair would soon begin the violent revolutionary cell known as the Symbionese Liberation Army.

• • •

Six days later, the general elections that were finally held in Argentina by the military junta that had been running the country since 1955 did not allow Juan Peron, who was still in exile in Spain, to run for office. However, his personally appointed substitute, left-wing Peronist Dr. Héctor Cámpora, did win the election. Cámpora's first acts were to grant amnesty to all political prisoners, re-establish relations with Cuba (which helped Castro end the U.S. blockade), and invite Peron to return to Argentina. For some reason, the *Propaganda Duo*, a clandestine, pseudo-Masonic, neo-Fascist, Italian organization, chartered an Alitalia jet to fly Peron back to Argentina. When the plane arrived at Ezeiza Airport in Buenos Aires, there were, according to police estimates, three and a half million people, mostly young left-wing Peronistas and Montoneros, to greet him. Camouflaged snipers opened fire on the crowd, killing 13 and wounding 365.

Dr. Cámpora resigned in July, and in the new election Peron himself ran, and won. Peron's new term was marred by battles between fascist members of his government and left-wing groups like the Montoneros and the People's Revolutionary Army.

• • •

Marlon Brando did not attend the 45th Academy Awards, but instead sent Apache actress Sacheen Littlefeather to accept, should he win the Best Actor award for *The Godfather*. He did win, and Littlefeather, in traditional garb, accepted. She was told she could not read the speech about the siege at Wounded Knee that Brando had written, and that she would be taken offstage and arrested if she spoke for more than a minute. With a global viewing audience of millions, she gave a short impromptu speech about the treatment of Native Americans in the film industry. Afterwards, backstage, she did read Brando's speech to the press. Her two speeches were considered a major victory for the American Indian Movement and rekindled the interest of the press and public in the occupation of Wounded Knee.

The siege became more and more intense as it dragged on through April. Government forces began stockpiling gasmasks and chemical agents that would induce vomiting. Local vigilantes began shooting at both the Natives and the police to try and initiate a firefight between them that would end the event once and for all. On the last day of the month, a cavalcade of Native cars attempted to bury Frank Clearwater, one of the protestors who had been shot by FBI snipers. The funeral, like so many things about this protest, turned into a debacle, with the blockading authorities and unsupportive Native leaders forbidding the burial because Clearwater was not an Oglala.

• • •

The same day was monumental elsewhere in American politics. That evening Richard Nixon, finally bowing to the reality of the swirling toilet bowl of his Watergate-infected Presidency, announced that he had accepted the resignations of his two closest advisors, John Ehrlichman and

H.R. Haldeman, and his Attorney General, Richard Kleindienst. He also announced that he had fired his White House Counsel, John Dean, after learning that Dean had flipped and was cooperating with the Watergate prosecutors. Nixon replaced Dean with Leonard Garment, who had been one of the key government negotiators with the natives both at Alcatraz and at Wounded Knee.

One of Garment's key directives from Nixon was to "bring an end to this Wounded Knee thing—it can't go on indefinitely." By May 8th, it was over. Armed troops in Armored Personnel Carriers entered the Reservation and most of the Natives were arrested and jailed. Dennis Banks, with the help of a geographically savvy Navajo warrior claiming to have spiritual guidance, managed to slip through the government blockade in the night and disappear into the Black Hills.

Banks was eventually caught and he and Russell Means, the leaders of the American Indian Movement, were put on trial. In what is considered the longest political trial in American history, the two were defended by star radical attorneys William Kunstler and Mark Lane. The trial was as messy and complicated as the original event, with the judge ultimately stating, "the misconduct of the government in this case is so aggravated that a dismissal must be entered in the interests of justice." The prosecution appealed, but the Eighth Circuit Court of Appeals denied the appeal and Banks and Means were freed. It was the end of the Occupation of Wounded Knee, and it also turned out to be the beginning of the end of the American Indian Movement. It had been a spectacular ride, and the few thousand members of AIM had certainly brought the problems of North America's most ignored population to the world's attention, but with the growing conservatism of the world, the aging population, and the beginning of a waning interest in activism, the power and influence of AIM began to disappear.

• • •

After the murder of Fred Hampton, constant police harassment, and the exile of Eldridge Cleaver, some Panthers decided to go underground to create a new secret organization they called the Black Liberation Army. The BLA dispensed with any of the public activities, like the Free Breakfast Program, that the Panthers had initiated. Their stated goal was simply "to take up arms for the liberation and self-determination of black people in the United States."

Joanne Chesimard had been involved in student and black activism since the mid 60s. In 1971 she changed her name to Assata Shakur. She rejected her "slave name" and said, "It sounded so strange when people called me Joanne. It really had nothing to do with me. I didn't feel like no Joanne, or no negro, or no *Amerikan*. I felt like an African woman." Shakur was accused of involvement in several robberies and murders of police officers and was considered the *de facto* head of the BLA. Robert Daley, Deputy Commissioner of the New York City Police, described her as "the soul of the gang, the mother hen who kept them all together, kept them moving, kept them shooting." Other officers claimed her role as the 'Black Joan of Arc' was exaggerated, that the police had themselves created the myth to "demonize" her because she was "educated, young, and pretty."

On May 2nd, she was driving on the New Jersey Turnpike with three others when she was stopped by the highway patrol. The car had a broken taillight but it sounds as if the main reason for the stop was the usual crime of 'driving while black'. The incident quickly escalated into a major gun battle with the New Jersey police. One policeman was killed, another injured, and Shakur shot in her shoulder and both arms. She was eventually captured and hospitalized. She claims that she was severely beaten and choked by the police while in the hospital.

She went through numerous trials and mistrials through the '70s, during which time she was held in various east-coast prisons, including, for a while, in solitary confinement as the only female prisoner in an otherwise all-male facility. During the first nine-week trial, hundreds of civil rights campaigners demonstrated daily on her behalf outside the courtroom, with Angela Davis and others claiming she was a political prisoner.

• • •

Meanwhile, on the west coast, Donald DeFreeze and his sidekick Mizmoon brought together eight other revolutionaries in June—most of them angry Vietnam vets or angry lesbians—to form the Symbionese Liberation Army. They claimed dedication to attacking "racism, sexism, ageism, capitalism, fascism, individualism, possessiveness, competitiveness and all other institutions that have made and sustained capitalism." Their slogan was "DEATH TO THE FASCIST INSECT THAT PREYS UPON THE LIFE OF THE PEOPLE." There is a body of thought that believes that DeFreeze was a police informant and an *agent provocateur*, working for the LAPD to destroy the Black Panther movement,[107] but if so, neither his lieutenants nor his famous victim ever suspected it. The gang began accumulating an arsenal of weaponry and building a list of potential targets. One was Raymond Procunier, the director of the California prison system; another was Marcus Foster, the superintendent of the Oakland school system; and a third was someone they simply called "that daughter of Hearst."

• • •

"That daughter of Hearst" would soon become the subject of the most famous kidnapping in history. As the SLA prepared for it, yet another trial regarding the most famous kidnapping in Canadian history began on June 13. It was the third and final trial of Jacques Rose, and like the others it was noisy political theater, conducted in Quebeçois *joual*. "In all my experience as a lawyer and a judge, I have never seen a trial like this one," said Judge Guy Mathieu. In the end he sentenced Rose's lawyer Robert Lemieux to two years and ten months for contempt, Rose's accomplice Francis Simard to a year, again for contempt, and Rose himself to eight years for his role in the kidnapping and killing of Québec Deputy Premier Pierre Laporte.

•   •   •

After the ramming of his boat in 1972 off Moruroa Lagoon, David McTaggart had sailed back to New Zealand and then flown to Vancouver to attempt to mount a legal campaign to get reparations from the French government. His efforts proved totally unsuccessful. *Au contraire,* the French announced they would resume nuclear testing in the summer. Even though he was now bankrupt, and his boat was still badly damaged, McTaggart determined to again sail into the nuclear exclusion zone to protest the tests. Greenpeace was able to get funding for a new voyage from churches, labor unions, and even the British Columbian government. McTaggart discovered that he also now had the tacit support of the New Zealand and Australian governments. This time, he and his crew member Nigel Ingram had their girlfriends, Ann-Marie Horne and Mary Lornie, with them. On July 10th, Greenpeace III left Auckland and, in a remarkably speedy display of sailing, were in the nuclear exclusion zone 21 days later. Only two days after that, the *Greenpeace III* was boarded by a rough team of French commandos, who beat McTaggart and Ingram with truncheons and smashed McTaggart in the eye.

McTaggart was so badly wounded and nearly blinded that he had to be flown for treatment first to Tahiti and then to Vancouver. His case got international attention. Canadian Prime Minister Pierre Trudeau raised hell with the French government both about the attack on *Greenpeace III,* and about the continuation of their nuclear testing in the Pacific. McTaggart moved to Paris to fight the French Navy in the courts. It was a long, difficult legal battle. One of the most important outcomes for the world was that because of McTaggart's actions, the French ended their atmospheric nuclear testing program in 1974.[108]

•   •   •

The intense battle over Women's Liberation continued. In August, the Cambridge Union, considered the oldest debating society in the world, resolved that, "This House Supports the Women's Liberation Movement" with feminist Germaine Greer pitted against conservative William Buckley. Buckley, in his typically arch manner, recalls that "memory reproaches me for having performed miserably, and for not having made any impression or dent in the argument. Ms. Greer carried the house overwhelmingly." Women might be winning debates in ivy-clad universities, but they were only making modest gains in the real world. When President Kennedy signed a bill banning wage discrimination in the early 1960s, women were making only 58 cents for every dollar earned by a man. By 1972, that had only improved marginally to 72 cents to the dollar.

• • •

On August 23rd, an unusual incident occurred in Stockholm, Sweden, that would be repeated many times through this period, primarily but not always by women. On this hot summer day an escaped prisoner named Jan-Erik Olsson, armed with a submachine gun, entered the Sveriges Kreditbanken in Norrmalmstorg Square. He demanded that the authorities release his friend Clark Olofsson from prison. The pair then held four hostages in the bank's vault for six days. To the amazement of the authorities, the hostages developed not only a close bond with their violent captors, but hostility toward the tactical police who were trying to save them. In part, this was a result of the way the authorities communicated. Hostage Kristen Enmark was granted a phone call to the Swedish Prime Minister Olaf Palme who told her that the government would not negotiate with criminals, and that "you will have to content yourself that you will have died at your post." Enmark told him, "I fully trust Clark and the robber. I am not desperate. They haven't done a thing to us. On the contrary, they have been very nice. But, you know, Olof, what I am scared of is that the police will attack and cause us to die." Another hostage said, "This is our world now, sleeping in this vault to survive. Whoever threatens this world is our enemy." The four hostages and two captors became very friendly, and even after the end of the event, the hostages refused to testify against their captors, and in fact raised money for their defense. This strange bond between captors and captives, perhaps a natural outgrowth of the shifting, amorphous loyalties in this revolutionary time period, became known as the Stockholm Syndrome. It was seen in many events in the period, most notably in the notorious kidnapping of Patricia Hearst.

• • •

Salvador Allende was the democratically elected President of Chile, but his proposals for the country continued to irritate Nixon, Kissinger, and the CIA. Particularly grating was his plan to nationalize American companies like IT&T that essentially controlled the Chilean economy. The CIA organized violent strikes and demonstrations against the government and condoned the murder of a powerful Chilean general who had vowed to defend democracy. On September 11th, a dissident general, Augusto Pinochet, with the support of the Nixon government and the CIA, staged a coup against Allende. The Presidential palace was strafed and bombed by fighter jets and attacked by armored troops.

As the shells were falling, Allende made a final radio address to the nation from the palace, saying "I will not resign. Foreign capitalism-imperialism united with reaction created the climate for the army to break with their tradition…*Long live Chile! Long live the people!* These are my last words. I am sure that my sacrifice will not be in vain. I am sure it will be at least a moral lesson, and a rebuke to crime, cowardice and treason." Allende then supposedly shot himself, with a rifle given to him by Fidel Castro, although documents uncovered in the aftermath of the 2010 earthquake in Chile indicate he was assassinated.

The Pinochet government was immediately recognized by the U.S. Government. Supporters of Allende were rounded up and imprisoned in the National Stadium, and many, including celebrated folksinger Victor Jara were killed. A CIA agent, Colonel Manuel Contreras was placed in charge of the Chilean Intelligence Service, and he promptly set up death squads to hunt down dissidents. An estimated 130,000 people were arrested during the first three years of the new dictatorship, and many thousands were killed, tortured, or "disappeared."

A week following the coup, the Weathermen reacted by exploding a bomb at the New York headquarters of IT&T.

• • •

The fight over Women's Liberation continued with the "Battle of the Sexes", a tennis match between the world's best female tennis player, Billy Jean King, and self-described 'tennis hustler' Bobby Riggs. Back in the 1940s, Riggs was the World's Number One male tennis player. Now, aged 55, he was considered well past his prime, but was still, of course, male. The prize was winner-take-all $100,000—over half a million in today's dollars. The event took place on September 20th in the Houston Astrodome, in front of 30,492 spectators and a television audience of 90 million. It was part spectacle, with both contestants entering the arena on Roman-style litters accompanied by prancing models. Riggs presented his opponent with a Sugar Daddy lollipop before the match. She gave him a squealing piglet, symbolic of his role as a Male Chauvinist Pig. It was also, though, considered a serious battle over one of the most contentious issues of the era. "I thought it would set us back 50 years if I didn't win that match," said King. "It would affect all of women's self-esteem." In the end, she did win—6-4, 6-3, 6-3.

• • •

Pablo Neruda, considered the National Poet of Chile, and, according to Gabriel Garcia Marquez, "the greatest poet of the 20th Century in any language", had been awarded the Nobel Prize for literature in 1971. A communist, and a strong supporter of Salvador Allende, Neruda was injected with what he (and a 2015 official Chilean Interior Ministry investigation) believed was poison, on orders from the new Pinochet regime. He died six days later, on September 23rd. Pinochet denied permission for Neruda's funeral to be made a public event, but thousands disobeyed the edict and crowded the streets to mourn his death.

• • •

October 6th was Yom Kippur, a major Jewish holiday of rest, fasting, and prayer. A coalition of Arab countries led by Egypt and Syria chose the day to invade the Sinai Peninsula and the Golan Heights—both areas that had been occupied by Israel since the 1967 Six-Day War. There were major Arab gains in the first days of the war, but the Israelis fought back, and there were considerable losses, and serious involvement by other nations, until a ceasefire was finally declared on October 25. Ultimately more than 2,500 Israelis were killed, about 8,000 wounded, between 8,000 and 18,000 (depending on the source) Egyptians and Syrians killed, and 9,000 captured. Many other nations became involved, and it was one of the major stand-offs of the Cold War between the U.S. and the Soviet Union. Off the coast of Israel and Egypt, 97 Soviet vessels including 23 submarines prepared for a battle with 60 American warships including three aircraft carriers. Cuba sent 4,000 troops. East Germany, Algeria, and Libya all sent fighter jets and tanks. North Korea and Pakistan sent jets and pilots. Saudi Arabia, Morocco and Sudan all sent troops and armored vehicles.

The biggest contribution to the war was from the United States which provided a major allocation of military supplies and $2.8 billion to Israel. The huge gift led to the Saudi Arabian embargo against the United States and four other countries who were perceived to be support-ing Israel—Canada, the United Kingdom, the Netherlands, and Japan. This embargo in turn led to the Oil Crisis of 1973 in which the price of oil increased by 300%. The crisis led to gasoline shortages, rationing, strikes, shootings, and bombings at American gas stations. It also had numerous effects on society, particularly in the United States. The speed limit was dropped to 55 mph, the country shifted to Daylight Saving Time year-round, and consumers stopped buying large gas-guzzling American cars, in favor of smaller, more fuel-efficient Japanese and European models, which in turn led to the decline of the American automobile industry. It also caused the stock market crash of 1973 – 74. Germany, the U.K., Italy, Switzerland and Norway all banned driving, flying, and boating on Sundays, and Holland jailed people who used more than their ration of electricity. France was hit particularly badly by the crisis. The prosperity of the *trente glorieuses*—the 30 years of postwar economic growth—was over. Unemployment was on the rise, and the sour mood of the country was famously described as "morose."

The oil sheiks probably made a more revolutionary change in the world than all the other actors we have been considering in this period. They certainly made the United States start to question its view of itself as the invincible center of the world, and along with the loss of the war in Vietnam shook the American sense of its 'exceptionalism'. Both the political right and left were rocked by the oil crisis. Paradoxically, it is sometimes easier to be a revolutionary when things are good than when things are bad. According to secret records not declassified until 2004, the United States considered invading the Middle East to militarily take control of the oil fields. Ultimately, hawkish elements in the government were constrained by consideration of how the Arabs, Russia, and the Third World would react to such a move. The crisis did, however, create a shift in U.S. military policy with America beginning to see the threat from the Arab countries of the Middle East as being as great as from traditional adversaries like the Soviet Union and China.

• • •

On November 6th, three Symbionese Liberation Army members, never identified but probably Donald Defreeze (now styling himself "General Field Marshall Cinque"), Mizmoon, and the diminutive, 4'11" Nancy Ling Perry murdered Oakland School Superintendent Marcus

Foster, the city's first black school administrator, because he had proposed that students carry identification cards and that police be brought in to curb school violence, both of which the SLA termed "fascist". Their communique, delivered to a radio station, declared, "To those who would bear the hopes and future of our people, let the voice of their guns express the words of freedom." The group had the nutty idea that killing Foster would gain them support and sympathy, but exactly the opposite happened. Even the most radical of urban revolutionaries, Bernardine Dohrn, disowned the action, releasing a statement saying, "We do not comprehend the execution of Marcus Foster and respond very soberly to the death of a black person who is not a recognized enemy of the people."

• • •

The authoritarian military dictatorship in Greece—a country that considered itself the founder of democracy—continued to be an embarrassment. Many Greeks were still imprisoned, while others, such as singer Melina Mercouri and future Prime Minister Andres Papandreou were in exile and vainly trying to lead the resistance from other parts of Europe. The widely seen Costa-Gavras film Z brought the situation to the attention of the world, but to no avail. The junta was supported by the American CIA which was represented by a secret operative in Athens named John Maury. American Vice President Spiro Agnew praised the junta as "the best thing to happen to Greece since Pericles ruled in ancient Athens."

Most Greeks disagreed. On November 14th, students at the National Technical University of Athens staged a sit-in, pledging to restore democracy to the country. Construction workers and farmers poured in to join the students. Using laboratory parts, the students constructed and began broadcasting from a clandestine radio transmitter. The junta put army snipers in high buildings across the city. They killed 24 people and injured hundreds more. On November 17th, a tank smashed through the gates of the school and the army took over the central square of the city. Brigadier Dimitrios Ioannidis, a soldier even more hardline than Colonel

Papadopoulos, the leader of the original 1967 'revolution' (more properly called a coup) took the opportunity to declare martial law, stage a counter-coup, and take power. Greece was in a state of crisis and chaos and would remain that way until July of the next year when Ioannidis would unsuccessfully attempt to stage yet another coup.

• • •

On November 19th, "Radio Free America" began broadcasting on an old Navy minesweeper, just outside the three-mile limit off Cape May, New Jersey. The station featured Reverend Carl MacIntyre, a well-known right-wing, anti-communist, anti-liberal preacher. MacIntyre's sermons and political rabble-rousing had been heard for years on hundreds of radio stations, but the FCC had just shut down his home base station, WXUR, citing its "flagrant disregard of the FCC's Fairness Doctrine." Consequently, the preacher hit the high seas to get his fundamentalist message out. His pirate radio station was just one of his many evangelical and reactionary activities. He also campaigned against the Stonewall Gay Rights activists, proposed re-building both the Temple of Jerusalem and Noah's Arc, defended My Lai war criminal Lt. William Calley, and led pro-Vietnam War 'Victory Marches' in Washington. His pirate radio station didn't last long as it too was shut down for interfering with the frequencies of licensed radio stations. An unabashed MacIntyre later recalled, "It was a crazy thing to do, but it was dramatic."

• • •

In November, Madame Mao, Zhang Chunqiao, Wang Hongwen and Yao Wenyan banded together as the "Gang of Four" primarily to defend Chairman Mao and fight Zhou Enlai. The gang also began a campaign called "Criticize Lin, Criticize Confucius" in which they slagged the memory of both the recently assassinated Lin Biao, and the revered Chinese philosopher, who died (of natural causes) in 479 BCE.

• • •

Two days after Christmas, a book was published that *TIME* Magazine called, "the best non-fiction book of the 20th Century." Aleksandr Solzhenitsyn's *The Gulag Archipelago* would have a profound effect on ending the most famous revolutionary regime in history. David Remnick, writing in *The New Yorker*, said of its influence, "It is impossible to name a book that has had a greater effect on the political and moral consciousness of the late 20th century."

Solzhenitsyn had been arrested in 1945 for making mildly derogatory remarks about Joseph Stalin in a private letter. He was sentenced to eight years imprisonment, which he served in a Gulag labor camp in Kazakhstan, and then internal exile for life. Following Nikita Krushchev's 1956 speech condemning the excesses of Joseph Stalin, especially the Gulag labor camps, Solzhenitsyn, along with thousands of other prisoners, was released. For the next 16 years Solzhenitsyn secretly and feverishly worked on his massive history of the death camps and his own experience. Since writing about the prison camps incurred the possibility of a return to the Gulag, Solzhenitsyn divided the manuscript into small segments and hid them all over Moscow. For years, he would go to the different locations to work on the book. In 1965, the KGB discovered part of the book and confiscated it, forcing the author to slowly and secretly reconstruct the manuscript.

After completing the book, Solzhenitsyn hid two copies with the daughter of Arnold Susi, a prisoner he had met in Lubyanka Prison in 1945, who had, since his release, become the Minister of Education of Estonia. The author hid another copy of the manuscript in Moscow. In August of 1973 the KGB arrested one of Solzhenitsyn's trusted typists, Elizaveta Voronyanskaya, who revealed to them under interrogation where they could find the manuscript. Within days of her release, she was found hanging in the stairwell of her apartment building; either a suicide or a murder.[109] Following her death, Solzhenitsyn knew he had to smuggle the book out to the west which he managed to do in September. The Russian language version was published in Paris on December 27th. English and French translations followed in the winter of 1974. Once the Soviets learned of the publication, Solzhenitsyn was stripped of his citizenship, expelled from Russia, and began to live in the United States.[110]

The book had a profound effect on the Russians who were able to secretly either read it or hear it read on Radio Liberty, the massive short-wave radio station sponsored by the U.S. State Department and the CIA and aimed at the USSR. It was not an easy task as the station was regularly jammed by the KGB. The book was absolutely banned in the USSR, but after its publication in France, unbound, hand-typed *samizdat* (illegal) manuscripts began circulating in the Soviet Union.[111] There were strict rules about how they could be read. Usually, readers had only 24 hours to consume the thick text before they had to secretly pass the dog-eared, mimeographed, treasured copy on to the next underground reader.

The harrowing book sold 30 million copies in 35 languages and is considered to have been a major contributor to the new focus on international human rights during the presidency of Jimmy Carter. American diplomat George F. Keenan called it "the most powerful single indictment of a political regime ever to be levied in modern times," and novelist Doris Lessing described it as "the book that brought down an empire." [112]

Empires don't fall easily, though. Regardless of the efforts of Mr. Solzhenitsyn, or the effects of the Beatles or of Western political rhetoric and sabre-rattling, it would be another 16 years before the Soviet empire fell.

Meanwhile, there was still lots of life left in the new revolution of the '60s and '70s.

1974

Patricia Hearst Kidnapped, James Bay Sabotaged,
Another British Coup Blue-skyed,
Patty Hearst Becomes Tania the Bank Robber,
Carnation Revolution, Cyprus Explodes,
Prairie Fire, Rochdale Busted, Selassie Deposed,
Carlos the Jackal, Argentine Maritime Attacks,
IRA Birmingham Bombing, Nixon Resigns.

On January 10th, after two of the members of the Symbionese Liberation Army were arrested, the rest of the gang tried to set fire to their hideout and split. If they hoped the fire would destroy any traces of their presence, they were unsuccessful. The police were able to identify the members of the SLA from the discarded trash in which they found clues to their future plans, and a list of possible targets that included "that daughter of Hearst."

The "daughter of Hearst" they were referring to was Patricia Hearst, the 19-year-old third daughter of Randolph Apperson Hearst and Catherine Wood Campbell. Her grandfather was the legendary William Randolph Hearst who 70 years earlier had created the largest newspaper, magazine, newsreel, and movie business in the world. The 1941 film *Citizen*

Kane is the story of his life. Although Hearst tried to destroy the film, he failed, and to this day it is widely considered to be one of the greatest movies ever made.

On February 4th, Patricia was with her fiancé Steven Weed in her duplex on the edge of the UC Berkeley campus when Donald Defreeze (aka Cinque), Bill Harris, and Angela Atwood broke in. They forced Patricia, wearing only a nightgown, into the trunk of their car, fired a few bullets at curious neighbors and sped away.

The gang locked Hearst in a closet in their new SLA headquarters, and three days later, sent a communiqué to radio station KPFA announcing that "The Court of the People" had seized Patty as a "prisoner of war" and denounced her father as a "corporate enemy of the people."

The story of Patricia Hearst's transformation from hostage to revolutionary urban guerrilla and her eventual capture on September 18, 1975 became, after Watergate, the biggest media event of the 1970s. Her face would appear many times on magazine covers—seven times on *Newsweek* alone.

While the SLA members took turns guarding the closet, they began talking to her about their radical goals. Patricia began to warm to them, and she gradually became impressed by how sincere they seemed and how genuinely they were leading a revolution that would transform society. On February 12th, the group released a tape that contained Cinque's demands and Patty's assertion that "These people aren't just a bunch of nuts. They've been really honest with me and they're perfectly willing to die for what they're doing. I'm here because I'm a member of a ruling class family." The SLA demand was that her father must provide $70 worth of food to every needy person in the state. He was to do this three times a week for the next four weeks. Estimates of the cost of such a giveaway were as much as $400 million. There was some back-and-forth negotiation and finally both sides agreed to a more modest food give-away, which the SLA wanted the Black Panthers to administer. The Panthers wanted nothing to do with what they perceived to be the nutty SLA. As an alternate solution,

Randolph Hearst set up an organization called People in Need. It would attract some well-meaning people, and some crazies. One of the crazies was Sara Jane Moore, who worked as a volunteer bookkeeper for the food program while simultaneously reporting on them to the FBI. She is the same Sara Jane Moore who would later attempt to assassinate President Gerald Ford. Another was Reverend Jim Jones, the cult leader and faith healer, who tried to insinuate himself and his cult into the food program.

It was a colossal and chaotic undertaking. There were delays, long lineups, fistfights, and people knocked cold by frozen turkeys hurled at unmanageable crowds from the back of trucks. Still, during the recession of 1973, tens of thousands of people were fed by the program. Conservatives roundly disapproved. California Governor Ronald Reagan made the heartless and memorable quip to a group of Republican supporters, "It's just too bad we can't have an epidemic of botulism."

The food program should have been enough to get the SLA to release their hostage, but it wasn't. Furthermore, it had become question-able whether Patricia Hearst even wanted to leave. She started to like her captors, and the feeling was reciprocated. Her primary guards, Angela Atwood (now known as 'General Gelina'), Nancy Ling Perry ('Fahizah'), and Willy Wolfe ('Cujo') reported to their comrades, "You're not going to believe this, but we like her."

Another tape shocked her parents and the world when Patty reported that the SLA had given her a gun to protect herself in case they were raided. She proclaimed, "I no longer fear the SLA, because they are not the ones who want me to die. The SLA wants to feed the people and assure safety and justice for the two men in San Quentin. I realize it is the FBI who want to murder me."

Like many of the revolutionary groups of this period, there was a very strong female and feminist component. There was only one married couple inside the cell, and ironically, they were the only two people not having sex with each other. For the rest, it was a merry-go-round of cou-pling. A month into the hostage-taking, Angela asked Patricia if she ever got horny. Patricia admitted that she did. Still blindfolded and physically weak, and perhaps brainwashed from weeks of confinement, she proposed that if she was to get it on with any of the comrades, it would be Cujo. Angela took this information back to the full group. After a revolutionary pow-wow, the gang brought her out and told her their feelings about sex. Free sex was encouraged. No-one was forced to have sex with anyone else, but if one comrade asked another, it was comradely to say yes.

"So, we want you to know," said General Gelina, "you can fuck any one of the men in the cell that you want to." To the laughter of all, Camilla Hall, the most enthusiastically lesbian of the group added, "Or any woman!"

So that is what happened. Hearst and Cujo began an affair—at first carnal, then a full-blown love affair. After Cujo was killed in the massive police shootout, Patricia described him as the "gentlest, most beautiful man I've ever known. We loved each other so much, and his love for the people was so deep that he was willing to give his life for them…Neither Cujo or I ever loved an individual the way we loved each other, probably because our relationship wasn't based on bourgeois, fucked-up values, attitudes, and goals. Our relationship's foundation was our commitment to the struggle and our love for the people. It's because of this that I still feel strong and determined to fight. I was ripped off by the pigs when they murdered Cujo, ripped off in the same way that thousands of sisters and brothers in this fascist country have been ripped off of the people they love. We mourn together, and the sound of gunfire becomes sweeter."

The radical Weather Underground were almost as shocked by the SLA's actions as were the police and the public, but not to be outdone, the newly feminist members of the group formed a "Women's Brigade" and in March they bombed a Department of Health, Education and Welfare building in San Francisco.

· · ·

The Caribbean, like almost everywhere in the world, saw largely female revolutionary political action in the 1970s. In Grenada, a group of nurses was striking in advance of the country's independence from Britain. Young political firebrand Maurice Bishop attempted to organize the nurses and other workers on the island under the banner of his political party, the New Jewel Movement. A mass demonstration on February 7th led to followers of Bishop being tear-gassed by police and pelted with stones and bottles by supporters of Sir Eric Mathew Gairy, the Premier of the country. Bishop's elderly father, while leading girls and boys away from the danger, was shot and killed in the melee.

Two weeks later, on the day before Independence, Bishop was arrested on charges of plotting an armed anti-government conspiracy. After being released on bail, Bishop high-tailed it for the United States, but eventually returned to become leader of the opposition in the Grenadian House of Representatives. Gairy, who became the nation's first Prime Minister, held onto power through terrorism and fraudulent elections. In 1979 Bishop staged a revolution and deposed Gairy. Bishop's government, which lasted for four years, introduced free public healthcare, and reduced illiteracy from 35% to 5%, and unemployment from 50% to 14%. However, the Reagan government was suspicious of Bishop's socialist ideals, and the Bishop government stifled the free press and would not hold elections.[130] In a 1983 coup, Bishop was himself deposed and executed by a People's Revolutionary Army firing squad along with three members of his cabinet and four followers. Days later, U. S. President Ronald Reagan launched a military invasion of the island.

• • •

Extreme and often violent labor unrest was another aspect of the turbulent era. This was true throughout the world but nowhere more so than in Canada, particularly Québec. In 1970, work had begun on what the Québec government considered the 'project of the century', the $3.8 billion James Bay electric generating system. It would ultimately become the largest hydro-electric generating plant in Canada (larger, even, than Niagara Falls) and the largest underground generating plant in the world. There was, however, a great deal of ill-will and controversy attached to its construction, with resistance from the local First Nations peoples whose land was flooded for the site, and action from the laborers who built the massive installation. On March 21st, Yvon Duhamel, a business agent for the International Union of Operating Engineers, led a group of rebellious workers who drove bulldozers into the power generators, and after badly damaging them, lit them on fire, causing $35 million damage. The unrest was caused by what the workers perceived to be poor working conditions, inter-union rivalry, and the arrogance of the American executives of the contractor, Bechtel Corporation, a multi-million-dollar conglomerate. It capped several years of violent labor unrest in the province, including the 1971 strike at the Montréal newspaper *La Presse*, which featured a window-smashing riot and a death; and the Québec Public Service Strike, which resulted in several of the labor leaders, including the head of the Québec Teachers Federation, going to jail. The violent action of the workers at the James Bay generating plant was considered to be one of the most extreme cases of workplace sabotage of all time. It led to the Royal Commission of Inquiry into Union Freedom in which everyone from Montréal hoodlums to Québec cabinet ministers were raked over the coals for their involvement in the events.

• • •

In England, an acrimonious coal miners' strike led Prime Minister Edward Heath to call an election, which he then lost to the Labour party. Harold Wilson was re-elected for a second term. As had happened in 1968, the results ignited another right-wing campaign by the Secret Service MI5 to smear Wilson who they continued to believe was a danger to the country. Peter Wright, the Scientific Officer at MI5 (the "Q" in James Bond terms) quoted one of the roughly 30 officers conspiring against the Prime Minister, "Wilson's a bloody menace and it's time the public knew the truth," and "We'll have him out, this time we'll have him out." [131] The MI5 plot against Wilson's Labour government was codenamed *Operation Clockwork Orange* after the Stanley Kubrick/Malcolm McDowell movie. The Cunard Line was approached about the possibility of requisitioning the luxury liner *QE2* for use as a prison ship to hold government officials, labor leaders, and journalists hostile to the new regime. [132] The Army, without telling the government, took over Heathrow Airport, ostensibly for training for a possible IRA attack, but, according to Marcia Williams, a senior aide to Wilson, in reality as a practice run for a military takeover of the country. [133] Again, as in 1968, there was talk of Lord Mountbatten being appointed head of an interim administration after Wilson had been deposed.

• • •

Whatever craziness the British might dream up, California could do them one better. By late March, the SLA had completely brainwashed their captive Patricia Hearst, and now wanted the world to know it. They officially invited her to join their gang, and when she agreed, they dramatically removed her blindfold, revealed their faces to her, and presented her with a new revolutionary name, and a submachine gun. The women in the group sewed a new SLA flag featuring their seven-headed cobra symbol and then took a Polaroid of Patty wearing fatigues and a beret and cradling her gun in her arms standing defiantly in front of it. After the photo was released, it was published in almost every newspaper in the world and it became, after the famous Alberto Korda photo of Che Guevara, the most iconic image of the era.

With her parents and almost everyone else in shock about the provocative photo, the SLA released another tape in which Patty left no doubt about which side she was now on. "I have been given the choice of #1) being released in a safe area; or #2) joining the forces of the Symbionese Liberation Army and fighting for my freedom and the freedom of all oppressed people. I have chosen to stay and fight." She went on to renounce her name Hearst and introduce her new 'revolutionary' name. "I have been given the name 'Tania' after a comrade who fought alongside Che in Bolivia for the people of Bolivia. I embrace the name with the determination to continue fighting with her spirit. There is no victory in half-assed attempts at revolution. I know Tania dedicated her life to the people. Fighting with total dedication and an intense desire to learn, which I will continue in the oppressed American people's revolution, it is in the spirit of Tania that I say, *Patria o muerte, venceremos! (Fatherland or death, we shall triumph!)*"

If that didn't get everyone's attention, the events of April 15th would. The gang was running low on money and wanted both to build up their coffers and make a splashy statement. They carefully cased out local banks. Security cameras had only just been introduced in banks and were still rare. The SLA became the first and last bank robbers in history to specifically look for a bank *with* a security camera, and then make sure that their star accomplice stood directly in front of it. At 9:51 AM, Donald DeFreeze and his gang of four women entered the bank and began screaming at the tellers to open their tills. While Mizmoon scooped up the cash from the drawers, Patty, wielding an M1 carbine, bellowed at the tellers, security guard, and customers, "This is Tania, Patricia Hearst. Up against the wall, motherfuckers. First person puts his head up, I'll blow his motherfucking head off."

The robbery was a success. Not only did they get $10,660 from the Hibernia Bank, but the images from the bank's security cameras confirmed the amazing news: Patricia Hearst, once an heiress-hostage, was now Tania, foulmouthed revolutionary bank robber. The extreme left adopted her as a heroine. The Berkeley *Barb*, under a banner headline reading PATTY FREE! and the photo from the bank security-camera proclaimed, "Patty Hearst has said her last goodbye to America's ruling class; to a life of privilege, wealth and power; and joined the guerrillas of the Symbionese Liberation Army in their war against the fascist corporate state." On the other hand, William Saxbe, Nixon's Attorney General, described her as a "common criminal," and Wanted Posters of her and the other robbers were placed in every post office in the country.

• • •

There was so much revolutionary political activity going on in the '70s that completely apolitical criminals often used it as a distraction and cover for their crimes. On March 22, John Patterson, the U.S. Vice-Consul in Hermosillo, Mexico was kidnapped. The consulate received a ransom note from the 'People's Liberation Army of Mexico' (a group no one had heard of before) demanding $500,000. President Nixon, who was immediately told about the kidnapping, was not shocked. Although only three months into 1974, Patterson was already the sixth American diplomat of the year to be taken hostage. In one of the worst cases, Black September had seized a number of U.S. diplomats in Khartoum, Sudan. They demanded the release of prisoners in the U.S., including Robert Kennedy's killer Sirhan Sirhan. When their demands were not met, they killed all of their hostages.

The hunt for what turned out to be the fictitious 'People's Liberation Army of Mexico' continued through April. The Mexican police did capture members of the '23rd of September Communist League' and brutally tortured them but learned nothing. The FBI, who were unable to crack the case, came up with a new theory, that it had been a "self-kidnapping", engineered by Patterson and his wife Andra to extort the half million bucks from the U.S. government. They were especially suspicious of Andra because of her past endorsements of liberal causes. According to a report submitted to Washington by one of the G-Men assigned to the case, she "admitted to participating in various 'rad-lib' demonstrations and was against the war in Vietnam and admitted to participating in demonstrations against the war." [113] The FBI not only liked this theory but released it to the press. One headline read: "POLICE ASSURE THAT DISAPPEARANCE OF U.S. VICE CONSUL IS A SELF-KIDNAPPING." The story described how the pair would be prosecuted once Patterson had been located.

In fact, it was not a 'self-kidnapping' and it had nothing to do with the fictitious 'People's Liberation Army of Mexico' or any other political group. It was instead a purely criminal kidnapping undertaken by an ex-sergeant in the U.S. Army. Bobby Joe Keesee had a strangely checkered past. In 1962, he had gone AWOL from the military and hijacked a plane to Cuba. The Cubans were convinced that he was a spy, so sent him back to America, where he was arrested. The defense mounted in his trial was that he *was* a spy, working for the CIA to destabilize the Castro regime. He got away with less than three years in jail for that caper. Then, in 1970, he ended up in Thailand where again he hijacked a plane, this time aiming for North Vietnam. As before, he was assumed to be an American spy. He was tortured by the North Vietnamese, then jailed in the notorious 'Hanoi Hilton.'

On March 14, 1973, he had been on the same plane with John McCain and the other celebrated POW's, returning from Hanoi to America. Unlike McCain and the others, though, the American government did not make a big fuss about his return but instead surreptitiously whisked him off the plane and away from the waiting press.

Now, a year later, he ended up in Mexico, kidnapping John Patterson. When his attempted kidnapping failed, Keesee murdered the diplomat and hid his body in the Mexican desert. Keesee was eventually caught. Even though he was clearly a sociopath, he got off easily. For somewhat mysterious reasons, the prosecution dropped the murder charge and while he did get 20 years for conspiracy to kidnap, he was out in 11. Twelve years later he was again arrested for yet another kidnapping and murder. This time he got a life sentence with no chance of parole.

• • •

On April 25th, the fancifully named Carnation Revolution ended the long regime of António Salazar in Portugal. The Portuguese empire began to dissolve. Mozambique, a Portuguese colony since 1505, became an independent communist state and began supporting the ZANU guerrillas fighting in neighboring Rhodesia against the white regime of Ian Smith.

• • •

The SLA began to feel that San Francisco was getting too dangerous, so on May 10th they split up into two cars and headed south to Los Angeles. Patty's father posted a $50,000 reward for the return of his daughter, and her fiancé Steven Weed proposed trying to get the help of Régis Debray, the French academic and associate of Che Guevara. Randolph Hearst responded to this idea by saying, "We need a goddamn South American revolutionary mixed up in this thing like a hole in the head," but Weed persisted. He got Debray's coordinates from Joan Baez, and headed off to Mexico to meet with him.

Once in Southern California, the Symbionese gang rented a small slummy house in the ghetto of South-Central Los Angeles. Seventy dollars a month. No electricity, no hot water. On May 16th, Bill and Emily Harris, and Patricia/Tania, were sent to buy heavy clothing and outdoor gear in preparation for future missions. Since they were now three of the most wanted people in America, they wore disguises—Patty a dark curly wig. They headed for a store called Mel's Sporting Goods. Patricia stayed in the van while the married couple bought what they needed and then Bill Harris stupidly shoplifted a shotgun shell bandolier to which he had taken a fancy. His theft was spotted by the clerk who followed him out of the store and accosted him on the street. Determined not to get stopped, Harris began battling the clerk. Another clerk and a passerby joined in the melee. Patricia saw what was happening and acted immediately. She didn't drive away. She didn't try to hide. Instead, she whipped out a submachine gun from the back seat and began spraying Mel's Sporting Goods. Thirty rounds of deadly bullets broke the windows of the store and ricocheted around the street. Her crazy move worked. The clerks gave up the attempted arrest, Bill and Emily ran to the van, jumped in, and they roared away.

The trio ditched the van, hijacked a Pontiac Trans-Am, then a Chevy Nova, then noticed a Ford Econoline van with a For Sale sign in the window and asked the owner, an 18-year-old named Tom Matthews, if they could take it for a test drive. He agreed, but concerned they might steal it, wanted to come with them. Off they went, driving around Los Angeles, with Bill quickly identifying himself as SLA, and asking the young man if he recognized the woman he was sitting beside in the back seat.

"Holy shit!" exclaimed Matthews. He realized that his companion was none other than Patricia Hearst, the most notorious fugitive in the world.

At that point, one of them remembered that they had left an obvious clue on the front seat of their original van—a parking ticket they had received right in front of their slum house. The LAPD had found the van, picked up the clue, and were on their way to the house. However, Defreeze, Cujo and their four female compatriots had heard the news of the Mel's Sporting Goods debacle on the radio, and quickly split. They drove deeper into the South-Central ghetto.

Both factions of the SLA were looking for a place to hide. The Harrises, Tania, and their new hostage opted for a drive-in movie theater, where they watched a double bill of *The New Centurions*, a drama about the LAPD (Matthews noted that the three comrades cheered every time a cop was shot) and *Thomasine & Bushrod*, a *Bonnie and Clyde* knock-off in which a young black couple go on a Robin Hood-style crime spree, stealing from rich white capitalists and giving to the poor. Although the gang's new hostage enjoyed hanging out with them, he asked that he be released the next day, as he had a baseball game to play. It was the first day of the California state high school championships.

Meanwhile, in the middle of the night, the Defreeze wing of the revolutionary gang found a house with its lights still on and they just boldly knocked on the door and asked if they could crash there. The occupants were all either smashed, stoned, or passed out, and they invited the newcomers in to join the party. Defreeze and his gang brought in their huge cache of weapons and ammunition and settled in. By the next day, children and neighbors came and went, bottles of wine were passed around, and Defreeze openly told them who he was. He told one of the visitors that there was likely going to be a shoot-out, and that he was prepared to die. However, he said, "We're going to take a lot of motherfucking pigs with us."

By a quarter-to-six in the evening, the police had the house completely surrounded. The FBI had a "sniffer dog" specially trained to identify the scent of Patricia Hearst, dead or alive. They made 18 demands to surrender, all met with silence, though an eight-year-old boy did come out, telling the police there were two men and four women still inside. The six began taking up positions for the inevitable shoot-out. A crowd, which the LAPD estimated at 4,000, assembled to watch the fireworks. TV crews with the just-invented live minicams transmitted live images of the stand-off back to KNXT, and from there to stations across the country. 'The whole world' was probably not watching, but much of the United States certainly was.

Just before six, the cops fired tear gas canisters, and the house erupted with gunfire from the trapped revolutionaries. The biggest police gun battle in the history of the U.S. began, live, before 4,000 spectators and hundreds of thousands more watching on television.

Three of the TV viewers were Patricia Hearst, and Bill and Emily Harris. They had released their hostage in the morning, stolen yet another car, then purchased another (their fifth!) and driven to—where else?—Disneyland. They found themselves a hideout—a motel across from the theme park—settled in and turned on the TV to watch the mayhem. In San Francisco, Patricia's mom and dad were also watching (likely assuming their daughter was inside the house with a machine gun), and in San Diego, watching too, was her fiancé Steven Weed, just back from his negotiations in Mexico with communist academic Régis Debray.

The police fired 83 tear gas canisters and 5,300 rounds of ammunition into the house. The SLA fired back with many thousands of rounds.

Within an hour, the building was on fire. The shooting stopped. The house burned to the ground. Once it had cooled investigators could find only tiny remnants of six dead revolutionaries, and no sign whatsoever of Tania.

Steven Weed raced up from San Diego to see if Patricia was in the house. He joined the huge crowd held back by police tape. Weed was recognized by one of the bystanders, who taunted him, "Tania's found her brown sugar now an' she don't need no more of your shit!"

Tania and the Harrises were in catatonic shock over the death of their comrades and their now utterly precarious position. "I was a soldier, an urban guerrilla in the people's army," Patricia would later write. "It was a role I had accepted in exchange for my very life. There was no turning back. The police or FBI would shoot me on sight, just as they had killed my comrades."

The trio hung out in Orange County for ten more days, watching as the Los Angeles D.A. announced all the new charges against them—kidnapping, armed robbery, assault to commit murder, etc., etc. They were friendless and nervous in Orange County, then the center of Republican conservatism in the country. On the Memorial Day weekend, America's most wanted revolutionary criminals merged into the busy holiday traffic and headed back north to their more familiar turf of Berkeley and San Francisco.

• • •

There was just as much mayhem going on in Ireland. On May 17th, the Protestant, Unionist Ulster Volunteer Force detonated three huge car bombs in Dublin and another in Monaghan, killing 33 people and injuring hundreds—the highest one-day death toll of the Troubles. Serious allegations were made that the British security forces aided the UVF in carrying out the bombings.

• • •

Meanwhile, the person who in retrospect seems to have been the real revolutionary of the era, Steve Jobs, was not lobbing bombs but rather touring India and seeking enlightenment. He returned in the summer with a shaved head and wearing Indian clothing, practicing Zen Buddhism, and living at the All One commune in Oregon. The apple orchard of the commune would eventually provide the name for Jobs' world-changing start-up computer company.

• • •

It was increasingly difficult for the dwindling cadre of the three living members of the SLA to find a place to stay or friends to support them in the Bay Area. They lucked out, however, when a radical journalist from Manhattan named Jack Scott decided he would try to link up with them. Scott was a prominent figure in a small subset of the radical politics of the era. He was the sports editor of the slick, muckraking *Ramparts* Magazine, and had written extensively on the exploitation of athletes in college and pro ranks. He'd managed to successfully get under the skin of Vice-President Spiro Agnew, a big sports fan, who denounced him for questioning the holy grail of American sport. Scott not only sympathized with the revolutionary politics of the SLA, but he thought getting the inside scoop on their wild story could make his career as a reporter and writer.[127] Scott flew to San Francisco, tapped into some connections that clandestinely linked him up with Tania and the Harrises, and offered them a hideout—a farmhouse in Pennsylvania. After considerable negotiation over whether he would allow them to bring their huge arsenal with them (he won; they didn't), the four of them, plus, of all people, Scott's mother and father, set off on a cross-country caravan to their new hideout. Patricia became more strident and dogmatic as her strange new life continued, cursing "the pigs" for having killed her lover, claiming that she had in fact staged her own kidnapping, writing a feminist tract, and compiling a "hit list" of people she felt had "betrayed the revolution", with Jane Fonda and Angela Davis at the top.

• • •

On June 13th, a week after Tania and gang left for the east, the Weathermen, citing the SLA as inspiration, detonated a large bomb that wrecked most of the 29th floor of the Gulf Oil headquarters in Pittsburgh. Also that month, the Italian Red Brigades killed two members of the Italian neo-fascist party, the *Movimento Sociale Italiano* during a raid on the MSI headquarters in Padua. However Italian police were able to infiltrate the *Brigate Rosse* using an ex-monk named *Frate Mitra* (Friar Machine Gun, alias Silvano Girotto). In September Red Brigade leader Renato Curcio was arrested by the infamous terrorist hunter General Carlo Chiesa and sentenced to 18 years in prison. Curcio would be busted from prison by his wife the following winter and General Chiesa would be murdered in 1982 in Palermo on orders from Mafia boss Salvatore Riina.

• • •

After a year of declining health, Argentine President Juan Perón died on July 1st. He was one of the longest serving leaders on the planet, having first been elected to political office in 1945. His funeral was a massive event, with hundreds of international leaders and 2,000 journalists in attendance. Over a million people lined the ten-mile funeral procession chanting, "Perón! Perón! Perón!" Perón's wife, Isabel ran the country until 1976, when she was deposed by yet another coup d'état. A right-wing junta took over and began the 'Dirty War', in which, according to international human rights organizations, as many as 30,000 were killed by state terrorism.

• • •

In Cyprus, on the other side of the world, Greek strongman Dimitrios Ioannidis, who had already staged two coups, (1967 and 1973), now staged yet another, this time against Cypriot President, Archbishop Makarios III, who he called "communistic" and "the Red Priest." This coup proved his undoing, as it triggered an invasion of Cyprus by Turkey, and yet another coup in Greece, which ended the many years of brutal dictatorship and finally returned democracy to the country. Ioannidis was charged with treason and with inciting the military commanders to commit criminal acts during the Athens Polytechnic student uprising. He was given the death sentence, later commuted to life, and spent 35 years in prison, from 1975 until his death in 2010.

The invasion of Cyprus by Turkey led to a particularly nasty war between Turkey and Greece, with about 10,000 people killed and 14,000 wounded. Two hundred thousand Greek Cypriots were expelled from northern Cyprus, and 50,000 Turkish Cypriots were expelled from the Republic of Cyprus.[125] There were hundreds of atrocities committed during the war, especially rapes, which were used to systematically soften resistance and clear civilian areas through fear. There was so much rape that the very conservative Cypriot Orthodox Church temporarily permitted abortion, especially of the very young girls who had been raped by the soldiers.[126]

• • •

On July 23rd, the Weathermen published their manifesto, *Prairie Fire*. The title came from Mao's line, "a single spark can ignite a prairie fire" and there were further references to Mao's thinking throughout the book, such as his theory of creating alliances between underground and above ground revolutionaries that would "help create a sea for the guerrillas to swim in." Five thousand copies of the book were distributed to bookstores, libraries, and coffee houses across America. A copy even made its way to the SLA hideout in Pennsylvania and was embraced enthusiastically by

Patricia Hearst. It was even studied in some of America's most radical colleges.

• • •

The acrimonious situation continued to escalate at Toronto's Rochdale College. In March, the court had granted permission to empty the 'free school' of all tenants. In May, 87 eviction notices were served, and in June another 151. Usually six or seven Sherriff's officers, plus police and receiver's staff would arrive with sledgehammers to open the doors and the tenants would be evicted. The doors would then be padlocked, but many would soon be broken into and the room re-occupied by another 'tenant'. On July 30th, there was a major riot at the school. After a drug bust on the tenth floor, some dealers and tenants blocked the exit of two policemen, who were locked inside. Electricity had been turned off and the elevators did not work. A group of 25 longhaired Rochdalians, including Wolf Sullivan, were in the elevator lobby of the tenth floor. Sullivan recalls, "A policeman came to rescue his colleagues and pointed his gun at everybody. He was visibly scared shitless and pointed the gun at Jackie Halliday's face. She was frozen as the cop held the gun and a long metal flashlight in front of him, and yelled, 'Get out of the way, bitch!' Jackie didn't move fast enough, and the cop slammed her head with both gun and flashlight. She turned a complete sideways somersault from the force of the hit. Apparently, the police were trying to provoke a riot by assaulting women so they could use deadly force. The lights were out and it was a terrifying experience."

The hippie tenants, though, refused to leave and Rochdale stayed alive and occupied for another year.

• • •

On August 4th, an Italian *Ferrovie dello Stato* train was bombed early in the morning, killing 12 and wounding 18. The neo-Fascist group *Ondine*

Nero claimed responsibility, announcing, "we wanted to show the nation that we can place a bomb anywhere we want, whenever and however we please. Let us see in autumn, we will drown democracy under a mountain of dead."

● ● ●

Abbie Hoffman, facing potentially monstrous jail time for a cocaine bust, skipped bail in the spring and in August ended up in a Los Angeles plastic surgery clinic with a yarn about being a Canadian TV personality getting on in years who needed a new face. With his looks transformed, he took on the new name and identity of 'Barry Freed' and went underground, living in the village of Fineview, New York in the 1,000 Islands on the St. Lawrence River. The notorious *luftmensch* lived in virtual exile for the next six years. When considering going on the lam he had always used the code words 'going swimming' if he thought he was being bugged. He was now living on the very extreme northern edge of America. It was a relatively short swim across the border if he had to do it.

● ● ●

An even more infamous American was also forced to disappear. On August 9th, facing certain impeachment by the U.S. House of Representatives, Richard Nixon resigned from office—the only President to ever do so. He was replaced by Gerald Ford, an amiable man once described by the ever-profane Lyndon Johnson as someone who "couldn't fart and chew gum at the same time." Ford's first action as President was to pardon Richard Nixon for the crimes that forced his resignation.

● ● ●

Richard Nixon had been President since 1969. Emperor Haile Selassie had ruled Ethiopia *since 1916*. He had survived 58 years of intrigue, rebellions, wars with neighbors, and an invasion by Italy. Still, he could not survive the coup-crazy '70s. Ethiopia had been enduring a terrible famine that began to weaken his regime. In the summer of '74, a group of military officers known as the Derg began infiltrating the government and nationalizing the emperor's private businesses and gradually stripping him of power. On September 11th, on national TV, the Derg broadcast a BBC documentary about the famine into which they had intercut scenes of the emperor grandly presiding over an elaborate wedding feast on the grounds of one of his many palaces. The reaction to their piece of *agit-prop* film was swift. The next day Selassie was unceremoniously shoved into a Volkswagen and whisked away from his palace.

The new leader, Mangistu Haile Mariam ordered the killing by firing squad of most members of Selassie's government and then on December 20 declared the country to be a socialist republic and all land to be public property. He picked a difficult time to revolutionize the country, for like most of the world, Ethiopia was suffering deeply from the oil crisis.

Selassie was imprisoned in a wing of the Grand Palace, where he apparently suffered under the demented belief that he was still emperor. On August 27, 1975, he was assassinated by soldiers of the new regime, and his body was buried on the palace grounds, reportedly under a latrine. Prominent Rastafarian leaders from Jamaica including Rita Marley attended his funeral, but many Rastafari refused to believe he was dead.

Mangistu became a violent tyrant, eliminating all opposition by having them strangled or shot. Thousands were killed and left to rot in the gutters of Addis Ababa. Some of the victims were as young as 11. He cut all ties with the west and aligned with the Soviet Union and Cuba. Modelling himself on Fidel Castro, dressed in combat fatigues with a gun on his hip and with cheetahs chained near his desk, he soon developed a cult of personality rivalling the Cuban leader. North Korea assisted in building giant monuments to Mangistu and the Revolution and organizing massive military parades around the capital. Mangistu's regime itself finally fell to a combination of a military coup and guerrilla attacks from neighboring Eritrea, and the dictator escaped to asylum in Zimbabwe.

• • •

The day after Selassie was deposed, on Friday the 13th of September, following orders of Fusako Shigenobu (the female leader of the Japanese Red Army) and Carlos the Jackal, three Japanese terrorists stormed the French Embassy in The Hague, the Netherlands. They demanded the release from France of one of their compatriots, plus a million dollars, and an airplane. Two days later, Carlos, in a related action, threw a grenade into *Le Publicis Drugstore* café in Paris, killing two and wounding 34 others. The two incidents convinced the French government to release the jailed Japanese terrorist, give them $300,000, and allow the hostage-takers to fly to Damascus. Syria allowed them into the country but forced them to give their ransom back as it did not believe that hostage-taking for money was a 'revolutionary' activity.

• • •

On September 18th, the St. Francis Hotel in San Francisco hosted a rather strange press conference that tried to make sense of what had happened to Timothy Leary. Although no-one knew all the details, it appeared that the Acid King had turned state's evidence on the groups that had sprung him from jail back in 1970—the Weathermen and the Brotherhood of Eternal Love. Jerry Rubin, Allen Ginsberg, Leary's 25-year-old son Jack, and his old partner Richard Alpert, (now going by the name Ram Dass) all denounced Leary as a "cop informant, a "paranoid schizophrenic" and a "liar." At the end of the event, Ken Kesey said that what it meant was, "The '60s are dead. That was just the funeral." Leary was still in jail, and for now he seemed to have lost all his friends and supporters.

• • •

The following day, September 19th, twenty members of Argentina's Montoneros, disguised as policemen, ambushed the limos of Jorge and Juan Borg, two of the owners of a huge Argentinian business conglomerate, Bunge and Borg. After killing their driver and bodyguard, they held the two businessmen for ransom in a safehouse of Argentine State Intelligence until June of 1975.

• • •

After their summer on the lam in Pennsylvania, on September 27 Patricia Hearst, the Harrises, and Jack Scott began a long trek back across the country. Because of the need for secrecy, Hearst was deposited in a motel near Las Vegas. There, she wiled away the hours watching, of all things, the old TV show *Sergeant Preston of the Yukon* in which Sergeant Preston, a Mountie, "always got his man"—an outcome that Tania no doubt hoped might apply to the RCMP, but not the FBI. Eventually she and the group, which had now grown to eight with the addition of five members of the Revolutionary Army bombing group, met up in Sacramento, rented a house, and began a six-month experiment in communal living, group sex, and living outside the law.

• • •

On October 5th, a subgroup of the Provisional IRA known as the Balcombe Street Gang exploded two 8-pound gelignite bombs in two pubs in Guildford, Surrey. The pubs were targeted because they were popular with British Army personnel stationed in Ireland. Four soldiers and one civilian were killed, and 65 people injured. Four people, who became known as the Guildford Four, were wrongfully convicted of the bombings and sentenced to long prison terms.

• • •

The *Fuerzas Armadas de Liberación Nacional* was founded in the late '60s following decades of persecution by the FBI of the Puerto Rican independence movement, including illegal imprisonments and assassinations. On October 26th, the FALN conducted their first bombing campaign, hitting the Marine Midland Bank in New York's financial district, then a few minutes later the Exxon Building at Rockefeller Center, then ten minutes after that one outside the Banco de Ponce, then one at the Union Carbide Building on 48th Street, then one at Lever House at Park Avenue and 53rd Street. Their goal was to "rid Puerto Rico of Yanki colonialism."

•   •   •

Argentina's Montoneros were in many ways the most ambitious of the world's terrorist revolutionaries. On November 1st, they took their bombing campaign to the water, killing General Commissioner Alberto Villar, the chief of the Argentine federal police, by exploding a bomb in his yacht. In 1975 they expanded their marine activities, which they modeled on the British commando raids of the 1940s. In August their frogmen placed a mine on an Argentine destroyer, and in December, they placed explosives on a yacht belonging to the Commander in Chief of the Argentine Navy.

•   •   •

On November 21st, bombs exploded in two pubs in Birmingham, England, killing 21 people and injuring 182. It was the worst bombing in England since World War II. The grotesque images of the slaughtered people inflamed the people of Birmingham who reacted with considerable venom against the 100,000 Irish living in the city. The Irish were ostracized from public places and subjected to physical assaults and death threats. In Northern Ireland there was a wave of revenge attacks by loyalist paramilitaries, who, within two days, killed five Catholic civilians. Soon after, the recently banned Ulster Volunteer Force took responsibility for eleven murders of Catholics in one day.

Six Irishmen were arrested and jailed for 16 years for the bombings, but in 1991 a Court of Appeal threw out the case. The incarceration is now considered one of the worst miscarriages of justice in British legal history.[114]

• • •

Once again, just as had happened so many times in the U.S. and South America, the reaction by the police and legal system was as extreme as the events themselves. As Planet Earth entered the last of these "ten years that shook the world," the battlelines between the revolutionaries and authorities continued to grow increasingly murky.

1975

Khmer Rouge Kill, Church Committee Convenes,
Arrested Acid Pusher a CIA Spook,
Killing Fields of Kampuchea, Saigon Falls,
Whales Saved, Jaws Released, Idi Amin Married,
Miami Showband Massacred, Rhodesia Abandoned,
Ford Shot, Patricia Hearst Captured, Cubans in Angola,
Operation Condor, OPEC Attacked.

On January 1st, the Khmer Rouge initiated their final offensive to capture the beleaguered Cambodian capital of Phnom Penh. They pounded the city with artillery and rocket fire until it finally fell on April 17th. By then, the country was virtually destroyed. The economy was in ruins, the rice harvest was only a quarter of what it had been before the war, the roads were cratered by bombs, and the people were starving. Two million refugees were now trying to live in Phnom Penh, a city that before the war had a population of 600,000. By 1975, most were without food, shelter, or jobs.

• • •

Carlos the Jackal was back in action, this time in Paris. On January 13th, he attacked two El Al airliners at Orly Airport with rocket-propelled grenades. The attack resulted in a 17-hour hostage situation that involved hundreds of police. Carlos fled during the gunfight. He was not seen until June when he was fingered by another member of the PLO who led two members of the French domestic intelligence service to him. Carlos shot all three men and escaped, first to Brussels and then to Baghdad.

• • •

Eleven days later, the Puerto Rican nationalist group the FALN bombed the Fraunces Tavern, a white-tablecloth restaurant in south Manhattan that had been popular with the revolutionaries of 1776 and was now frequented by bankers and stockbrokers. Forty were badly injured, and four were killed in the deadliest terrorist attack in the U.S. since an anarchist bomb had killed 35, also in Manhattan's Wall Street district, in 1920.

• • •

On January 27th, the U.S. Congress created the Church Committee to investigate widespread reports of the excesses of the American intelligence services in the '60s and early '70s. The list was long. The committee's investigations revealed the existence of *Operation Shamrock*, in which there was widespread illegal tapping of phones and opening of mail by the NSA, and multiple assassination attempts on foreign leaders by the CIA. These included attempts to kill Patrice Lumumba of Zaire, Rafael Trujillo of the Dominican Republic, Fidel Castro of Cuba, Ngo Dinh Diem of South Vietnam, and General René Schneider of Chile.

• • •

Two days later, threats were phoned in by the Weather Underground about bombs at the State Department in Washington, and at the Navy

Induction Center in Oakland, California. The State Department bomb did explode, damaging twenty offices and causing flooding from broken water systems. The Oakland center was evacuated but no bomb exploded. A bomb-sniffing dog was led in to search but found nothing. Later, though, an officer found the bomb in a false ceiling. Disposal experts towed it out by a rope and blew it up on the street in front of the building.

• • •

Further questions were again asked about the CIA following the arrest of the elusive Ronald Stark in Bologna, Italy. After the bust of Timothy Leary, and the subsequent surrender of Billy Hitchcock in 1973 that led to the downfall of the acid-dealing gang the Brotherhood of Eternal Love, the DEA was focused on Stark, who they claimed had created over 50 million hits of LSD. Stark was a genius con man who could talk circles around almost anyone in any of the ten languages he spoke. Now, after years of living a high-flying life cavorting with Sicilian mafiosi, political extremists of both the left and right, and secret service officials of different countries, it seemed that Stark was caught. However, even though he was captured with 4,600 kilos of marijuana, morphine, and cocaine, plus formulas for the manufacture of LSD, he didn't last long in prison. Judge Giorgio Floridia released Stark because of "an impressive series of scrupulously enumerated proofs" that Stark was in fact a CIA agent. The Italian judge stated that "Many circumstances suggest that from 1960 onwards Stark belonged to the American secret services." [128]

It is a wildly shocking hypothesis. It again raised the idea that the entire drug culture of the '60s was a creation of the CIA, and that elements within the agency had manipulated the distribution of LSD and other drugs to dismember the counterculture/anti-war movement. Stark himself had hinted at his close connection with the agency, once telling an associate he was going to shut down his Paris drug lab because the CIA had warned him that French police were preparing a bust.

By the mid-70s, prominent counterculture heroes like William Burroughs, White Panther leader John Sinclair, and novelist/Merry Prankster Ken Kesey all bought into the notion that they had been duped and that the entire acid craze had been started and nurtured by the CIA. The Acid King himself, Timothy Leary, smiling broadly as always, once spoke at a conference saying, "The LSD movement was started by the CIA. I wouldn't be here now without the foresight of the CIA scientists. It was no accident. It was all planned and scripted by the Central Intelligence, and I'm all in favor of Central Intelligence." John Lennon agreed. After learning that CIA Director Richard Helms ordered the shredding of all the documentation of the agency's drug and mind control projects in 1973, Lennon stated, "We must always remember to thank the CIA and the Army for LSD. That's what people forget…they invented LSD to control people and what they did was give us freedom." He then added, paraphrasing the William Cowper hymn, "Sometimes things work in mysterious ways, their wonders to perform."

• • •

February 4th was the one-year anniversary of the kidnapping of Patricia Hearst. She and Bill Harris celebrated by staking out a Sacramento bank. In the process they were accosted by a passerby, who facetiously asked, "Does anyone ever tell you that you look like Patty Hearst?" Bill Harris, stunned that Hearst's wig and freckles disguise did not seem to be working, quickly replied, "Oh, people say that all the time. This is my wife, and you're right—she does look like Patty Hearst."

Three weeks later, the gang returned to the bank, and robbed it of $3,700. It was a clean, well-planned robbery and no-one was killed or injured. They bagged enough loot to pay for materials with which to create new bombs. Their next heist would not be so successful.

• • •

As a sign that the violent activities of the past ten years were possibly coming to an end, on February 10th the IRA and the British declared a ceasefire in Northern Ireland. Any optimism that this may have engendered was soon shattered. Northerners felt that a ceasefire without guaranteed talks was a mistake and that the British had just strung the IRA along. The very next day there was an IRA killing in County Tyrone, and killings by either the IRA or the UVF continued on a weekly basis right through the year. By mid-1975 Northern Ireland had been turned into an armed camp. There were two-meter-high fences separating Catholic and Protestant areas of Belfast and military checkpoints everywhere.

One of the highest profile killings was of Ross McWhirter, the creator and editor of *The Guinness Book of Records.* Even though his book was sponsored by the famous Irish beer company, McWhirter had very hardline views on the Irish and he had personally posted a £50,000 reward for information about the IRA bombings in Guildford and Birmingham. Two members of the Balcombe Street Gang of the IRA shot and killed him at his home in Bush Hill Park.

• • •

On February 18th, *Brigate Rossa (Red Brigade)* co-founder Margherita Cagol led a commando raid on the prison that was holding her husband, Renato Curcio, and successfully got him out. Curcio remained at large until he was re-captured in January,1976.

• • •

Three days after the Italian prison break-out, U.S. Attorney General John Mitchell was found guilty of conspiracy, obstruction of justice, and perjury and was sentenced to two-and-a-half to eight years for his role in the Watergate break-in and cover-up. It was another classic image of this unique era—the highest law enforcement official in the land, now himself behind bars. Mitchell ultimately served 19 months in a minimum-security prison in Alabama before being released on parole for medical reasons.

• • •

As in all revolutions, there was often internecine warfare between various factions of the revolutionary movements. In Zambia, the squabbling between the ZANU and the ZANLA wings of the guerrillas fighting to free Rhodesia was a great irritant to Zambian president Kenneth Kaunda and his security forces, especially as the friction appeared to be aggravated by the efforts of undercover Rhodesian agents. On March 18th, an ex-British SAS operative and now CIA assassin named Alan "Taffy" Brice bombed a car belonging to leader of ZANU Herbert Chitepo. The explosion killed Chitepo, his bodyguard, and the child of a next-door neighbor. It was a hugely successful undercover operation that resulted in Kaunda jailing 1,300 guerrillas.

• • •

On April 1st, Prime Minister Lon Nol resigned and left Cambodia. It was naïvely hoped that his departure might make possible a negotiated settlement with the Khmer Rouge. His successor was in office for only three weeks. The U.S. Congress voted against any resumption of American air support. On April 12th, America helicoptered out all their embassy personnel. Although the remaining members of the Cambodian royal family were offered rides, they chose to stay and share the fate of their people. They trusted the Khmer Rouge's promise that they would be welcomed in helping to build the new Cambodia. Within a week of the fall of Phnom Penh, they were all beheaded.

The communists renamed the country Kampuchea. In the style of the French revolutionaries, who in 1792 abolished the calendar and declared the date to be Year One, the Cambodian revolutionaries declared that the date was no longer 1975, but rather Year Zero (in Khmer, *Chhnam*

Saun). All culture, industry, and tradition that had previously existed in Cambodia was to be destroyed. The Khmer language, for instance, was immediately altered. Severe penalties were meted out for anyone using the old formal forms of address. Everyone was now to be greeted only with the word *mitt* (comrade). The revolution began with a massive purge of all intellectuals, business-owners, doctors, and government officials. Teachers were much hated and hundreds were executed, as were artists, musicians, and filmmakers. Christian priests, Muslims, and Buddhist monks, all regarded as 'social parasites' were shot. The death toll soon vastly exceeded that of the Reign of Terror that had followed the French Revolution.

Pol Pot was perhaps the most extreme and violent batshit crazy revolutionary of this very violent period. "There is a continuous, non-stop struggle between revolution and counter-revolution," he proclaimed. "We must keep to the standpoint that there will be enemies 10 years, 20 years, 30 years into the future…[but] if we constantly take absolute measures, they will be scattered and smashed to bits."

The new regime began, almost unbelievably, by forcing the evacuation to the countryside of the two million people now living in the capital city. Patients from the hospitals were tipped out into the street like garbage. One witness described it as, "the greatest caravan of human misery I have ever seen." French missionary François Ponchaud wrote "I shall never forget one cripple who had neither hands nor feet, writhing along the ground like a severed worm, or a weeping father carrying his ten-year-old daughter wrapped in a sheet around his neck like a sling, or the man with his foot dangling at the end of a leg to which it was attached by nothing but skin." Those who wouldn't leave were simply shot. Children, though, were valued. Thousands were conscripted into the Khmer Rouge and indoctrinated to commit mass murder and other atrocities in the killing fields that lay ahead.

• • •

On April 2nd, the Puerto Rican FALN bombing campaign continued. Four bombs exploded one after another in New York City—the New York Life Insurance Building at Madison and 27th; the Metropolitan Life Insurance Building at Park and 25th; the Bankers Trust Company at Park Avenue and 48th St.; and the American Bank and Trust Company at 46th St and Fifth Avenue.

• • •

In yet another sign that the era was coming to an end, Chinese leader Chiang Kai-shek died on April 5th. Chiang had been one of the major revolutionary leaders of China in the 1920s and 30s, but after his nationalist movement was defeated by Mao's communists in 1949, he and his army retreated to Taiwan, which he then ruled for the next 25 years as an authoritarian dictator. His strongly anti-communist stance meant that for a long time the West recognized him as being the leader of the only legitimate government of all of China, but after Mao's 'Red' China was admitted to the United Nations in 1971 and mainland China was visited by Richard Nixon in 1972, Chiang's star quickly began to fade.

• • •

The American revolution was still alive and kicking. In April, in Los Angeles, filmmakers Emile de Antonio, Haskell Wexler, and Mary Lampson began filming *Underground*, a feature-length documentary profile of the Weathermen. It is a most unusual film largely consisting of interviews with members of the group in which the viewer sees only the filmmakers asking the questions and not the subjects, who are all hidden. When the FBI learned of the film, they subpoenaed the three filmmakers hoping to be able to confiscate the material and gain information about the location of the Weathermen. The trio, with the legal assistance of lawyers paid for by filmmakers Warren Beatty, Jack Nicholson, Shirley MacLaine, and Elia

Kazan, managed to get the subpoenas repealed, on the basis of the rights of journalists to maintain the confidentiality of their sources.

• • •

Meanwhile the real underground technological revolution continued. Steve Jobs and Steve Wozniak joined the Homebrew Computer Club, where they began work on the design of the Apple computer that would be released the following year. Their garage-based start-up outfit, that is today the largest company in the world, was officially formed on April 1st, 1976, and the first computers sold soon after.

• • •

On April 21st, the eight members of the SLA, including Patricia Hearst, robbed the Crocker National in Carmichael, California. A customer, Myrna Opsahl, was killed. Emily Harris' dismissal of Ms. Opsahl as being "just a bourgeois pig" caused a bitter schism in the group. With potential murder charges now looming, the group abandoned Sacramento and hightailed it back to their original stomping grounds in San Francisco.

• • •

Following the departure from Vietnam of most of the Americans and all of their Australian allies by the end of 1973, the South Vietnamese Army were left to fight the North Vietnamese and the Vietcong as best they could. Their best was not good enough. The Americans gave them many warplanes and tanks, but like everyone in the world they were hit hard by the oil crisis, and without fuel, their planes were grounded and useless. On the other hand, with the end of the American bombing of Hanoi, Russian ships were able to land dozens of new tanks in the North Vietnamese port along with the fuel to run them.

In early 1975 the CIA and U.S. Army Intelligence believed that the South Vietnamese could hold out for another year, but this proved to be grievously wrong. The People's Army of Vietnam drove south toward Saigon. The South Vietnamese government grew increasingly ineffectual and corrupt and on April 19th, President Nguyễn Văn Thiêu made a series of confused and contradictory commands that sent the country into chaos. Thousands of deserting troops and millions of panicked civilians headed for coastal cities like Dà Nẵng where they tried to board ships to flee the country. Only a fraction of them succeeded. As the North Vietnamese pounded the coastal cities with artillery, the cities fell, "like a row of porcelain vases sliding off a shelf." When Thieu's hometown of Phan Rang fell, the retreating ARVN troops showed their disgust by demolishing his family's ancestral shrines and graves.

On April 21st, Thieu made a rambling and incoherent speech in which he excoriated the U.S. calling it, "inhumane, not trustworthy and irresponsible", and then, close to tears, he resigned. Two days later he boarded a plane and, with the help of the CIA, escaped to Taiwan. With the South Vietnamese government and army in complete disarray, the PAVN pushed south, and on April 30th the city of Saigon fell, finally ending the 10,000-day war.

The world watched incredible imagery of the largest helicopter evacuation in history. There were indelible televised shots of frightened people on the roof of the American embassy trying to jam into overloaded helicopters. Then, with no room left on the aircraft carriers that took the evacuees, there were even more startling images of sailors pushing an estimated ten million dollars-worth of Huey choppers off the decks into the South China Sea.

North Vietnam had won the war. North and South Vietnam unified and remain as a single country to this day. The "Domino Theory" that was always presented as the reason for the American presence in Vietnam never happened. The costs to the country were enormous. The U.S. dropped 19 million gallons of herbicide on Vietnam that wiped out almost all the country's ancient triple-canopy forests. The U.S. destroyed 9,000 of South Vietnam's 15,000 hamlets. In the north, U.S. bombing destroyed all six industrial cities, 28 of 30 provincial towns, and 96 of 116 district towns. More than 3,800,000 Vietnamese people and 58,280 Americans died in the war. The Americans always claimed they needed to capture the 'hearts and minds' of the Vietnamese. The reality is that they never tried very hard to do so, and they certainly didn't succeed. In fact, they did not even capture the 'hearts and minds' of Americans, nor the rest of the world. In the end, it was the moral force of the revolutionary anti-war movement in America and around the world that led to the defeat of the American military, and of South Vietnam.

• • •

While Saigon was falling, Greenpeace was preparing a bold new mission. The group's provocative actions against nuclear testing in previous years had been successful, but it was their anti-whaling activities that cemented their position as the preeminent activist environmental organization of the era. On April 27th, a Greenpeace group—sailing on the same halibut seine-fishing boat they had used for the Amchitka protest in 1971, left the Vancouver waterfront. By now their activities had captured the support of many people. Serenaded by 17 bands, 23,000 gathered to see them off.

For 62 days off the coast of California, they searched for the Japanese or Soviet Russian whaling fleets. Finally, on June 20th, they came upon the Russian fleet—a factory ship and numerous large chaser boats. They discovered the carcasses of numerous dead teenage whales that were all under the legal-size limit. The activists then drove their inflatable Zodiacs between the harpoon guns of the ships and the spouting whales. After some hesitation, the Russian harpooners began firing. Robert Hunter, one of the founders and leaders of Greenpeace, recalled, "the guy with the harpoon must have been a good shot, or we were awfully lucky. The spear went right over our head, missed us by only six or seven feet." [117]

The new concept of putting their bodies and their small inflatable boats between the whales and the harpoons of the Soviet whalers fired the public imagination and Greenpeace became one of the most successful radical agents for change of all time. The *New York Times* reported that, "for the first time in the history of whaling, human beings had put their lives on the line for whales." Their actions didn't immediately end whaling, but they eventually (for the most part) did.

• • •

As Saigon fell, so did other symbols of the previous ten years. On May 15th, seven Sheriff's officers with sledgehammers backed by two dozen policemen entered Toronto's Rochdale College to evict the final hold-out tenants of the wild experiment in communal education. By the end of the month, everyone was gone. The interior was trashed. It reeked of marijuana and was littered with broken beer bottles. Janitors and a construction crew began to clean up. The last issue of the Rochdale newspaper wryly commented, "Drug dealing is now the domain of the professionals—lawyers, doctors, etc. Let's hope they never get to live in the same building." Ironically, they quite possibly do. Within two years, the high-rise re-opened as an apartment block designed for assisted living for senior citizens.

• • •

In Italy, the revolution was not over. On June 2nd, the *Brigate Rossa* was back in the news after Margherita Cagol led a small team who kidnapped rich industrialist (and, according to them, fascist), Vallarino Gancia. The carabinieri were soon on their tail, and the next day the kidnappers were apprehended at the rural safe house where they were hiding their victim. In the shoot-out that followed, both Cagol and a policeman were killed. Most of the gang were arrested and jailed, but Cagol's husband (and the co-founder with her of the Red Brigades) Renato Curcio was still, since his jailbreak earlier in the year, at large. He remained on the lam until 1976, when he was captured, tried, convicted, and imprisoned. That was by no means, though, the end of the *Brigate Rossa*.

A new generation took the reins of the underground organization, and on March 16th, 1978 staged their wildest operation, the kidnapping and eventual assassination of former Italian Prime Minister Aldo Moro. Years later, new controversy swirled about his death. Former U.S. Deputy Assistant Secretary of State for Management Steve Pieczenik, who during the 55 day hostage-taking was advising the Italian government on the crisis, claimed in a documentary interview that "we had to sacrifice Aldo Moro to maintain the stability of Italy," and that the CIA had been involved in having the *Brigate Rosse* kill Moro, since the former Prime Minister was revealing under pressure the existence of a top secret American and European paramilitary anti-Soviet organization code-named *Gladio*.[118]

· · ·

Patricia Hearst and her SLA comrades had a surprisingly quiet spring and early summer. The five women in the group, emboldened by the radical feminism that was permeating the era, began an internal feminist study group, using a new Marxist text, the *Dialectic of Sex* as their guide, and questioning the need for any male leadership of the group. "We had developed our own combat skills and were equal to the men in that respect," said Patricia, "and therefore we no longer needed them to lead the revolution. Our position on equality in sexual relationships held that sex should be the result of natural friendships. A woman should not feel inhibited about sleeping with a woman she likes, any more than she would when sleeping with a man for whom she cared." The sexual shenanigans between the comrades continued through the hot California summer.

· · ·

On June 9th, an incident occurred at the British Columbia Maximum Security Penitentiary that seemed to mirror events of the era such as the Patty Hearst story, the Attica prison riot, and the 'Stockholm Syndrome' bank robbery. Three inmates, all doing serious time, took 15 people hostage in an attempt to escape from the ancient prison. Most of the hostages were social workers—described in the correctional system as 'classification officers.' The leader of the cons, Andy Bruce, demanded that one of them volunteer as spokesperson for the hostages. Mary Steinhauser stepped forward. It was a dangerous role, since she and Bruce would be first in the line of fire should shooting break out. Steinhauser was an extraordinarily empathetic person. She was a trained psychiatric nurse who had only worked in the institution for a few months but had developed productive relationships with many of the cons. Bruce, one of her clients, had made 23 visits to her office over the previous month. The prison guards were less friendly—in fact were brazenly hostile to Steinhauser and the other social workers.

The incident received intense attention locally, across Canada and internationally, as a group of lawyers, journalists and radio hosts unsuccessfully attempted to negotiate a peaceful outcome. After a stand-off of 41 hours, a team of prison guards, later accused of being reckless and trigger-happy, charged the office and vault and began shooting.

The prison and the police later reported that what precipitated the incident was that Bruce had sliced the neck of his hostage. The autopsy later showed this to be a lie—she was not cut. Instead, according to a paramedic witness, George High, the prison guards began firing as soon as they entered the office. After Bruce was hit twice, Mary Steinhauser crawled in front of him, screaming, "Don't shoot him!", at which point, according to High, one of the guards shouted, "Kill her, kill her." [119] Steinhauser was fatally shot in the heart.

The guard who was most suspected as the shooter was Albert Hollinger, the leader of the TACT squad. Hollinger quickly rounded up all the guns that his squad had used and, against all rules, unloaded the spent shells and mixed up the guns so that none could be definitively traced to the killing. A jury later exonerated the guards of any blame in the death of Mary Steinhauser. The incident has been extensively examined and debated. An official commission, a book[120], a play, two feature film scripts (one by this author), and a musical stage presentation have all explored the social and political ramifications of the tragic event, which symbolized to many the conflicts and passions of the era.

• • •

On June 14th, the Puerto Rican nationalist group FALN set off two bombs in Chicago—one at the First National Bank, and one at the United Bank of America. Two days later, David Gilbert of the Weathermen set off a bomb at the Banco de Ponce, suggesting that the Weathermen and the FALN were linking forces.

• • •

In what was considered a victory for the ten years of activism of Cesar Chavez' United Farmworkers, California Governor Jerry Brown signed the California Agricultural Labor Relations Act, considered the most favorable labor bill in the U.S. The new bill did not end Chavez' activism, and he would soon begin his 'Thousand Mile March' from San Diego up the California coast.

• • •

In Argentina, the Montoneros, who since September of 1974 had held wealthy businessmen Jorge and Juan Born hostage, received $60 million U.S., considered the largest ransom payment ever paid in modern times, to finance their revolutionary activities. They also demanded and received $1.2 million worth of food and clothing to be given to the poor.[129]

• • •

June 20th saw the wide release of *Jaws*, the film that signaled the end of the 1965 – 75 period of cultural experimentation. None of the previously familiar tropes of either the *Nouvelle Vague*, the underground film movement, or the 'New Hollywood' were in the film. There was no sex.

Director Steven Spielberg had tellingly cut a scripted adulterous affair provided by the screenwriters. There were barely any women in the film and not a single non-white character. There was no brooding angst, no pseudo-sophisticated wordplay. It is true that there was, in classic '70s fashion, a quasi-countercultural young hero, played by Richard Dreyfus, going up against the establishment—the town's mayor, (Murray Hamilton), police chief (Roy Scheider), and the grouchy old-time fisherman (Robert Shaw), but of course the real story is the human characters going up against the great white shark. The film changed the zeitgeist of the times. *Jaws* created the concept of the blockbuster, and thus mostly destroyed the potential for production of many more of the radical films of the 65 – 75 period, films like *Five Easy Pieces, Easy Rider, Carnal Knowledge, The Apprenticeship of Duddy Kravitz,* or the European films of Fellini, Godard, or Bergman. *Jaws*, which was made for $9 million, grossed $472 million. The notion of making films that would appeal to European revolutionaries or would play in university film societies or Manhattan art houses mostly withered away. *Jaws* created a template that would be the new model for Hollywood to make billions from the culturally conservative films of the late 70s and 80s like *Star Wars* and *Raiders of the Lost Ark.*

• • •

A year after the Carnation Revolution in Portugal, the former Portuguese colony of Mozambique became independent. It was now led by the Frelimo Party, dedicated not just to bringing socialism to the country but to supporting all efforts to bring down the white-supremacist government of its neighbor Rhodesia.

• • •

Meanwhile in Uganda Idi Amin bestowed a new title on himself. He was now: *His Excellency, President for Life, Field Marshall Al Hadji, Doctor Idi Amin Dada, VC, DSO, MC, CBE, King of Scotland, Lord of all the Beasts of the*

Earth and Fishes of the Seas and Conqueror of the British Empire in Africa in General and Uganda in Particular. (The "Fishes of the Seas" part is particularly rich, since Uganda is one of the few nations on earth that is totally landlocked). The various medals he displayed were self-invented knockoffs of British military medals. For instance, 'VC' did not stand for the usual Victoria Cross, but rather for something he created called the Victorious Cross.

He had married five women (some of whom died under mysterious circumstances) and reportedly fathered 54 children.

In July, he staged a wedding to Sarah Kyolaba, nicknamed 'Suicide Sarah.' She was a 19-year-old go-go dancer with the 'Revolutionary Suicide Mechanized Regiment Band.' The wedding, costing two million British pounds, was held during the Kampala summit meeting of the Organization of African Unity. Yasser Arafat, Chairman of the Palestine Liberation Organization, served as best man. Sarah was already pregnant from a previous boyfriend. The child was born on Christmas Day. Idi Admin declared the child as his own and it is believed the boyfriend was either beheaded or jailed.

Amin took up the sport of rally race driving, with Sarah as his navigator. Smart competitors made sure that he and Sarah won the rallies.

• • •

On July 31st, at a fake army checkpoint, members of the Ulster Volunteer Force and soldiers from the British Army ambushed a van containing the Miami Showband, a popular Irish musical group. The soldiers tried to plant an explosive disguised as being from the IRA, but while installing it in the van, the bomb exploded. The UVF men and soldiers then opened fire on the band, killing three of them as well as two bystanders. British Army Intelligence was later shown to have been involved in organizing the bombing. *Irish Times* diarist Frank McNally described the massacre as "an incident that encapsulated all the madness of the time."

• • •

In a year of considerable disaster, August 8th would have brought more bad news, except that what happened that day was kept a state secret by the Chinese government until 2005. Between 85,000 and 240,000 people died when the Banqiao Dam in Henan, China collapsed. An area of three million acres (12,000 square kilometers) was flooded, 30 cities were inundated and 6.8 million houses were destroyed. The dam break, caused by intense rainfall from Typhoon Nina, led to the third biggest flood in the history of the world, and was later listed as Number One in the Discovery Channel show "The Ultimate Ten Technological Disasters" of the world. Although partially blamed on engineering flaws in the construction of the dam during Mao's "Great Leap Forward", most of the blame for the catastrophe was laid upon the abandonment of any concern for the structure during the Cultural Revolution, when all focus was on revolutionary purity, and none on the dull work of the maintenance of infrastructure.

By now the Cultural Revolution was beginning to wither away. Its effects had been almost entirely negative. The endless purges had not only been devastating to the civic and political leaders, the army, the hospitals, and the schools, but they had also destroyed the economy. In 1975, Chinese cities could barely produce half of the commodities needed by the population. Starvation on a mass scale was common in many parts of China until 1976, when things slowly began to improve. It was not atypical for villagers to try to exist on less than eight kilos of food per month.

Thousands of hungry people and large gangs of beggars roamed the countryside. Others became what were known as *Wuming* (*Nameless*). They were people who had survived the broken homes and shattered schools of the Revolution but had now given up on all other aspects of life and obsessively devoted themselves to art. They received paint and brushes from the government on the assumption they would produce the standard approved portraits of Mao. Instead, they secretly and endlessly made paintings of nature—collective art therapy.

Others secretly sublimated their worship of Chairman Mao into the religions of the past. There was a resurgence not only of Christianity,

Buddhism, Taoism, and Islam, but also of folk religions—each with their own local gods and deities. With the government offices in charge of religious affairs in turmoil, all manner of religions and cults reorganized and resurfaced, a phenomenon that would explode following the death of Mao. It would eventually lead to the growth of Falun Gong, a movement that the Communist Party felt was so threatening to the state that it was outlawed and thousands of its adherents jailed.

• • •

The previous year, seismologists predicted a very large earthquake near the city of Tangshan, 150 kilometers east of Beijing. Through the summer of '75, the Chinese noticed the strange behavior of animals. Snakes appeared 'frozen' on the roads, rats seemed to be 'drunk', and chickens refused to enter their coops. Once again, though, due to the more pressing demands of the Cultural Revolution, both the scientific and natural warnings were ignored. The following year on July 28th, the second deadliest earthquake in the history of the world convulsed the region and between half a million and 700,000 were killed. In China, earthquakes are thought to be harbingers of other big events, and indeed, a little over a month later, there was one. On September 9th, Chairman Mao died. It was not the end of Maoism, nor the end of the Cultural Revolution, but it was the beginning of the end.

• • •

In August, the SLA got into the bombing business. Bill Harris was now using *The Anarchist Cookbook* to cook up some bombs, and on August 7th Patricia Hearst and Josephine Soliah laid a bomb under a police car in front of the Mission police station. It failed to detonate but 13 days later outside the Marin County Sheriff's office the pair planted two bombs that did explode. The SLA claimed responsibility for the bombings, saying they were a warning "to the fascist dogs who murder our children in cold blood." They ended the communiqué with their familiar, all-caps catch phrase: 'DEATH TO THE FASCIST INSECT THAT PREYS UPON THE LIFE OF THE PEOPLE.'

The gang celebrated by going to the movies. They went to see *In the Year of the Pig*, Emile de Antonio's documentary about the Vietnam war. Bill Harris embarrassed the rest of the group by bellowing encouragement to the Vietcong soldiers in the film, and shouting, "Eat lead, pigs!" at images of American soldiers. Patricia, fearful of being seen after Harris' noisy display, resisted his suggestion that they go on to see a second film. "Ask me to do anything, ask me to rob a bank with you," she told him, "But don't ask me to go to a movie theater and get arrested watching fucking *Citizen Kane*."

• • •

In September, Henry Kissinger traveled to Pretoria. He secretly told South African Prime Minister John Vorster that the U.S. had launched what it called *Operation Savannah*, a covert CIA military operation in Angola to attempt to defeat the *Movimento Popular de Libertação de Angola*. He also told Vorster that the U.S. would attempt to overcome the resistance of the rest of the world to allow the International Monetary Fund to grant South Africa $460 million. In return, Kissinger asked Vorster to end South African military assistance to its neighbor, Rhodesia. As a sop to the Democrats, the Republican Administration had decided to back away from its support of the openly racist Rhodesia. Vorster, entering the height of the battles with the young students of Soweto, reluctantly agreed to the terms. Without the support of South Africa and the United States, and with sanctions from Europe and the rest of Africa, Rhodesia's days were numbered.

• • •

On September 5th, there was a dramatic assassination attempt of President Gerald Ford at the State Capitol Building in Sacramento,

California. Lynette "Squeaky" Fromme had been one of the first and most loyal followers of Charlie Manson. She was not charged in the Tate-LaBianca murders, but did attend every day of Manson's trial, burned an X into her forehead in solidarity with him, and served 90 days for attempting to feed a hamburger laced with LSD to one of the trial witnesses to try to prevent her from testifying. By 1975 she had become an environmental activist of sorts. When she learned that Ford, in typical Republican fashion, was trying to roll back the provisions of the Clean Air Act, she took an ancient, WWI-vintage Colt .45 to Sacramento and attempted to shoot Ford at virtually point-blank range. She did not cock the gun properly, though, and it did not fire. She was jailed for 34 years but was released in 2009, and now lives with another ex-con in upstate New York.

• • •

Even the most remote parts of the world joined in the period's passion for change. On September 16th, Papua New Guinea threw off its colonial shackles and became independent, though it remained within the British Commonwealth. The country had been ruled by Germany, England, and Australia, but most of it is so remote and hidden that the colonial masters had virtually no effect on the lives of much of the population. The Australians, though, had managed to reduce the traditional ritual warfare between the mountain tribes. With independence, the ritualistic battling returned, though with a new twist. The colorful imagery on the battle shields that are an integral part of the warfare now changed from traditional abstract designs to modern Western images, sometimes automotive or beer company logos, but more frequently images of the comic book character 'The Phantom', who was adopted as a heroic symbol by the more primitive and warlike elements of the new country.

• • •

The FBI hated their inability to solve the Patty Hearst case. The reason for their failure was perhaps simple. The G-Men of this period had a very hard time infiltrating the baby boomers, the counterculture, and the radical left. "One thing bothers me terribly," San Francisco FBI director Charlie Bates told journalist Shana Alexander. "In the 16-to-25 age group, *everybody's* anti-law enforcement. No-one will even speak to you. I dunno why…the reasons are more complicated than the problem. You knock and say, 'FBI, can I talk to you, please? And they shout, 'Bug off!' and slam the door." (They probably did not use the word, 'bug').

Their luck changed when Walter Scott, brother of Jack Scott and himself a rather mysterious ex-mercenary who had worked for Colonel Gaddafi in Libya, walked into the Scranton, Pennsylvania office of the FBI and drunkenly spilled the beans about his brother's connections with the SLA. The news was received skeptically but was eventually passed on from Scranton to San Francisco. The FBI found and questioned Jack Scott, but he refused to cooperate. Instead, he held a press conference, alongside his friend, professional basketball star Bill Walton, and stated, "The events of Watergate, and the U.S. involvement in Vietnam, the present economic situation, and the almost daily revelations about the FBI and the CIA have convinced us that we are confronted with a morally bankrupt government. We believe a position of total non-collaboration with this government is our moral responsibility. We have no intention of talking with the FBI now, or in the future." [121]

The FBI figured out a way of going around Scott's refusal to cooperate, and on September 18th they nabbed first Bill and Emily Harris while they were out jogging (the latest new craze of the mid-70s). An hour later, they smashed through the backdoor of a San Francisco apartment and grabbed one of two women sitting talking at the kitchen table and held a gun to her head. As the second bolted for the bedroom, where her guns were stashed, the agent shouted at her, "Freeze! I'll blow her head off!" She stopped. The agent asked her, "Are you Patty Hearst?"

"Yes," she confessed. She then peed her pants in fear.

She was taken to the San Mateo County Jail where she was booked on charges of armed robbery and using a weapon in a felony. She gave her name as both Patricia Campbell Hearst and as Tania, and when asked her occupation, she described herself as "Urban Guerrilla." Jailed, and waiting for a bail hearing, she was allowed to write letters to her lover and fellow SLA member Steve Soliah, who had also been picked up in the dragnet. "As long as we stay strong and free these pigs can't fuck with us," she wrote. "They can imprison our bodies but not our hearts & minds. I look forward to a lifetime of struggle—there will be a revolution in Amerikkka and we'll be helping to make it."

Five days later, there was yet another bizarre chapter to the Hearst story with yet another attempted assassination of President Gerald Ford. Sara Jane Moore was fascinated by Patty Hearst. She had worked as a volunteer bookkeeper for People in Need, the organization Patty's father had set up to distribute food for the Symbionese Liberation Army. At the same time, she was also spying on the organization as an informant for the FBI. Now, 18 months later, Moore had a new fixation—the President of the United States. Moore's own gun had been confiscated by the police the day before her assassination attempt, so on the morning of the attempted killing she had to go out and buy a new one. Police analysis later determined that it was only because the sights were off on the new gun that Moore missed.

Ford now held the record—two unsuccessful attempts on his life within 17 days, both by women.

• • •

On October 27th Puerto Rico's clandestine paramilitary group *Fuerzas Armadas de Liberación Nacional* set off ten bombs—two in Washington, five in New York, and three in Chicago, causing damage of a quarter of a million dollars. The modus operandi of the FALN was to explode bombs (they fired off 130 in total) and then publish a communiqué taking credit for them and declaring their opposition to "the colonial forces of the United

States" and the "Yanki capitalist monopoly" on the island. This time their missive also included thanks to Fidel Castro for his "moral support" of the group. Castro had frequently stated his belief that if Puerto Rico was ever hit by a major crisis, the U.S. would abandon the territory. This was a prediction that some said came true with the Trump administration's tepid and bungled response to the devastation of the island by Hurricane Maria in 2017.

• • •

On October 31ˢᵗ, in what became known as the "Halloween Massacre", President Gerald Ford confirmed the American government's swing to the right by appointing George H.W. Bush as head of the CIA, Dick Cheney as Chief of Staff, and Donald Rumsfeld (a "ruthless little bastard", according to Richard Nixon) as Secretary of Defense. The hardline trio would dominate Republican administrations for the next 20 years.

• • •

After learning that the U.S. had begun sending arms to Angola for use by CIA-backed mercenaries, Cuba countered by sending combat troops to support the communist-aligned People's Movement for the Liberation of Angola. The MPLA controlled the country, but were under attack by two other groups, UNITA and FNLA. The fight became a proxy battle of the Cold War, with UNITA, the FNLA, the U.S., and South Africa on one side, and the MPLA, Cuba, Yugoslavia, and the Soviet Union on the other. It lasted for 16 years. It is possibly the first time in the history of the world that a small Third World country sent a major military force across an ocean to fight in a liberation war on another continent. The Cuban forces grew to 18,000 in 1975 and to 60,000 by 1988. Cuban casualties in the bush war totaled over 10,000 dead, wounded, or missing. The Cuban presence in Angola was much more than military. They also sent a large team of doctors, 1,300 volunteer teachers, professors, engineers, and construction workers. They built 2,000 new houses and 50 new bridges and invited up to 18,000 Angolan students on full scholarship to study in Cuba.

Nelson Mandela spoke about the Cuban involvement in Angola at the 38th anniversary of the Cuban revolution, saying, "The Cuban people hold a special place in the hearts of the people of Africa. The Cuban internationalists have made a contribution to African independence, freedom, and justice unparalleled for its principled and selfless character. We in Africa are used to being victims of countries wanting to carve up our territory or subvert our sovereignty. It is unparalleled to have another people rise to the defense of one of us. The defeat of the apartheid army [in Angola] was an inspiration to the struggling people of South Africa!" [122]

• • •

On November 14th, an RV camper owned by Marlon Brando and on loan to the American Indian Movement was pulled over by an Oregon State Trooper. Inside were AIM leaders Leonard Peltier, Dennis Banks, Annie Mae Aquash and others, as well as a cache of guns and explosives. Peltier and Banks escaped, but Aquash and the others were arrested and returned to South Dakota. Aquash was released in December but disappeared weeks later and was found dead in a snow bank with a bullet hole in her head. She was possibly killed because other members of AIM suspected her of being an FBI informer. Leonard Peltier fled to Canada but was ultimately caught. He was extradited from Alberta to the U.S on charges of the murder of two FBI agents. Even though Canada's Solicitor General, Warren Allmand later said the extradition documents provided by the FBI contained false information, Peltier received two life sentences, and an additional seven years for a 1979 jailbreak. He is still in prison despite pleas for clemency from such luminaries as Mother Teresa, Nelson

Mandela, Bishop Tutu, the Dalai Lama, Jesse Jackson, and numerous human rights organizations.

• • •

Also in November, after the police reacted heavy-handedly to the recent political and racial turmoil, San Francisco voters approved a series of ballot initiatives to curb police power. The police angrily responded by going on a ticket-writing blitz, issuing three times as many parking tickets as normal. Activists responded by pouring liquid steel into the locks of hundreds of city parking meters.

It was another serio-comic end to the age of revolution. By the next year Bernardine Dohrn was releasing a communiqué claiming that she and her co-conspirators had "followed the classic path of white so-called revolutionaries who sold out the revolution." Meanwhile the FBI agents who had led the investigation of the Weathermen were now themselves being investigated and subpoenaed for their break-ins and other excesses. To protect themselves, they threw out or burned thousands of pages of evidence and notes of their investigations. In the end a Washington grand jury handed down indictments not against the field agents but against their superiors—Acting Director L. Patrick Gray, Acting Associate Director Mark Felt, and Assistant Director Ed Miller. The irony was profound. After a seven-year bombing campaign, it was the leaders of the FBI, not the Weathermen, who were going to trial.

• • •

A horrific new era had only just begun in South America. By the end of 1975, right-wing military dictatorships were ruling Paraguay, Brazil, Bolivia, Uruguay, and Chile, and then Argentina a few months later. In November, security and military officials from the six countries met in Santiago to secretly plot what they called *Operation Condor*, a collaborative effort to wipe out all political opposition in the so-called 'Southern Cone' of South America. During the ten years of the program, with help from U.S. Secretary of State Henry Kissinger, the U.S. Army, and the CIA, they imprisoned 400,000 people, killed 60,000 and, according to the Archive of Terror "disappeared" another 30,000. *Operation Condor* was run by the Pinochet regime in Chile, but the worst of the torture and excesses took place in Argentina and Paraguay. In Argentina, favorite interrogation techniques included taking children away from their parents and 'disappearing' them and taking groups of suspects out to sea in helicopters and hurling them one by one into the ocean.

In Paraguay, U.S. Army officer Lieutenant Colonel Robert Thierry led an American team in assisting the Paraguayans in building a detention and interrogation center called *La Technica*. The jail became a well-known torture center. President Alfredo Stroessner's secret police, led by the obese chief torturer Pastor Coronel, bathed their captives in tubs of human excrement and vomit, and shocked them in the rectum with electric cattle prods. They dismembered communist party secretary Miquel Angel Soler alive with a chainsaw while President Stroessner listened on the phone. Stroessner then demanded that tapes of detainees screaming in pain be played for their family members.

Operation Condor basically ended the Montoneros in Argentina, the Tupamaros in Uruguay, and any semblance of freedom in the bulk of South America. It was yet another sign that the political climate had profoundly changed as the world entered the last half of the '70s and then slid into the conservative, non-revolutionary '80s.

• • •

On December 21ˢᵗ, in the wildest event of the year, Carlos the Jackal led a six-person team (including Gabriele Kröcher-Tiedemann) that attacked the meeting of the leaders of OPEC (the Organization of Petroleum Exporting Countries) at their headquarters in Vienna. They killed three and took 60 as hostages. Once again, Carlos got away with it after forcing the government of Austria to read a communiqué outlining the Palestinian cause on radio and TV, and then flying the kidnappers and their hostages to Algiers. It is believed that Carlos got a huge amount of money—somewhere between $20 and $50 million—from an undisclosed "Arab president" widely thought to be Libya's Muammar al-Gaddafi, for returning the hostages safely. Carlos didn't buy that tired old Robin Hood shit about stealing from the rich and giving to the poor. Carlos stole from the rich and kept for himself.

The Vienna kidnapping was an outrageously brazen action; an appropriately outlandish climatic finale to these revolutionary and violent ten years that shook the world.

WHATEVER HAPPENED TO:

In the random, loose spirit of the times, here is an update on the lives of many of the prominent figures of the late '60s and early '70s, in the years after 1975.

Carlos the Jackal was involved in dozens of major attacks and bombings, mostly in France, throughout the late '70s and '80s. The PLO was angered that he did not execute the two senior hostages—the finance minister of Iran and the oil minister of Saudi Arabia—in December of 1975, so expelled him from the organization. Carlos returned to Europe and became a freelance terrorist and then a secret agent for the STASI—the East German Secret Police.

He bounced around Eastern Europe, the Middle East, and Africa throughout the '80s and '90s, with no country willing to let him stay for long. A legendary CIA agent named Billy Waugh led a long search, and finally located the Jackal in 1994 in Khartoum, Sudan. Police in the African nation convinced Carlos that the Americans were going to attempt an assassination and that he should accept their offer of a safe house and bodyguards. While he slept, the bodyguards injected him with a tranquilizer and turned him over to agents of the French secret police who flew him back to Paris. In 1997 he was found guilty of three 1975 murders and was sentenced to life with no possibility of parole. After receiving another life sentence in 2011 and a third in 2017, the Jackal was returned to Clairvaux Prison, which will presumably now be his permanent abode.

Carlos' Japanese co-conspirators in the terrorist activities of the mid '70s were also eventually captured. **Kasue Yoshimura** joined up with the Shining Path movement in the remote mountains of Peru but was eventually arrested in 1998 by agents of the Peruvian counter-terrorist unit DIRCOTE. Her compatriot **Fusako Shigenobu** hid out in Takatsuki City, Osaka for 26 years following the 1974 attack on the French Embassy. She was finally captured on November 8, 2000 and in 2006 was sentenced to 20 years in prison, where she remains, despite several unsuccessful appeals.

Since his birth in 1898, Chinese Premier **Zhou Enlai** survived through thick and thin in an extraordinarily eventful life, even managing to survive the complexities of the seven years of the Cultural Revolution. He died on January 8, 1976. His boss, Chairman **Mao Zedong** also died in 1976, on September 7th. Mao is believed to be responsible for between 40 and 80 million deaths. His own death (at 83) was a result of lung and heart disease caused by chain-smoking, compounded by Parkinson's Disease and Lou Gehrig's Disease. His body is interred at the Mausoleum of Mao Zedong in Beijing.

Jiang Qing, also known as **Madame Mao**, was arrested following the death of Mao and charged with being a member of a counter-revolutionary clique, the so-called Gang of Four. She was sentenced to death, but in 1983 her sentence was commuted to life. She committed suicide in May, 1991.

Assata Shakur was charged and found guilty of numerous crimes due to her activities in the early 1970s with the Black Liberation Army. She received a life sentence as well as a consecutive 26 to 33-year sentence. She was serving her term at the Clinton Correctional Facility in New Jersey until November 2, 1979 when a group known as "The Family" consisting of two Black men, and two white women, (one of them the Italian revolutionary Silvia Baraldini), broke her out of the prison. Shakur hid out in Pittsburgh, then in the Bahamas, then in Cuba. The FBI and the State of New Jersey posted a two-million-dollar reward for her capture, and she became the first woman ever to be listed on the FBI Most Wanted Terrorists list. She calls herself "a 20th Century escaped slave, living in Cuba, one of the largest, most resistant and most courageous *Palenques* (Maroon Camps) that has ever existed on the face of this planet." [123] She is still living in Cuba today.

Many members of Puerto Rico's **Fuerzas Armadas de Liberación Nacional** were captured and received long prison sentences for their bombings in the 1970s. On August 11th, 1999, President Bill Clinton granted clemency to 16 of them whose bombings had not caused any injuries. The petition for clemency had been supported by ten Nobel Peace Prize laureates, several archbishops, and past President Jimmy Carter, but it was vigorously opposed by the FBI, the Fraternal Order of Police, and others.

Bernardine Dohrn and **Bill Ayers** finally surrendered to authorities in Chicago on December 3, 1980. Dohrn, once described by J. Edgar Hoover as "La Passionaria of the Lunatic Left" did not repent. "This was a time when the unspeakable crimes of the American government were exposed and resisted by unprecedented numbers of its own people," she told the press. "Resistance by any means necessary is happening and will continue within the U.S. and around the world." She was released on bond, and a month later was found guilty and sentenced to three years' probation and a fine of $1,500. The extremely light sentence did not go over well with the police. "What really galls me," said Don Strickland of Squad 47, "is we did all this stuff, risking our lives every day, putting our lives on the line. And we end up being the villains! And these Weathermen scumbags end up being the fucking Robin Hoods!" Investigator Lou Vizi bitched, "The Weather Underground had done a hundred bombings, and they were never prosecuted for one of them. That's amazing. I mean, absolutely amazing. You know who got prosecuted? Us. The FBI."

FBI Associate Director **Mark Felt** was indeed finally found guilty in 1980 of violating civil rights and authorizing illegal residential break-ins in his pursuit of the Weathermen, but he received only a feather-light fine of $5,000. He was ultimately pardoned by Ronald Reagan. In 2005, on his deathbed, he revealed that he was "Deep Throat", the secret source that allowed reporters Bob Woodward and Carl Bernstein to uncover the Watergate scandal that ultimately led to the resignation of Richard Nixon in 1974.

Following his resignation, President **Richard Nixon** went into seclusion in California. In 1977, he agreed to sit for an interview with British talk-show host David Frost, for a fee (in today's dollars) of $3 million. Nixon admitted to Frost that he had "let down the country" and that "I brought myself down. I gave them a sword and they stuck it in. And they twisted it with relish. I guess if I'd been in their position, I'd have done the same thing." Nixon suffered a stroke on April 18, 1994, and died four days later at age 81.

After travelling in exile through Algeria, Lebanon, Tanzania, and other African countries, **Sekou Odinga**, considered by many to be both "the most amazing" and "the most badass" of the Black Panthers, lived undetected and underground until 1981 when he was finally captured and convicted. He received a consecutive 25-year to life state sentence and a 40-year federal sentence. He was released from prison on November 25, 2014.

Timothy Leary was released from prison on April 21, 1976, by California Governor Jerry Brown. In 1982 he formed an improbable partnership with Nixon's Watergate burglar **G. Gordon Liddy** who had been instrumental in the early '60s in the effort to bust Leary's Millbrook commune. The pair toured with a left-wing/right-wing debate schtick that earned them both a hefty income. Leary continued to do drugs but stopped proselytizing for psychedelics and instead began to campaign for space colonization and extending the human lifespan. After he was diagnosed with inoperable prostate cancer, Leary attempted to organize to have his body cryogenically frozen after his death, but in the end he was cremated. He died on May 31, 1996.

The main Greenpeace organizers of the early '70s continued their environmental activism in different ways. **Robert Hunter**, called by *TIME* magazine "one of the eco-heroes of the 20th Century", became the environmental reporter for the CITY-TV chain of television stations. Although it lost its edge many years ago, CITY was originally a very radical television station that started in 1972 in Toronto and expanded across Canada and into South America. **David McTaggart** threw in his sailing anchor and became the chairman of Greenpeace International, moving the Greenpeace headquarters from Vancouver to Amsterdam and enlarging the organization enormously. He retired in 1991 and died ten years later. **Paul Watson** left Greenpeace to start the Sea Shepherd fleet of anti-whaling, anti-poaching ships. More than anyone else from the 1965 – 75 protest era, he continues his radical activism today in just as intense a manner as he did in the '70s.

Eighty-three convicted Québec **separatist militants** and two dozen supporters spent a total of 282 years behind bars. Those who went into exile spent a total of 134 years in Cuba, Algeria, or France.

James Cross, held hostage in Montréal by the FLQ for 59 days in the fall of 1970, returned to England after his release. He returned to work for the British Foreign Service but never took another foreign posting. He died of Covid-19 on January 6th, 2021, a victim of the Pandemic.

In 1996 the Montréal *Gazette* revealed that **Gaétan Desrosiers**, who in 1966 had pled guilty to murder in connection with an FLQ bombing, was earning $91,300 as the equivalent of Assistant Deputy Minister in the Parti Québécois government.

Rhéal Mathieu, imprisoned in 1967 for a term of nine years and six months for his role in a string of FLQ bombings was still at it in

October 2000 when he was arrested for the fire bombings of three Second Cup coffee shops in Montréal as a protest against their English name.

Michelle Duclos, the central figure in the attempted bombing of the Statue of Liberty in 1965, was appointed to various government positions in Québec beginning in 1985, and in 2002 she became Non-resident Representative to Algeria of the Government of Québec.

Separatism continued as a very active political force in Québec. On October 29th, 1995, a referendum on separatism was defeated in Quebec with the narrowest of margins. The "No" votes were 50.6% vs 49.4% voting "Yes" to separation..

The British ended the policy of internment of suspected IRA members in December, 1975, but there were still huge numbers of detainees in jails in Northern Ireland and England. **Bobby Sands** was sentenced in 1977 to 14 years for explosives charges. He refused to wear the prison uniform which he considered a sign of criminal, not political incarceration. Although he was locked up naked, he continued to participate in numerous political protests. While in prison he wrote a number of essays and songs, one of which, *Back Home in Derry* became a hit in Ireland when it was recorded to the tune of Gordon Lightfoot's *The Wreck of the Edmond Fitzgerald.* In 1981, he began a hunger strike from prison. Shortly thereafter, he was elected as M.P. to the British Parliament. He died from the effects of the hunger strike on May 5, 1981, without ever having taken his seat in the Commons. Bobby Sands became the most celebrated martyr of The Troubles.

Shootings and bombings in Northern Ireland continued for another 20 years. The most notorious incident was the killing of **Lord Louis Mountbatten** by an IRA bomb that exploded on his fishing boat in August of 1979. "The Troubles" finally ended with the Good Friday Agreement of 1998.

Though he 'retired' following his serious motorcycle accident in 1966, **Bob Dylan** returned to recording and touring and has been on what is called his 'never-ending tour' since the 1990s. He has released 39 studio albums and 94 singles. He won the Nobel Prize for Literature in 2018. The handwritten original lyrics to *Like a Rolling Stone* were sold at auction for $2 million, a world record for a popular music manuscript.

Andy Warhol suffered from the effects of the 1968 attempted assassination for the rest of his life. Nevertheless, he continued to produce a vast quantity of art, publish the successful magazine *Interview*, and play a central role in celebrity culture until his death on February 22nd, 1987.

After her release from prison in 1971, **Valerie Solanas** continued to stalk Andy Warhol. She was re-arrested and eventually moved to California and lived a life of homelessness and mental illness. She died of pneumonia, on April 28, 1988 in the Bristol Hotel in the Tenderloin neighborhood of San Francisco.

The stories of **Jane Fonda**'s anti-war activism, some true, many utterly false, have never abated. By 2002, there were 7,000 Jane Fonda hate sites on the Internet. She, however, continued to thrive. She became the most prominent star of the home-video explosion of the early 80s with her best-selling fitness tapes. She has continued to perform in dozens of major projects for film and television. In 1991 she married billionaire CNN founder, yachtsman, rancher, and philanthropist Ted Turner. She has remained a committed activist, fighting for feminist and environmental causes and against the Iraq War and Donald Trump.

Roosevelt Douglas, one of the students imprisoned in Canada after the Sir George Williams Affair of 1968, went on to become Prime Minister of Dominica. Another of the protestors, **Anne Cools**, was jailed for two months for her involvement in the event, and then, years later, in 1984, was appointed by Pierre Trudeau as the first Black Senator in Canada.

The genocide of **Pol Pot**'s Khmer Rouge revolution continued from 1976 until 1979. Vast numbers of people were tortured, primarily in the Tuoi Sieng prison camp. Around 17,000 people passed through the torture chambers and were then taken to sites outside of Phnom Penh known as the 'Killing Fields' where they were executed. Some were shot, but to save

bullets, most were killed with pickaxes. Between 1.6 and 1.8 million people were executed—nearly a quarter of the country's population. Another
300,000 starved to death.

The Khmer Rouge also destroyed almost all the buildings, churches,
cathedrals and Buddhist temples built before the revolution. It is only
through very good luck that they did not destroy the national treasure, the
temple complex at Angkor Wat. The violent Pol Pot dictatorship was overthrown in 1979 and Cambodia began very slowly to rebuild itself.

Of the many thousands of Cambodians who were processed through
Tuoi Sieng prison, only 12 were known to have survived. They were artists,
saved by Pol Pot so they could create a seven-meter-high gold and silver
statue of the leader in the center of the ruined capital. The monument
was never completed. Pol Pot was finally arrested and sentenced to life
imprisonment in 1997. He died, either of heart failure, or suicide by drug
overdose on April 15, 1998.

The 'Yippies' self-immolated in 1968. **Abbie Hoffman** and **Jerry
Rubin** had different fates. Hoffman went underground in 1974 and lived
for a while in the Virgin Islands. After plastic surgery to alter his appear-
ance, he assumed the name 'Barry Freed' and hid out in California and
Mexico and then in a house on the St. Lawrence River in upstate New
York where he kept a boat at the ready in case he had to make a run for
Canada. He was very involved in environmental issues including the health
of the St. Lawrence River. In the '80s he emerged from hiding, fought for
new causes, and taught new, young organizers in Nicaragua, the U.S., and
Canada. On April 12, 1989, he was found dead from an overdose of 150
phenobarbital tablets. His death was ruled a suicide. His fellow Chicago
Seven defendant David Dellinger disputed the ruling, saying, "I don't
believe for one moment the suicide thing," and claimed that Hoffman had
"numerous plans for the future." Hoffman had often lectured about the
CIA's covert activities, including assassinations disguised as suicides.

Jerry Rubin moved from guerrilla politics and theater to become
an adherent of some of the personal growth developments of the 1970s

such as the mind-control movement/cult EST. He dropped his wild outfits of the 1960s to don a suit and tie and become a Wall Street stockbroker. He also was one of the earliest investors in Apple Computers and became a multi-millionaire. During the 1980s he embarked on a debating tour with his old partner Hoffman titled 'Yippie vs Yuppie'. On November 14, 1994, while attempting to cross Wilshire Boulevard in Los Angeles he was struck by a car and killed.

Patricia Hearst transformed herself from a gun-toting revolutionary back into a Hearst aristocrat. Her family hired the famous defense lawyer F. Lee Bailey to defend her. His defense was not thought to be superlative and on March 20, 1976, the jury found her guilty of bank robbery and using a firearm in the commission of a felony. On September 24th, Judge William Orrick sentenced her to seven years. However, the very rich usually have ways of avoiding jail. In this case her family put up $1.25 million in security to get her released on bail. One of the conditions was that she had to have round the clock protection from four security guards, all of whom were ex-police officers. Within two months she married, of all people, her court-appointed police bodyguard Bernard Shaw (a man she would have referred to for most of 1974 and '75 as a "pig"). After extensive lobbying by the Hearst family, President Jimmy Carter commuted her sentence on January 29, 1979. That wasn't enough for Hearst. In the 1990s, she began a campaign for full executive clemency. There was very divided opinion about this in American law enforcement. Robert S. Mueller III, then a U.S. Attorney in San Francisco, later of course the famous investigator of the Trump presidency, wrote a scathing letter of objection. "The record at trial," he wrote, "was clear that Hearst's gun was loaded and that she was not only a willing participant in that robbery but participated with zeal because of her commitment to 'revolutionary' causes. The attitude of Hearst has always been that she is a person above the law and that based on her wealth and social position, she is not accountable for her conduct despite the jury's verdict." Notwithstanding Mueller's (and others') objections, on January 20, 2001, his last day in office, President Bill Clinton granted her a full pardon. She has written a book about the ordeal (which almost resulted in new charges being laid), produced a Travel Channel TV special about her grandfather's Hearst Castle, performed cameos in five of John Waters' campy movies, and today is an enthusiastic dog-owner, entering her Shih Tzus in events such as the Westminster Dog Show. She is now a widow, a mother of two, and a grandmother. Her father died a billionaire in 2000, so it is fair to say she will likely never have to rob any more banks to keep the wolf from the door.

Bill O'Neal, the informant who gave the FBI and the Chicago police the information needed for the assassination of Black Panther Illinois Chairman Fred Hampton, stayed under the cover of the U.S. Federal Witness Protection Program until he submitted to an interview for the documentary series *Eyes on the Prize*. Immediately after its broadcast on PBS on January 15th, 1990, he committed suicide.

Gudrum Ensslin, **Andreas Baader** and other members of the **Baader-Meinhof Gang** (aka the Red Army Factions) were held in the Stammheim Prison in Stuttgart, Germany, until 1977. New, younger members of the RAF tried to spring them from the jail by kidnapping Hanns-Martin Schleyer and holding him hostage for a prisoner exchange. Schleyer had been a member of the Nazi SS and was a prominent well-known German business leader, admired by some and hated by many others. The *New York Times* described him as a "caricature of an ugly capitalist." [124] The prisoner exchange was turned down and hours later, on October 17th, Ensslin, Baader, and Jan-Carl Raspe were discovered dead in their cells. Ensslin was found hanging, the other two were shot. A fourth member, Irmgard Möller allegedly stabbed herself four times in the chest with a stolen knife. She recovered from her injuries and later claimed that the deaths were not suicides, as the prison claimed, but extrajudicial killings undertaken by the government. Then and now, the German government denies this. On learning of the deaths, the Red Army Factions who were holding Schleyer murdered him and left his body in a parked car in France. The notorious members of the Baader-Meinhof Gang have been portrayed in numerous plays, books, and movies. For instance, the character of the narcissist assassin played by Kevin Kline in the 1988 film *A Fish Called Wanda* was a parody based on Andreas Baader.

As the Irish Troubles escalated, **Bernadette Devlin** continued to fight for the Catholic Republicans. On January 16, 1981 she and her husband Michael McAliskey were objects of an assassination attempt by members of the Ulster Freedom Fighters, a cover name for the terrorist Ulster Defense Association. Devlin was shot nine times in front of her children. She believes the assassination was ordered by the British authorities, and that the army patrol of the 3rd Battalion Parachute Regiment who showed up after the shooting waited for half an hour, doing nothing and waiting for her to die. She was finally transported to a Belfast hospital intensive care unit and survived.

In 2003 she was barred from entering the U.S. and deported on the grounds that the State Department had declared her "a serious threat to the security of the United States." Today, she is still involved in political activity, mostly on behalf of foreign migrant workers in Ireland.

Warren Beatty did indeed eventually get the millions of dollars needed to make *Reds*, his pet-project epic film about the Russian Revolution. He not only got the financing from Hollywood, but from the one of the largest and most conservative industrial conglomerates ever, Gulf + Western, which owned Paramount Pictures in the '70s. Beatty recalls that Charles Bludhorn, the multi-millionaire Chairman of Gulf + Western had huge reservations about the film. According to Beatty, "Rumors were flying that this was a pro-communist picture, with a communist hero, and that was very disconcerting for this big conglomerate. There couldn't have been more hostility to communism at that time in history, with everything shifting to the right." Finally, Bludhorn made a proposal to Beatty, in his cement-thick Austrian accent:

"Vat iz diz vilm goink to cozt?"

"I can't really tell you," replied Beatty.

"Name zee figure."

"Why would I do that? That would be dishonest."

"Let's say diz vilm iz goink to cozt twenty-fife million," said the man known affectionately as 'The Mad Austrian of Wall Street.'

"Okay. 25 million."

"Do me a vayvor. Take diz twenty-fife million. Go to Mexico. Keep diz twenty-vor million vor yorzelf. Spend diz vun million on a vilm. Juzt don't make diz film."

"Charlie, I have to make this movie."

Beatty finally persuaded Charles Bludhorn to give him $32 million of Gulf + Western's money to make *Reds* (roughly $79 million in today's dollars.) Beatty ended up directing the film as well as starring, writing, and producing. He became a relentless, driven, and obsessive during the production, at one point demanding 80 takes of a scene with Maureen Stapleton, which prompted the query from the veteran star, "Are you out of your fucking mind?"

After years of work, the film was finally released on December 4, 1981. The commie epic was not a smash success, but it did gross over $40 million, and so, as Beatty later remarked, "it made a little money" for Gulf + Western.

FOOTNOTES

1 Mitchell, David Fontaine, *The Monumental Plot* in *The Journal of Counter Terrorism*, Volume 16, No. 4, 2010

2 Kellner, Douglas, *Ernesto, "Che" Guevara*, Chelsea House Publishers, 1989

3 Stone, Oliver & Kuznick, Peter, *The Concise Untold History of the United States*, New York: Gallery Books, 2014

4 Lee, Martin A. & Shlain, Bruce, *Acid Dreams: The Complete Social History of LSD, the CIA, the Sixties and Beyond*, New York: Grove Press, 1985

5 Stone, Oliver & Kuznick, Peter, *The Concise Untold History of the United States*, New York: Gallery Books, 2014

6 Moritz (ed), *Current Biography Yearbook*, 1970, p. 260

7 Hilburn, Robert, *Johnny Cash: The Life*, New York: Little Brown and Company, 2013

8 Amnesty International, *Amnesty International Annual Report 1972-1973*, London: Amnesty International Publications

9 Jackson, Andrew Grant, *1965: The Most Revolutionary Year in Music*, New York: Thomas Dunne Books / St. Martin's Press, 2015

10 Leigh, David, *The Wilson Plot*, London: William Heinemann Ltd., 1988

11 Siegel, Fred, *The Revolt Against the Masses: How Liberalism Has Undermined the Middle Class*, New York: Encounter Books, 2014

12 Naimark, Norman, *The Russians in Germany: A History of the Soviet Zone of Occupation, 1945-1949*, Cambridge: Belknap Press, 1995

13 Edelman, Susan, *"Journalist's tell-all on mobster tied to JFK might have got her killed"*, *New York Post* – December 4, 2016

14 *'Mad Mike' Hoare Obituary: African mercenary of Irish extraction*, *The Irish Times*, February 15, 2020

15 Lee, Martin A. & Shlain, Bruce, *Acid Dreams: The Complete Social History of LSD, the CIA, the Sixties and Beyond,* New York: Grove Press, 1985

16 Shoreline Productions (Amazon Prime Video), *RFK in the Land of Apartheid,* 2010

17 Lee, Martin A. & Shlain, Bruce, *Acid Dreams: The Complete Social History of LSD, the CIA, the Sixties and Beyond,* New York: Grove Press, 1985

18 Barnouin, Barbara and Yu Changgen, *Zhou Enlai: A Political Life:* Hong Kong: Chinese University of Hong Kong

19 Bosworth, Patricia, *Jane Fonda – The Private Life of a Public Woman* Boston: Houghton Mifflin Harcourt, 2011

20 *Le Nouvel Observateur,* September 20, 1967

21 *Le Monde,* September 6, 1967

22 Seale, Bobby, *Seize the Time: The Story of the Black Panther Party and Huey P. Newton* Baltimore: Black Classic Press, 1991 pp 395-401

23 Bourseiller, Christope, *Les Maoïstes, La Folle Histoire des Gardes Rouges Français,* Paris: Plon, 1996 p.18

24 Berton, Pierre, *1967 – The Last Good Year,* Toronto: Doubleday Canada, 1997, p 201

25 King, Jessica, *"U.S. in First Effort to Clean up Agent Orange in Vietnam",* CNN News, August 10, 2012

26 Stone, Oliver & Kuznick, Peter, *The Concise Untold History of the United States,* New York: Gallery Books, 2014

27 Ibid

28 Burrough, Bryan, *Days of Rage – America's Radical Underground, the FBI and the Forgotten Age of Revolutionary Violence,* New York: Penguin Books, 2015

29 Blum, William, *Killing Hope: U. S. Military and CIA Interventions since World War II,* Common Courage Press

30 Tompkins, Colin, *"In the Outlaw Area"*, *The New Yorker*, New Yorker - January 1, 1966

31 Berton, Pierre: *1967, The Last Good Year*, Toronto: Doubleday Canada, 1997, p 324

32 Biskind, Peter, *Star: The Life and Wild Times of Warren Beatty*, New York: Simon & Shuster, 2010

33 Hoffman, Abbie, *Steal This Book*, New York: Grove Press, 1971 (reprinted by Da Capo Press, 2002)

34 Hoffman, Abbie, *The Autobiography of Abbie Hoffman*, New York: Four Walls Eight Windows, 1980

35 Albert, Judith and Stewart, Edward, *The Sixties Papers: Documents of a Rebellious Decade*, New York: Praeger Publishers, p 442

36 Stone, Oliver & Kuznick, Peter, *The Concise Untold History of the United States*, New York: Gallery Books, 2014

37 *"Eartha's Shouts Stun Lady Bird into Tears"*, *Chicago Tribune*, January 18, 1968

38 Hanyok, Robert J., *Spartans in Darkness*, Washington, R.C.: Center for Cryptographic History, NSA, 2002, p.94

39 Adams, Eddie, *"Eulogy: General Nguyen Ngoc Loan"*, *TIME* Magazine, July 27, 1998

40 Belinda Davis et al *Changing the World, Changing Oneself: Political Protest and Collective Identities in West Germany and the US in the 1960s and 1970s.* Oxford: Berghahn Books, 2013

41 Peyrefitte, Alain, *C'était de Gaulle* Paris: Editions de Fallois-Fayard, 1994

42 *Le Monde*, May 16, 1998

43 *"How Political Hatred During the Cultural Revolution Led to Murder and Cannibalism in a Small Town in China"*, *South China Morning Post*, May 11, 2016

44 Jenish, D'Arcy, *The Making of the October Crisis – Canada's Long Nightmare of Terrorism at the Hands of the FLQ*, Toronto: Penguin Random House Doubleday Canada, 2018

45 Smith, Karen D., *"American Soldiers Testify in My Lai Court Martial" Amarillo Globe-News*, December 6, 2000

46 Bourke, Joanna, *An Intimate History of Killing: Face-to-Face Killing in Twentieth Century Warfare* New York: Basic Books, 1999

47 Lawson, Steven F and Payne, Charles M., *Debating the Civil Rights Movement 1945-1968*, New York: Rowman & Littlefield pp148-149

48 *Transcript of the Martin Luther King Jr. Assassination Conspiracy Trial*

49 Hoffman, Abbie, *The Autobiography of Abbie Hoffman*, New York: Four Walls Eight Windows, 1980 p. 140

50 Haun, Harry, *"Age of Aquarius"*, *Playbill*, April 2009

51 Brody, Richard, *Everything is Cinema – The Working Life of Jean-Luc Godard*, New York: Holt Paperbacks, 2008

52 Ziegler, Philip, *Mountbatten*, London: Perennial Library, January 1, 1986

53 Penrose, Barrie and Courtier, Roger, *The Pencourt File* London: Secker & Warburg, February 1, 1978

54 Langguth, A.J., *Our Vietnam*, New York: Simon & Schuster, 2000 p 422

56 Newfield, Jack, *Robert Kennedy: A Memoir*, New York: Penguin Group, 1988 p. 394

57 Tscheschlok, Eric G., *Long Road to Rebellion: Miami's Liberty City Riot of 1968* Florida Atlantic University, 1995

58 Churchill, Lindsay, *Becoming the Tupamaros – Solidarity and Transnational Revolutionaries in Uruguay and the United States* Nashville: Vanderbilt University Press, 2014, p.34

59 Jenish, D'Arcy, *The Making of the October Crisis – Canada's Long Nightmare of Terrorism at the Hands of the FLQ*, Toronto: Penguin Random House Doubleday Canada, 2018 p.139

60 Hoffman, Abbie, *The Autobiography of Abbie Hoffman*, New York: Four Walls Eight Windows, 1980 p. 143

61 Hoffman, Abbie, *Revolution for the Hell of It*, New York: Thunder's Mouth Press, 1968, p.107

62 Hoffman, Abbie, *Ibid*, p. 106

63 Hoffman, Abbie: *The Autobiography of Abbie Hoffman*, New York: Four Walls Eight Windows, 1980 p. 160

64 Lovell, Julia. *Maoism, A Global History*, London: Vintage, 2019

65 Brokaw, Tom, *Boom! Voices of the Sixties*, New York: Random House, 2007

66 Careaga, Rogelio Antonio, *The Peruvian Coup d'état of 1968:The Goals and Policies of the Military Government*, Ann Arbor: University Microfilms International

67 Agee, Philip, *Inside the Company – CIA Diary*, New York: Bantam Books, 1977

68 Jenish, D'Arcy, *The Making of the October Crisis – Canada's Long Nightmare of Terrorism at the Hands of the FLQ*, Toronto: Penguin Random House Doubleday Canada, 2018

69 Stone, Oliver & Kuznick, Peter, *The Concise Untold History of the United States*, New York: Gallery Books, 2014

70 *"Chasing the Moon", American Experience* PBS, July 10, 2018

71 *"Earthrise: How the Iconic Image Changed the World", The Guardian, December 24, 2018*

72 *"John N. Mitchell dies at 75; Major Figure in Watergate", New York Times,* November 10, 1988

73 Easton, Robert Olney, *Black Tide, The Santa Barbara Oil Spill and its Consequences*, New York: Delacorte Press

74 Clark, K.C. & Hemphill, Jeffrey, *The Santa Barbara Oil Spill, A Retrospective*, Honolulu: University of Hawaii Press, 2002

75 Lüthi, Lorenz, *The Sino-Soviet Split: Cold War in the Communist World*, Princeton: Princeton University Press, 2010

76 Summers, Anthony, *Drunk in Charge, www.theguardian.com*, September 2, 2000

77 Summers, Anthony, *Drunk in Charge, www.theguardian.com*, September 2, 2000

78 *Police Ombudsman for Northern Ireland Report*, Belfast, October 4, 2001

79 Stone, Oliver & Kuznick, Peter, *The Concise Untold History of the United States*, New York: Gallery Books, 2014

79a McCann, Eamonn, *War and an Irish Town*, Chicago: Haymarket Books, 2018

80 Burrough, Bryan, *Days of Rage – America's Radical Underground, the FBI and the Forgotten Age of Revolutionary Violence*, New York: Penguin Books, 2015

81 Devlin, Bernadette, *The Price of My Soul*, New York: Alfred A. Knopf, 1969

82 Maddow, Rachel, *Blowout*, New York: Crown Publishing, 2019, p. 17

83 Ibid, p. 19

84 Zhai Zhenhua, *Red Flower of China*, New York: Soho Press, July, 2003, p. 199

85 Smith, Paul Chaat & Warrior, Robert Allen, *Like a Hurricane – The Indian Movement From Alcatraz to Wounded Knee*, New York: The New Press, 1996, p. 24

86 Churchill, Ward & Vander Wall, Jim, *Agents of Repression: The FBI's Secret Wars Against the Black Panther Party and the American Indian Movement*, Boston, South End Press

87 Gitlin, Todd, *The Sixties – Years of Hope, Days of Rage*, New York: Bantam Books, 1987

88 Collier, Peter & Horowitz, David, *Destructive Generation: Second Thoughts About the Sixties*, New York: Encounter Books, 2005

89 Browne, Alastair Storm & Karinch, Maryann, *Cosmic Careers – Exploring the Universe of Opportunities in the Space Industries*, New York: Harper Collins, 2021

90 Wormser, Gerard, *Sartre Adversaire de la Non-Violence*, *"Alternatives Non-Violence" Number 106*, June 2006

91 Means, Howard, *67 Shots: Kent State and the End of American Innocence*, Boston: Da Capo Press, 2016

92 *"Kill a Few": Nixon's Cold-blooded Take on Kent State*, Miller Center of Public Affairs, February 17, 2021

93 Lee, Martin A. & Shlain, Bruce, *Acid Dreams: The Complete Social History of LSD, the CIA, the Sixties and Beyond*, New York: Grove Press, 1985

94 Trudeau, Pierre, *Memoirs*, Toronto: McClelland & Stewart, 1993 pp 167, 211

95 De Vault, Carole with William Johnson, *The Informer*, Toronto: Fleet Books, 1982

96 Jenish, D'Arcy, *The Making of the October Crisis – Canada's Long Nightmare of Terrorism at the Hands of the FLQ*, Toronto: Penguin Random House Doubleday Canada, 2018

97 Shigenobu, Fusako, *A Personal History of the Japanese Red Army*, Tokyo: Kawada, 2009

98 Bernstein, Carl & Woodward, Bob, *All the President's Men*, New York: Simon & Schuster, 1974 p. 105

99 MacLaine, Shirley, *You Can Get There From Here*, Toronto/New York: Bantam Books, 1975

100 Matthiessen, Peter, *In the Spirit of Crazy Horse: The Story of Leonard Peltier and the FBI's War on the American Indian Movement*, New York: Penguin, 2001

101 Conacher, Brian, *As the Puck Turns: A Personal Journey Through the World of Hockey*, Toronto: Wiley & Sons, 2007

102 Macnab, Geoffrey, *"Last Tango in Paris: Can it Arouse the Same Passions Now?"*, *The Independent*, March 11, 2010

103 Smith, Paul Chaat & Warrior, Robert Allen, *Like a Hurricane – The Indian Movement From Alcatraz to Wounded Knee*, New York: The New Press, 1996, p. 147

104 Gopnik, Blake, *Warhol*, New York: HarperCollins, 2020, p 738

105 *"He Was No Hippie: Remembering Manson, Prison, Scientology and Mind Control" Raw Story*, November 26, 2017

106 Stone, Oliver & Kuznick, Peter, *The Concise Untold History of the United States*, New York: Gallery Books, 2014

107 Headley, Lake and Hoffman, William, *Vegas P.I.: The Life and Times of America's Great Detective* 1993: Running Press

108 France briefly resumed nuclear testing at Mururoa in 1995-96.

109 Thomas, Donald, *Aleksandr Solzhenitsyn: A Century in the Life* London: Abacus

110 *Ibid*

111 *Ibid*

112 Solzhenitsyn, Aleksandr, *The Gulag Archipelago* (Foreword) New York, Harper Perennial, 1973

113 Koerner, Brendan, *The Diplomat Who Disappeared, Atlantic* Magazine, May, 2021

114 *Birmingham Pub Bomb Inquests Will Not Resolve Enduring Injustice, Court Told*, ITV News, July 17, 2018

115 Lee, Martin A. & Shlain, Bruce, *Acid Dreams: The Complete Social History of LSD, the CIA, the Sixties and Beyond*, New York: Grove Press, 1985

116 Isaacs, Arnold, *Without Honor: Defeat in Vietnam and Cambodia*, Baltimore: John Hopkins University Press, 1983

117 *Roots of Greenpeace: Bodies on the Line*, CBC – *The Fifth Estate* 1976

118 Emmanuel Amara, *Les Derniers Jours d'Aldo Moro* (Rue 89) and Hubert Artus, *Pourquoi le Pouvoir Italien a Lâche Aldo Moro, Exécuté en 1978* (Rue 89)

119 Berry, Steve, *Who Killed Mary Steinhauser?* Vancouver *Province*, November 2, 2003

120 Franz, Margaret, *Between Blade & Bullet – The Mary Steinhauser Story*, Victoria: Friesen Press, 2021

121 Toobin, Jeffrey, *American Heiress – The Wild Saga of the Kidnapping, Crimes and Trial of Patty Hearst*, New York: Doubleday, 2016

122 Mandela, Nelson & Castro, Fidel, *How Far We Slaves Have Come*, New York: Pathfinder, 1991

123 Rodriguez, Dylan, *Forced Passages: Imprisoned Radical Intellectuals and the U.S. Prison Regime*, Minneapolis: University of Minnesota Press, 2006

124 Gimlette, John, *Panther Soup, Travels Through Europe in War and Peace* 2011- Random House p 628

125 Paul Sant Cassia, *Bodies of Evidence: Burial, Memory, and the Recovery of Missing Persons in Cyprus.* Berghahn Books, p.55

126 *Ibid*

127 Richardson, Peter, *A Bomb in Every Issue – How the Short Unruly Life of Ramparts Magazine Changed America*, New York: The New Press, 2009, p.68

128 Lee, Martin A. & Shlain, Bruce, *Acid Dreams: The Complete Social History of LSD, the CIA, the Sixties and Beyond,* New York: Grove Press, 1985

129 In 1532, Francisco Pizarro was paid the equivalent of $2 billion in gold for the release of Inca leader Atahualpa.

130 Mendoz, Jorge L. *Grenada, La Nueva Joya del Caribe* Havana: Editorial de Ciencias Sociales, 1982

131 Wright, Peter, *Spycatcher* London: William Heinemann, 1987

132 Leigh, David, *The Wilson Plot,* London: William Heinemann Ltd., 1988, p. 223

133 Wheeler, Brian, *"Wilson Plot: The Secret Tapes"* BBC News, March 9, 2006

BIBLIOGRAPHY

Agee, Philip, *Inside the Company – CIA Diary*, New York: Bantam Books, 1977

Arscott, David, *The 60s – A Very Peculiar History*, Brighton: The Salariya Book Company, 2012

Bernstein, Carl & Woodward, Bob, *All the President's Men*, New York: Simon & Schuster, 1974

Berton, Pierre, *1967 – The Last Good Year*, Toronto: Doubleday Canada, 1997

Biskind, Peter, *Star: The Life and Wild Times of Warren Beatty*, New York: Simon & Shuster, 2010

Bockris, Victor, *The Life and Death of Andy Warhol*, New York: Bantam Books, 1989

Bosworth, Patricia, *Jane Fonda – The Private Life of a Public Woman*, Boston: Houghton Mifflin Harcourt, 2011

Bouchehri, Regina et al, *The Cuba Libre Story*, Looks/ZDF-Info/Interscope (Netflix)

Brody, Richard, *Everything is Cinema – The Working Life of Jean-Luc Godard*, New York: Holt Paperbacks, 2008

Brokaw, Tom, *Boom! Voices of the Sixties*, New York: Random House, 2007

Burrough, Bryan, *Days of Rage – America's Radical Underground, the FBI and the Forgotten Age of Revolutionary Violence*, New York: Penguin Books, 2015

Churchill, Lindsay, *Becoming the Tupamaros – Solidarity and Transnational Revolutionaries in Uruguay and the United States*, Nashville: Vanderbilt University Press, 2014

Davis, Angela, *An Autobiography*, New York: International Publishers, 1974

Debray, Régis: *Revolution in the Revolution?*, Havana: Casa de las Americas, 1967

De Vault, Carole with William Johnson, *The Informer*, Toronto: Fleet Books, 1982

Devlin, Bernadette, *The Price of My Soul*, New York: Alfred A. Knopf, 1969

Dikötter, Frank, *The Cultural Revolution*, New York: Bloomsbury Publishing, 2016

Feeney, Brian, *A Short History of The Troubles*, Dublin: The O'Brien Press, 2004

Franz, Margaret, *Between Blade & Bullet – The Mary Steinhauser Story*, Victoria: Friesen Press, 2021

Gitlin, Todd, *The Sixties – Years of Hope, Days of Rage*, New York: Bantam Books, 1987

Goodman, Amy, Gonzalez, Juan, *"Jesse Jackson on 'Mad Dean Disease', the 2000 Elections and Rev. Dr. Martin Luther King"*, Democracy Now!, January 15, 2004

Gopnik, Blake, *Warhol*, New York: HarperCollins, 2020

Grimes, William, *"Fritz Teufel, A German Protestor in the '60s, Dies at 67"*, *New York Times*, August 7, 2010

Hagan, Matthew, *"The Man Who Told Québec the Truth"*, *Maclean's* Magazine, July 1, 1975

Harris, Richard L., *Che Guevara: A Biography*, Santa Barbara: ABC-Clio LLC, 2011

Hoffman, Abbie, *Revolution For The Hell of It*, New York: Thunder's Mouth Press, 1968

Hoffman, Abbie, *Steal This Book*, New York: Grove Press, 1971 (reprinted by Da Capo Press, 2002)

Hoffman, Abbie, *The Autobiography of Abbie Hoffman*, New York: Four Walls Eight Windows, 1980

Jackson, Andrew Grant, *1965: The Most Revolutionary Year in Music*, New York: Thomas Dunne Books/ St. Martin's Press, 2015

Jenish, D'Arcy, *The Making of the October Crisis – Canada's Long Nightmare of Terrorism at the Hands of the FLQ*, Toronto: Penguin Random House Doubleday Canada, 2018

Joyce, Bruce & Weil, Marsha, *Models of Teaching*, Englewood Cliffs, New Jersey: Prentice-Hall, Inc., 1972

Kandell, Jonathon, *"The Talk of Paris; 'Morose' Describes it All: Weather, Politics, Crime"*, *New York Times*, August 1, 1978

Lee, Martin A. & Shlain, Bruce, *Acid Dreams: The Complete Social History of LSD, the CIA, the Sixties and Beyond*, New York: Grove Press, 1985

Leigh, David, *The Wilson Plot*, London: William Heinemann Ltd., 1988

Lovell, Julia, *Maoism: A Global History*, London: Vintage, 2019

MacFarquar, Roderick & Schoenhals, Michael, *Mao's Last Revolution*, Boston: Harvard University Press, 2008

Maddow, Rachel, *Blowout*, New York: Crown Publishing, 2019

Macintyre, Ben, *The Spy and the Traitor*, Toronto: McClelland and Stewart/ Penguin Random House, 2019

MacLaine, Shirley, *You Can Get There From Here*, Toronto/New York: Bantam Books, 1975

Mailer, Norman, *The Armies of the Night*, New York: Plume/Penguin, 1968

Mitchell, David Fontaine, *The Monumental Plot* in *The Journal of Counter Terrorism*, Volume 16, No. 4, 2010

Newton, Huey, *To Die For the People*, San Francisco: City Lights Books, 2009

O'Donnell, Lawrence, *Playing With Fire – The 1968 Election and the Transformation of American Politics*, New York: Penguin Books, 2017

Pollen, Michael, *How to Change Your Mind – What the New Science of Psychedelics Teaches Us About Consciousness, Dying, Addiction, Depression and Transcendence*, New York: Penguin Press, 2018

Richardson, Peter, *A Bomb in Every Issue – How the Short Unruly Life of Ramparts Magazine Changed America*, New York: The New Press, 2009

Schumacher, Michael, *There but for Fortune – The Life of Phil Ochs*, New York: Hyperion Press, 1996

Shoreline Productions (Amazon Prime Video), *RFK in the Land of Apartheid*, 2010

Smith, Paul Chaat & Warrior, Robert Allen, *Like a Hurricane – The Indian Movement From Alcatraz to Wounded Knee*, New York: The New Press, 1996

Solzhenitsyn, Aleksandr, *The Gulag Archipelago* New York, Harper Perennial, 1973

Stone, Oliver & Kuznick, Peter, *The Concise Untold History of the United States*, New York: Gallery Books, 2014

Tetley, William, *The October Crisis, 1970*, Montréal/Kingston: McGill-Queen's University Press, 2010

Tompkins, Colin, *"In the Outlaw Area"*, *The New Yorker*, January 1, 1966

Toobin, Jeffrey, *American Heiress – The Wild Saga of the Kidnapping, Crimes and Trial of Patty Hearst*, New York: Doubleday, 2016

Trudeau, Pierre, *Memoirs* Toronto: McClelland & Stewart, 1993

UPI, *"British Embassy Fired by Peking Red Guards"*, *Desert Sun*, Volume 41, Number 15, August 22, 1967

Waugh, Billy, *Hunting the Jackal*, New York: Avon Books/Harper Collins, 2005

Westmoreland, William C., *A Soldier Reports*, Garden City, N.Y.: Doubleday, 1978

Wilkinson, Daniel, *Silence on the Mountain: Stories of Terror, Betrayal and Forgetting in Guatemala*, Boston: Houghton Mifflin, 2002

INDEX

ACKNOWLEDGEMENTS

My great thanks to my three beta-readers, Ian Perrin, Larry Jeffery and Vic Lacorte.

Also, thanks to publishing consultants Tom Harnett, Steven Spatz and Maryann Karinch.

Most especially, much gratitude and thanks to Phillippa Baran, who took time out from her own soon-to-be-published book on her late brother, figure skater, Olympian and artist Toller Cranston, to read Ablaze. She found and fixed the many split infinitives, misplaced commas and over-used present participles in my original writing, so that you, dear reader, didn't have to see them. If any are left, the blame is mine.

THE AUTHOR

Peter Rowe is an award-winning writer, director, producer, and cinematographer who has worked all over the world. His previous books include *Music vs The Man*, published in 2020 by Armin Lear Press and *Adventures in Filmmaking*, published in 2013 by Pinewood Independent Publishing. Both are available at online booksellers.

He has written the screenplays for numerous films including *Treasure Island* (1999), *Lost!* (1986) and *Shipwrecked on a Great Lake* (2014). He has more than 180 films to his credit as director/producer including the 49-part TV series, *Angry Planet* (2007-2015).

Rowe was 18 years old in 1965 and 28 in 1975. In those formative years he experienced, lived, observed, processed and absorbed many of the incidents described in *Ablaze – Ten Years That Shook The World*.

He can be reached at peter@peterrowe.tv

Online Praise for *Music vs The Man*

A super read about musicians we thought we knew! *Music vs The Man* is a superb book written for anyone who's seen the raunchy side of music and musicians fighting against the law. It peels away the outer layers and gets deep into the troubles afflicting well-known musicians, from classical to current. Why are they harassed by the law so often? Why did world leaders obsess about Elvis and John Lennon? Peter Rowe writes from the point of view of a participant in most of the music of the 20th Century because he seems to have been in the midst of it. He writes about Jimi Hendrix performing at the Isle of Wight Festival – a concert that attracted 650,000 people – and casually mentions that "This writer was on the stage, just a few feet away from Hendrix, filming him for a documentary." As seen from this book, Peter Rowe was everywhere and he writes from personal experience. It's hard not to blast through this book because it's so bizarre and outrageous in so many places. You get hooked. But it's better to go slow and savor each chapter, preferably with the music of each performer streaming in the background. Music vs The Man gives insight into the music while the music give insight to the stories. Peter Rowe provides a whole different view of the musicians we thought we knew so well.

Great behind the scenes in the music world! Peter Rowe's *Music vs the Man* is an extraordinary set of stories skillfully written, covering musicians from Beethoven and Bach to John Lennon, Paul Robeson, Billie Holiday, Chuck Berry, Frank Sinatra, Michael Jackson, Paul McCartney, Elvis Presley, and dozens more. Throughout the book Rowe gives us lots of meticulously researched insider stories on everything from groupies, politicians, jailhouses, racism, drugs, and rock n roll — stories that kept me turning pages from beginning to end. I highly recommend this book for music fans, history buffs, and anyone who wants a fascinating look behind the scenes in the world of musicians and their battles with The Man.

I love this book! This is a great book. If you were there, you remember. This brings it all back. If you were there but too wrecked, this fills in the gaps. If you weren't there, this puts you there. It triggers the memories. It informs. I love this book.

Music vs The Man is available at all online booksellers.